PRACTICAL MATHEMATICS

REVISED EDITION
CONSUMER APPLICATIONS

Holt, Rinehart and Winston, Inc.

Austin   Orlando   San Diego   Chicago   Dallas   Toronto

Authors

Marguerite M. Fredrick
Computer Consultant, K–12
Pleasantville Union Free School District
Pleasantville, New York
Formerly Math Chairperson, 7–12
The Ursuline School
New Rochelle, New York

Robert D. Postman
Professor and Chairperson
Mathematics Education
Mercy College
Westchester, New York

Steven J. Leinwand
Mathematics Consultant, K–12
Connecticut State Department of Education
Hartford, Connecticut

Laurence R. Wantuck
Mathematics Supervisor, K–12
Broward County Schools
Fort Lauderdale, Florida

For Photo and Art Credits, see page 486.

Printed in the United States of America

ISBN: 0-03-076791-1

4 5 6 7 8 040 99 98 97

CONTENTS

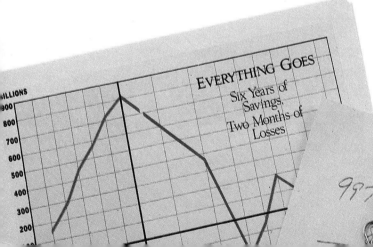

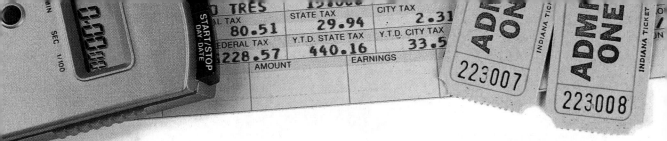

CHAPTER 3   PART-TIME AND SUMMER JOBS

CHAPTER 4   FULL-TIME WORK

CHAPTER 5   RECREATION AND SPORTS

CHAPTER 9 AUTOMOBILE EXPENSES

CHAPTER 10 TRANSPORTATION

CHAPTER 11 TAXES

CHAPTER 12   HOUSING

CHAPTER 13   TRADE INDUSTRIES

CHAPTER 14   OTHER PROFESSIONS

CHAPTER 17 PROBABILITY

CHAPTER 18 EQUATIONS

Copy and complete.

1. $87 = 8$ tens ■ ones $= 7$ tens ■ ones
2. $92 =$ ■ tens 2 ones $=$ ■ tens 12 ones
3. $326 = 3$ hundreds ■ tens 6 ones $= 2$ hundreds ■ tens 6 ones
4. $583 = 5$ hundreds 8 tens ■ ones $= 5$ hundreds 7 tens ■ ones

Copy and complete.

5. $2.8 = 2$ ones and ■ tenths $= 1$ one and ■ tenths
6. $4.1 =$ ■ ones and 1 tenth $=$ ■ ones and 11 tenths
7. $1.74 = 1$ one and ■ tenths 4 hundredths $= 1$ one and ■ tenths 14 hundredths
8. $9.23 = 9$ ones and 2 tenths ■ hundredths $= 9$ ones and 1 tenth ■ hundredths

Add or subtract.

9. $5 + 3$
10. $6 + 2$
11. $8 + 4$
12. $5 + 8$
13. $8 + 7$
14. $9 + 6$
15. $7 + 7$
16. $9 - 5$
17. $8 - 4$
18. $12 - 3$
19. $14 - 6$
20. $11 - 9$
21. $16 - 7$
22. $16 - 9$
23. $18 - 9$

Multiply or divide.

24. 3×6
25. 4×4
26. 6×5
27. 5×9
28. 8×6
29. 4×9
30. 7×9
31. $15 \div 5$
32. $28 \div 7$
33. $32 \div 4$
34. $8\overline{)64}$
35. $6\overline{)42}$
36. $7\overline{)56}$
37. $8\overline{)72}$
38. $9\overline{)81}$

Compute.

39. $2 + 5 + 3$
40. $3 + 7 + 8$
41. $12 + 0 + 4$
42. $9 + 6 + 7$
43. $5 \times 3 + 6$
44. $2 \times 9 + 3$
45. $8 \times 0 + 3$
46. $8 \times 3 + 0$

Write the ratio in fraction form.

47. squares to all shapes
48. circles to all shapes
49. triangles to all shapes
50. circles and squares to all shapes

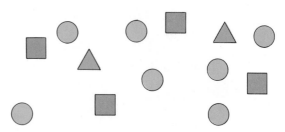

Write the ratio as a percent.

51. 6 per 100
52. 17 per 100
53. 80 per 100
54. 8 out of 100
55. 21 out of 100
56. 75 out of 100

PAPER -AND- PENCIL COMPUTATIONS

Many people enjoy participating in or watching a baseball game. How are numbers used in baseball, both during the game and in keeping performance records?

1.1 ADDING WHOLE NUMBERS AND DECIMALS

Addition Vocabulary:	ADDEND + ADDEND = SUM	ADDEND +ADDEND SUM

SKILL 1 *Adding 2 whole numbers*

Add: 4,068 + 5,794

1. Add ones. Regroup.	2. Add tens. Regroup.	3. Add hundreds.	4. Add thousands.
1 4,068 +5,794 2	1 1 4,068 +5,794 62	1 1 4,068 +5,794 862	1 1 4,068 +5,794 9,862

SKILL 2 *Column addition with whole numbers*

Add: 453 + 4,802 + 327

Remember to line up the places when you write the example in vertical form.

1. Add ones. Regroup.	2. Add tens.	3. Add hundreds. Regroup.	4. Add thousands.
1 453 4,802 + 327 2	1 453 4,802 + 327 82	1 1 453 4,802 + 327 582	1 1 453 4,802 + 327 5,582

SKILL 3 *Adding 2 decimals*

Add: 4.6 + 3.7

1. Line up the decimal points and the decimal places.	2. Write the decimal point for the sum.	3. Add as you would whole numbers.
4.6 +3.7	4.6 +3.7	1 4.6 +3.7 8.3

SKILL 4 Column addition with decimals

Add: 5.16 + 8.7 + 4.02

1. Line up the decimal points and the decimal places.

   THINK: 8.7 = 8.70

2. Write the decimal point for the sum.

3. Add as you would whole numbers.

```
    5.16            5.16            5.16
    8.70            8.70            8.70
  +4.02           +4.02          +4.02
                                  17.88
```

PRACTICE EXERCISES

Add.

1. $\begin{array}{r} 521 \\ +236 \end{array}$	**2.** $\begin{array}{r} 837 \\ +185 \end{array}$	**3.** $\begin{array}{r} 908 \\ +\ 39 \end{array}$	**4.** $\begin{array}{r} 2{,}346 \\ +7{,}385 \end{array}$

5. $\begin{array}{r} 7{,}368 \\ +\ \ 612 \end{array}$ **6.** $\begin{array}{r} 568 \\ +2{,}394 \end{array}$

7. $\begin{array}{r} 18.5 \\ +11.3 \end{array}$ **8.** $\begin{array}{r} 0.86 \\ +1.62 \end{array}$ **9.** $\begin{array}{r} 9.47 \\ +6.8 \end{array}$ **10.** $\begin{array}{r} 0.73 \\ +0.64 \end{array}$ **11.** $\begin{array}{r} 2.5 \\ +29.63 \end{array}$ **12.** $\begin{array}{r} 16.2 \\ +35.97 \end{array}$

13. $\begin{array}{r} 802 \\ 311 \\ +\ 89 \end{array}$ **14.** $\begin{array}{r} 875 \\ 918 \\ +6{,}213 \end{array}$ **15.** $\begin{array}{r} 4{,}275 \\ 5{,}728 \\ +\ \ 982 \end{array}$ **16.** $\begin{array}{r} 1{,}805 \\ 4{,}633 \\ +5{,}065 \end{array}$ **17.** $\begin{array}{r} 5{,}024 \\ 810 \\ +\ \ 265 \end{array}$ **18.** $\begin{array}{r} 411 \\ 6{,}807 \\ +\ \ 253 \end{array}$

19. $\begin{array}{r} 7.3 \\ 4.2 \\ +3.5 \end{array}$ **20.** $\begin{array}{r} 9.6 \\ 8.7 \\ +0.4 \end{array}$ **21.** $\begin{array}{r} 38.6 \\ 19.8 \\ +24.2 \end{array}$ **22.** $\begin{array}{r} 2.94 \\ 3.65 \\ +13.08 \end{array}$ **23.** $\begin{array}{r} 13.2 \\ 14.57 \\ +\ 0.7 \end{array}$ **24.** $\begin{array}{r} 0.5 \\ 17.83 \\ +\ 0.27 \end{array}$

25. 4,892 + 3,605

26. 567 + 9,028

27. 3,841 + 187

28. 19.3 + 48.6

29. 9 + 8.5

30. 18.34 + 9.7

31. 4,387 + 8,062 + 964

32. 4,361 + 904 + 627

33. 2,053 + 87 + 763

34. 12.3 + 8.9 + 17.1

35. 9.6 + 13.05 + 10

36. 2.5 + 0.18 + 12.08

Solve.

37. Ron spent $28.36 at the sports store and $16.09 at the clothing store. How much did he spend all together?

38. Margaret sold 189 ice cream cones on Friday, 308 on Saturday, and 67 on Sunday. How many cones did she sell all together?

39. It is 789 mi from Houston, Texas, to Atlanta, Georgia, and 2,496 mi from Atlanta to San Francisco, California. How many miles is it all together from Houston to San Francisco?

40. During the first week, 10.8 in. of snow fell. During the second week 18 in. of snow fell, and 0.8 in. fell during the third week. What was the total snowfall for these 3 weeks?

1.2 SUBTRACTING WHOLE NUMBERS AND DECIMALS

Subtraction Vocabulary:
Addition and subtraction are related operations.

ADDEND + ADDEND = SUM

SUM − ADDEND = ADDEND (DIFFERENCE)

SUM
−ADDEND
ADDEND (DIFFERENCE)

SKILL 1 Subtracting whole numbers

Subtract: 8,674 − 6,319

1. Regroup tens. Subtract ones.	2. Subtract tens.	3. Subtract hundreds.	4. Subtract thousands.
6 14 8,6 7 4 −6,3 1 9 5	6 14 8,6 7 4 −6,3 1 9 5 5	6 14 8,6 7 4 −6,3 1 9 3 5 5	6 14 8,6 7 4 −6,3 1 9 2,3 5 5

SKILL 2 Subtracting whole numbers across zeros

Subtract: 8,012 − 7,635

1. Regroup tens. Subtract ones.	2. No hundreds to regroup. Regroup thousands.	3. Regroup hundreds.	4. Complete the subtraction.
0 12 8,0 1 2 −7,6 3 5 7	7 10 0 12 8,0 1 2 −7,6 3 5 7	9 10 7 10 0 12 8,0 1 2 −7,6 3 5 7	9 10 7 10 0 12 8,0 1 2 −7,6 3 5 3 7 7

SKILL 3 Subtracting decimals

Subtract: 9.2 − 0.7

1. Line up the decimal points and the decimal places.	2. Write the decimal point for the difference.	3. Regroup ones. Subtract tenths.	4. Subtract ones.
9.2 −0.7	9.2 −0.7	8 12 9.2 −0.7 .5	8 12 9.2 −0.7 8.5

Subtract: 6.3 − 2.15

1. Line up the decimal points and the decimal places.	2. Write the decimal point for the difference.	3. Regroup.	4. Subtract.
THINK: 6.3 = 6.30			

$$
\begin{array}{r} 6.30 \\ -2.15 \\ \hline \end{array}
\qquad
\begin{array}{r} 6.30 \\ -2.15 \\ \hline \end{array}
\qquad
\begin{array}{r} 6.\overset{2\;10}{\cancel{3}\cancel{0}} \\ -2.15 \\ \hline \end{array}
\qquad
\begin{array}{r} 6.\overset{2\;10}{\cancel{3}\cancel{0}} \\ -2.15 \\ \hline 4.15 \end{array}
$$

PRACTICE EXERCISES

Subtract.

1. 683 −251	**2.** 872 −839	**3.** 964 − 87	**4.** 4,829 −1,237	**5.** 8,658 −2,672	**6.** 5,216 − 397

7. 5,007 −3,129	**8.** 8,730 −5,372	**9.** 4,900 − 634	**10.** 7.2 −3.6	**11.** 7.34 −4.92	**12.** 78.5 −39.58

13. 0.83 −0.57	**14.** 68.21 −46.3	**15.** 81.1 −79.3	**16.** 90.7 −39.8	**17.** 30.06 − 4.87	**18.** 20.08 −17.3

19. 937 − 425

20. 602 − 418

21. 537 − 189

22. 4,862 − 3,794

23. 6,238 − 429

24. 3,072 − 1,691

25. 8,006 − 5,237

26. 6,521 − 875

27. 5,307 − 87

28. 43.6 − 18.7

29. 58.32 − 29.54

30. 53.1 − 40.2

31. 90.08 − 69.79

32. 36.2 − 14.17

33. 50.3 − 15.82

34. 9 − 6.3

35. 27 − 12.89

36. 60 − 7.35

Solve.

37. It is 2,078 mi from Dallas, Texas, to Seattle, Washington. You have already traveled 1,693 mi. How many more miles do you need to travel?

38. Your class needs to raise $2,004 for a class trip. So far the class has $796. How much more money does the class need to raise?

39. You need to buy some school supplies. The total cost of the supplies is $9.06. You have $7.98. How much more money do you need?

40. In March, there were 3.69 in. of rain. In April, 4 in. of rain fell. How much more rain fell in April than in March?

1.3 MULTIPLYING WHOLE NUMBERS AND DECIMALS

Multiplication Vocabulary:	FACTOR × FACTOR = PRODUCT	FACTOR ×FACTOR PRODUCT

SKILL 1 *Multiplying whole numbers*

Multiply: 6 × 38

1. Multiply ones.
   Regroup.

$$\begin{array}{r} \overset{4}{38} \\ \times\ 6 \\ \hline 8 \end{array}$$

2. Multiply tens.
   Then add 4 tens.

$$\begin{array}{r} \overset{4}{38} \\ \times\ 6 \\ \hline 228 \end{array}$$

SKILL 2 *Multiplying whole numbers with zeros*

Multiply: 9 × 407

1. Multiply ones.
   Regroup.

$$\begin{array}{r} \overset{6}{407} \\ \times\ 9 \\ \hline 3 \end{array}$$

2. Multiply tens.
   Then add 6 tens.
   **THINK: 0 tens + 6 tens
   = 6 tens**

$$\begin{array}{r} \overset{6}{407} \\ \times\ 9 \\ \hline 63 \end{array}$$

3. Multiply
   hundreds.

$$\begin{array}{r} \overset{6}{407} \\ \times\ 9 \\ \hline 3,663 \end{array}$$

SKILL 3 *Multiplying whole numbers and decimals in tenths*

Multiply: 7 × 3.4

1. Multiply as you would whole
   numbers.

$$\begin{array}{r} \overset{2}{3.4} \\ \times\ 7 \\ \hline 238 \end{array}$$

2. Count the number of decimal
   places in the factors. There
   are that many decimal places
   in the product.

$$\begin{array}{r} 3.4 \leftarrow 1 \text{ decimal place} \\ \times\ 7 \leftarrow 0 \text{ decimal place} \\ \hline 23.8 \leftarrow 1 \text{ decimal place} \end{array}$$

SKILL 4 Multiplying whole numbers and decimals in hundredths

Multiply: 8×1.73

1. Multiply as you would whole numbers.

$$\begin{array}{r} {}^{5\ 2} \\ 1.73 \\ \times\quad 8 \\ \hline 1384 \end{array}$$

2. Count the number of decimal places in the factors. There are that many decimal places in the product.

$$\begin{array}{r} 1.73 \leftarrow 2 \text{ decimal places} \\ \times\quad 8 \leftarrow 0 \text{ decimal place} \\ \hline 13.84 \leftarrow 2 \text{ decimal places} \end{array}$$

PRACTICE EXERCISES

Multiply.

1. 24 × 2	**2.** 12 × 4	**3.** 34 × 3	**4.** 39 × 3	**5.** 26 × 9	**6.** 89 × 7
7. 213 × 2	**8.** 401 × 3	**9.** 418 × 3	**10.** 372 × 9	**11.** 609 × 5	**12.** 307 × 8
13. 3.2 × 3	**14.** 2.4 × 2	**15.** 0.9 × 2	**16.** 0.5 × 6	**17.** 6.8 × 3	**18.** 8.2 × 9
19. 4.32 × 2	**20.** 1.31 × 4	**21.** 0.32 × 6	**22.** 0.65 × 7	**23.** 7.07 × 4	**24.** 1.35 × 8

25. 4×52 26. 3×81 27. 8×37 28. 9×16

29. 3×221 30. 6×167 31. 9×618 32. 7×442

33. 8×3.6 34. 5×7.3 35. 3×1.3 36. 6×1.9

37. 8×0.65 38. 2×7.12 39. 4×3.75 40. 9×3.39

41. 3×80 42. 7×104 43. 2×907 44. 8×408

45. 5×1.02 46. 8×6.07 47. 4×0.09 48. 9×0.03

Solve.

49. It is 379 mi from Los Angeles to San Francisco. You made this trip 7 times. How many miles did you travel?

50. You bought 6 lb of vegetables that cost $0.79 per lb. How much money did you spend?

51. Your class is selling school shirts for $5.39 each. The class sold 8 shirts during the first hour of the sale. How much money was collected during that hour?

52. During one year, the annual consumption of fresh citrus fruits was about 94.8 lb per person. About how many pounds did a family of 4 consume that year?

1.4 DIVIDING WHOLE NUMBERS AND DECIMALS

> Division Vocabulary: DIVIDEND ÷ DIVISOR = QUOTIENT AND (R)REMAINDER
> $$\text{DIVISOR)}\overline{\text{DIVIDEND}}^{\;\text{QUOTIENT (R)REMAINDER}}$$

SKILL 1 — *Dividing 3-digit numbers by 1-digit numbers*

Divide: 648 ÷ 3

1. Divide hundreds.

```
    2
3)648
    6
```

2. Divide tens.

```
   21
3)648
   6
    4
    3
    1
```

3. Divide ones.

```
  216
3)648
   6
    4
    3
   18
   18
    0
```

SKILL 2 — *Dividing 4-digit numbers by 1-digit numbers*

Divide: 2,417 ÷ 3

1. Divide hundreds.

```
     8
3)2,417
   2 4
```

2. Divide tens.

```
    80
3)2,417
   2 4
     1
     0
     1
```

3. Divide ones.

```
   805 R2
3)2,417
   2 4
     1
     0
    17
    15
     2
```

SKILL 3 — *Dividing decimals by whole numbers*

Divide: 18.3 ÷ 6

1. Place the decimal point in the quotient directly above the decimal point in the dividend.

2. Divide as you would whole numbers. Write additional zeros in the dividend as needed.

```
    3.05
6)18.30
  18
    3
    0
   30
   30
    0
```

SKILL 4 *Rounding decimal quotients*

Divide and round to the nearest hundredth: $3.4 \div 7$

1. Place the decimal point in the quotient directly above the decimal point in the dividend.

2. Divide one place beyond the place you are rounding to.
   THINK: Divide to thousandths, round to hundredths.

$$\begin{array}{r} 0.485 \\ 7\overline{)3.400} \\ \underline{2\ 8}\downarrow \\ 60 \\ \underline{56}\downarrow \\ 40 \\ \underline{35} \\ 5 \end{array}$$

3. Round the quotient.
   Remember: $\approx$ means *is approximately equal to.* $0.485 \approx 0.49$

PRACTICE EXERCISES

Divide.

1. $2\overline{)84}$
2. $3\overline{)39}$
3. $2\overline{)37}$
4. $6\overline{)282}$
5. $8\overline{)751}$

6. $4\overline{)872}$
7. $5\overline{)530}$
8. $7\overline{)723}$
9. $6\overline{)8,790}$
10. $2\overline{)6,210}$

11. $8\overline{)6,616}$
12. $3\overline{)2,249}$
13. $6\overline{)15.3}$
14. $8\overline{)6.8}$
15. $7\overline{)6.3}$

16. $4\overline{)8.12}$
17. $5\overline{)0.52}$
18. $6\overline{)11.22}$
19. $7\overline{)30.87}$
20. $9\overline{)8.37}$

21. $83 \div 4$
22. $71 \div 6$
23. $842 \div 2$
24. $3,748 \div 4$
25. $6,790 \div 9$

26. $7.2 \div 5$
27. $5.6 \div 4$
28. $8.19 \div 9$
29. $12.34 \div 4$
30. $23.5 \div 8$

Divide and round to the nearest tenth.

31. $9.92 \div 4$
32. $7.41 \div 3$
33. $5.48 \div 8$
34. $7.63 \div 9$
35. $20.3 \div 6$

Divide and round to the nearest hundredth.

36. $8.32 \div 6$
37. $8.59 \div 4$
38. $6.93 \div 8$
39. $6.87 \div 7$
40. $39.7 \div 3$

Solve.

41. An 8-oz box of chocolates costs $3.92. How much is the cost per ounce?

42. The total cost of a restaurant dinner for 6 people was $73.80. How much was each person's equal share?

43. It is about 2,628 mi from Los Angeles to Washington, DC. You made the trip in 6 d, traveling the same distance each day. How many miles did you travel each day?

44. During one year, a family of 5 consumed about 750.2 lb of fresh vegetables. About how much was that per family member?

1.5 FRACTIONS, DECIMALS, AND PERCENTS

Percent Vocabulary:	**Percent (%)** means **per hundred.**
	18% means 18 per hundred, 0.18, or $\frac{18}{100}$.

SKILL 1 *Renaming decimals as percents*

Rename 0.9 as a percent.

1. Multiply by 100 by moving the decimal point
   2 places to the right. Write additional
   zeros if necessary.   0.9 0

2. Write the percent sign.   90%

Other Examples

$0.89 \rightarrow 0.89 \rightarrow 89\%$ $0.034 \rightarrow 0.034 \rightarrow 3.4\%$ $8.4 \rightarrow 8.40 \rightarrow 840\%$

SKILL 2 *Renaming fractions as percents*

Rename $\frac{1}{5}$ as a percent.

1. Write the fraction as a decimal.
   Divide the numerator by the denominator. $\frac{1}{5} \rightarrow 5\overline{)1.0}^{\,0.2}$
   Write additional zeros if necessary.

2. Write the decimal as a percent. $0.20 \rightarrow 20\%$

Other Examples

$2\frac{1}{5} = 2 + \frac{1}{5} \rightarrow 200\% + 20\% = 220\%$ $\frac{5}{8} \rightarrow 8\overline{)5.000}^{\,0.625} = 62.5\%$

SKILL 3 *Renaming percents as decimals*

Rename 3% as a decimal.

1. Divide by 100 by moving the decimal point
   2 places to the left. Write additional $3\% \rightarrow 00 3\%$
   zeros if necessary.

2. Remove the percent sign.   0.03

Other Examples

$43\% \rightarrow 043\% \rightarrow 0.43$ $5.7\% \rightarrow 005.7\% \rightarrow 0.057$ $287\% \rightarrow 287\% \rightarrow 2.87$

SKILL 4 *Renaming percents as fractions*

Rename 80% as a fraction.

1. Write the percent as a fraction with a denominator of 100.

$$80\% = \frac{80}{100}$$

2. Write the fraction in lowest terms.

$$\frac{80}{100} = \frac{80 \div 20}{100 \div 20} = \frac{4}{5}$$

Other Examples

$$75\% = \frac{75}{100} = \frac{75 \div 25}{100 \div 25} = \frac{3}{4}$$

$$150\% = \frac{150}{100} = \frac{150 \div 50}{100 \div 50} = \frac{3}{2} = 1\frac{1}{2}$$

PRACTICE EXERCISES

Rename as a percent.

1. $\frac{23}{100}$ 2. $\frac{12}{100}$ 3. $\frac{7}{100}$ 4. $\frac{3}{100}$ 5. $\frac{186}{100}$ 6. $\frac{600}{100}$

7. 0.63   8. 0.07   9. 0.058   10. 0.2   11. 9   12. 6.21

Rename as a decimal and as a percent.

13. $\frac{1}{4}$ 14. $\frac{4}{5}$ 15. $\frac{7}{8}$ 16. $\frac{3}{8}$ 17. $\frac{2}{5}$ 18. $\frac{7}{10}$

19. $3\frac{1}{2}$ 20. $7\frac{3}{4}$ 21. $9\frac{1}{8}$ 22. $4\frac{5}{8}$ 23. $5\frac{3}{5}$ 24. $8\frac{3}{10}$

Rename as a decimal.

25. 24%   26. 56%   27. 18%   28. 4%   29. 2%   30. 9%

31. 2.8%   32. 0.8%   33. 0.05%   34. 300%   35. 438%   36. 703%

Rename as a fraction.

37. 70%   38. 60%   39. 85%   40. 140%   41. 110%   42. 180%

Complete the table of estimated job opening changes from 1980 to 1990.

Occupation	Percent	Fraction	Decimal
Welder	up 25%	up $\frac{1}{4}$	43. up ■
Librarian	up 5%	44. up ■	up 0.05
Secretary	45. up ■	46. up ■	up 0.32
Computer technician	up 112%	47. up ■	48. up ■
High school teacher	49. down ■	down $\frac{7}{50}$	50. down ■

1.6 FINDING THE PERCENT OF A NUMBER

SKILL 1 *Expressing percents as decimals*

You can express any percent as a decimal.

Find 40% of 19.

1. Write the problem as a number sentence.

40% of 19 is ■
↓   ↓
40% × 19 = ■

2. Rename the percent as a decimal.
   THINK: 40% = 0.40 = 0.4

0.4 × 19 = ■

3. Solve.

0.4 × 19 = 7.6

So 40% of 19 is 7.6.

SKILL 2 *Expressing percents as fractions*

Sometimes it is easier to express a percent as a fraction.

This table shows the equivalent fractions for some percents.

$25\% = \frac{1}{4}$	$50\% = \frac{1}{2}$	$75\% = \frac{3}{4}$	
$20\% = \frac{1}{5}$	$40\% = \frac{2}{5}$	$60\% = \frac{3}{5}$	$80\% = \frac{4}{5}$
$16\frac{2}{3}\% = \frac{1}{6}$	$33\frac{1}{3}\% = \frac{1}{3}$	$66\frac{2}{3}\% = \frac{2}{3}$	$83\frac{1}{3}\% = \frac{5}{6}$
$12\frac{1}{2}\% = \frac{1}{8}$	$37\frac{1}{2}\% = \frac{3}{8}$	$62\frac{1}{2}\% = \frac{5}{8}$	$87\frac{1}{2}\% = \frac{7}{8}$

Find 75% of 16.

1. Write the problem as a number sentence.

75% of 16 is
↓   ↓

2. Rename the percent as a fraction.
   THINK: $75\% = \frac{3}{4}$

75% × 16 = ■
$\frac{3}{4}$ × 16 = ■

3. Solve.
   THINK: $\frac{1}{4} \times 16 \rightarrow 16 \div 4 = 4$

   $\frac{3}{4} \times 16 \rightarrow 3 \times 4 = 12$

   $\frac{3}{4} \times 16 = 12$ So 75% of 16 is 12.

PRACTICE EXERCISES

Find the answer. Express the percent as a decimal.

1. 10% of 40
2. 20% of 30
3. 20% of 600
4. 60% of 50
5. 40% of 15
6. 30% of 320
7. 90% of 36
8. 80% of 52
9. 50% of 73
10. 5% of 65
11. 2% of 95
12. 8% of 57

Find the answer. Express the percent as a fraction.

13. 25% of 24
14. 20% of 25
15. 50% of 36
16. 60% of 45
17. 75% of 56
18. 40% of 85
19. 80% of 75
20. 75% of 24
21. $16\frac{2}{3}$% of 36
22. $12\frac{1}{2}$% of 16
23. $33\frac{1}{3}$% of 39
24. $66\frac{2}{3}$% of 54

Find the answer. Decide whether to express the percent as a decimal or as a fraction.

25. 60% of 35
26. 30% of 36
27. 80% of 50
28. 40% of 35
29. $33\frac{1}{3}$% of 36
30. 75% of 60
31. $87\frac{1}{2}$% of 72
32. 20% of 62
33. $37\frac{1}{2}$% of 64
34. 25% of 400
35. $62\frac{1}{2}$% of 120
36. $16\frac{2}{3}$% of 39

Solve.

37. The trip between 2 towns is exactly 90 mi. You have gone 40% of this distance. How far have you gone?

38. Roy is reading a book that has 320 pages. He has already read 90% of the book. How many pages has he already read?

39. It takes Cara 35 min to walk to school. It takes Sue 80% of Cara's time. How long does it take Sue?

40. Larry's math test score was 90. Andrew's test score was 20% less. How much less was Andrew's score?

41. A sports watch originally cost $96. It is now being sold for $87\frac{1}{2}$% of its original price. How much does the watch cost now?

42. A ski outfit originally cost $71.20. It is now being sold at 30% off. How much has been deducted from the original cost of the outfit?

43. After a taste test, 40% of the 30 people interviewed preferred a new vegetable drink over orange juice. The rest preferred orange juice. How many people preferred the vegetable drink? How many people preferred orange juice?

44. At a store promotion, 150 free televisions were to be given away to persons who arrived during the first 15 min after the store opened. On the first day, 30% of the televisions were given away. How many televisions was that? How many were left for the following days?

PROBLEM Solving STRATEGY

1.7 INTERPRETING DATA FROM TABLES AND GRAPHS

Situation:

The sales staff at Donney Motors keeps records of their car and truck sales. Contests are sometimes held to encourage special efforts to sell various cars and trucks. How can these records be used to identify a salesperson's performance?

Strategy:

You can use information in a **table** or a **bar graph** to solve a problem.

Applying the Strategy:

A. The salesperson who sold the greatest number of trucks in October won a videocassette recorder. Who was it?

THINK: Look at the column labeled "Number of Trucks Sold."

1. Which number is the greatest?   22
2. Which name is on the same line as 22?   Ruth

OCTOBER SALES

Salesperson	Number of trucks sold
Ruth	22
Art	15
John	9
Eric	12
Mindy	4

Ruth sold the greatest number of trucks in October and won the VCR.

B. Eric sold the greatest number of cars and trucks last year and won a free trip. How many cars and trucks did he sell?

THINK: Look at the bar above Eric's name.

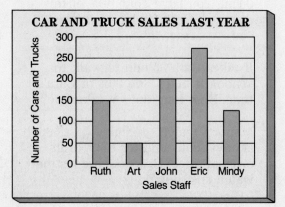

1. Between which 2 numbers does the bar lie?

Between 250 and 300

2. Is the bar nearer to 250 or 300?

It is halfway between 250 and 300.

3. What number is halfway between 250 and 300?

$250 + 300 = 550$
$550 \div 2 = 275$

Eric sold 275 cars and trucks last year.

PRACTICE EXERCISES

Use the table of October Sales for Exercises 1–3.

1. How many trucks did Art sell?   2. How many trucks did Mindy sell?

3. How many more trucks did Art sell than Mindy?

Use the bar graph of Car and Truck Sales Last Year for Exercises 4–7.

4. How many did Ruth sell?   5. How many did Mindy sell?

6. What was the total number sold by Ruth and Mindy together?

7. Who sold the same number last year as Ruth and Mindy together?

The sales staff posted this bar graph to show the numbers of cars and trucks Donney Motors leased last year.

8. Which type was leased the most?

9. How many station wagons were leased?

10. How many more hatchbacks were leased than 2-door sedans?

11. What fraction of the vehicles leased were 4-door sedans? Write this as a percent.

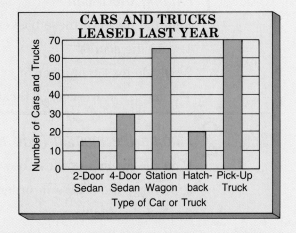

12. Use the information in the table at the right to construct a bar graph. Use this vertical scale: 0, 5, 10, 15, 20, 25, 30, 35.

DECEMBER SALES

Salesperson	Ruth	Art	John	Eric	Mindy
Number of cars sold	10	25	30	15	20

1.8 MEAN, MEDIAN, AND MODE

> **Vocabulary:** **Mean (average)**—The sum of a group of numbers divided by number of addends.
> **Median**—The middle number when a group of numbers is arranged in order from least to greatest.
> **Mode**—The number that occurs most frequently in a group of numbers.

SKILL 1 *Finding the mean*

Find the mean of these basketball player's scores: 48, 36, 51, 72, 58.

1. Add the scores. $48 + 36 + 51 + 72 + 58 = 265$

2. Divide by the number of scores. $265 \div 5 = 53$

The mean, or average, of these scores is 53.

SKILL 2 *Finding the median (odd number of scores)*

Find the median of these bowling scores: 126, 108, 145, 108, 117.

1. Arrange the scores in order.   108   108   117   126   145

2. Find the middle score.   117

The median of these scores is 117.

SKILL 3 *Finding the median (even number of scores)*

Find the median of these bowling scores: 139, 106, 145, 113, 128, 109.

1. Arrange the scores in order.   106   109   113   128   139   145

2. Find the middle score.

    THINK: There is no one middle number.   113   128

3. Find the mean of the two middle scores. $113 + 128 = 241$
$241 \div 2 = 120.5$

The median of these scores is 120.5.

SKILL 4 *Finding the mode*

Find the mode of these race times: 9.3, 9.6, 9.2, 10.2, 9.6, 10.1, 9.5.

Find the time that occurs most often.   9.6 occurs twice.

The mode of these scores is 9.6.

PRACTICE EXERCISES

Find the mean.

1. 86, 90, 94

2. 420, 185, 874

3. 4.2, 8.5, 2.6

4. 15, 34, 19, 52

5. 172, 550, 293, 413

6. 1.2, 6.3, 9.5, 10.2

7. 20, 18, 6, 10, 16

8. 2.7, 1.8, 4.5, 5.1, 3.4

Find the median.

9. 7, 13, 25, 46, 8

10. 9, 12, 7, 24, 3, 18

11. 1.3, 6.2, 8.9, 2.4, 5.6

12. 2.3, 5.4, 0.7, 1.6, 4.6, 3.7

Find the mode.

13. 1, 3, 5, 9, 3, 6, 7, 8

14. 2.6, 3.5, 0.8, 4.7, 6.2, 0.8, 1.2

Find the mean, the median, and the mode. Round the mean and median to nearest tenth.

15. 56, 78, 92

16. 108, 135, 87

17. 6.3, 2.5, 10.1

18. 81, 78, 56, 31

19. 302, 220, 220, 208

20. 14.8, 16.2, 4.8, 12.1

21. 75, 93, 89, 75, 84

22. 158, 213, 107, 213, 213

23. 6.1, 5.9, 4.2, 5.9, 10.7

Solve.

24. At noon each day last week, Fran took temperature readings. They were 16°F, 23°F, 10°F, 9°F, and 14°F. What are the mean and median of these temperatures?

25. Six judges scored a diving contest. On one dive, 2 judges gave a 7.5. The other scores were 8.0, 7.9, 6.8. and 7.3. What are the mean, median, and mode of these scores?

EXTENSION   Using a Tally

Each time Ed played miniature golf, he made a tally mark next to his score.

1. How many games did Ed play?

2. What are his two mode scores?

3. What is his median score?

What is the total of the scores of:

4. 69?   **5.** 68?   **6.** 67?

7. What is his mean score?

ED'S GOLF SCORES

Score	Total	Score	Total
72 I	72	69 ++++II	
71 I	71	68 III	
70 ++++II	490	67 II	

CHAPTER REVIEW

Vocabulary Choose the letter of the word(s) that completes the sentence.

1. Percent means ■. [10]

   a. Per ten   **b.** Tenths   **c.** Per hundred

2. The sum of a group of numbers divided by the number of addends is called the ■. [16]

   a. Mean   **b.** Median   **c.** Mode

3. The middle number when a group of numbers is arranged in order from least to greatest is called the ■. [16]

   a. Mean   **b.** Median   **c.** Mode

Skills Add. [2]

4. $682 + 327$ 5. $6,981 + 2,217$ 6. $741 + 2,037 + 667$

7. $4.7 + 3.6$ 8. $5.81 + 7.99$ 9. $3.16 + 4.2 + 3.55$

Subtract. [4]

10. $753 - 541$ 11. $9,832 - 6,754$ 12. $5,003 - 2,324$

13. $9.6 - 6.4$ 14. $11.07 - 9.21$ 15. $10.6 - 3.58$

Multiply. [6]

16. 2×43 17. 6×725 18. 7×209

19. 3×6.5 20. 5×3.23 21. 4×8.02

Divide. [8]

22. $468 \div 2$ 23. $644 \div 7$ 24. $6,072 \div 8$

25. $7.8 \div 3$ 26. $0.6 \div 4$ 27. $40.02 \div 5$

Rename as a percent. [10]

28. $\frac{6}{100}$ 29. $\frac{57}{100}$ 30. $\frac{400}{100}$ 31. 0.87 32. 0.09 33. 7

Rename as a decimal. [10]

34. 43% 35. 98% 36. 4% 37. 0.6% 38. 600% 39. 153%

Find the answer. [10, 12]

40. 40% of 25 41. 70% of 96 42. $12\frac{1}{2}\%$ of 48

CHAPTER TEST

Angel Pastor ♡'s Christine Alzeri

Add.

1. 682 + 527 **2.** 8,732 + 1,487 **3.** 23.6 + 7.5 **4.** 16.7 + 0.89 + 3.65

Subtract.

5. 739 − 486 **6.** 4,376 − 2,923 **7.** 48.7 − 32.81 **8.** 50.06 − 17.39

Multiply.

9. 4 × 321 **10.** 7 × 803 **11.** 4 × 8.2 **12.** 7 × 6.08

Divide.

13. 652 ÷ 4 **14.** 2,464 ÷ 3 **15.** 7.2 ÷ 4 **16.** 4.68 ÷ 9

Divide and round to the nearest hundredth.

17. 9.27 ÷ 4 **18.** 3.86 ÷ 7 **19.** 7.31 ÷ 6 **20.** 5.08 ÷ 6

Rename as a percent.

21. 0.75 **22.** 0.062 **23.** 4.87 **24.** $\frac{2}{5}$ **25.** $\frac{3}{4}$

Rename as a decimal and as a fraction.

26. 60% **27.** 95% **28.** 5% **29.** 160% **30.** 250%

Find the answer. Express the percent as a decimal or as a fraction.

31. 30% of 70 **32.** 40% of 45 **33.** $33\frac{1}{3}$% of 42 **34.** 75% of 64

Group of numbers: 15, 12, 10, 15

Find:

35. the mean **36.** the median **37.** the mode

Use the bar graph for Exercises 38–40.

38. Who sold the greatest number of cars and trucks?

39. How many cars and trucks did Ruth sell?

40. How many more cars and trucks did Mindy sell than Art?

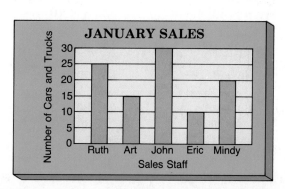

JANUARY SALES

PreSkills TEST

Round to the nearest ten.

1. 58   **2.** 62   **3.** 27   **4.** 34   **5.** 95

Round to the nearest hundred.

6. 138   **7.** 594   **8.** 737   **9.** 461   **10.** 975

Round to the nearest thousand.

11. 8,659   **12.** 9,823   **13.** 1,844   **14.** 2,425   **15.** 6,432

Round to the nearest tenth.

16. 0.86   **17.** 0.68   **18.** 0.128   **19.** 0.268   **20.** 0.985

Round to the nearest hundredth.

21. 0.067   **22.** 0.084   **23.** 0.0524   **24.** 0.037   **25.** 0.098

Round to the nearest whole number.

26. $2\frac{3}{4}$ **27.** $8\frac{1}{5}$ **28.** $9\frac{1}{2}$ **29.** $36\frac{2}{3}$ **30.** $57\frac{3}{16}$

Add or subtract.

31. $\begin{array}{r} 20 \\ +17 \\ \hline \end{array}$ **32.** $\begin{array}{r} 50 \\ +38 \\ \hline \end{array}$ **33.** $\begin{array}{r} 700 \\ +125 \\ \hline \end{array}$ **34.** $\begin{array}{r} 400 \\ +369 \\ \hline \end{array}$ **35.** $\begin{array}{r} 900 \\ +873 \\ \hline \end{array}$

36. $\begin{array}{r} 2,000 \\ +3,000 \\ \hline \end{array}$ **37.** $\begin{array}{r} 6,000 \\ +4,000 \\ \hline \end{array}$ **38.** $\begin{array}{r} 10,000 \\ +40,000 \\ \hline \end{array}$ **39.** $\begin{array}{r} 30,000 \\ +50,000 \\ \hline \end{array}$ **40.** $\begin{array}{r} 70,000 \\ +20,000 \\ \hline \end{array}$

41. $\begin{array}{r} 65 \\ -30 \\ \hline \end{array}$ **42.** $\begin{array}{r} 88 \\ -40 \\ \hline \end{array}$ **43.** $\begin{array}{r} 592 \\ -300 \\ \hline \end{array}$ **44.** $\begin{array}{r} 910 \\ -500 \\ \hline \end{array}$ **45.** $\begin{array}{r} 798 \\ -700 \\ \hline \end{array}$

46. $\begin{array}{r} 5,000 \\ -3,000 \\ \hline \end{array}$ **47.** $\begin{array}{r} 8,000 \\ -4,000 \\ \hline \end{array}$ **48.** $\begin{array}{r} 60,000 \\ -50,000 \\ \hline \end{array}$ **49.** $\begin{array}{r} 40,000 \\ -20,000 \\ \hline \end{array}$ **50.** $\begin{array}{r} 90,000 \\ -60,000 \\ \hline \end{array}$

Multiply or divide.

51. 6×30 **52.** 8×10 **53.** 54×500 **54.** 8×900

55. 30×100 **56.** 50×500 **57.** 70×800 **58.** 90×400

59. $40 \div 4$ **60.** $20 \div 4$ **61.** $700 \div 7$ **62.** $400 \div 5$

63. $60 \div 30$ **64.** $80 \div 40$ **65.** $100 \div 20$ **66.** $200 \div 50$

Chapter 2

THE CALCULATOR AND ESTIMATION

You will probably be using a calculator to work the exercises in this book. Why have people always been interested in inventing devices for computing numbers?

When you want to compute quickly and accurately with greater numbers, you can use a calculator.

The four basic operations can be performed easily.

Operation	Calculator Entry	Display
Add: 49,567 + 78,078	4 9 5 6 7 + 7 8 0 7 8 =	127,645
Subtract: 34.014 − 5.708	3 4 . 0 1 4 − 5 . 7 0 8 =	28.306
Multiply: 908 × 0.045	9 0 8 × . 0 4 5 =	40.86
Divide: 0.078)4.9452	4 . 9 4 5 2 ÷ . 0 7 8 =	63.4

You can use a calculator to do a series of operations without using the = key (**is equal to**) after each operation.

EXAMPLE 1

Compute: $45.09 - 6 + 4.7 - 18$

Operation	Calculator Entry	Display
1. Subtract.	4 5 . 0 9 − 6 +	39.09
	Get ready to add.	
2. Add.	4 . 7 −	43.79
	Get ready to subtract.	
3. Subtract.	1 8 =	25.79

So $45.09 - 6 + 4.7 - 18 = 25.79$.

The CE key (**Clear Entry**) can help you when you have entered a wrong number into the calculator.

EXAMPLE 2

Correct, then complete the following computation on a calculator.

Multiply: $4.5 \times 78 \times 0.09$ Error

	Calculator Display
Calculator Entry: 4 . 5 × 8 7	87
1. Press CE to clear 87 from the calculator.	0
2. Complete the computation.	
Enter: 7 8 ×	351
Enter: . 0 9 =	31.59

So $4.5 \times 78 \times 0.09 = 31.59$.

FOR DISCUSSION

1. For which operations will the order in which you enter two numbers not affect the answer? Why?

2. The entry below was made on two different calculators. One calculator displayed the answer 6.15. The other calculator displayed the answer 16.4. Explain the different answers.
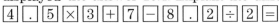

PRACTICE EXERCISES

Use a calculator to compute.

1. 234,634 + 33,568 + 995,400
2. 1,294,588 − 346,183
3. 4,983 × 8,834
4. 27,587 ÷ 49
5. 256.3 + 89.375 + 5,832.6
6. 735.8 − 35.635
7. 93.53 × 7.394
8. 425.36 × 18.3
9. 39.447 + 874.336 − 175.68
10. 46.84 × 7.03 ÷ 2
11. 114,289 divided by 1,126
12. 36.5 divided into 65,700
13. 678.68 divided by 7.6
14. 0.4 divided into 0.028

Divide and round to the nearest tenth.

15. 737 ÷ 15
16. $18.2\overline{)375}$
17. 13,275 ÷ 1,083
18. $3.79\overline{)463}$

Divide and round to the nearest hundredth.

19. 14.83 ÷ 0.21
20. $2.9\overline{)0.37}$
21. 72.6 ÷ 0.046
22. $53.8\overline{)2.847}$

Compute from left to right.

23. 687.3 + 39.4 − 398.46 − 4.236
24. 933.6 − 3.498 + 364.9 − 483.78
25. 76.2 × 3.9 ÷ 7.5 × 35
26. 28.64 ÷ 0.2 × 0.45 ÷ 15

Solve.

27. George spent $27.80 for a pair of pants and $14.50 for a shirt. He paid a sales tax of $2.54. How much did he spend in all?

28. Joe's car odometer read 27,314 mi when he left for vacation. Three weeks later, the odometer read 35,278 mi. How far had Joe traveled?

29. Susan is reimbursed 27.5¢ per mi when she drives for business purposes. She drove 85 mi last week. How much was she reimbursed?

30. Gary ordered 500 sheets of paper. When they arrived, they formed a pile 4.5 cm high. How thick was each sheet?

You may often find it easier to compute mentally than to use pencil and paper or even a calculator. You can add mentally by using numbers that are **multiples of 10** and then adjusting.

EXAMPLE 1

You are buying a shirt for $19 and a jacket for $44. Mentally compute the cost of the shirt and the jacket.

Add: $19 + $44

THINK: $19 is $1 less than $20. $20 + $44 = $64

So $19 + $44 is $1 less than $64, or $63.

The shirt and the jacket will cost $63.

You can subtract mentally in the same way.

EXAMPLE 2

Subtract:

a. 94 − 18

THINK: 18 is 2 less than 20.

94 − 20 = 74
So 94 − 18 is 2 more
than 74, or 76.

b. 465 − 190

THINK: 190 is 10 less than 200.

465 − 200 = 265
So 465 − 190 is 10
more than 265, or 275.

Mental computation is also commonly used when you multiply or divide by **powers of 10,** such as 10, 100, or 1,000.

EXAMPLE 3

Multiply: 100 × 87.3

THINK: The product must be greater than 87.3, so move the decimal point to the right.

$100 × 87.30 = 8,730$

2 zeros   2 places right

EXAMPLE 4

Divide: 38,430 ÷ 1,000

THINK: The quotient must be less than 38,430, so move the decimal point to the left.

$38,430 ÷ 1,000 = 38.43$

3 places left   3 zeros

FOR DISCUSSION

1. Ricky argues that mental computation is a waste of time, since he has a calculator. How would you convince Ricky that he is wrong?

2. Enter 245.8 into your calculator. Press $\div$ $\boxed{10}$ $\boxed{=}$. Read the display. Press $\boxed{=}$. Read the display. Press $\boxed{=}$ and read. What is happening?

PRACTICE EXERCISES

Use mental computation to add or subtract.

1. $56 + 19$	**2.** $25 + 48$	**3.** $263 + 390$	**4.** $467 + 310$
5. $343 + 590$	**6.** $36¢ + 29¢$	**7.** $\$638 + \$206$	**8.** $\$6.55 + \$3.39$
9. $1.20 + 0.62$	**10.** $6.57 + 2.99$	**11.** $80 - 38$	**12.** $47 - 19$
13. $586 - 420$	**14.** $376 - 102$	**15.** $80¢ - 29¢$	**16.** $\$875 - \$280$
17. $\$200 - \$61$	**18.** $\$1.70 - \$0.61$	**19.** $4.63 - 1.98$	**20.** $7.80 - 4.38$

Use mental computation to multiply or divide.

21. 10×127	**22.** $100 \times 4{,}806$	**23.** 10×37.24	**24.** 100×6.8
25. $1{,}000 \times 2.8$	**26.** 100×759.5	**27.** $1{,}000 \times 0.43$	**28.** 10×0.532
29. $3{,}200 \div 100$	**30.** $6.5 \div 10$	**31.** $0.27 \div 100$	**32.** $19.4 \div 10$
33. $459 \div 1{,}000$	**34.** $28.5 \div 100$	**35.** $4.3 \div 1{,}000$	**36.** $2{,}045 \div 100$

Solve using mental computation.

37. The tax on a $37.60 blouse is $2.82. What is the cost of the blouse including tax?

38. A $550 refrigerator is marked down $59. How much does the refrigerator now sell for?

39. An average person can lift 90 lb. If a forklift can lift 1,000 times as much, how much can the forklift lift?

40. A box contains 425 g of cereal. How much will a bowl containing one-tenth of the cereal weigh?

41. Chin bought groceries that cost $1.46, 80¢, and 69¢. How much did he spend in all?

42. The 100 members of a band agree to split the $7,340.00 cost of their trip. What is each member's share?

EXTENSION   Multiplying Mentally by 50 and by 25

Multiply: 50×2.8

THINK: $100 \times 2.8 = 280$

Since $50 = 100 \div 2$,
then $50 \times 2.8 = 280 \div 2 = 140$.

Multiply: 25×16.4

THINK: $100 \times 16.4 = 1{,}640$

Since $25 = 100 \div 4$,
then $25 \times 16.4 = 1{,}640 \div 4 = 410$.

Use mental computation to multiply.

1. 50×4.6	**2.** 50×84	**3.** 25×4.8	**4.** 25×240
5. 50×0.9	**6.** 50×120	**7.** 25×0.72	**8.** 25×360
9. 0.24×50	**10.** 1.08×50	**11.** 404×25	**12.** 82.8×25

2.3 ESTIMATING SUMS AND DIFFERENCES

A common way to **estimate** sums is to round each number to its **greatest place** and then add mentally.

EXAMPLE 1

About how much is the total population of Fairview County?

Town	Greenfield	Salem	Goshen	Wells
Population	21,284	3,487	38,372	10,480

1. Round.

$$
\begin{array}{rcr}
21{,}284 & \to & 20{,}000 \\
3{,}487 & \to & 3{,}000 \\
38{,}372 & \to & 40{,}000 \\
+10{,}480 & \to & +10{,}000 \\
\hline
\end{array}
$$

2. Add.   73,000

73,000 is a good estimate for the total population.

When adding decimals or money amounts, estimate by rounding each number to its **greatest nonzero place**.

EXAMPLE 2

Estimate:

a. 31.07 + 0.6 + 3.87

1. Round.

$$
\begin{array}{rcr}
31.07 & \to & 30 \\
0.6 & \to & 0.6 \\
+ \ 3.87 & \to & + \ 4 \\
\hline
\end{array}
$$

2. Add.   34.6

b. Estimate: 95¢ + $2.09 + $5.75

1. Round.

$$
\begin{array}{rcr}
\$0.95 & \to & \$1 \\
\$2.09 & \to & \$2 \\
+\$5.75 & \to & +\$6 \\
\hline
\end{array}
$$

2. Add. $9

The same estimating rules are used for subtraction.

EXAMPLE 3

Estimate:

a. 27,387 − 2,163

1. Round.

$$
\begin{array}{rcr}
27{,}387 & \to & 30{,}000 \\
- \ 2{,}163 & \to & - \ 2{,}000 \\
\hline
\end{array}
$$

2. Subtract.   28,000

b. 0.37 − 0.097

1. Round.

$$
\begin{array}{rcr}
0.37 & \to & 0.4 \\
-0.097 & \to & -0.1 \\
\hline
\end{array}
$$

2. Subtract.   0.3

FOR DISCUSSION

1. How is mental computation different from estimation?

2. To estimate $4.80 + $2.25 + $3.40, Gail used $5 + $2 + $3 = $10. Gail's mother rounded up and used $5 + $3 + $4 = $12. What are some advantages of doing estimation the second way?

PRACTICE EXERCISES

Estimate the sum or difference.

1. 47 +29	**2.** 378 +128	**3.** 4,572 +8,752	**4.** 572 628 + 84	**5.** 27,480 4,749 +32,564
6. $6.84 + 3.14	**7.** $7.85 + 0.98	**8.** $2.18 0.95 + 1.32	**9.** 4.98 +5.1	**10.** 893.5 + 37.75
11. 4.78 0.7 +1.26	**12.** 0.099 +0.43	**13.** 778 −259	**14.** 432 − 19	**15.** 286 − 63
16. 88,271 −27,557	**17.** 72,800 − 4,290	**18.** $0.82 − 0.17	**19.** $28.14 − 14.80	**20.** $13.72 − 0.84
21. 9.3 −2.87	**22.** 248.2 − 24.9	**23.** 1.37 −0.0294	**24.** 4.89 −0.75	**25.** 0.56 −0.096

26. 47,564 + 6,891   **27.** $795.66 + $24.13   **28.** 0.028 + 0.0095

29. 61,285 − 8,721   **30.** $795.77 − $9.56   **31.** 0.082 − 0.0099

Solve.

32. Ben bought lunch for $3.08. About how much change did he get from $5.00?

33. Robin bought a radio for $46.30. About how much change did she get from $100.00?

34. A television is advertised at Bob's Appliances for $379. The same television is on sale at Acme Audio for $285. About how much can be saved by buying it at Acme?

35. One store sells microwave ovens for $229.50. Another sells them for $309.88. About how much can be saved by buying the less expensive microwave oven?

Use the Fair Attendance sign for Exercises 36–37.

FAIR ATTENDANCE	
Friday	18,275
Saturday	37,587
Sunday	22,812

36. About how many people attended in all?

37. About how many more people attended the fair on Saturday than on Friday?

THE CALCULATOR AND ESTI

2.4 ESTIMATING PRODUCTS AND QUOTIENTS

A common way to estimate products and quotients is to round each number to its **greatest place** and then compute mentally.

EXAMPLE 1

There were 285 wildlife pamphlets left to be distributed. Six friends shared the task. About how many pamphlets must each person hand out if they share the job?

1. Round.   285 rounds to 300. Since 6 is a 1-digit number, it does not need to be rounded.

2. Divide. $300 \div 6 = 50$.

So each person will hand out about 50 pamphlets.

EXAMPLE 2

a. Estimate: $2{,}789 \times 48$

1. Round. $3{,}000 \times 50$

2. Multiply. $150{,}000$

b. Estimate: $22{,}270 \div 39$

1. Round. $20{,}000 \div 40$

2. Divide.   500

When multiplying or dividing decimals or money amounts, estimate by rounding each number to its **greatest nonzero place.**

EXAMPLE 3

a. Estimate: $78 \times \$0.29$

1. Round. $80 \times \$0.30$

2. Multiply. $24

b. Estimate: $324.8 \div 4.87$

1. Round. $300 \div 5$

2. Divide.   60

FOR DISCUSSION

1. Chicken costs $1.29 per lb. When Rob purchased 3.7 lb, the price sticker read $6.24. How did Rob know immediately that he was being overcharged?

2. Laura calculated that 3.2×16.8 is 5.376. Estimate and explain why Laura's answer cannot be correct.

PRACTICE EXERCISES

Estimate the product or quotient.

1. 7×23	**2.** 2×192	**3.** 612×289	**4.** $4,812 \times 44$
5. $7 \times \$1.98$	**6.** $52 \times \$12.75$	**7.** $480 \times \$4.90$	**8.** $360 \times \$19.95$
9. 8×9.7	**10.** 82×5.8	**11.** 713×3.87	**12.** 8.9×3.13
13. 4.845×84.1	**14.** 27.19×8.47	**15.** $67 \times \$0.39$	**16.** $385 \times \$0.82$
17. 32×0.638	**18.** 185×0.89	**19.** 0.43×0.18	**20.** 0.65×0.34
21. $87 \div 3$	**22.** $413 \div 8$	**23.** $182 \div 21$	**24.** $216 \div 39$
25. $3,485 \div 11$	**26.** $875 \div 182$	**27.** $7,742 \div 390$	**28.** $\$11.80 \div 5$
29. $\$625.50 \div 3$	**30.** $\$43.60 \div 22$	**31.** $\$198.75 \div 38$	**32.** $\$293 \div 53$
33. $39.21 \div 23$	**34.** $87 \div 2.87$	**35.** $292 \div 6.14$	**36.** $957.5 \div 46$
37. $7.8 \div 4.3$	**38.** $35.7 \div 5.4$	**39.** $286.4 \div 2.88$	**40.** $962.1 \div 19.3$

Use the menu for Exercises 41–44.

41. About how much will 6 hot dogs cost?

42. About how much will 5 juices cost?

43. About how many hot dogs can be bought for $6.00?

44. About how many hamburgers can be bought for $18.00?

MENU

Hot dogs	$1.15
Hamburgers	$1.89
Juice	$0.79

Solve.

45. Denim cloth sells for $7.79 per yd. About how much will 8 yd of denim cloth cost?

46. Cassette tapes cost $6.75 each. About how much will 12 tapes cost?

47. School sweaters cost $18.50 each. About how many sweaters can be bought for $57.00?

48. Men's suits cost $175.50 each. About how many suits can be bought for $820.00?

Sonya sometimes baby-sits for a neighbor after school. Since she is interested in an approximation of how much time she has worked, an estimate will be sufficient. Estimating sums and differences is often used with mixed numbers because they are easily rounded up or down to the **nearest whole number.**

EXAMPLE 1   About how many hours did Sonya baby-sit last week?

1. Round. $7\frac{1}{2} \rightarrow 8$

   $3\frac{1}{4} \rightarrow 3$

   $+5\frac{3}{4} \rightarrow +6$

2. Add. $\overline{17}$

Sonya baby-sat about 17 h.

SONYA'S HOURS
Mon. ——— $7\frac{1}{2}$ h
Tues. ——— $3\frac{1}{4}$ h
Wed. ——— $5\frac{3}{4}$ h

EXAMPLE 2

a. Estimate: $67\frac{7}{8} - 41\frac{3}{4}$
                  $\downarrow$ $\downarrow$
   1. Round. $68 - 42$
   2. Subtract. 26

b. Estimate: $12\frac{13}{16} - 7\frac{3}{8}$
                  $\downarrow$ $\downarrow$
   1. Round. $13 - 7$
   2. Subtract. 6

Rounding mixed numbers is also helpful when estimating products and quotients.

EXAMPLE 3

a. Estimate: $4 \times 7\frac{3}{4}$
                       $\downarrow$
   1. Round. 4×8
   2. Multiply. 32

b. Estimate: $8\frac{7}{8} \times 3\frac{1}{8}$
                  $\downarrow$ $\downarrow$
   1. Round. 9×3
   2. Multiply. 27

EXAMPLE 4

a. Estimate: $1{,}000 \div 19\frac{7}{8}$
                           $\downarrow$
   1. Round. $1{,}000 \div 20$
   2. Divide.   50

b. Estimate: $14\frac{3}{4} \div 3\frac{1}{16}$
                  $\downarrow$ $\downarrow$
   1. Round. $15 \div 3$
   2. Divide.   5

FOR DISCUSSION

When estimating $48\frac{3}{4} - 26\frac{1}{9}$, Nancy rounded to the nearest 10 and subtracted $50 - 30$. Jill rounded to the nearest whole number and subtracted $49 - 26$. Compare and contrast these two methods.

PRACTICE EXERCISES

Estimate the answer.

1. $7\frac{3}{4} + 10\frac{3}{4}$

2. $2\frac{1}{4} + 8\frac{7}{8}$

3. $27\frac{1}{6} + 3\frac{7}{8}$

4. $43\frac{3}{8} + 22\frac{5}{6}$

5. $2\frac{2}{3} + 5\frac{1}{4} + 6$

6. $4\frac{4}{5} + 6\frac{5}{6} + 10\frac{1}{3}$

7. $2\frac{1}{2} + 8\frac{1}{4} + 17\frac{7}{8}$

8. $15\frac{1}{4} + 8\frac{4}{5} + 14\frac{9}{10}$

9. $12\frac{2}{3} - 7\frac{3}{4}$

10. $6\frac{3}{4} - 2\frac{5}{8}$

11. $3\frac{3}{4} - 3\frac{1}{8}$

12. $19\frac{7}{8} - 10\frac{1}{3}$

13. $100 - 17\frac{1}{8}$

14. $37\frac{4}{5} - 18\frac{1}{5}$

15. $97\frac{1}{3} - 26\frac{5}{8}$

16. $77\frac{3}{5} - 52\frac{5}{6}$

17. $6\frac{3}{4} \times 5$

18. $8\frac{1}{3} \times 4\frac{7}{8}$

19. $7\frac{4}{5} \times 9\frac{1}{6}$

20. $100 \times 8\frac{5}{8}$

21. $200 \times 3\frac{7}{8}$

22. $\frac{7}{8} \times 30\frac{1}{4}$

23. $29\frac{1}{2} \times 2\frac{1}{16}$

24. $39\frac{1}{2} \times 29\frac{11}{16}$

25. $16\frac{1}{4} \div 1\frac{7}{8}$

26. $55\frac{3}{4} \div 7\frac{7}{8}$

27. $59\frac{3}{5} \div 6\frac{1}{5}$

28. $1,000 \div 4\frac{7}{10}$

29. $2,000 \div 9\frac{3}{4}$

30. $27\frac{5}{8} \div 1\frac{7}{8}$

31. $72\frac{3}{8} \div 35\frac{7}{8}$

32. $89\frac{4}{5} \div 44\frac{15}{16}$

Use the chart for Exercises 33–36.

33. About how many hours did Jody work altogether?

34. About how many more hours did Jody work on Saturday than on Sunday?

35. If Jody works twice as long next Saturday, about how long will she work?

36. At this rate, about how many 3-d work periods will Jody need to work before she has worked 75 h?

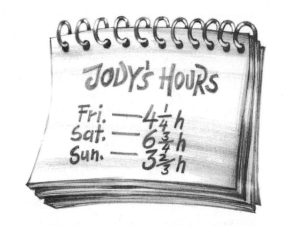

Solve.

37. A piece of pipe $42\frac{3}{4}$ in. long is cut from a piece $75\frac{1}{4}$ in. long. About how much pipe is left?

38. A hiker covered $24\frac{8}{10}$ mi in $4\frac{3}{4}$ h. About how fast was she traveling?

39. Aaron worked $45\frac{1}{2}$ h last week and $39\frac{3}{4}$ h this week. About how many hours did he work during the 2 wk?

40. Sue is cutting pieces of ribbon $8\frac{1}{8}$ in. long. About how many pieces can she cut from a 6-ft length of ribbon?

Matt has just filled the gas tank in his car with 9.8 gal of gasoline. He has driven 213 mi since his last fill-up and wants to check his gas mileage.

Matt could use a calculator and actually divide 213 by 9.8, getting 21.734693, or 21.7 mi per gal. But of what practical value is an answer that exact? An estimate would do here.

EXAMPLE 1 About how many miles per gallon did Matt's car get?

THINK: Miles per gallon means 213 mi divided by 9.8 gal.

1. Round. $213 \div 9.8 \approx 200 \div 10$

2. Divide. 20 mi per gal

Matt's car got about 20 mi per gal.

Another use for estimation is in judging the reasonableness of answers, especially those computed on calculators or cash registers.

EXAMPLE 2 Karen's lunch bill came to $5.75. She gave the cashier $20.00 and received $12.25 in change. Was this a reasonable amount of change?

THINK: The change will be $20.00 − $5.75.

1. Round. $20 − $5.75 ≈ $20 − $6

2. Subtract. $14 in change

No, $12.25 was not a reasonable amount of change.

Estimation is also used when we want to be sure we have enough money to make purchases. When estimating the cost of a purchase, round all money amounts up, getting an **overestimate.**

EXAMPLE 3 Willie selected 3 ties for $8.40 each and 2 sweaters for $29.50 each. Will $80 be enough to buy these items?

1. Estimate the cost of the ties. 3 × $8.40 ≈ 3 × $9 = $27

2. Estimate the cost of the sweaters. 2 × $29.50 ≈ 2 × $30 = $60

3. Add the estimates. $27 + $60 = $87

Since $80 < $87, $80 will not be enough to buy these items.

FOR DISCUSSION

1. Name other situations in which you would round up all amounts in order to estimate. Tell why.

2. Name situations in which estimates would not be appropriate. Tell why.

PRACTICE EXERCISES

Estimate to choose the reasonable answer.

1. 487 + 357 + 621   **a.** 148   **b.** 1,483   **c.** 2,483

2. 6.2 + 15.9 + 0.3   **a.** 22.4   **b.** 2.2   **c.** 224

3. 5,946 − 2,873   **a.** 307   **b.** 8,819   **c.** 3,073

4. 15.87 − 0.6   **a.** 9.87   **b.** 5.81   **c.** 15.27

5. 27 × $18.50   **a.** $49.95   **b.** $4,995   **c.** $499.50

6. 7.81 × 0.32   **a.** 2.4992   **b.** 24.992   **c.** 0.24992

7. 58.24 ÷ 3.2   **a.** 18.2   **b.** 1.82   **c.** 182

8. $18,540 ÷ 45   **a.** $41.20   **b.** $412   **c.** $4,120

Solve.

9. Beth needs $48 for a new dress. If her allowance is $5 per wk, about how many weeks will it take her to save the $48?

10. Ethan spent $7.85 on books. About how much change did he receive when he gave the clerk $20.00?

11. A car went 487 mi on 19.6 gal of gasoline. About how many miles per gallon is that?

12. About how far can a car go on 15 gal of gasoline if it averages 29.3 mi per gal?

Use the ad and estimate for Exercises 13–16.

13. Will $15.00 be enough to buy 3 pairs of socks?

14. Will $15.00 be enough to buy a scarf and a belt?

15. Will $15.00 be enough to buy 2 pairs of socks and a tie?

16. Is $30.00 enough to buy 1 of each item?

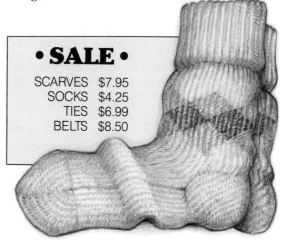

• **SALE** •

SCARVES $7.95
SOCKS $4.25
TIES $6.99
BELTS $8.50

PROBLEM
Solving
STRATEGY

2.7 WHICH WAY TO COMPUTE?

Situation:

Suppose you are asked to find the cost of 5 pairs of socks at $1.95 a pair plus a sales tax of $0.40. Which way would you use to compute the answer?

Strategy:

Use paper and pencil skills, a calculator, or mental computation skills depending on the situation, the numbers involved, or your own personal preference.

Applying the Strategy:

Joan took out a pencil and computed:

$$\begin{array}{r} \$1.95 \\ \times \quad 5 \\ \hline \$9.75 \\ + \ 0.40 \\ \hline \$10.15 \end{array}$$

Jill took out a calculator and computed:

$$\boxed{5}\boxed{\times}\boxed{1}\boxed{.}\boxed{9}\boxed{5}\boxed{+}\boxed{.}\boxed{4}\boxed{=}$$
$$\boxed{\quad 10.15 \quad}$$

Jackie thought:
$1.95 is $2 less 5¢.
So 5 pairs are $10 less 25¢, or $9.75, plus 40¢.

40¢ is 25¢ plus 15¢.
So $9.75 plus 25¢ is $10, plus 15¢ is $10.15.

Notice that Joan, Jill, and Jackie all got the same answer.

Other Situations

A. What is the best way to compute the amount of change that Ray received if he paid $5.00 for a $2.97 meal?

> Ray can easily compute this mentally.
> He thinks: $2.97 is 3¢ less than $3.00.
> $5.00 − $3.00 is $2.00.

So $5.00 − $2.97 is $2.00 plus 3¢, or $2.03.

B. What is the best way for Alvin to compute the new balance in the class treasury? The balance was $357.82. He made a deposit of $182.14 and then made a withdrawal of $78.50.

> Alvin needs an exact answer, and the numbers are too great to use mental computation. So he uses his calculator or paper and pencil to get $461.46.
> $$\boxed{3}\boxed{5}\boxed{7}\boxed{.}\boxed{8}\boxed{2}\boxed{+}\boxed{1}\boxed{8}\boxed{2}\boxed{.}\boxed{1}\boxed{4}\boxed{-}\boxed{7}\boxed{8}\boxed{.}\boxed{5}\boxed{=}\boxed{\quad 461.46 \quad}$$

C. What is the best way for Mr. Lee to compute the total length of pipe?

One piece is $4\frac{3}{4}$ ft long, and the other is $2\frac{7}{8}$ ft long.

If Mr. Lee wants an exact answer, it is unlikely that he will use mental computation or convert to decimals and use a calculator. He will probably use paper and pencil.

$$\begin{array}{r} 4\frac{3}{4} \ = \quad 4\frac{6}{8} \\ +2\frac{7}{8} \ = \ +2\frac{7}{8} \\ \hline 6\frac{13}{8} = 7\frac{5}{8} \text{ ft} \end{array}$$

FOR DISCUSSION

1. Show how Alvin could have solved his problem with paper and pencil instead of a calculator. Discuss which method you prefer and why.

2. Show how Mr. Lee could have solved his problem using a calculator. Discuss why this answer is different from what Mr. Lee found.

PRACTICE EXERCISES

Identify whether you would most likely use *paper and pencil, a calculator,* or *mental computation* to compute.

1. Find the change from $10.00.

2. Find the tip for a waiter.

3. Balance a checkbook.

4. Find the walking time to school.

5. Find the total cost of 2 items that cost $127.95 and $264.85.

6. Find the cost of 17 items in the grocery store.

7. Find how much gasoline you need for a trip across the country.

8. Find the average weight of the students in your class.

Use 2 different methods to compute. Identify the most efficient method.

9. The change from $10.00 for an $8.95 record.

10. The actual distance between 2 cities that are $2\frac{1}{4}$ in. apart on a map with a scale of 1 in. = 40 mi.

11. The cost per person if 30 people spent a total of $150.

12. The cost per person if 27 people spent a total of $200.

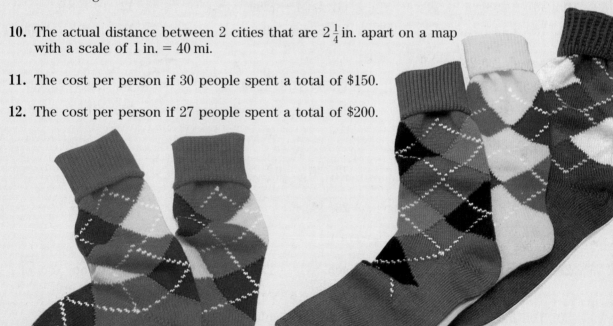

CHAPTER REVIEW

Vocabulary   Choose the letter of the word(s) that completes the sentence.

1. The ■ calculator key can be used when you have entered the wrong number into the calculator.   [22]

    a. Is equal to   **b.** Clear entry   **c.** Clear

2. You can estimate with whole numbers and decimals by rounding each number to its ■ place.   [26, 28]

    a. Last place   **b.** Greatest nonzero place   **c.** Least nonzero place

3. You can estimate with mixed numbers by rounding each number to the ■.   [30]

    a. Greatest nonzero place   **b.** Nearest tenth   **c.** Nearest whole number

Skills   Use a calculator to compute.   [22]

4. $4{,}689 + 8{,}873 + 472$

5. $36{,}748 - 7{,}974$

6. 58.93×39.58

7. $38.5\overline{)938.63}$

8. $7 + 39.88 - 15.938$

9. $5.02 \times 21.25 \div 5$

Compute mentally.   [24]

10. $357 + 298$

11. $\$394 - \$290$

12. 10×8.9

13. 100×14.7

14. $866 \div 100$

15. $37{,}480 \div 1{,}000$

Estimate.   [26, 28]

16. $6{,}835 + 3{,}128$

17. $14.87 + 7.299$

18. $13.89 - 4.935$

19. 29×63

20. $67 \times \$7.88$

21. $387.5 \div 3.74$

Estimate.   [30]

22. $3\frac{2}{3} + 22\frac{1}{4}$

23. $46\frac{7}{8} - 9\frac{3}{4}$

24. $63\frac{1}{3} - 12\frac{1}{4}$

25. $300 \times 3\frac{7}{8}$

26. $9\frac{4}{5} - 1\frac{1}{3}$

27. $26\frac{5}{8} - 2\frac{15}{16}$

Write *yes* or *no*.   [32]

28. Records are on sale for $6.79 each. Will $25 be enough to buy 4 records?

29. Will $30.00 be enough to buy 6 books that cost $3.98 each?

30. You multiply 8.73×2.57. Is a calculator display of 11.30 reasonable?

CHAPTER TEST

Use a calculator to compute.

1. $498.38 + 98.47$ **2.** $42{,}827 - 28{,}894$ **3.** $489 \times 3{,}983$ **4.** $8.72\overline{)780.44}$

5. $596.35 - 56.217 + 482.1$ **6.** $141.82 - 15.6 + 302.88$ **7.** $56.2 \times 6.25 \div 0.05$

Use mental computation to add or subtract.

8. $453 + 210$ **9.** $563 - 98$ **10.** $\$45 + \$39$ **11.** $\$5.00 - \$2.98$

Use mental computation to multiply or divide.

12. 100×23 **13.** $1{,}000 \times 8.27$ **14.** $78.4 \div 10$ **15.** $6.4 \div 100$

Estimate the sum or difference.

16. $875 + 786$ **17.** $687 - 312$ **18.** $5.24 + 18.9$ **19.** $53.2 - 18.66$

20. $\$4.86 + \$8.52$ **21.** $\$0.83 - \$0.38$ **22.** $32\frac{1}{6} + 9\frac{3}{4}$ **23.** $97\frac{2}{3} - 20\frac{1}{4}$

Estimate the product or quotient.

24. 62×78 **25.** $217 \div 18$ **26.** 6.385×9.82 **27.** $62.38 \div 2.8$

28. $29 \times \$7.85$ **29.** $\$839.50 \div 18$ **30.** $14\frac{7}{8} \times 1\frac{7}{8}$ **31.** $35\frac{1}{16} \div 6\frac{15}{16}$

Estimate to choose the reasonable answer.

32. $86 + 74.9 + 365.4$ **a.** 5.263 **b.** 526.3 **c.** $5{,}263$

33. $18.26 - 5.8$ **a.** 12.46 **b.** 15.46 **c.** 23.46

34. 2.3×12.8 **a.** 2.944 **b.** 29.44 **c.** 294.4

35. 6.34×0.86 **a.** 5.4524 **b.** 54.524 **c.** 545.2

36. $5{,}860 \div 15$ **a.** 3.907 **b.** 39.07 **c.** 390.7

Use the ad for Exercises 37–40.

37. About how much will 2 pens and 4 erasers cost?

38. About how much will 4 pencils and 5 notebooks cost?

39. Will $4.00 be enough to buy 10 erasers?

40. About how many pens can you buy for $3.00?

SALE

Pencils 19¢   Pens 59¢
Erasers 39¢
Notebooks 98¢

Add.

1. $23 + $28

2. $56 + $87

3. $138 + $76

4. $207 + $906

5. $18.27 + $16.30

6. $84.26 + $13.97

7. $125.62 + $9.87

8. $379.05 + $298

Subtract.

9. $78 − $26

10. $92 − $38

11. $416 − $47

12. $801 − $136

13. $39.48 − $13.17

14. $86.27 − $54.38

15. $316.32 − $58.26

16. $410.09 − $89

Multiply.

17. 9 × $8

18. 7 × $1.40

19. 6 × $8.90

20. 2 × $4.08

21. 16 × $3.86

22. 39 × $5.17

23. 12 × $17.36

24. 28 × $11.07

Divide.

25. $32 ÷ 5

26. $66 ÷ 8

27. $23 ÷ 4

28. $270 ÷ 3

29. $146 ÷ 8

30. $24.48 ÷ 6

31. $85.25 ÷ 5

32. $696.40 ÷ 4

Rename as a decimal.

33. 45%

34. 78%

35. 19.4%

36. 72.41%

37. 4.56%

38. 0.08%

39. 7.51%

40. 7.15%

Find the answer to the nearest cent.

41. 25% of $100

42. 30% of $50

43. 8% of $55

44. 6.5% of $94

45. 7.15% of $78.50

46. 7.51% of $149.75

Chapter 3

PART-TIME AND SUMMER JOBS

Many teenagers hold part-time or summer jobs. How can these jobs help prepare them for full-time work when they are older?

You need a part-time job. You want to earn some money to buy things and go places with your friends. You begin your job search by visiting stores and restaurants near your home.

You apply for several different jobs. For each job you have to fill out a **job application** like the one below. Later you will have to come back for a personal interview.

Copy the top of this job application.
Supply all this information about yourself.

Name _____ Phone _____

Address _____
        Street   Town   State   Zip

Social Security Number_____

Position applied for_____

Circle last grade completed   5 6 7 8 9 10 11 12

Other Jobs You Have Held

Employer	Job	Dates	Supervisor
_____	_____	_____	_____
_____	_____	_____	_____
_____	_____	_____	_____

You went on an **interview** for a part-time job at a drugstore and you were hired. The manager told you that you would earn $12.75 for each day you worked after school during the week. You would also earn $31.88 for working all day Saturday.

EXAMPLE

You decide to work 2 d after school and all day Saturday. How much money will you earn each week?

THINK: You make $12.75 each weekday and $31.88 on Saturday.

Add. $12.75 + $12.75 + $31.88 = $57.38

You will earn $57.38 per wk.

1. What information should you find out about a job? Why?

2. What kinds of questions might you be asked during a job interview?

PRACTICE EXERCISES   Remember to estimate whenever you use your calculator.

Solve.

1. Sue earns $18 working after school in a department store. She earns $33.75 working in the store on Saturday. She worked 1 d after school and 1 Saturday. How much did she earn that week?

2. Ron has a part-time job in a bakery. He earns $15.25 when he helps the baker. He earns $12.95 when he works at the sales counter. He helped the baker for 1 d and worked at the counter 2 d. How much did he earn?

3. Fred works part-time at a cleaners. Last week, he worked extra hours and earned $14.50 more than he usually does. He usually earns $70.50. How much did he earn last week?

4. Marita usually earns $50 per wk working weekdays at a movie theater. Last week, she earned $84.50 because she worked all day Saturday. How much did she earn last Saturday?

5. Sarah usually earns $80.25 per wk working in a pizza parlor. This week, she took some time off. She earned $9.50 less than she usually does. How much did she earn?

6. Morey works part-time at a fast food restaurant. Last week, he earned $40.45. That was $19.75 less than he usually earns. How much does he usually earn?

This chart shows the wages of some people who work Saturdays in the Recreation Program.

Assistant Director	$45
Arts and Crafts Instructor	$35
Sports Coach	$35
Junior Counselor	$25.50

7. How much more does an Assistant Director earn each Saturday than a Junior Counselor?

8. Eirin worked 2 Saturdays as a Sports Coach and 1 Saturday as a Junior Counselor. How much did she earn?

9. Derek worked 1 Saturday as an Assistant Director and 2 Saturdays as an Arts and Crafts Instructor. How much did he earn?

10. Fran usually earns $87 per mo. Last month, she missed 1 Saturday as an Assistant Director. How much did she earn last month?

11. Last Saturday, there were 2 Assistant Directors, 1 Arts and Crafts Instructor, and 3 Junior Counselors working. What was the payroll that day?

You want to try to find a job that pays more than the **minimum wage.** The minimum wage is set by federal law. It is the least amount of money that a person can be paid per hour. You are interested in this want ad.

★ ★ **CASHIER** ★ ★

DOWNTOWN RECORD STORE
M – Th   6:00 – 9:00 P.M.

$4.85/h

EXAMPLE 1   If you got this job, how much would you earn each week?

THINK: Monday—Thursday: 4 d   6:00—9:00 P.M.: 3 h

PAY = HOURS WORKED × HOURLY WAGE

1. Multiply to find how many work hours. $4 \times 3 = 12$ h

2. Multiply to find your weekly pay. $12 \times \$4.85 = \$58.20$

You would earn $58.20 per wk.

Your friend Brian is interested in this want ad for a summer job.

CAMP VANGUARD

Counselor in Training

JULY–AUGUST
8 weeks   6 days a week
$864 Season—Room and Board

EXAMPLE 2   If Brian took this job, how much money would he earn each week? Each day?

THINK: Season rate: $864   Weeks: 8   Days per week: 6

1. Divide to find the weekly pay. $\$864 \div 8 = \$108$

Brian would earn $108 per wk.

2. Divide to find the daily pay. $\$108 \div 6 = \$18$

Brian would earn $18 per d.

FOR DISCUSSION

Why do you think a camp counselor can usually earn more by working at a day camp than at a sleep-away camp?

Remember to estimate whenever you use your calculator.

Use these want ads for Exercises 1–6.

P/T Fred's Franks
Afternoons
12 hours weekly
$55.80 weekly

P/T Counter Help
★ *Jan's Cleaners* ★
T, W, Th 4:00 – 8:00 P.M.
$4.25/h

WILLOW LAKE DAY CAMP
Counselor 7 weeks
JULY–AUGUST
$1,512 season

1. What is the hourly wage for working at Fred's Franks?

2. What is the weekly pay for working at Jan's Cleaners?

3. What is the weekly pay for working at Willow Lake Day Camp?

4. Which of these jobs has the highest weekly pay?

5. Which job has the higher hourly wage, working for Jan's Cleaners or for Fred's Franks?

6. Assuming an 8-h work day and 6 d per wk, about what is the hourly wage for working at Willow Lake Day Camp?

Use these want ads for Exercises 7–14.

Temporary Help
Holiday Sale Days
RAY'S DEPT. STORE
15 hours a week
$65.55 weekly

Hamburger Barn
Counter Person
After School
M-F 6:00 – 9:00 P.M.
$4.30/h

CAMP CRESTMONT
JUNIOR COUNSELOR
July – August
Room & Board
$960 Season

7. Which of these is a summer job? A permanent part-time job? A temporary part-time job?

8. As a junior counselor at Camp Crestmont, you would work for 8 wk. What is the weekly pay?

9. What is the hourly wage at Ray's Department Store?

10. How much will you earn each week working at the Hamburger Barn?

11. How much will you earn working for 50 wk at the Hamburger Barn?

12. You would work for 48 d at Camp Crestmont. What is the daily pay?

13. Which job has the highest weekly pay?

14. Which job has the highest hourly wage? Assume an 8-h work day and 6 d per wk at Camp Crestmont.

Many students your age have jobs that involve tips. A **tip** is the amount of money a customer leaves as a gift for a person who has provided service. The word TIPS comes from these four words— To Insure Prompt Service. Usually, the better the service, the greater the tip.

If a job involves tips, there may not be any hourly wage. If there is an hourly wage, it will probably be less than the minimum wage.

People usually leave a tip as a percent of the bill according to these standards.

Poor Service   10% or less
Average–Good Service   15%
Excellent Service   20%

EXAMPLE 1

You eat at a restaurant and the meal costs $18.00. You want to leave a 15% tip. How much should you leave?

Multiply to find the tip.

THINK: 15% = 0.15 $0.15 \times \$18.00 = \$2.70$

You should leave a $2.70 tip.

You can also compute the tip mentally.

1. Find 10% of $18.00.
   THINK: 10% = 0.1 $0.1 \times \$18.00 \rightarrow \$1\underset{\smile}{8}.00 \rightarrow \$1.80$

2. Find 5% of $18.00.   (5% = $\frac{1}{2}$ of 10%)   5% of $18 = $\frac{1}{2}$ of $1.80 = \$0.90$

3. Add. $\$1.80 + \$0.90 = \$2.70$

EXAMPLE 2

Your wage at a resort is $2.15 per h. The resort adds 15% to each bill. You receive that amount as a tip. One day, you worked 5 h and served meals costing $325. How much did you earn that day?

1. Multiply to find your earnings from wages. $5 \times \$2.15 = \$10.75$

2. Multiply to find your earnings from tips. $0.15 \times \$325 = \$48.75$

3. Add to find your total earnings. $\$10.75 + \$48.75 = \$59.50$

You earned $59.50.

FOR DISCUSSION

Discuss the importance of hourly wage, food prices, and the number of customers when choosing a restaurant job that involves tips.

PRACTICE EXERCISES   Remember to estimate whenever you use your calculator.

Solve.

1. You ate at a restaurant and the meal cost $14.00. You want to leave a 15% tip. How much should you leave?

2. You served a meal that cost your customers $47.25. You are expecting a 20% tip from them. How much are you expecting?

Six students worked at a resort on Saturdays. The table below shows the hourly wages, hours worked, and the costs of the meals served on 1 Saturday. The resort adds 15% to the cost of the meals. Each person gets that amount as a tip. Find each person's earnings.

Employee	Hourly wage	Hours worked	Cost of meals	Earnings from wages	Tips	Total earnings
Janice	$2.05	6	$180	3. ■	4. ■	5. ■
Rob	$2.05	5	$160	6. ■	7. ■	8. ■
Sven	$2.10	7	$240	9. ■	10. ■	11. ■
Susan	$2.10	8	$520	12. ■	13. ■	14. ■
Ted	$2.15	6.5	$380	15. ■	16. ■	17. ■
Arlene	$2.15	6	$439	18. ■	19. ■	20. ■

EXTENSION   Finding What Percent Tip Is Given

You served a meal that cost your customers $25.75. They gave you a $4.50 tip. You are curious to know what percent $4.50 is of $25.75.

1. Divide. $4.50 ÷ $25.75 = 0.1747572

2. Rename the decimal as a percent.   0.1747572 = 17.47572%

3. Round to the nearest tenth.   17.47572% ≈ 17.5%

Your customers left you a 17.5% tip.

Find the percent of tip to the nearest tenth of a percent.

1. Cost of meal: $18.50
   Tip: $2.80

2. Cost of meal: $28.00
   Tip: $3.60

3. Cost of meal: $58.25
   Tip: $10.50

You got your first paycheck. When you took it out of the envelope, you noticed that it was for less than you had earned. You headed into the bookkeeper's office to find out why.

The bookkeeper explained: "We all have amounts withheld from our paychecks. There are taxes, including FICA, withheld. **FICA** stands for **Federal Insurance Contributions Act,** or **Social Security.** Remember when you got your job here? You had to get a Social Security card with your Social Security number. You are the only person alive with that number."

"The money you contribute to Social Security is used to provide the following benefits:
1. retirement income
2. income for disabled persons who can no longer work
3. survivor's benefits for the dependents of a worker who dies
4. medical costs for persons covered by Medicare

The money you contribute is not yours, but the government knows how much you have paid. Each month, a percent of a paycheck is withheld for Social Security. In a recent year, that amount was **7.65%** of your pay."

EXAMPLE 1

You earned $300 last month. How much was withheld for Social Security?

THINK: The withholding rate is 7.65%   7.65% = 0.0765

Multiply to find the amount withheld.   0.0765 × $300 = $22.95

The amount withheld was $22.95.

You could use estimation to check the reasonableness of your answer.

THINK: 7.65% is between 7% and 8%.   0.07 × $300 = $21

7% = 0.07   8% = 0.08   0.08 × $300 = $24

The amount withheld was between $21 and $24.

So, $22.95 is reasonable.

EXAMPLE 2

Your friend Alicia earned $475 last month.
How much was withheld for Social Security?
How much was left over after paying Social Security?

1. Multiply to find the amount withheld. $0.0765 \times \$475 = \$36.3375$

The amount withheld was $36.34.

2. Subtract to find the amount left over. $\$475 - \$36.34 = \$438.66$

Alicia had $438.66 left over after paying Social Security.

FOR DISCUSSION

1. In what type of situations do you think you would need to give your Social Security number?

2. Many people believe that Social Security benefits are only for senior citizens. How can Social Security benefit young families?

PRACTICE EXERCISES   Remember to estimate whenever you use your calculator.

Use the rate of 7.65% to find the Social Security withholding for the earnings. Round the amount to the nearest cent.

1. $200   2. $700   3. $4,200   4. $6,200   5. $945

6. $382   7. $837   8. $62.78   9. $489.28   10. $183.47

Remember that the people named in the table worked in a resort.
The resort added 15% to the cost of meals and gave it to each person as a tip.

Find the earnings from wages, tips, total pay, and the FICA withheld for each person. Round each amount to the nearest cent.

Employee	Hourly wage	Hours worked	Cost of meals	Earnings from wages	Tips	Total pay	FICA withheld
Janice	$2.05	15	$900	11. ■	12. ■	13. ■	14. ■
Rob	$2.05	10	$750	15. ■	16. ■	17. ■	18. ■
Sven	$2.10	12	$800	19. ■	20. ■	21. ■	22. ■
Susan	$2.10	20	$1,100	23. ■	24. ■	25. ■	26. ■
Ted	$2.15	20.5	$1,320	27. ■	28. ■	29. ■	30. ■
Arlene	$2.15	15	$1,845.96	31. ■	32. ■	33. ■	34. ■

PROBLEM
Solving
STRATEGY

3.5 GUESSING AND CHECKING

Situation:

Carol works part time at the Golden Arch Diner. A customer left Carol a tip of $1.90 in quarters and nickels. She was given 18 coins in all. How many coins of each kind did she receive?

Strategy:

Guessing and checking can help you arrive at a solution.

Applying the Strategy:

Guess 1

Carol received
3 quarters and 15 nickels.

Check

$3 \times \$0.25 = \quad \$0.75$
$15 \times \$0.05 = \underline{+ \ 0.75}$
$\qquad\qquad\qquad \$1.50$

THINK: $\$1.50 < \$1.90$
Make another guess. Try more quarters to raise the total.

Guess 2

Carol received
6 quarters and 12 nickels.

Check

$6 \times \$0.25 = \quad \$1.50$
$12 \times \$0.05 = \underline{+ \ 0.60}$
$\qquad\qquad\qquad \$2.10$

THINK: $\$2.10 > \$1.90$
Make another guess. Try fewer quarters to raise the total.

Guess 3

Carol received
5 quarters and 13 nickels.

Check

$5 \times \$0.25 = \quad \$1.25$
$13 \times \$0.05 = \underline{+ \ 0.65}$
$\qquad\qquad\qquad \$1.90$

Carol received 5 quarters and 13 nickels.

FOR DISCUSSION

Ernie has a part-time job at a bakery. He worked a total of 35 h in 2 wk. During the first week, he worked 5 h more than the second week.

1. You want to know how many hours Ernie worked in each of the 2 wk. What facts are you given?

2. Explain why 25 h the first week and 10 h the second week cannot be correct.

PRACTICE EXERCISES   Remember to estimate whenever you use your calculator.

Check each guess. Choose the correct guess.

1. Rosa has a part-time job at a supermarket. She worked a total of 44 h in 2 wk. During the first week, she worked 8 h more than the second week. How many hours did Rosa work in each of the 2 wk?

   a. Guess: 16 h, 24 h

   b. Guess: 18 h, 26 h

   c. Guess: 26 h, 18 h

2. Ted works part-time at the Star Diner. A customer gave him an $0.85 tip in quarters and nickels. He was given 9 coins. How many coins of each kind did he receive?

   a. Guess: 3 quarters, 6 nickels

   b. Guess: 2 quarters, 7 nickels

   c. Guess: 1 quarter, 8 nickels

Solve the problem by using guessing and checking.

3. Jacob worked a total of 170 h in 2 mo. During the first month, he worked 20 h more than the second month. How many hours did Jacob work in each of the 2 mo?

4. A customer left Adrian a tip of $3.25 in quarters and dimes. He was given 16 coins in all. How many coins of each kind did he receive?

5. Diana has a part-time job at a gas station. She earned a total of $70 in 2 wk. During the first week, she earned $20 less than the second week. How much did Diana earn in each of the 2 wk?

6. Sarah works part-time at Bill's Deli. She worked 72 h in April and May. She worked one-half as many hours in April as she did in May. How many hours did Sarah work in each month?

7. Christine works at the Mountain View Restaurant on weekends. A customer left her a tip of $2.55 in quarters, dimes, and nickels. She was given 18 coins in all. How many coins of each kind was Christine given?

8. Isaac works at the General Store on Mondays and Tuesdays. Last week, he worked a total of $9\frac{3}{4}$ h for both days. He worked 135 min longer on Monday than on Tuesday. How long did Isaac work each day?

3.6 INVESTIGATING WANT ADS

DECISION MAKING

The first step in selecting a job is to locate and compare the want ads you are interested in.

PROBLEM A

Rebecca is looking for a part-time job. She cut out these want ads.

COUNTER HELP	HIGH SCHOOL STUDENT	SALES CLERK
Big Time Burger	Light Stock Work	Dime Department Store
Mon. – Fri. 5:00 – 7:00 P.M.	*Morse's Pharmacy*	*Experience Necessary*
Saturday 8:00 – 11:00 P.M.	T, W 4:00–8:00 P.M.	Fri. 4–10 Sat. 9–4
$4.25/h	**$34.00/wk**	**$4.50/h**

DECISION-MAKING FACTORS

Weekly schedule   Hours per week   Hourly wage   Weekly pay   Job responsibilities

DECISION-MAKING COMPARISONS

Complete the table to compare the 3 jobs.

	Big Time Burger	Morse's Pharmacy	Dime Department Store
Weekly schedule	M–F 5–7, S 8–11	1. ■	2. ■
Hours per week	3. ■	8 h	4. ■
Hourly wage	$4.25	5. ■	6. ■
Weekly pay	7. ■	$34	8. ■
Job responsibilities	9. ■	10. ■	Sales clerk

MAKING THE DECISIONS

11. If Rebecca's main interest were weekly pay, which job would be best?

12. If Rebecca's main interest were hourly wage, which job would be best?

13. If Rebecca likes to work around food, which job would be best?

14. If Rebecca has never worked before, which job could she not get?

15. If Rebecca cannot work more than 12 h a week, which job would be best?

16. If Rebecca likes to work with people, which job would be the worst?

PROBLEM B

You are looking for a summer job in a day camp (5 d per wk). You marked these want ads A, B, and C. Now you need to decide which job is best for you.

A

CAMP COUNSELOR
$4.50/h
8 hours per day
Supervise 15 8-year-olds
HS junior/senior
Some overnight trips

B

APPLE DAY CAMP
Nature Counselor
Work with 8 to 12-year-olds
Planned program of activities
9:00–4:30 $35/day

C

ARTS & CRAFTS COUNSELOR
$1,200 for 7 wk, M-F
35 h per wk
Plan, organize,
direct activities

DECISION-MAKING FACTORS

Length of work day   Weekly pay   Hourly wage
Job responsibilities   Other information

DECISION-MAKING COMPARISONS

Complete the table to compare the 3 jobs.

	Camp A	Camp B	Camp C
Length of day	8 h	17. ■	18. ■
Weekly pay	19. ■	$175	20. ■
Hourly wage	$4.50	21. ■	22. ■
Job responsibilities	23. ■	24. ■	Plan, organize, direct arts and crafts activities
Other information	25. ■	26. ■	Plan *own* activities

MAKING THE DECISIONS

27. If your main interest were weekly pay, which camp would be best?

28. If your main interest were hourly wage, which camp would be best?

29. If your main interest were nature, which camp would be best?

30. If you like to work with children under 10, which camp would be best?

31. If your main interest were arts and crafts, which camp would be best?

32. If you like to plan your own activities, which camp would be best?

33. Only you can decide which job has the best combination of pay and other factors. Which of these camp jobs would be best for you? Why?

CHAPTER REVIEW

Vocabulary   Choose the letter of the word(s) that completes the sentence.

1. The pay you earn is found by multiplying the number of hours worked by the ▪. [42]

   a. Number of days worked   **b.** Hourly wage   **c.** Tips

2. The amount of money a customer leaves for a person who has provided service is called a ▪. [44]

   a. Hourly wage   **b.** Total pay   **c.** Tip

3. Another name for the Federal Insurance Contributions Act is ▪. [46]

   a. Payroll deductions   **b.** Social Security   **c.** Paycheck

Skills   Find the answer.

4. The hourly wage is $4.30. John worked 7 h. How much did he earn? [42]

5. The hourly wage is $4.85. May worked 9 h. How much did she earn? [42]

6. Serita worked 6 h and earned $31.50. What is her hourly wage? [42]

7. Sal worked 9 h and earned $39.15. What is his hourly wage? [42]

8. Andrew received a 15% tip for serving a $25 meal. How much was his tip? [44]

9. Opray received a 15% tip for serving a $28.65 meal. How much was her tip? [44]

10. A meal you ordered cost $24.00. You left a 15% tip. How much did you leave? [44]

11. Jacqueline earned $3.05 per h for 6 h plus 15% in tips on $220 of meals. What was her total pay? [42, 44]

12. Enrico earned $2.95 per h for 6 h. He also earned tips of 15% on $275 of meals. What was his total pay? [42, 44]

13. Ann earned $2.90 per h for 5 h plus 15% in tips on $318.65 of meals. What was her total pay? [42, 44]

14. Mark's total pay was $400. How much was withheld for Social Security? [46]

15. Manuel earned $8.75 per h for 25 h. How much was withheld for Social Security? [46]

16. Regina earned $3.10 per h for 7 h plus 15% in tips on $417 worth of served meals. What was her total pay? How much was withheld for Social Security? [46]

17. Ira earned $3.40 per h for 5 h plus 15% in tips on $225 worth of served meals. What was his total pay? How much was withheld for Social Security? [46]

Find the total pay.

1. Monday: $18
    Tuesday: $16

2. Monday: $21
    Tuesday: $16
    Friday: $37

3. Monday: $10.95
    Tuesday: $10.95
    Saturday: $28.49

4. Hours worked: 6
    Hourly wage: $4.30

5. Hours worked: 11
    Hourly wage: $3.85

6. Hours worked: 8.5
    Hourly wage: $4.65

Find the hourly wage.

7. Amount earned: $34.65
    Hours worked: 7

8. Amount earned: $29.10
    Hours worked: 6

9. Amount earned: $38.52
    Hours worked: 9

How much was the tip?

10. Cost of meal: $27
    Tip: 10%

11. Cost of meal: $34.50
    Tip: 15%

12. Cost of meal: $64.54
    Tip: 15%

Find the total pay.

13. Hours worked: 6
    Hourly wage: $3.85
    Tips: $15.50

14. Hours worked: 7
    Hourly wage: $3.50
    Tips: $28.50

15. Hours worked: 4.5
    Hourly wage: $3.40
    Tips: $38.65

Find the total pay and the amount withheld for Social Security.
Use 7.65% as the withholding rate.
Round each amount to the nearest cent.

16. Hours worked: 5
    Hourly wage: $4.26

17. Hours worked: 6
    Hourly wage: $2.85
    Cost of meals: $235
    Tip: 15%

18. Hours worked: 8
    Hourly wage: $3.05
    Cost of meals: $485
    Tip: 18%

Solve the problem using guessing and checking.

19. Anna worked a total of 150 h in 2 mo.
    During the first month, she worked
    20 h more than the second month.
    How many hours did Anna work in
    each of the 2 mo?

20. A customer left Bob a tip of $2.30 in
    quarters and dimes. He was given 14
    coins in all. How many coins of each
    kind did he receive?

MONEY TIPS

Transportation costs should be considered when you want to know your actual take-home pay.

LET'S LOOK AT THE FACTS

If you use public transportation, it will cost you money to go to and from your job. Look at the comparison table below for 3 different part-time jobs.

	Diana's Health & Fitness Center	Pattycake Bake Shop	Winston National Bank
Weekly pay	$200	$190	$150
Distance from your home	3 mi	4 mi	2 mi
Transportation (1 way)	1 express bus	2 local buses	1 local bus

LET'S DISCUSS WHY

1. Compute how much transportation would cost weekly (5 d) for each of the 3 jobs if a local bus ride costs $1.00 and an express bus ride costs $4.00.

2. Subtract the cost of weekly transportation from each weekly pay. Which job would leave you with the greatest actual take-home pay?

3. How might you reduce transportation costs to the Bank? To the Bake Shop?

4. For each job, how much money could you save if you walked to work every morning and took public transportation only at night?

LET'S SEE WHAT YOU WOULD DO

5. You and 3 friends all work at the Bake Shop on the same days and during the same hours. How could the 4 of you get to work besides taking the bus?

6. You are eager to save as much money as possible each week from a part-time job in order to buy a stereo cassette player and some new clothes. If you would not mind walking up to 4 mi per d, which of the jobs could you take to get an actual take-home pay of $180?

 **STANDARD AND SCIENTIFIC CALCULATORS**

There are 2 kinds of calculators, standard and scientific. They perform a series of calculations differently.

A **standard calculator** performs operations in the order in which they are entered.

Evaluate $6 + 4 \times 3$, using a standard calculator.

If you enter $\boxed{6}\boxed{+}\boxed{4}\boxed{\times}\boxed{3}\boxed{=}$, a standard calculator will display an incorrect answer of 30. First, it adds 6 and 4 to give 10. Then it multiplies 10 by 3.

To obtain the correct answer on a standard calculator, you must follow the correct order of operations.

Procedure	Calculator Entry	Calculator Display
1. Perform the multiplication.	$\boxed{4}\boxed{\times}\boxed{3}\boxed{=}$	12.
2. Perform the addition.	$\boxed{+}\boxed{6}\boxed{=}$	18.

So $6 + 4 \times 3 = 18$.

A **scientific calculator** performs operations according to the correct order of operations. If you enter $\boxed{6}\boxed{+}\boxed{4}\boxed{\times}\boxed{3}\boxed{=}$ on a scientific calculator, the display will show the correct answer, 18.

1. Using $6 + 4 \times 3$, determine whether your calculator is standard or scientific.

Use a calculator to evaluate.

2. $12 + 3 \times 4$

3. $18 + 5 \times 3$

4. $2 \times 6 - 3$

5. $12 + 9 \div 3$

6. $135 + 10 \div 5$

7. $16.9 + 8.6 \div 2$

8. $432 + 15.6 \times 3$

9. $152 + 8.1 \times 9$

10. $200 + 49.6 \div 12.4$

11. $36 + 46 + 1.8 \times 5$

12. $8.6 - 4.5 + 2.3 \times 7$

13. $16 \div 2 \times 4 + 8.5$

There is a 1-digit number missing in the number sentence. First estimate, then use your calculator to find the missing number.

14. $12 + 4 \times \blacksquare = 24$

15. $6.8 + 3 \times \blacksquare = 30.8$

16. $41 + 7 \times \blacksquare = 76$

17. $60 - 35 + 5 \times \blacksquare = 45$

Rename as a decimal.

1. $35\frac{1}{2}$ 2. $17\frac{3}{4}$

3. $35\frac{1}{4}$ 4. 27%

5. 4.5% 6. 2.7%

Identify the correct operation.

7. To find how much greater one number is than another

8. To find the total amount of 3 unequal measures

9. To find the total amount of 24 equal measures

10. To find the size of each equal portion of an amount

Subtract.

11. $258.99 − $37.56 − $74.57 12. $5,389 − $368.90 − $35

Multiply.

13. 8 × $4.67 14. 5 × $2.74 15. 52 × $3.58 16. 30 × $472

17. 1.5 × $4.50 18. 1.5 × $8.90 19. 25.5 × $6.75 20. 35.75 × $12.50

Divide. Round to the nearest cent.

21. $18,900 ÷ 12 22. $673.40 ÷ 40 23. $26)\overline{\$8,940}$ 24. $24)\overline{\$23,800}$

Find the elapsed time.

25. Find 7:15 A.M. to 3:45 P.M. 26. From 8:10 A.M. to 5:15 P.M.

27. From 9:20 A.M. to 2:10 P.M. 28. From 8:45 A.M. to 3:30 P.M.

Add or subtract.

29. $2\frac{1}{2} + 5\frac{3}{4} + 6$ 30. $5 + 7\frac{1}{2} + 5\frac{3}{4}$

31. $37\frac{1}{2} - 5\frac{3}{4}$ 32. $20 - 6\frac{1}{4}$

Find the answer.

33. 80% of $385 34. 40% of $36.50

35. $6\frac{1}{2}$% of $4,500 36. 3.5% of $53,860

Chapter 4

FULL-TIME WORK

In many factories, workers must punch in and punch out on a time clock. What factors, other than regular hours worked, could determine how much a factory worker is paid for a week's work?

4.1 HOURLY WAGES AND OVERTIME PAY

You work as a mechanic in a large garage and earn $8.40 per h. For any hours you work above 40 h per wk, you are eligible for **overtime pay** at a rate of $1\frac{1}{2}$ times your regular hourly wage.

EXAMPLE 1

What is your regular weekly pay if you work $37\frac{1}{2}$ h each week?

THINK: Hours worked: $37\frac{1}{2}$, or 37.5   Hourly wage: $8.40

HOURS WORKED × HOURLY WAGE =   PAY

37.5   × $8.40   = $315.00

Your regular weekly pay is $315.00.

EXAMPLE 2

During a very busy week, you were asked to work 46 h. What was your total pay for that week?

1. Multiply to find the regular pay.   40 × $8.40 = $336.00

2. Find the overtime pay.

   • Subtract to find the overtime hours.   46 − 40 = 6 h
   • Multiply to find the overtime rate.   1.5 × $8.40 = $12.60 per h
   • Multiply to find the overtime pay.   6 × $12.60 = $75.60

3. Add to find the total pay. $336.00 + $75.60 = $411.60

Your total pay for the 46 h was $411.60.

FOR DISCUSSION

1. Why do you think workers have asked for overtime pay at a higher rate than their regular hourly wage?

2. Why does the government set a minimum wage? How does this affect you?

Remember to estimate whenever you use your calculator.

Find each employee's regular pay. Round the amount to the nearest cent.

Employee	Hours worked	Hourly wage	Regular pay
Henderson	40	$4.85	1. ■
Rodriquez	25	$7.39	2. ■
Martin	$37\frac{3}{4}$	$5.40	3. ■

Employee	Hours worked	Hourly wage	Regular pay
Lieberman	$16\frac{1}{4}$	$6.12	4. ■
Washington	$32\frac{1}{2}$	$12.80	5. ■
Jones	$34\frac{3}{4}$	$18.42	6. ■

Complete the table. Use an overtime rate of $1\frac{1}{2}$ times the hourly wage
for work over 40 h. Round each amount to the nearest cent.

Employee	Hours worked	Hourly wage	Regular pay	Overtime pay	Total pay
Carter	38	$6.48	7. ■	8. ■	9. ■
Honesdale	43	$5.00	10. ■	11. ■	12. ■
Chang	$46\frac{3}{4}$	$8.20	13. ■	14. ■	15. ■
Hernandez	$52\frac{1}{2}$	$7.48	16. ■	17. ■	18. ■
Santini	$49\frac{1}{4}$	$18.42	19. ■	20. ■	21. ■

Solve.

22. Sarah earned $230 for 40 h of work. What was her hourly wage?

23. Jim earned $313.50 for 32 h of work. What was his hourly wage?

24. Cheryl earns $7.58 per h. If her regular pay last week was $272.88, how many hours did she work?

25. Bart earns $6.30 per h. If his regular pay last week was $236.25, how many hours did he work?

EXTENSION   Overtime Hours

Matt earns $9.00 per h. His total weekly pay, including overtime, was $414.00.

1. For how many hours did he earn $9.00 per h?

2. What was his regular pay?

3. What was his overtime pay?

4. What was his overtime rate of pay?

5. How many overtime hours did he work?

You are a freelance proofreader for a large publisher. You work at home and earn $8.50 per h. You keep track of the hours you work on a **time sheet** that you submit weekly to the publisher.

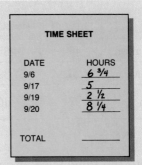

TIME SHEET	
DATE	**HOURS**
9/6	6 3/4
9/17	5
9/19	2 ½
9/20	8 ¼
TOTAL	_____

EXAMPLE 1 According to your time sheet, how many hours did you work during the week? How much did you earn?

1. Add to find the total hours. $6\frac{3}{4} + 5 + 2\frac{1}{2} + 8\frac{1}{4} = 22\frac{1}{2}$ h

You worked a total of $22\frac{1}{2}$ h.

2. Multiply to find the earnings. $22\frac{1}{2} \times \$8.50 = 22.5 \times \$8.50 = \$191.25$

You earned $191.25.

Many workers "punch in" and "punch out" on a **time clock** that records their arrival and departure times on a weekly **time card.** The time card is then used to determine how many hours were worked. Times from time cards are usually rounded *down* to the nearest quarter hour.

Employee	Sarah Williams	
Employee	# 2733	
Week of	10/7	
DATE	**IN**	**OUT**
10/7	8:02	4:05
10/8	7:55	4:52
10/10	9:01	3:34
10/11	8:12	4:17
TOTAL HOURS		_____

EXAMPLE 2 Sarah works as a cashier in a food store and earns $5.18 per h. Use her time card to determine how many hours she worked. Then find her regular pay for the week.

1. Round to find the hours worked.

10/7:	8 to 4 is	8 h
10/8:	7:45 to 4:45 is	9 h
10/10:	9 to 3:30 is	$6\frac{1}{2}$ h
10/11:	8 to 4:15 is	$8\frac{1}{4}$ h

2. Add to find the total hours. $31\frac{3}{4}$ h

According to Sarah's time card, she worked $31\frac{3}{4}$ h.

3. Multiply to find the regular pay. $31\frac{3}{4} \times \$5.18 = 31.75 \times \$5.18 = \$164.465$

Sarah's regular pay for this week was $164.47.

FOR DISCUSSION

1. What are the advantages of using a time clock in a factory?

2. Why are hours worked usually rounded down to the nearest quarter hour?

PRACTICE EXERCISES   Remember to estimate whenever you use your calculator.

Complete the table to find the hours worked. Round down to the nearest quarter hour.

Employee	Time in	Time out	Rounded time in	Rounded time out	Hours worked
Meyer	7:10 A.M.	3:16 P.M.	1. ■	2. ■	3. ■
Labeau	7:54 A.M.	4:57 P.M.	4. ■	5. ■	6. ■
Modica	8:19 A.M.	3:43 P.M.	7. ■	8. ■	9. ■
Jefferson	7:32 A.M.	1:13 P.M.	10. ■	11. ■	12. ■
Anderson	8:41 A.M.	5:14 P.M.	13. ■	14. ■	15. ■

Write a time sheet for the person, including the total. Use the time sheet in Example 1 as your model. Then answer the question.

16. Rob worked 6 h on Mon., $5\frac{1}{2}$ on Tues., $4\frac{1}{4}$ on Wed., $7\frac{1}{2}$ on Thurs., and $4\frac{3}{4}$ on Fri. If Rob is paid $4.75 per h, how much did he earn?

17. Julie worked $5\frac{1}{4}$ h on Mon., $3\frac{1}{2}$ on Tues., $8\frac{3}{4}$ on Thurs., and $7\frac{1}{4}$ on Fri. If Julie earns $6.86 per h, how much did she earn?

Use the time cards below for Exercises 18–19.

Employee	Sam Longo	
Employee	# 25830	
Week of	12/15	
DATE	IN	OUT
12/15	8:10	4:08
12/16	7:55	2:58
12/17	8:16	4:29
12/18	7:57	4:45
12/19	8:57	12:31
TOTAL HOURS		

Employee	Tina Baker	
Employee	# 4755	
Week of	11/20	
DATE	IN	OUT
11/20	7:05	3:58
11/21	7:30	5:01
11/22	8:01	5:32
11/23	7:22	4:46
11/24	6:55	4:31
TOTAL HOURS		

18. How many hours did Sam work? If he earns $7.55 per h, what was his pay?

19. How many hours did Tina work? If she earns $5.35 per h, what was her pay?

4.3 SALARY

You take a job as a computer-service technician that pays a **salary** of $18,500 per y. You will be paid weekly.

EXAMPLE 1

What is your pay per week?

THINK: Your salary is divided into 52 equal pay periods.

YEARLY SALARY ÷ NUMBER OF PAY PERIODS = PAY PER PERIOD

$18,500 ÷ 52 = $355.76923

Your pay per week is $355.77.

Many people are paid **biweekly,** or every other week. This means they will receive 26 paychecks per y. Other workers are paid **semimonthly.** These workers receive 2 paychecks per mo, or 24 paychecks per y.

EXAMPLE 2

Kathleen takes a job that pays $21,800 per y. If she is paid semimonthly, what is the amount of each paycheck?

THINK: Semimonthly means 24 equal pay periods per year.

Divide to find the pay per period. $21,800 ÷ 24 = $908.33333

Kathleen's semimonthly paycheck is $908.33.

Some jobs are advertised with a weekly pay or an hourly wage. It is often necessary to convert these to annual salaries to compare jobs.

EXAMPLE 3

Richard needs to choose between a job advertised at $16,250 per y and another advertised at $350 per wk. Which job has the greater annual salary?

1. Multiply to find the annual salary.   52 × $350 = $18,200

2. Compare the annual salaries. $18,200 > $16,250

The $350-per-wk job has the greater annual salary.

FOR DISCUSSION

What are some advantages to being paid biweekly instead of monthly?

Remember to estimate whenever you use your calculator.

Complete the table.

Employee	Annual salary	Pay period	Pay per period
Parker	$8,750	weekly	1. ■
Smith	$12,300	biweekly	2. ■
Oliviero	$14,890	semimonthly	3. ■
Yeh	$24,700	monthly	4. ■

Complete the table.

Employee	Pay period	Pay per period	Annual salary
Rogers	weekly	$247.55	5. ■
Silverbear	biweekly	$638.85	6. ■
Halbacher	semimonthly	$487.32	7. ■
Cohen	monthly	$1,587.95	8. ■

Which job pays more? How much more?

Job A

9. $450 per wk

10. $8,450 per y

11. $439 semimonthly

12. $8.95 per h (40 h per wk)

13. $12.25 per h (40 h per wk)

14. $10.95 per h (35 h per wk)

Job B

$25,800 per y

$775 per mo

$420 biweekly

$16,400 per y

$28,600 per y

$18,500 per y

Solve.

15. Kelly has been offered one job that pays $740 per mo and another that pays $9,200 per y. Which job pays more per year? How much more?

16. Jeff presently earns $230 per wk. He is offered another job that pays $13,200 per y. How much will his salary increase per year? How much more will he earn per week?

17. Roger earns a salary of $22,800 per y. He works a 40-h week. What is his hourly wage?

18. Nicole earns $7.65 per h for a 35-h week. How much more per year will she earn if she is promoted to a job that pays an annual salary of $16,750?

In some industries, workers are paid based on the number of items they produce or jobs they complete. This is called **piecework** since workers' wages depend on the number of pieces or jobs completed.

EXAMPLE 1

Suppose you are paid $4.67 for each garment you complete while working in a clothing factory. If you complete an average of 2 garments per h, what is your average pay for a 40-h work week?

THINK: Work week: 40 h   Items produced: 2 per h   Piece rate: $4.67

PIECE RATE × ITEMS PRODUCED = PAY

1. Multiply to find the average number of items produced. $40 \times 2 = 80$ items

2. Multiply to find the pay. $\$4.67 \times 80 = \$373.60$

You earn about $373.60 for a 40-h week.

EXAMPLE 2

Alex works part time at home, typing papers for others on his word processor. Alex charges $1.75 per page and averages 9 pages per h. Alex needs to earn $250 per wk. About how many hours must he work each week? About how many pages will he need to type each week?

THINK: Piece rate: $1.75   Items produced: 9 per h
            Pay needed: $250 per wk

1. Multiply to find the average pay per hour. $\$1.75 \times 9 = \$15.75$ per h

2. Divide to find the number of hours needed. $\$250 \div \$15.75 = 15.873015$ h

Alex must work about 16 h to earn $250.

3. Multiply to find the number of typed pages needed. $16 \times 9 = 144$ pages

Alex will need to type about 144 pages to earn $250.

FOR DISCUSSION

1. How does the piecework system motivate workers?

2. What are some advantages and disadvantages of the piecework system?

Remember to estimate whenever you use your calculator.

Find the pay for the job.

	Piece rate	Items produced
1.	$1.75	7 garments made
2.	$12.40	13 machine parts made
3.	$20	9 cleaned carpets
4.	$1.25	400 proofread pages
5.	$3.50	25 typed pages
6.	$2.00	15 grocery deliveries

	Piece rate	Items produced
7.	$0.08	450 delivered newspapers
8.	$45.00	120 illustrations
9.	$4.75	300 washed cars
10.	$6.35	55 packed cartons
11.	$63.50	18 car tune-ups
12.	$85.75	25 repaired televisions

Solve.

13. Becky is paid $1.25 per shirt. She averages 5 shirts per h. What is her average pay for a 35-h week?

14. Juan earns 4.2¢ for each circuit. He averages 120 circuits per h. What is his average pay for a 30-h week?

15. Leon assembles an average of 12 machines per d. He is paid $15.60 per machine. What is his average pay for a 5-d week?

16. Jennifer averages 5 deliveries per h and earns $2.40 per delivery. What is her average pay for a 35-h week?

17. Blair is paid 16¢ for each telephone call. She earned $148.16 last week. How many calls did she make?

18. Jake earns $5.25 for each lawn he mows. About how many lawns must he mow in order to earn $200 per wk?

19. Roberta earns $35 per illustration. It takes her about $1\frac{1}{2}$ h to complete each illustration. How many illustrations must she complete to earn $525? How many hours will this take her?

20. Guido is paid 85¢ per page to proofread manuscripts. He proofreads about 15 pages per h. About how many hours must he work in order to earn over $400 per week? About how many pages will he need to proofread to earn this much?

EXTENSION   Mixed Rates of Pay

Eric is paid $265 per wk plus 80¢ for each part he machines.

1. What is Eric's piecework pay for machining 97 parts?

2. What is Eric's total pay for a week in which he machines 97 parts?

3. What is his average hourly wage if he works a 35-h week?

You have taken a job selling magazine subscriptions. It offers a commission of $8.25 for each subscription sold. A **commission** is an amount of money paid for selling a product or a service.

EXAMPLE **1**

What would your commission be if you sold 60 subscriptions?

THINK: Commission rate: $8.25 per subscription
Total sales: 60 subscriptions

COMMISSION RATE × TOTAL SALES = COMMISSION

$8.25 × 60 = $495.00

Your commission would be $495.00.

The **commission rate** is often a percent of the total value of sales. Remember to change the percent to a decimal or a fraction before multiplying.

EXAMPLE **2**

A sign in a carpet-store window advertises a sales position that earns a commission of $5\frac{1}{4}\%$. How much commission would you earn on sales of $6,000?

THINK: $5\frac{1}{4}\% = 0.0525$

COMMISSION RATE × TOTAL SALES = COMMISSION

0.0525 × $6,000 = $315

You would earn a commission of $315.

In the above situations, the only pay was a commission, known as **straight commission.** Some jobs offer a combination of **salary and commission.**

EXAMPLE **3**

A sales position at an appliance store offers a base pay of $250 per wk plus a 12% commission on sales. How much would you earn on weekly sales of $1,750?

1. Multiply to find the commission.

   THINK: 12% = 0.12   0.12 × $1,750 = $210

2. Add to find the total earnings. $210 + $250 = $460

You would earn $460.

FOR DISCUSSION

If you could earn $300 per wk plus a 3% commission or a straight commission of 7%, which job would you choose? Why?

Remember to estimate whenever you use your calculator.

Find the commission on the sale.

	Commission rate	Total sales
1.	$5.35 per order	25 orders
2.	25¢ per box	650 boxes
3.	9%	$7,280
4.	40%	$82.75

	Commission rate	Total sales
5.	3%	$26,359
6.	$12\frac{1}{2}$%	$642.30
7.	19%	$3,983
8.	$6\frac{3}{4}$%	$935.40

Solve.

9. Dwight is paid a commission of $3.75 for each class ring he sells. How much did he earn by selling 74 class rings?

10. Sylvia is in automobile sales. She earns a commission of 3.2% on the value of her auto sales. How much did she earn on sales of $46,280?

11. Ellen sells cosmetics and earns a weekly pay of $230 plus a commission of 12% on sales. How much did she earn last week when she sold $1,200 worth of cosmetics?

12. Will earns a monthly pay of $825 plus a commission of $4\frac{1}{2}$% on sales. How much did he earn last month when his sales were $13,850?

13. Luis is paid $245 per wk plus a 12.5% commission on all sales over $500. His sales last week totaled $1,340. What were his total earnings?

14. Emily earns $775 per mo plus a $3\frac{3}{4}$% commission on sales over $5,000. What were her total earnings last month when she had sales of $14,250?

EXTENSION   Graduated Commission

In some situations, a different rate of commission is paid for different levels of sales. This is called **graduated commission.**

Each month, Lance receives a graduated commission of 8% on his first $5,000 of sales, 10% on his next $5,000, and 12% on sales over $10,000. Last month, Lance's sales totaled $14,250.

1. What was Lance's commission on the first $5,000?

2. What was Lance's commission on the next $5,000?

3. How much in sales over $10,000 did Lance have last month?

4. How much commission did Lance receive on the sales over $10,000?

5. What was Lance's total commission for the month?

For a 40-h work week, you earn a **gross pay** of $376.00. Your "take-home pay," or **net pay,** was only $252.92 because of **payroll deductions.**

City of Hampton		Employee Earnings Statement	
Employee _Your Name_		Social Security # 000-00-0000	
Earnings		_Taxes/Deductions_	
Regular Earnings:	$376.00	Federal Taxes:	$54.40
		FICA:	28.76
Overtime Earnings:	0.00	State Tax:	9.52
		Insurance:	17.60
Gross Earnings:	$376.00	Retirement:	8.30
		Union Dues:	4.50
Week ending 10/25		NET PAY:	$252.92

EXAMPLE 1

How much was deducted from your gross pay?

THINK: Gross pay: $376.00   Net pay: $252.92

GROSS PAY − NET PAY = TOTAL DEDUCTIONS

$376.00   − $252.92   = $123.08

A total of $123.08 was deducted from your gross pay.

The two highest deductions are for **Federal Withholding Tax** and for **Social Security Tax (FICA).**

EXAMPLE 2

How much will be deducted from your pay over the course of a year (52 weekly paychecks) for each tax?

THINK: Weekly Federal Withholding: $54.40
Weekly Social Security: $28.76

Multiply to find each annual deduction.

Federal Withholding Tax → 52 × $54.40 = $2,828.80
Social Security Tax → 52 × $28.76 = $1,495.52

One way to judge the size of your payroll deductions is to compute the percentage of your gross pay that you take home.

EXAMPLE 3

What percent of your gross pay is your net pay?

THINK: $252.92 is what percent of $376.00?

1. Divide to find a decimal. $252.92 ÷ $376.00 = 0.6726595

2. Rename the decimal as a percent.   0.6726595 = 67.26595%

Your net pay is about 67%, or about $\frac{2}{3}$ of your gross pay.

FOR DISCUSSION

1. Why is Federal Withholding Tax deducted from your pay?
2. Why is Social Security Tax deducted from your pay?

PRACTICE EXERCISES

Remember to estimate whenever you use your calculator.

Complete the table.

Employee	Hours worked	Hourly wage	Gross pay	Federal tax	Social Security	Other deductions	Net pay
Burbridge	36	$4.25	1. ■	$14.71	$11.70	$3.50	2. ■
Samuelson	40	$7.85	3. ■	$56.37	$24.02	$24.53	4. ■
Alloca	35	$9.50	5. ■	$60.42	$25.44	$31.25	6. ■
O'Donnell	$27\frac{1}{4}$	$4.25	7. ■	$9.75	$8.86	$6.37	8. ■
Garcia	$15\frac{3}{4}$	$5.27	9. ■	$0	$6.35	$2.00	10. ■

Josh works $37\frac{1}{2}$ h per wk at $10.73 per h. His Federal Withholding Tax is $75.40 and his Social Security Tax is $30.78. He also has $8.50 deducted each week for union dues, and he pays $15.30 per wk for insurance. Complete the earnings statement below for Josh.

Employee Josh Evans   Social Security # 000-00-0000

Earnings   *Taxes/Deductions*

Regular Earnings: 11. ■   Federal Taxes: 13. ■
Overtime Earnings: 0.00   FICA: 14. ■
Gross Earnings: 12. ■   Insurance: 15. ■
                                      Union Dues: 16. ■
Week ending 11/18
                                      NET PAY: 17. ■

What is Josh's annual deduction for:

18. Federal Withholding Tax?   19. Social Security Tax?   20. Insurance?

21. What percent of his gross pay does Josh take home?

Solve.

22. Ken has $4.30 deducted twice a month for union dues. How much is deducted per year?

23. Robin's net weekly pay is $248.55. If her gross pay is $325.00, what percent of her gross pay is her net pay?

4.7 HEALTH INSURANCE

Most employees receive some form of **health insurance** as a "fringe benefit" of their employment. Their employer pays all or part of the cost of this insurance, which usually covers the cost of doctors, hospitals, and medicine, and sometimes of dental and eye care.

A common feature of health-insurance policies is a **deductible**—the amount that the person insured must pay. The insurance company then pays all or part of the remaining balance.

EXAMPLE 1   Your employer provides you with health insurance that has a $175 deductible. The insurance company will then pay 80% of the remaining medical expenses up to $20,000. After minor surgery, you incur medical expenses of $1,245. How much will your insurance carrier pay, and how much will you pay?

THINK: The insurance company will pay 80%, or 0.8, of the costs after subtracting the deductible.

1. Find the insurance company's share.

   • Subtract the deductible. $1,245 − $175 = $1,070

   • Multiply by the rate.   0.8 × $1,070 = $856

The insurance company will pay $856 of the bill.

2. Subtract to find your share. $1,245 − $856 = $389

Your share of the bill will be $389.

Sometimes the cost of health insurance is split between an employee and his or her employer. The employee's share is taken out as a **payroll deduction.**

EXAMPLE 2   Norma's company pays 60% of the cost of her family-coverage health insurance. The monthly premium for the insurance is $147.20. What is Norma's monthly payroll deduction for health insurance? How much does she pay per year for health insurance?

THINK: Her employer pays 60%.
       Norma's share is 40%, or 0.4, of the premium.

1. Multiply to find Norma's share.   0.4 × $147.20 = $58.88

Norma's monthly deduction is $58.88.

2. Multiply to find the annual cost.   12 × $58.88 = $706.56

Norma pays $706.56 per y for health insurance for her family.

1. Why do health-insurance policies usually have deductibles?

2. Why is health insurance usually less expensive when purchased for a large group than when purchased for an individual?

PRACTICE EXERCISES   Remember to estimate whenever you use your calculator.

Complete the table.

Medical bill	Deductible amount	% of Coverage over deductible	Amount paid by insurer	Amount paid by you
$475	$165	80%	1. ■	2. ■
$88	$150	80%	3. ■	4. ■
$245	$125	70%	5. ■	6. ■
$2,485	$175	90%	7. ■	8. ■
$746	$100	65%	9. ■	10. ■

Complete the table.

Monthly premium for insurance	% Paid by employer	Monthly deduction for insurance	Annual cost
$38.70	50%	11. ■	12. ■
$46.00	80%	13. ■	14. ■
$128.50	75%	15. ■	16. ■
$72.80	90%	17. ■	18. ■

Solve.

19. Terry's insurance pays 80% of all costs. Last year, Terry ran up doctor bills of $47.50, $73.00, and $26.75. How much did Terry pay her doctor?

20. Dans's bills were $275 for a doctor, $897 for the hospital, and $92.30 for medicine. If his policy has a $150 deductible and pays 80% of all costs over $150, how much did Dan pay?

21. From each of Janet's weekly paychecks, $4.50 is deducted for health insurance. If her employer is paying 80% of the cost of this insurance, what is the total annual premium for Janet's health insurance?

22. Ted's health insurance costs a total of $87.50 per mo, but his employer pays 70% of the premium. If Ted paid $283.50 for medical expenses last year, how much did he pay for health care, including insurance?

People buy **life insurance** for themselves or for others to provide financial protection against loss of income in the event that the person insured dies.

Key life insurance terms are:

Beneficiary—the person who receives the insurance money
Face value—the amount of money received from the policy

There are 2 major types of life insurance:

Term insurance policies provide protection for a limited period of time—usually 5, 10, 15, or 20 y—and can then be renewed at higher premiums. Term insurance is the simplest and least expensive form of life insurance.

Straight life insurance policies provide permanent lifetime protection for as long as you pay your premiums.

Life insurance rates vary depending on the age and gender of the insured person, and the face value of the policy.

SOME ANNUAL PREMIUMS FOR $1,000

Age at issue		Term Insurance		Straight life
Male	Female	10-Year	20-Year	
20	23	$2.86	$3.90	$13.67
25	28	$3.27	$5.74	$15.78
30	33	$3.72	$7.83	$18.87
35	38	$4.42	$10.22	$23.37
40	43	$5.87	$14.58	$28.51
45	48	$7.42	$18.46	$32.17

EXAMPLE

Ronald is 25 y old and wants to buy $30,000 of insurance. What would his annual premium be for 10-y term insurance? For straight life?

1. Multiply to find the annual premium for 10-y term. $30 \times \$3.27 = \$98.10$

Ronald's annual premium would be $98.10 for 10-y term insurance.

2. Multiply to find the annual premium for straight life. $30 \times \$15.78 = \$473.40$

Ronald's annual premium would be $473.40 for straight life insurance.

FOR DISCUSSION

1. Why do term insurance rates increase as you get older?

2. Why are the premiums for straight life insurance higher than for term insurance?

PRACTICE EXERCISES

Remember to estimate whenever you use your calculator.

Use the premium table to compute the annual premium for each policy.

	Type of policy	Age	Gender	Face value
1.	10-y term	25	Male	$35,000
2.	Straight life	28	Female	$50,000
3.	Straight life	20	Male	$25,000
4.	20-y term	23	Female	$40,000
5.	10-y term	30	Male	$75,000
6.	Straight life	40	Male	$75,000
7.	20-y term	38	Female	$50,000
8.	Straight life	48	Female	$50,000

Solve.

9. How much less per year would a 35-year-old male pay for $25,000 of 20-y term insurance than for straight life?

10. Jack purchased $150,000 of 20-y term insurance at age 25. What will his total premiums be over the 20 y?

EXTENSION   Decreasing Term Insurance

As people get older, their need for financial protection often decreases. For this reason, **decreasing term insurance** is also available for less cost than level term insurance. As each year passes, the amount of insurance coverage decreases.

1. Sam bought $40,000 of 10-y decreasing term insurance. How much insurance coverage will he have in the 4th year of the policy?

2. Rachel bought $60,000 of 10-y decreasing term insurance. How much insurance coverage will she have in the 7th year of the policy?

COVERAGE PER $1,000 INITIAL VALUE OF 10-Y DECREASING TERM INSURANCE

Year	Coverage	Year	Coverage
1	$1,000	6	$555
2	$940	7	$460
3	$860	8	$340
4	$730	9	$250
5	$660	10	$140

4.9 BUYING INSURANCE

DECISION MAKING

Two of the hardest decisions young people must make are deciding what type of life insurance to purchase and how much coverage to get.

PROBLEM

Jeff and Susan are both 20 y old, and they were just married. Susan has life insurance through her company; Jeff does not. They believe that while they are young and healthy, and before they have children, it would be wise to purchase life insurance for Jeff on their own. They need to decide what type of insurance they can afford at this time.

DECISION-MAKING FACTORS

Type of policy   Cost of policy   Term of policy

Cash value is the monetary value of your policy if, at some time, you choose to cancel it.

Renewable policies can be automatically renewed for additional periods of time without requiring a physical examination.

Insurance Options

1. Savings Bank Life Insurance (SBLI)
   - 5-y Non-renewable term
   - $2.60 per $1,000 per y

2. Jefferson Insurance Co.
   - 10-y Renewable term
   - $3.40 per $1,000 per y

3. McKinley Insurance Co.
   - Straight life for $9.50 per $1,000 per y
   - Cash value per $1,000:

     $90 after 10 y

     $160 after 15 y

     $270 after 20 y

     $690 at age 65

DECISION-MAKING COMPARISONS

Compare the 3 options by completing the table.

Factor	SBLI	Jefferson	McKinley
Type of policy	1. ■	term	2. ■
Cost per $1,000	$2.60	3. ■	4. ■
Term of insurance	5. ■	10 y	6. ■
Cash value—yes or no	7. ■	8. ■	yes
Renewable—yes, no, or not applicable	no	9. ■	10. ■

MAKING THE DECISIONS

11. Jeff and Susan decide that Jeff should have $50,000 worth of insurance. What is the annual premium for a $50,000 policy under each option?

12. Which policy should they purchase if cost is the only factor?

13. What is the cash value of a $50,000 straight life policy from McKinley after 10 y? Remember: Cash values are per $1,000.

14. What is the net cost of this McKinley policy if Jeff and Susan deduct the cash value from the total premiums paid over 10 y?

15. Is the net cost of the McKinley policy more or less expensive than 10 y of the Jefferson policy?

16. Jeff learns that when he is 5 y older, the cost of a new SBLI policy will rise to $4.90 per $1,000 per y. Compare the total cost of the SBLI and the Jefferson policies over the 10 y. Which is the better buy? Remember: For 10 y, Jeff will need 2 consecutive SBLI policies of 5 y each.

17. If you were Jeff, which policy would you purchase? Why?

Vocabulary Choose the letter of the word(s) that completes the sentence.

1. For work above 40 h per wk, many employees often receive $1\frac{1}{2}$ times their regular wage, or ▪. [58]

   a. Overtime pay   **b.** Hourly wage   **c.** Piecework

2. An amount of money paid for selling a product or service is called ▪. [66]

   a. Regular pay   **b.** Commission   **c.** Annual salary

3. After payroll deductions, most people's ▪ is much less than their gross pay. [68]

   a. Biweekly pay   **b.** Social Security deduction   **c.** Net pay

Skills Find the answer.

4. Celia worked 40 h at $5.40 per h. What was her regular pay? [58]

5. Joe worked $37\frac{1}{2}$ h at $7.50 per h. What was his regular pay? [58]

6. Ellen worked $44\frac{1}{2}$ h at $6.20 per h. Her overtime rate is $1\frac{1}{2}$. What was her total pay? [58]

7. Bob earns an annual salary of $14,500. What is his weekly pay? [62]

8. Ted earns an annual salary of $23,500. What is his biweekly pay? [62]

9. Sharon's weekly pay is $385. What is her annual salary? [62]

10. Sarah earns a piece rate of $12.50 per delivery. How much did she earn by making 7 deliveries? [64]

11. Eli earns a 15% commission on sales. How much did he earn on sales of $3,680? [66]

12. David earns a $6\frac{1}{2}$% commission on sales. How much did he earn on sales of $159,000? [66]

13. John's gross pay was $548.96. His net pay was $458.75. How much was deducted from his paycheck? [68]

14. Kelly has $89.30 deducted each week for Social Security. How much is deducted in a year? [68]

15. Calvin earns $8.25 per h for a 40-h week. If his deductions total $71.90, what is his net pay? [68]

16. Your health insurance has a $150 deductible, after which it pays 80% of all costs. How much will your insurance pay on a $265 bill? [70]

17. At $12.84 per $1,000, what is the annual premium for a $75,000 straight life insurance policy? [72]

Find the earnings.

1. Hours worked: 38
   Hourly wage: $5.35

2. Hours worked: 42
   Hourly wage: $7.45
   Overtime rate: $1\frac{1}{2}$

3. Hours worked: $47\frac{1}{2}$
   Hourly wage: $6.60
   Overtime rate: $1\frac{1}{2}$

4. Hours worked: 5, $4\frac{1}{2}$, $8\frac{3}{4}$
   Hourly wage: $18.75

5. Hours worked: 3, $6\frac{1}{2}$, $5\frac{3}{4}$, $8\frac{1}{4}$
   Hourly wage: $20.50

6. Hours worked: 7:15 A.M. to 3:30 P.M.
   Hourly wage: $4.58

7. Hours worked: 8:00 A.M. to 5:30 P.M.
   Hourly wage: $7.25

8. Piece rate: $7.50   Items produced: 73 interviews

9. Commission rate: 30¢   Total sales: 850 boxes

10. Commission rate: $4\frac{1}{2}$%   Total sales: $4,325

Solve.

11. June packs an average of 12 cartons per h. She is paid 60¢ per carton. About how much does she earn for a 35-h work week?

12. Miguel worked 10 h and earned $175 constructing fencing. If he averages 8 yd per h, how much is he paid for each yard of fencing?

13. Grace's annual salary is $12,680. What is her weekly pay?

14. Dave's biweekly pay is $793.68. What is his annual salary?

15. Dawn works a 40-h week at $6.34 per h. If her deductions total $86.47, what is her net pay?

16. Lee's gross pay last week was $493.54. If his net pay was $386.47, how much was deducted from his pay?

17. Hal's health insurance pays 80% of his medical bills with a $130 deductible. How much did he pay on a $2,850 bill?

18. Tracy's employer pays 75% of the cost of her health insurance. How much does she pay per year if the total biweekly premium is $35.70?

19. Rita has $80,000 straight life insurance. It costs $3.87 per $1,000. What is her annual premium?

20. Diane has $50,000 10-y term life insurance. It costs $5.32 per $1,000. How much will she pay over the 10-y period?

Add or subtract.

1. $15 + $28   **2.** $92.65 + $7.38   **3.** $15.85 + $9.14

4. $72.83 + $49.86   **5.** $183.75 + $27.89   **6.** $32 − $9.75

7. $58.79 − $16.32   **8.** $80.85 − $17.91   **9.** $143.65 − $62.99

10. $16.50 + $30 + $45.75   **11.** $110 + $8.80 + $41.30 + $10

Multiply.

12. 8 × $9.65   **13.** 7 × $16.38   **14.** 4 × $3.48   **15.** 9 × $18.09

16. 80 × $9.65   **17.** 60 × $23.56   **18.** 35 × $48.02   **19.** 73 × $71.63

Divide.

20. $84 ÷ 12   **21.** $96 ÷ 24   **22.** $527 ÷ $31   **23.** $972 ÷ $27

24. $37.60 ÷ 16   **25.** $37.49 ÷ 23   **26.** $71.06 ÷ 34   **27.** $56.96 ÷ 64

Find the answer.

28. 25 is what percent of 50?   **29.** 15 is what percent of 60?

30. 16.5 is what percent of 82.5?   **31.** 56 is what percent of 14?

Use the table for Exercises 32–37.

32. How much did a gallon of gas cost in February?

33. How much did a gallon of gas cost in September?

34. During which month was gas most expensive?

35. During which month was gas least expensive?

36. In which months did gas cost more than $1.25?

37. In which 2 months did gas cost the same?

COST OF GAS PER GALLON

Month	Price
January	$1.21
February	$1.27
March	$1.19
April	$1.16
May	$1.23
June	$1.28
July	$1.31
August	$1.26
September	$1.17
October	$1.15
November	$1.19
December	$1.14

RECREATION AND SPORTS

There are many types of recreation. What factors would determine how you spend your free time? How would a limited budget affect your choices?

One summer night, you went to the movies with your parents, your brother, and your sister. You and your sister are students over age 12. Your brother is 10 y old.

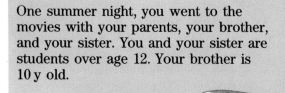

QUADPLEX MOVIES

Adults	$6.25
Students (over 12)	$4.75
Students (12 and under)	$3.50
Children (under 5)	FREE

All prices include tax.

EXAMPLE 1

How much did it cost for your family to go to the movies? How much change did you get from $30?

THINK: 2 adults, 2 students over 12, 1 student 12 and under

1. First estimate the total cost. $6 + $6 + $5 + $5 + $4 = $26

2. Add to find the total cost.
$$\$6.25 + \$6.25 + \$4.75 + \$4.75 + \$3.50 = \$25.50$$

Compare $25.50 to the estimate. The answer is reasonable. It cost $25.50 for your family to go to the movies.

3. Subtract to find the amount of change. $30.00 − $25.50 = $4.50

You got $4.50 in change.

Sometimes you will buy tickets that each cost the same amount.

EXAMPLE 2

You and 6 of your friends are going to attend a concert. Each ticket, including tax, costs $18.75. What is the total cost for all 7 people? How much change will you get from $140?

1. First estimate the total cost. $7 \times \$20 = \$140$

2. Multiply to find the total cost. $7 \times \$18.75 = \$131.25$

Compare $131.25 to the estimate. The answer is reasonable.

3. Subtract to find the amount of change. $140.00 − $131.25 = $8.75

You will get $8.75 in change.

FOR DISCUSSION

Many people get tickets for concerts, plays, and musicals from large ticket brokers. Why do you think brokers charge more per ticket than theaters?

Remember to estimate whenever you use your calculator.

Use these movie prices for Exercises 1–6.

	Theater A	Theater B	Theater C
Adults	$6.25	$7.25	$5.75
Students (over 12)	$4.75	$3.75	$5.75
Students (12 and under)	$3.50	$3.75	$4.25
Children (under 5)	$2.00	FREE	$1.25

> Jones family: 2 adults, 1 student over 12, 1 student 12 or under, 1 child under 5

1. How much would it cost for the Jones family to go to Theater A? How much change would they get from $25?

2. How much would it cost for the Jones family to go to Theater B? How much change would they get from $30?

3. How much would it cost for the Jones family to go to Theater C? How much change would they get from $40?

> Wong family: 1 adult, 3 students over 12, 1 child under 5

4. How much would it cost for the Wong family to go to Theater A? How much change would they get from $40?

5. How much would it cost for the Wong family to go to Theater B? How much change would they get from $30?

6. How much would it cost for the Wong family to go to Theater C? How much change would they get from $25?

Solve.

7. Tickets to the school play cost $7. How much will it cost for 8 people to go?

8. Tickets to the laser-light show cost $9.50. How much will it cost for 6 people to go?

9. Sondra bought 6 tickets to a concert. Tickets cost $13.75 each. How much did she pay? How much change did she get from $100?

10. The Planetarium sells tickets in books of 12. Each ticket costs $4.35. How much did Ray spend for a book of tickets? How much change did he get from $60?

11. Lorraine wants to buy 11 tickets to an ice-skating exhibition. Tickets cost $9.85 each. She plans to buy them from a ticket broker who charges $2.50 extra for each ticket. She has $88. How much more does she need?

12. The regular price of a theater ticket is $19.80. Ann has **twofer coupons.** Each one lets her buy 2 tickets for the price of 1. How much would 9 tickets cost if Ann uses her twofer coupons?

You are at Future Land Park. You can either pay one price for an **all-day pass** or pay separately for each ride.

FUTURE LAND PARK

All-Day Pass	$14.25
Tilt Slide	$ 1.75
Looper	$ 2.50
Water Trough	$ 1.75
Coaster-to-Coaster	$ 3.50

EXAMPLE 1

You want to go twice each on the Water Trough and the Coaster-to-Coaster. You want to go on the other rides once. How much would you save by buying an all-day pass instead of paying for each ride?

1. Multiply to find the costs of the Trough and the Coaster rides.

$2 \times \$1.75 = \$3.50$
$2 \times \$3.50 = \$7.00$

2. Add to find the total cost of all of the rides.

$\$1.75 + \$2.50 + \$3.50 + \$7.00 = \$14.75$

3. Subtract to find the amount saved.

$\$14.75 - \$14.25 = \$0.50$

You would save $0.50 by buying an all-day pass.

Sharon went to the ballpark to pick up some baseball tickets for future games. Tickets for the better seats are more expensive.

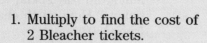

TICKET PRICES

Bleachers	$4.35
Grandstand	$6.25
Reserved Seat	$8.75
Box Seat	$10.50
Tax included.	

EXAMPLE 2

Sharon had $30. She bought 2 Bleacher tickets, 1 Grandstand ticket, and 1 Reserved Seat ticket. How much money did she have left?

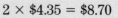

1. Multiply to find the cost of 2 Bleacher tickets.

$2 \times \$4.35 = \$8.70$

2. Add to find the total cost of all of the tickets.

$\$8.70 + \$6.25 + \$8.75 = \$23.70$

3. Subtract to find the amount left.

$\$30.00 - \$23.70 = \$6.30$

She had $6.30 left.

Sometimes you may be able to calculate the cost of tickets mentally.

EXAMPLE **3** Tad bought tickets for all 3 days of the Women's Tennis Tournament. Tickets cost $9.95 per d. How much did he spend?

THINK: $10.00 is $0.05 more than $9.95.

1. Multiply. $3 \times \$10 = \$30$ $3 \times \$0.05 = \$0.15$

2. Subtract to find the total cost. $\$30.00 - \$0.15 = \$29.85$

Tad spent $29.85 on tickets.

FOR DISCUSSION

Amusement parks sometimes charge large groups, like a whole class, a **group rate.** Do you think that the cost per person with a group rate is more or less than the regular cost per person? Why?

PRACTICE EXERCISES   Remember to estimate whenever you use your calculator.

Use the Safari Park ticket prices.
You can ride all the Safari Park rides as many times as you wish for $18.50. Find the total cost of the given ride tickets. Decide if you should pay for each ride separately or pay the $18.50.

SAFARI PARK TICKETS	
Tilt Slide	$1.75
Looper	$2.50
Water Trough	$1.75
Coaster-to-Coaster	$3.50
Giant Swing	$2.25
Puddle Jumper	$2.75
Merry-Go-Round	$1.25

1. 2 Tilt Slides
3 Water Troughs
1 Coaster
4 Merry-Go-Rounds

2. 3 Coasters
2 Jumpers
3 Swings

3. You have $15. How many times could you ride the Puddle Jumper?

4. You have $14. How many times could you ride the Tilt Slide?

Use the baseball ticket prices on page 86. Find the total cost of the given tickets and the amount of change.

5. 1 Bleacher
2 Grandstands
2 Box Seats
Change from $50?

6. 3 Bleachers
2 Reserved Seats
1 Box Seat
Change from $45?

7. 2 Grandstands
2 Reserved Seats
1 Box Seat
Change from $60?

Solve by computing mentally.

8. You bought 7 baseball tickets for $6.95 each. How much change did you get from $50?

9. You want to buy 6 soccer tickets for $8.75 each. You have $50. How much more money do you need?

Stamp collecting is a popular hobby. The rarest United States stamp is the "inverted jenny" 24-cent stamp printed in 1918. One hundred of these stamps were printed upside-down by mistake. This stamp is now worth over $80,000.

You do not need to buy expensive stamps to be a collector. You could start with just a few stamps.

EXAMPLE 1 You have $5.00 to start your collection. The stamp shop has packets of stamps on sale for $0.35 each. How many packets can you buy? How much change will you get?

   1. First estimate the number of packets.

      THINK: $0.35 ≈ $0.40

      3 packets cost 3 times the cost of 1. $3 \times \$0.40 = \$1.20 ≈ \$1.00$
      15 packets cost 5 times the cost of 3. $5 \times \$1.00 = \$5.00$

   You can buy about 15 packets with $5.00.

   2. Divide to find exactly how many packets. $\$5.00 \div \$0.35 = 14.285714$

   You can actually buy 14, not 15, packets with $5.00.

   3. Multiply to find the cost. $14 \times \$0.35 = \$4.90$

   4. Subtract to find the change. $\$5.00 - \$4.90 = \$0.10$

   You will get $0.10 in change.

Constructing models is another popular hobby. Some people construct miniature doll houses. Others construct model cars or planes.

EXAMPLE 2 You need these materials to finish your model. What is the total cost of these materials? How much change will you get from $15?

Materials Needed

$3 \frac{1}{2}$-in. dowels

1 bag balsa wood

2 bottles paint

1 paint brush

1 package decals

HOBBY SHOP
PRICE LIST

¼-in. dowel	$0.49
½-in. dowel	$1.89
1 bag balsa wood	$2.95
1 jar paste	$0.75
1 bottle paint	$1.05
1 paint brush	$0.59
1 pkg. decals	$1.50
Prices include tax.	

1. Multiply to find the cost of the dowels. $3 \times \$1.89 = \$5.67$

2. Multiply to find the cost of the paint. $2 \times \$1.05 = \$2.10$

3. Add to find the total cost.
$$\$5.67 + \$2.95 + \$2.10 + \$0.59 + \$1.50 = \$12.81$$

The total cost of the materials is \$12.81.

4. Subtract to find the change. $\$15.00 - \$12.81 = \$2.19$

You will get \$2.19 in change.

FOR DISCUSSION

What types of costs might be involved for photography? Your favorite hobby?

PRACTICE EXERCISES   Remember to estimate whenever you use your calculator.

Find the total cost of the purchases.

1. *Hobby: Stamp collecting*
   Stamps: \$7.20
   Tweezers: \$1.29
   Display book: \$12.95

2. *Hobby: Painting*
   Canvas: \$6.00
   Brushes: \$7.50
   Paints: \$21.85

3. *Hobby: Sewing*
   Pattern: \$4.45
   Fabric: \$18.70
   Thread: \$1.69
   Zipper: \$2.89

Solve.

4. Juan has \$18.00 to spend on stamp packets that sell for \$1.85 each. How many packets can he buy? How much change will he get?

5. Debra has \$21.00 to spend on clay that costs \$3.75 per lb. How many pounds can she buy? How much change will she get?

6. Michael belongs to a book club. He orders 4 special books for \$0.99 each and spends an additional \$32.50 for other books. The shipping and handling costs are \$15.25. What is the total cost of his order?

7. Lois wants to buy 4 packets of stamps that cost \$2.85 each, 1 stamp that costs \$2.89, and a stamp catalog that costs \$15.95. She has \$24.35. How much more money does she need?

Use the Hobby Shop price list on page 88. Find the total cost of the materials. Then find the amount of change.

8. $1\frac{1}{2}$-in. dowel

   3 bags balsa wood

   1 bottle paint
   2 pkgs. decals
   Change from \$15?

9. $5\frac{1}{4}$-in. dowels

   $1\frac{1}{2}$-in. dowel

   3 jars paste
   2 bottles paint
   Change from \$10?

10. 3 bags balsa wood

    $1\frac{1}{2}$-in. dowel

    3 bottles paint
    4 paint brushes
    Change from \$20?

Some sports cost almost nothing while others can be very expensive.

TOTAL COST = EQUIPMENT COSTS + USE FEES + TRANSPORTATION COSTS

EXAMPLE 1 You decide to go swimming once a week for the next 28 wk. You pay $28.95 for a swimsuit and $4.29 for goggles. You pay $25 to join the swim club, and it costs $2.75 each time you go swimming. The bus you take to and from the swim club costs $1.30 per round trip. What is the total cost of this sports activity?

1. Add to find the cost of the equipment.

$28.95 + $4.29 = $33.24

2. Multiply to find the cost of the swim sessions.

$28 \times $2.75 = $77.00

3. Add to find the total cost of using the swim club.

$25 + $77 = $102.00

4. Multiply to find the cost of the bus transportation.

$28 \times $1.30 = $36.40

5. Add to find the total cost.

$33.24 + $102 + $36.40 = $171.64

The total cost of this sports activity is $171.64.

For some sports, you may need to decide whether to buy or to rent equipment.

EXAMPLE 2 Sarah's ski club dues include transportation to and from the ski slopes and the lift tickets. It costs $20 to rent skis and $15 to rent poles and boots. It would cost her $169.50 to buy skis, $67.95 to buy boots, and $18 to buy poles. She hopes to go skiing with the club 6 times. Would it be less expensive to rent or to buy the equipment?

1. Add to find the cost of 1 day's rental. $20 + $15 = $35

2. Multiply to find the cost of 6 days' rentals. 6 × $35 = $210

3. Add to find the cost of buying equipment.
$169.50 + $67.95 + $18 = $255.45

4. Compare the rental and buying costs. $210 < $255.45

It is less expensive to rent the ski equipment.

FOR DISCUSSION

Name some sports that you think are inexpensive and some that are expensive. Tell why.

PRACTICE EXERCISES   Remember to estimate whenever you use your calculator.

Complete the table to find the total cost of the sports activity.

Sports activity	Equipment cost	Use fees	Round-trip transportation cost	Total cost
Ice-skating	$59.50	1. 10 visits at $3.50/visit = ■	$0.85	2. ■
Tennis	$83.95	3. $45 membership + 25 h at $9.50/h = ■	$0.00	4. ■
Swimming	$28.95	5. $35 membership + 18 visits at $4.50/visit = ■	$1.35	6. ■
Racquetball	$76.85	7. $75 membership + 30 h at $6.50/h = ■	8. 25 trips at $0.90/trip = ■	9. ■
Bowling	$48.79	10. 39 games at $2.75/game = ■	11. 14 trips at $2.60/trip = ■	12. ■

Solve.

13. Julio goes ice-skating. He can either rent or buy skates. Skates sell for $45.90 and rent for $1.75 per h. Each week, Julio skates for about 28 h. Is it less expensive for him to rent or to buy skates?

You have decided to join a health club and to take a fitness class. As a member of a health club, you can usually go whenever you wish to use the exercise machines and other facilities. As you inquire about the costs of clubs and classes, you should also make sure that the activities are properly supervised.

You pay a **membership fee** to belong to a health club. The **cost per visit** is the membership fee divided by the number of visits.

COST PER VISIT = MEMBERSHIP FEE ÷ NUMBER OF VISITS

EXAMPLE 1

You want to join the All-American Health Club. The annual membership fee is $418. You expect to go about 3 times per wk for a year. What would be your cost per visit to the nearest cent?

1. Multiply to find the number of visits.

   THINK: 1 y = 52 wk $3 \times 52 = 156$

2. Divide to find the cost per visit. $\$418 \div 156 = \$2.6794871$

It would cost you about $2.68 per visit.

As a member of the health club, you still need to pay for any fitness classes you join. For many fitness classes, the cost per class decreases as the term of time for which you sign up increases.

EXAMPLE 2

You want to sign up for an aerobics class that meets 3 times per wk. The class costs $101.25 for 15 wk (45 classes) or $138.75 for 25 wk (75 classes). How much less would the cost per class be if you signed up for 25 wk instead of 15 wk?

1. Divide to find the cost of a 15-wk class. $\$101.25 \div 45 = \$2.25$

2. Divide to find the cost of a 25-wk class. $\$138.75 \div 75 = \$1.85$

3. Subtract to find the difference. $\$2.25 - \$1.85 = \$0.40$

It would cost $0.40 less per class if you signed up for the longer term of 25 wk.

FOR DISCUSSION

Is it more important to know the total club membership fee or to compute your own cost per visit? Why?

Find the cost per visit to the nearest cent. Then find the cost per visit
including the transportation cost.

Health club	Membership fee	Expected number of visits	Cost per visit	Transportation cost per visit	Cost per visit including transportation
USA Health	$233/y	98/y	1. ■	$1.80	2. ■
Slim Studio	$9.50/wk	4/wk	3. ■	$0.90	4. ■
Aerobics Unlimited	$19/mo	11/mo	5. ■	$2.80	6. ■
The Fitness Center	$462 for 3 y	63/y	7. ■	$0.00	8. ■
Health City	$193 for 6 mo	3/mo	9. ■	$3.15	10. ■

Find how much can be saved, to the nearest cent, by signing up for the
longer-term class.

11. Judo
$210 for 15 wk (30 classes)
$340 for 26 wk (52 classes)

12. Jazz Dance Workout
$98 for 5 wk (15 classes)
$125 for 8 wk (24 classes)

13. Weight Training
$680 for 24 wk (72 classes)
$1,200 for 48 wk (144 classes)

14. Floor Exercises
$220 for 12 wk (36 classes)
$420 for 25 wk (100 classes)

EXTENSION   Percents of the Total Cost

What percent of the total cost did you spend on equipment, on fees,
and on transportation for this sports activity?

Total cost: $230   Equipment: $83   Fees: $118   Transportation: $29

Divide each cost by the total cost.

$83 ÷ 230 = 0.3608695, or 36%   Equipment was 36% of the total cost.

$118 ÷ 230 = 0.5130434, or 51%   Fees were 51% of the total cost.

$29 ÷ 230 = 0.1260869, or 13%   Transportation was 13% of the total cost.

Find the percent of the total cost spent on equipment, on fees, and on
transportation. Round each percent to the nearest percent.

1. Total cost: $234.50   Equipment: $54.00   Fees: $153.50   Transportation: $27.00

2. Total cost: $256.20   Equipment: $62.00   Fees: $169.50   Transportation: $24.70

5.6 INTERPRETING A REMAINDER

Situation:

Last week, the Brookdale Fitness Club held registration for its exercise classes. Each class can hold a maximum of 18 students. If 140 people registered, how could the classes have been arranged?

Strategy:

When you divide to solve a problem, be sure that you answer the question that was asked.

Applying the Strategy:

Divide 140 by 18.

Notice the different answers to each of the questions below.

$$\begin{array}{r} 7 \text{ R14} \\ 18\overline{)140} \\ \underline{126} \\ 14 \end{array}$$

A. How many exercise classes would have been filled to the maximum by 140 students?

   Use only the quotient.   7 classes would have been filled to the maximum.

B. How many students would have been in the last class?

   Use only the remainder.   14 students would have been in the last class.

C. How many exercise classes would have been needed to hold all 140 students?

   Raise the quotient by 1.   THINK:
   7 full classes + 1 class with 14 students
   8 classes would have been needed in all.

D. What fraction of the last class would have been filled?

   Use a fractional remainder.   THINK: $\dfrac{\text{students in last class}}{\text{students in full class}} \rightarrow \dfrac{14}{18} = \dfrac{7}{9}$

   $\dfrac{7}{9}$ of the last class would have been filled.

PRACTICE EXERCISES

Write the letter of the correct answer.

1. Each weight-lifting class can hold a maximum of 8 students. If 38 students want to register, how many students will be in the last, or smallest, class?
   a. Use only the quotient.
   b. Use only the remainder.
   c. Raise the quotient by 1.

2. How many advanced exercise classes can be formed from 52 students if exactly 12 students can be in each class?
   a. Use only the quotient.
   b. Use only the remainder.
   c. Raise the quotient by 1.

The Brookdale Fitness club gives each student a tee shirt to wear during classes. Dan packed 12 tee shirts in each carton. He had 285 tee shirts to pack.

3. How many cartons did Dan fill?

4. How many tee shirts did he put in the last partially filled carton?

5. How many cartons did Dan use to pack 285 tee shirts?

6. What fraction of the last carton was filled?

Solve by interpreting a remainder.

7. Sample classes are held during registration week. Each sample class costs $3. Tim has $10 to spend on sample classes. How many classes can he attend?

8. There are 78 floor mats in a shipment that arrived at the club. Each exercise room fits 8 mats. After fitting 9 rooms, what fraction of the 10th room can be fitted with mats?

9. One towel is needed for each of the 185 new students at the club. If a package contains 12 towels, how many packages are needed?

10. The 40 students in a calisthenics class were divided into groups of 4 pairs for a floor exercise. How many groups were set up?

5.7 SELECTING A SPORT

You do not need to be a good athlete to participate in and enjoy a sport. In fact, there is probably a sport for everyone.

PROBLEM

Derek is trying to decide in which sport to participate. He is interested in tennis, racquetball, skiing, and bowling. He listed the features of each sport to help him decide which one to choose.

Tennis	The equipment costs about $90. I'll have to pay $5.00 per h to play outside and $16.00 per h to play inside. I'll need to travel about 15 min to the tennis courts at a cost of about $1.25 for a round trip. Of the 4 sports, tennis ranks 3rd in the amount of exercise I'll get.
Racquetball	The equipment costs about $45. I'll have to pay $18 per h to play. The indoor racquetball courts are a short walk from my home. Racquetball ranks 1st in the amount of exercise I'll get.
Skiing	The equipment costs about $275. I'll have to pay $35 for a lift ticket every day I ski. I will probably want to ski about 5 h each day. It takes me about 2 h to get to the ski slopes at a cost of about $7.50 for a round trip. Skiing ranks between tennis and racquetball in the amount of exercise I'll get.
Bowling	The equipment costs about $55. I'll have to pay $2.75 for each game I play. I can bowl about 3 games per h for 2 h. It takes me about 1 h to get to the bowling alley at a round trip cost of $3.00. Bowling trails well behind tennis in the amount of exercise I'll get.

DECISION-MAKING FACTORS

Indoor or outdoor   Cost per hour   Travel time   Travel cost   Amount of exercise

DECISION-MAKING COMPARISONS

Compare the 4 sports, based on 40 h of participation, by completing the table. Remember to include equipment cost in the cost per hour.

Factor	Tennis	Racquetball	Skiing	Bowling
Indoor or outdoor	Both	1. ■	2. ■	3. ■
Cost per hour	$7.25 outdoor $18.25 indoor	4. ■	5. ■	6. ■
Round-trip travel time	7. ■	Few min	8. ■	9. ■
Travel cost	10. ■	11. ■	12. ■	$60.00
Amount of exercise	13. ■	14. ■	Ranks 2nd	15. ■

MAKING THE DECISIONS

Which sport would Derek choose if:

16. He wanted to play indoors and outdoors?

17. Cost per hour were the only factor?

18. Being close to home were the only factor?

19. Travel costs were the only factor?

20. If Derek did not want to spend more than $12 per h, which sports would he eliminate?

21. If Derek wanted the sport that would give him the most exercise, which sport would he choose?

22. If Derek wanted to exert himself as little as possible, which sport would he choose?

23. If Derek decided against racquet sports, which sports could he eliminate?

24. Which one of these sports would you choose? Name at least 3 reasons why.

Vocabulary   Choose the letter of the word(s) that completes the sentence.

1. If you want to pay only 1 price to go on all of the rides in an amusement park, you can buy ▪.   [86]

   a. An all-day pass   **b.** Individual tickets   **c.** A season pass

2. Amusement parks often charge large groups of people a ▪.   [86]

   a. Season pass   **b.** Use fee   **c.** Group rate

3. Membership fees and costs for a sports activity are called ▪.   [90]

   a. Equipment costs   **b.** Use fees   **c.** Transportation costs

Skills   Find the answer.

4. Use the movie-price list on page 84. An adult, two 14-year-olds, and a 3-year-old went to the movies. What was the total cost?   [84]

5. You and 3 friends went to a concert. Each ticket cost $23.50, including tax. What was the total cost?   [84]

6. Use the Future Land Park ticket prices on page 86. Ana wants to go twice on each of the rides. How much would she save by buying an all-day pass?   [86]

7. Use the baseball-ticket prices on page 86. Robert bought 2 Box Seat tickets, 2 Grandstand tickets, and 2 Bleachers tickets. How much money did he have left from $50?   [86]

8. Tony bought stamps for $5.50, a display book for $9.99, and tweezers for $0.89. How much did Tony spend?   [88]

9. Anita's hobby is photography. She bought a camera for $75.59, film for $7.20, and a camera case for $21.10. How much did Anita spend?   [88]

10. Lisa went bowling and spent $2.75 a game for 13 games. She spent $4.75 on shoe rental and $4.70 on transportation. How much did Lisa spend?   [90]

11. Ron joined a racquetball club for $55 and played for 28 h at $7.75 per h. The equipment cost $32, and Ron paid $13 for transportation. How much did Ron spend?   [90]

12. Fran joined a health club for $144 per y. She expects to visit the club 7 times per mo. What is the cost per visit?   [92]

13. A 10-class karate course costs $65. The 25-class course costs $149. How much can you save per class by signing up for 25 classes?   [92]

Find the total cost of the purchases.

1. Wood: $5.75
    Paste: $0.65
    Paint: $2.99
    Paintbrush: $1.59

2. Paper: $ 6.20
    Charcoal: $ 2.25
    Pencils: $ 1.89
    Easel: $15.50

3. Seeds: $ 9.95
    Shovel: $12.00
    Fertilizer: $ 6.50
    Wheelbarrow: $25.99

Find the total cost of the tickets and
the amount of change.

TICKET PRICES	
Bleachers	$ 4.35
Grandstand	$ 6.25
Reserved Seat	$ 8.75
Box Seat	$10.50
Tax included.	

4. 6 Grandstands
    3 Reserved Seats
    2 Box Seats
    Change from $100?

5. 3 Bleachers
    1 Box Seat
    2 Grandstands
    4 Reserved Seats
    Change from $80.00?

Complete the table to find the total cost of the sports activity.

Sports activity	Equipment cost	Use fees	Round-trip transportation cost	Total cost
Bowling	$42.50	6. 18 games at $3.25/game = ■	$5.10	7. ■
Tennis	$92.39	8. $75 membership + 25 h at $10.75/h = ■	$30.55	9. ■
Swimming	$58.99	10. $99 membership + 12 visits at $2.75/visit = ■	11. 12 trips at $1.60/trip = ■	12. ■

Complete the table to find the cost per visit to the nearest cent.

Health club	Membership fee	Expected number of visits	Cost per visit	Transportation cost per visit	Cost per visit including transportation
Health Club	$327/y	109/y	13. ■	$2.35	14. ■
Gym Center	$218 for 6 mo	16/mo	15. ■	$0.80	16. ■
Slim Salon	$402 for 2 y	9/mo	17. ■	$1.40	18. ■

Solve.

19. How much can be saved per class by
    signing up for 45 classes for $180
    instead of 24 classes for $100?

20. How many 12-person exercise classes
    can be filled by 40 people?

MONEY TIPS

Season tickets to sports events can save you money if you attend many games.

LET'S LOOK AT THE FACTS

Some people buy season tickets instead of buying tickets for 1 game at a time. This will cost less if you plan to attend many or all games. Read the ticket prices shown here carefully.

BASEBALL TICKET PRICES

TICKET	SEAT	PRICE	NUMBER OF GAMES
Single	Box	$10.00	1 only
Single	Reserved	$ 8.50	1 only
Season	Box	$750	79 - all home games
Season	Reserved	$600	79 - all home games
Season	Box	$408	47 - all weekday games
Season	Box	$187	30 - Mon/Wed/Thu games

IMPORTANT NOTE: Season price covers the cost of 79 <u>tickets</u>. Two doubleheaders are played at home, so that the season price covers the cost of 81 <u>games</u>.

LET'S DISCUSS WHY

1. Why do you think baseball teams offer season tickets?

2. Besides saving money, why do you think some people prefer buying season tickets?

3. Some people attend more weekday games. Others attend more weekend games. What might be some reasons for this?

4. What would be the price of 1 box ticket at the season ticket price? Is it more or less than a single box ticket? Why?

5. What is the price of 1 ticket of a season ticket for all 47 weekday games? For 30 weekday games? In each case, how much would you save over single box ticket prices?

6. How much would single box tickets cost for all weekday games? What percent discount would you get with a season ticket?

LET'S SEE WHAT YOU WOULD DO

7. You want to attend all weekday games. Your friend wants to attend only weekend games. In how many ways could you both buy the tickets you want? Which way would save both of you the most money?

8. You bought a full-season ticket for $750. Your boss transfers you to an out-of-town branch office for the month of August. You will miss some games, and the ticket is nonrefundable. What can you do to avoid losing money?

CALCULATOR PERCENT ON A CALCULATOR

Some calculators have a **percent key**, %. When you use the percent key on most calculators, do not press the is-equal-to key, =. You can use a calculator to find a percent of a number.

Find 30% of 60.

Procedure	Calculator Entry	Calculator Display
1. Enter the base number for which you must find the percent.	6 0	60.
2. Enter the × key.	×	60.
3. Enter the percent, including the % key.	3 0 %	18.

So 30% of 60 = 18.

Some calculators do not have a % key. If your calculator does not, first rename the percent as a decimal. Then multiply.

Find 125% of 40. Do not use the percent key, %.

Procedure	Calculator Entry	Calculator Display
1. Enter 1.25. **THINK:** 125% = 1.25	1 . 2 5	1.25
2. Multiply by 40.	× 4 0 =	50.

So 125% of 40 = 50.

Use a calculator to find the answer.

1. 45% of 100

2. 15% of 400

3. 125% of 500

4. 28% of 66

5. 8% of 90

6. 175% of 1,750

7. 325% of 0.6

8. 2.5% of 420

9. 0.05% of 18

10. 13.2% of 650

11. 450% of 9.8

12. 0.03% of 5

Use a calculator to solve.

13. For Sunday's game, 92% of the 52,000 tickets were sold. How many were sold?

14. Alex put down a 15% deposit on a $480 gym membership fee. How much did he pay?

Write the money amount to the nearest cent.

1. $1.072

2. $4.638

3. $8.5552

4. $12.0318

5. $34.7966

6. $83.24913

Rename as a percent. Round to the nearest percent.

7. 0.194

8. 0.327

9. 0.2318

10. 0.7551

11. 0.5983

12. 0.2914

Rename as a decimal.

13. 4%

14. 5%

15. 6%

16. 8%

17. 15%

18. 18%

19. $5\frac{1}{2}$%

20. $7\frac{1}{2}$%

21. $8\frac{1}{2}$%

22. 104%

23. 108%

24. 110%

Add.

25. $10.50 + $18.25 + $13.89

26. $9.35 + $31.65 + $42.69

27. $110.63 + $1.85 + $6.25

28. $216.40 + $5.36 + $11.75

Subtract.

29. 69¢ − 20¢

30. 83¢ − 25¢

31. 59¢ − 15¢

32. $35.29 − $16.50

33. $115.50 − $20.75

34. $249 − $25.80

Divide. Round to the nearest tenth of a cent.

35. 79¢ ÷ 3

36. 55¢ ÷ 4

37. $1.75 ÷ 4

38. $2.25 ÷ 8

39. $5.45 ÷ 12

40. $9.95 ÷ 20

Find the answer to the nearest cent.

41. 4% of $35

42. 6% of $15.50

43. $5\frac{1}{2}$% of $98

44. $7\frac{1}{2}$% of $20.89

BASIC PURCHASES

Most people like to buy new clothes. What factors would determine your choices if you had a limited amount of money to spend?

6.1 BUYING AUDIO AND VIDEO EQUIPMENT

You have been saving for a new stereo system. The system you want regularly sells for $329.99, but is now on sale for 20% off.

The amount that an item on sale has been reduced is called the **markdown,** or **discount.** When this amount is expressed as a percent, it is called the **discount rate.**

EXAMPLE 1

How much will the stereo cost on sale?

THINK: Discount rate: 20% or 0.2   Regular price: $329.99

DISCOUNT RATE × REGULAR PRICE = DISCOUNT

REGULAR PRICE − DISCOUNT = SALE PRICE

1. Multiply to find the discount. $0.2 \times \$329.99 = \$65.998 \approx \$66.00$

2. Subtract to find the sale price. $\$329.99 - \$66.00 = \$263.99$

The stereo will cost $263.99 on sale.

Sometimes the discount rate needs to be computed.

EXAMPLE 2

An AM/FM stereo cassette player that regularly sells for $84.99 is on sale for $59.98. What is the discount rate for this sale?

THINK: Regular price: $84.99   Sale price: $59.98

DISCOUNT ÷ REGULAR PRICE = DISCOUNT RATE

1. Subtract to find the discount. $\$84.99 - \$59.98 = \$25.01$

2. Divide to find the discount rate. $\$25.01 \div \$84.99 = 0.2942699$

3. Rename the decimal as a percent. $0.2942699 = 29.42699\%$

The discount rate is about 29%.

Most **retail** stores buy their merchandise **wholesale** and increase the price before selling it to their retail customers. This increase in price is called the **markup,** and is often expressed as a percent of the wholesale price.

EXAMPLE 3

A store buys a VCR for $175 and marks the price up 40%. For what will the store sell the VCR?

THINK: Markup rate: 40% or 0.4   Wholesale price: $175

1. Multiply to find the markup. $0.4 \times \$175 = \$70$

2. Add to find the retail price. $\$175 + \$70 = \$245$

The store will sell the VCR for $245.

The same color TV is advertised at one store for $200 less 20%, and at another store for $230 less 25%. Which store offers the greater discount? Which offers the better buy?

PRACTICE EXERCISES

Remember to estimate whenever you use your calculator.

Find the sale price to the nearest cent.

Item	Regular price	Discount rate	Sale price
Cassette recorder	$25.99	30%	1. ■
Turntable	$178.50	25%	2. ■
19″ color TV	$339.99	20%	3. ■
4-head VCR	$399.50	33%	4. ■
Digital receiver	$429.50	15%	5. ■

Find the discount rate to the nearest percent.

Item	Regular price	Sale price	Discount rate
Video-cassette tape	$3.99	$3.29	6. ■
B/W TV	$79.99	$59.99	7. ■
Stereo cabinet	$69.90	$55.00	8. ■
AM/FM car stereo	$89.99	$79.99	9. ■
Large-screen TV	$1,299.00	$949.99	10. ■

Find the retail price to the nearest cent.

Item	Wholesale price	Markup rate	Retail price
Compact-disc player	$75.00	80%	11. ■
VCR	$129.95	50%	12. ■
Video camera	$760.00	45%	13. ■
Color TV	$249.99	24%	14. ■

Solve.

15. A stereo regularly sells for $229.00. The regular discount is 10%. During a sale, it is reduced an additional 25%. What is the final price?

16. A store buys a VCR for $120. It marks the item up 60% and then sells it at a 10% discount. What is the final retail price?

6.3 SALES TAX

The most common form of tax we pay is the **sales tax.** Sales tax is computed as a percent of the total sales of goods and services. The money raised from the sales tax is a major source of revenue in many states and municipalities. So the sales tax rate varies from state to state and from city to city.

$7\frac{1}{2}$% Sales Tax Table

Amount of sales tax		Amount of sales tax		Amount of sales tax	
0.01 - 0.06	0.00	8.40 - 8.73	0.65	17.27 - 17.30	1.30
.07 - .19	.01	8.74 - 8.86	.66	17.40 - 17.63	1.31
.28 - .33	.02	8.87 - 8.97	.67	17.54 - 17.66	1.32
.34 - .46	.03	9.00 - 9.13	.68	17.67 - 17.79	1.33
.47 - .53	.04	9.14 - 9.26	.69	17.80 - 17.93	1.34
.60 - .73	.05	9.27 - 9.39	.70	17.94 - 18.06	1.35
.74 - .85	.06	9.40 - 9.53	.71	18.07 - 18.19	1.36
.87 - .90	.07	9.54 - 9.66	.72	18.20 - 18.33	1.37
1.00 - 1.13	.08	9.67 - 9.79	.73	18.34 - 18.46	1.38
1.14 - 1.26	.09	9.80 - 9.93	.74	18.47 - 18.59	1.39
1.27 - 1.30	.10	9.94 - 10.06	.75	18.60 - 18.73	1.40
1.40 - 1.53	.11	10.07 - 10.19	.76	18.74 - 18.86	1.41
1.54 - 1.66	.12	10.20 - 10.33	.77	18.87 - 18.99	1.42
1.67 - 1.79	.13	10.34 - 10.46	.78	19.00 - 19.13	1.43
1.80 - 1.93	.14	10.47 - 10.59	.79	19.14 - 19.26	1.44
1.94 - 2.06	.15	10.60 - 10.73	.80	19.27 - 19.39	1.45
2.07 - 2.19	.16	10.74 - 10.86	.81	19.40 - 19.53	1.46
2.20 - 2.33	.17	10.87 - 10.99	.82	19.54 - 19.66	1.47

EXAMPLE 1

How much sales tax will you pay on a $10.80 book if the sales tax rate is $7\frac{1}{2}$?

THINK: $7\frac{1}{2}$% = 0.075

Method 1

Use the partial table. Since $10.80 is between $10.74 and $10.86, the sales tax will be $0.81.

Method 2

Multiply to find the tax.
0.075 × $10.80 = $0.81
The sales tax will be $0.81.

EXAMPLE 2

About how much sales tax will you pay on a purchase of $42.75 worth of records if the sales tax rate is 3%?

THINK: $1\% = \frac{1}{100}$ $\frac{1}{100}$ of $42.75 = $42.75 ÷ 100 = $0.4275, or about $0.43.

Multiply mentally: 3% of $42.75 is about 3 × $0.43, or $1.29.

The sales tax will be about $1.29.

EXAMPLE 3

If the sales tax rate is 4%, what is the total cost of a $19.50 pair of sneakers?

THINK: 4% = 0.04   104% = 1.04

Method 1

1. Multiply to find the sales tax.

   0.04 × $19.50 = $0.78

2. Add to find the total cost.

   $19.50 + $0.78 = $20.28

Method 2

THINK: Adding 4% makes the total cost 104% of the original price.

Multiply to find the total cost.

1.04 × $19.50 = $20.28

The total cost of the sneakers will be $20.28.

Some people travel to other states or municipalities to do their shopping. Why do you think they do this? What hidden expenses are involved?

PRACTICE EXERCISES

Remember to estimate whenever you use your calculator.

Use the partial sales tax table on page 108 to find the $7\frac{1}{2}$% sales tax on the purchase price.

1. $2.22 2. $18.32 3. $10.85 4. $17.75 5. $1.95 6. $19.10

Find the sales tax to the nearest cent.

Purchase price	Sales tax rate	Sales tax
$23.50	4%	7. ■
$98.99	5%	8. ■
$375.00	6%	9. ■

Purchase price	Sales tax rate	Sales tax
$165.95	$2\frac{1}{2}$%	10. ■
$46.85	$5\frac{1}{2}$%	11. ■
$3,575.00	$8\frac{1}{4}$%	12. ■

Complete the table to find the estimated sales tax and exact sales tax. Round each amount to the nearest cent.

Purchase price	Sales tax rate	Estimated sales tax	Exact sales tax
$21.30	3%	13. ■	14. ■
$31.80	4%	15. ■	16. ■
$80.98	5%	17. ■	18. ■

Complete the table to find the sales tax and total cost. Round each amount to the nearest cent.

Purchase price	Sales tax rate	Sales tax	Total cost
$17.50	5%	19. ■	20. ■
$85.99	$4\frac{1}{2}$%	21. ■	22. ■
$257.00	6%	23. ■	24. ■
$4,786.50	$8\frac{1}{2}$%	25. ■	26. ■
$10,612.75	$7\frac{1}{4}$%	27. ■	28. ■

Many people shop at home by buying items through **catalogs.**

You find some winterwear that you really like in a catalog and decide to order 1 medium blue coat and 2 pairs of size 10 white stirrup pants.

EXAMPLE

Complete the order form for this purchase. Find the total cost.

1. Enter the information needed on the top 2 lines.

2. Total the price and shipping weight.

3. Use the partial delivery charges table to find the delivery charge for Zone 3.

4. Add the handling charge and the 5% sales tax to find the total amount.

WINTERWEAR

TOGGLE COAT plays soft, brushed cotton flannel against rugged wide wale cotton corduroy. Polyester fiberfill; cotton flannel lining. Machine wash.
Misses: S(4-6), M(8-10), L(12-14).
B9157 1291 - Peach.
B9157 1289 - Blue.
B9157 1192 - Pink.
B9157 1290 - White.
State color and size letter.
(3 lb 12 oz) 64.00

STIRRUP PANTS with V yoke below the waist. Leg tapers to the ankle, elastic stirrups. Wide wale cotton corduroy. Machine wash.
Misses: 4, 6, 8, 10, 12, 14.
B9157 2230 - Peach.
B9157 2228 - Blue.
B9157 2231 - Pink.
B9157 2229 - White.
State color and size.
(1 lb 12 oz) 38.00

BOOTS finish the long line. Woven cotton outside with warm acrylic pile lining. Rubber soles. B(Medium) full sizes: 5, 6, 7, 8, 9, 10.
For ½ sizes, order next largest full size.
W9157 1479 - Peach.
W9157 1476 - Blue.
W9157 1480 - Pink.
W9157 1478 - White.
State color, size and B width.
(2 lb 4 oz) 50.00

---

name of item	item number	color	size	qty.	price each		total price		ship. wt.	
TOGGLE COAT	B9157 1289	BLUE	M	1	64	00	64	00	3	12
STIRRUP PANTS	B9157 2229	WHITE	10	2	38	00	76	00	3	8

Find your Zone at right ▶	**DELIVERY CHARGES**				total for merchandise	$ 140	00	7 lb	4 oz
Shipping Weight ▼	Zone 1	Zone 2	Zone 3	Zone 4	total delivery charge		8	25	
Minimum charge	$ 3.75	$ 4.00	$ 4.25	$ 4.50					On charge orders, we do this part for you. Credit orders are subject to credit approval.
2 lb 1 oz to 5 lb	5.25	5.50	6.00	6.50	handling charge	$	1	00	
5 lb 1 oz to 10 lb	7.00	7.50	8.25	9.00					
10 lb 1 oz to 15 lb	8.75	9.50	10.25	11.50	**add sales tax of 5%**		7	00	
15 lb 1 oz to 20 lb	10.00	10.75	12.00	14.75	**TOTAL AMOUNT**	$ 156	25		
20 lb 1 oz to 25 lb	11.50	12.50	13.75	16.50					

FOR DISCUSSION

1. What are some advantages and disadvantages of catalog shopping?

2. Why do you often pay more for an item when you purchase it through a catalog?

PRACTICE EXERCISES   Remember to estimate whenever you use your calculator.

Use the partial delivery charges table on page 110 to find the delivery charge for the order.

1. 6 lb 4 oz to Zone 2

2. 22 lb to Zone 4

3. 1 lb 15 oz to Zone 2

Use the catalog information on page 110 to find the total cost to Zone 1.

4. 1 pair of boots

5. 1 pair of stirrup pants

6. 2 toggle coats

Use the catalog information at the right and the delivery charges table on page 110 to complete an order form for the order. Then find the total cost.

7. 1 large blue-denim jacket to Zone 3

8. Size 31 pleated cords, 1 pair gray and 1 pair blue, to Zone 2

9. 1 medium navy sweater and 2 large blue oxford shirts to Zone 4

10. 1 small blue-denim jacket, 2 size 29 black pleated cords, and 2 small green sweaters to Zone 1

Solve. Remember to include the delivery charge, the handling charge, and the sales tax.

11. How much is saved by ordering a denim jacket at the sale price?

12. How much is saved by buying a pair of pleated cords in a store with a 5% sales tax instead of ordering them from the catalog to Zone 4?

D.   THE JACKET IS 30% OFF. Denim on the outside, flannel on the inside, and corduroy on the collar. Zip front, snap cuffs, corduroy elbow patches. Two pockets. Pure cotton; dry clean. Blue.
Chests: S(34-36); M(38-40); L(42-44); XL(46). State size letter. (3 lb)
A4656 1146T...............Reg. $70   NOW 49.00

THE SWEATER IS $15 OFF. It's loaded with paisley. Pure wool; long sleeves. Hand wash.
Chests: S(34-36); M(38-40); L(42-44); XL(46).
B4258 4855 - Navy.   B4258 4856 - Green.
State color, size letter.   (1 lb 6 oz)
Reg.............................$55   NOW 39.99

OXFORD CLOTH SHIRT IS 20% OFF. Strong on stripes, with button-down collar; chest pocket; long sleeves. In yarn-dyed cotton/polyester. Machine wash.
Neck sizes: S(14-14 1/2); M(15-15 1/2); L(16 - 16 1/2); XL(17-17 1/2).
State color, size letter.
B4258 1002 - Blue/Green Stripe (shown)
B4258 1001 - Green/Burgundy Stripe
(12 oz)........................Reg. $30   NOW 24.00

PLEATED CORDS ARE 25% LESS than in many stores. In colors as versatile as they are uncommon. Pure cotton, with straight legs; back pockets. 35" finished bottoms. Machine wash.
Waists: 29, 30, 31, 32, 33, 34, 36, 38.
B4756 6200 - Taupe
B4756 6198 - Mallard Blue
B4756 6199 - Willow Gray
B4756 6788 - Black
State color, size. (1 lb 10 oz)
Elsewhere..................$38.   NOW 28.50

The weekly trip to the supermarket provides an excellent opportunity to shop wisely and save money. Since there are so many opportunities for errors in labeling or at the checkout line, it is very useful to estimate food costs.

EXAMPLE 1

Cut-up frying chicken is on sale for $1.99 per lb. One package is labeled 2.86 lb and marked $7.42. Does this price make sense?

THINK: Almost 3 lb at about $2.00 per lb

Multiply to estimate the cost. $3 \times \$2.00 = \$6.00$

So $7.42 does *not* make sense. It is too much.

Another way to shop wisely is to purchase the most economically-sized package of a certain food. A good way to determine which package or container is the better buy is to compare the **unit prices.**

EXAMPLE 2

Raisin bran is available in 15-oz boxes for $1.89 or in 20-oz boxes for $2.29. Which is the better buy? Divide to find the cost per ounce for each package.

15-oz box
$\$1.89 \div 15 = \$0.126$,
or 12.6¢ per oz

20-oz box
$\$2.29 \div 20 = \$0.1145$,
or 11.5¢ per oz

The 20-oz box is the better buy.

Another way to save money on food is to use **coupons.**

EXAMPLE 3

The 6-oz container of frozen orange juice sells for 79¢. How much will you pay for the juice if you use your "15¢ off" coupon during the double-coupon promotion at the store?

THINK: During the promotion, the coupon doubles in value to 30¢.

Subtract to find the sale price.   79¢ − 30¢ = 49¢

You will pay only 49¢ for the juice.

FOR DISCUSSION

1. Why do people sometimes buy frozen dinners? Why are these dinners usually more expensive than food prepared at home?

2. Why do people sometimes buy items that are not on their shopping lists? What do supermarkets do to encourage this type of buying?

PRACTICE EXERCISES Remember to estimate whenever you use your calculator.

Estimate to determine whether the labeled price *does* or *does not* make sense.

1. 2 lb of apples at 89¢ per lb $1.78

2. 3.4 lb of hamburger at $1.49 per lb $3.29

3. 0.76 lb of salami at $2.79 per lb $2.69

4. a 10.6-lb turkey at 89¢ per lb $9.43

5. 1.24 lb of cole slaw at 49¢ per lb 89¢

6. a 3.89-lb steak at $2.79 per lb $10.85

Find the unit prices to the nearest tenth of a cent. Identify which is the better buy.

7. 6 oz for 49¢
10 oz for 69¢

8. 9 oz for 89¢
14 oz for $1.49

9. 5 oz for 75¢
10 oz for $1.25

10. 20 oz for $1.79
32 oz for $2.99

11. 24 oz for $2.69
35 oz for $3.49

12. 12 oz for $3.36
18 oz for $4.70

13. 15 oz for $2.69
1 lb 9 oz for $4.29

14. 24 oz for $1.59
2 lb 5 oz for $2.39

15. 6.5 lb for $5.85
10 lb for $8.75

16. 1.75 lb for $3.79
2.5 lb for $4.99

17. 1 L for $1.19
2.5 L for $2.49

18. 0.5 L for 79¢
2 L for $2.79

Find the total cost of the shopping list.

19.
2 cans tomato sauce at 39¢ each
4 lb hamburger at $1.59 per lb
2.3 lb grapes at $1.19 per lb
1 box muffins at $1.79
1 can coffee at $3.89

You have a "50¢ off" coupon on the coffee during a double-coupon sale.

20.
1 box detergent at $3.89
2 boxes cereal at $1.79 each
5 cans beans at 2 for 89¢
1.45 lb sliced ham at $2.79 per lb
3 cans tuna at $1.09 each

You have a "25¢ off" coupon on the cereal and a "50¢ off" coupon on the detergent during a double-coupon sale.

EXTENSION Yearly Savings

Small savings each week can add up quickly. Large bottles of apple juice can be purchased for $1.69 for the name brand and $1.09 for the store brand. If you consume 2 bottles of apple juice each week, how much can you save in a year by buying the store brand?

COUNTRY SANDWICH SHOP

SANDWICHES

Tuna $2.75
Roast Beef 3.75
Ham 3.45
Egg Salad 2.50
Steak 3.95

SPECIALS

Tuna Sandwich
Special $4.20
(includes potatoes,
medium juice)
Steak Sandwich
Special 4.90
(includes salad or
cole slaw, medium juice)

SIDE ORDERS

Potatoes . . . .$ .95
Onions 1.25
Salad 65
Cole Slaw 75

BEVERAGES

Juice . . . . .small .50
   medium .70   large .90
Milk .60   Coffee .45
         Tea .45

You and a friend shop for lunch at the Country Sandwich Shop. You order a roast beef sandwich, potatoes, and a medium juice. Your friend orders an egg salad sandwich and a large juice.

EXAMPLE 1 Will $12 be enough to cover both lunches? Estimate the total cost.

Your lunch: roast beef sandwich $3.75 ⎫
                potatoes   0.95 ⎬ About $6.00
                medium juice   0.70 ⎭

Friend's lunch: egg salad sandwich   2.50 ⎫ + About $4.00
                large juice   0.90 ⎭
                                              ‾‾‾‾‾‾‾‾‾‾‾‾‾
                                              About $10.00

So $12 should be enough for the lunches.

EXAMPLE 2 Including a 5% sales tax and a 15% tip, exactly how much will the lunches cost?

1. Add to find the total cost.

$$\$3.75 + \$0.95 + \$0.70 + \$2.50 + \$0.90 = \$8.80$$

2. Multiply to find the sales tax.

THINK: 5% = 0.05 $0.05 \times \$8.80 = \$0.44$

3. Multiply to find the tip.

THINK: 15% = 0.15 $0.15 \times \$8.80 = \$1.32$

4. Add the total cost, the sales tax, and the tip. $\$8.80 + \$0.44 + \$1.32 = \$10.56$

The entire lunch with sales tax and tip will cost $10.56.

1. Why do you think the Tuna Sandwich Special is less expensive than ordering each of the items separately?

2. In some cities the sales tax rate is about 8%. Why do many people just double the sales tax to compute a 15% or 16% tip?

PRACTICE EXERCISES   Remember to estimate whenever you use your calculator.

Use the Country Sandwich Shop menu to estimate whether the meal should cost *more than $5.00* or *less than $5.00*.

1. Tuna sandwich, coffee

2. Steak sandwich, onions, milk

3. Tuna Sandwich Special, tea

4. Steak Sandwich Special, small juice

5. Ham sandwich, cole slaw, coffee

6. Egg salad sandwich, potatoes, milk

Use the menu to compute the cost of the meal, including a 6% sales tax and a 15% tip. Then find the amount of change from $20.

7. Roast beef sandwich
   Salad
   Large juice

8. Ham sandwich
   Potatoes
   Coffee

9. 2 Tuna sandwiches
   Onions
   2 Medium juices

10. Ham sandwich
    Roast beef sandwich
    2 Cole slaws
    2 Coffees

11. Tuna Sandwich Special
    2 Egg salad sandwiches
    1 Milk
    2 Medium juices

12. 2 Steak Sandwich Specials
    2 Salads
    2 Large juices

Solve.

13. A meal costs $21.50. The sales tax rate is 8%. Find the sales tax. Mentally compute a 16% tip.

14. A meal costs $28.00. The 16% tip is $4.48. Mentally compute the 8% sales tax.

15. A complete lunch consists of 1 sandwich, 1 side order, and 1 beverage. What is the difference between the cost of the most expensive lunch and the least expensive lunch?

16. Suppose a family of 4 eats lunch at the Country Sandwich Shop. Make up an order that comes close to $20.00, including a 5% sales tax and a 15% tip.

6.7 COMPARING FOOD COSTS

After a busy day it is often easiest to just take out food or to go out to a nearby restaurant for dinner. But not preparing dinner at home can become very costly.

PROBLEM

Les and Wanda have been ordering take-out food and eating in restaurants frequently. Because they are trying to save money for a new car, they decide to examine a sample of their meal costs (excluding tax) to see if they can cut expenses. They made the following notes.

Chicken dinner at home:	4 pieces of chicken	$3.60	Time: 50 min
	Salad ingredients (serves two)	$2.00	Not very convenient
	1 package potatoes	$1.59	
	Rolls	$0.40	
	Juice (two glasses)	$0.40	
Chicken dinner from Barney's Take-Out:	4 pieces of chicken	$2.00 each	Time: 10 min
	Salads	$1.50 each	Very convenient
	Potatoes	$0.90 per order	
	Rolls	Included	
	Juice	$0.75 per person	
Chicken dinner at the Capital Diner:	Complete dinner (includes chicken, salad, potatoes, roll)	$9.95 each	Time: 35 min Convenient
	Juice	$1.00 per glass	
	Tip	15%	

DECISION-MAKING FACTORS

Cost   Time   Convenience   Quality of food

DECISION-MAKING COMPARISONS

Compare the 3 options by completing the table.

Factor	Home	Barney's Take-Out	Capital Diner
Cost for two: Chicken	1. ■	2. ■	Included
Salad	3. ■	$3.00	4. ■
Potatoes	$1.59	5. ■	6. ■
Rolls	7. ■	Included	8. ■
Juice	9. ■	10. ■	$2.00
Total cost	11. ■	$14.30	12. ■
Time	50 min	13. ■	14. ■
Convenience	15. ■	16. ■	Average

MAKING THE DECISIONS

Where should Les and Wanda get their dinner:

17. If cost were the only factor?   18. If time were the only factor?

19. If convenience were the only factor?

20. How much can Les and Wanda save by eating at home instead of using Barney's Take-Out?

21. If they have been using Barney's Take-Out an average of twice a week, how much could they save in a year by preparing dinner at home?

22. How much could Les and Wanda save by preparing dinner at home instead of going to the Capital Diner?

23. If they have been going to the diner about once a week, how much could they save in a year by preparing dinner at home?

24. Where do you think the quality of the food is the highest? Why?

25. Is the cost of the food alone an accurate measure of the cost of preparing dinner at home? What other costs might be included?

26. Is the time for food preparation alone an accurate measure of the time involved in preparing a meal at home? Why?

CHAPTER

REVIEW

Vocabulary   Choose the letter of the word(s) that completes the sentence.

1. The sale price of an item is found by subtracting the ■ from the regular price.   [104]

   a. Sales tax   **b.** Markup   **c.** Discount

2. To determine which package of food is the better buy, compare the ■.   [112]

   a. Package prices   **b.** Unit prices   **c.** Package sizes

3. To find the total cost of a meal in a restaurant, include the sales tax and the ■.   [114]

   a. Tip   **b.** Markup   **c.** Coupon value

Skills   Find the answer.

4. A knit shirt that regularly sells for $11.99 is now on sale at 10% off. What is the sale price?   [104]

5. A ski sweater that regularly sells for $58.00 is now on sale at 20% off. What is the sale price?   [104]

6. A cardigan sweater that regularly sells for $35.00 is now on sale for $32.50. How much can be saved by buying 2 sweaters on sale?   [106]

7. Lana bought a $300 television set. The sales tax rate is 6%. What was the total cost?   [108]

8. Fred bought a $25 book. The sales tax rate is $7\frac{1}{2}$%. What was the total cost?   [108]

9. Karen bought a cassette player for $75.50. The sales tax rate is $5\frac{1}{2}$%. What was the total cost?   [108]

10. A chef's-salad lunch special is $4.50. Including a 5% sales tax and a 15% tip, what is the total cost?   [114]

11. A tuna-sandwich lunch special is $3.75. Including a $7\frac{1}{2}$% sales tax and a 15% tip, what is the total cost?   [114]

Find the sales tax to the nearest cent. Then find the total amount.   [110]

12.   Merchandise: $50.00
        Delivery and handling: $4.10
               Sales tax rate: 6%

13.   Merchandise: $150.00
        Delivery and handling: $16.25
               Sales tax rate: $5\frac{1}{2}$%

Which is the better buy?   [112]

14. 3 oz for 95¢ or 8 oz for $2.40

15. 1.56 lb for $1.34 or 3 lb for $2.64

Find the discount to the nearest cent. Then find the sale price.

1. Regular price: $12.59
Discount rate: 10%

2. Regular price: $400
Discount rate: 30%

3. Regular price: $179.89
Discount rate: 25%

Find the markup to the nearest cent. Then find the retail price.

4. Wholesale price: $50
Markup rate: 75%

5. Wholesale price: $125.50
Markup rate: 30%

6. Wholesale price: $360.99
Markup rate: 50%

Use the ad to answer Exercises 7–11.

7. Sal bought 2 clock radios on sale. How much change did he get from $75?

How much can be saved with the sale?

8. Digital clock radio   **9.** Jeans jacket

Jacket
Regular $18.75 NOW $15.99

Digital Clock Radio
Regular $45 NOW $36

Find the discount rate to the nearest percent.

10. Digital clock radio   **11.** Jeans jacket

Find the sales tax to the nearest cent. Then find the total amount.

12.   Merchandise: $100.00
Delivery and handling: $8.50
Sales tax rate: 5%

13.   Merchandise: $75.89
Delivery and handling: $6.25
Sales tax rate: $7\frac{1}{2}$%

Find the unit prices. Then determine which is the better buy.

14. 4 oz for 39¢
7 oz for 67¢

15. 10 oz for 79¢
15 oz for $1.17

16. 1.2 lb for $2.50
3 lb for $6.03

Solve.

17. Turkey is on sale for $1.49 per lb. One package is labeled 2.79 lb and marked $5.40. Does this make sense?

18. You buy bread for $1.19 and 1.5 lb of fruit for 39¢ per lb and use a "20¢ off" coupon. What is the total cost?

Use the menu to find the cost of the meal, including a 5% sales tax and a 15% tip. Round all amounts to the nearest cent.

19. 1 Egg salad
1 Tuna
2 Salads

20. 2 Ham and cheese
2 Tuna
3 Potatoes

THE SANDWICH SHOPPE			
SANDWICHES		**SIDE ORDERS**	
Egg salad	$1.95	Salad	$0.90
Tuna	2.25	Potatoes	0.85
Ham and cheese	3.10	Coleslaw	0.65
BEVERAGES			
Milk 0.75	Juice 0.50	Soda 0.80	

MONEY TIPS

You can get the best buys on some items if you buy them at certain times of the year.

LET'S LOOK AT THE FACTS

February, March, and April are considered some of the best months to buy some items. Read the list of sale items for each month.

FEBRUARY
- Air conditioners
- Curtains
- Humidifiers
- Housewares
- Lamps
- Stereo equipment
- Storm windows
- Used cars

MARCH
- Children's shoes
- Garden supplies
- Hosiery
- Infants' clothing
- Luggage
- Winter coats
- Winter sports equipment

APRIL
- Painting equipment
- Spring cleaning supplies
- Fabrics
- Lawn and garden furniture

LET'S DISCUSS WHY

Winter Coats

1. Which month is a sale month?

2. During which months are they worn?

3. When do you think stores would like to empty out their inventory of them? What would they replace them with in the store?

4. Why are winter coat sales held in March?

5. During which other month(s) of the year might winter coats also be on sale? Why?

Air Conditioners

6. Which month is a sale month?

7. During which months are they used most often?

8. By which time do you think some stores would like to make room for newer models?

9. By which time do you think other stores would like to use these sales to bring in customers after the holiday sales?

10. Why are air conditioner sales held in February?

11. During which other month(s) of the year might air conditioners also be on sale? Why?

LET'S SEE WHAT YOU WOULD DO

12. Next summer, you plan to repaint your house, to plant a garden, and to furnish your patio. Which items could you buy on sale in February, March, or April? Tell why each would be on sale at that time.

ESTIMATION SKILLS

DECIMAL SUMS APPROXIMATELY EQUAL TO 1

Front-end estimation of some sums can be adjusted by examining decimals for sums that are approximately equal to 1.

1. Add the whole numbers for a first estimate.

2. Examine the decimals.

3. Adjust the first estimate.

Examples

```
  ②.6
  ②.5    THINK: 0.6 + 0.5 is  about 1.
  ①.7
+ 0.2 9   THINK: 0.7 + 0.29 is about 1.
```
First estimate: ⑤   +   about 2 = 7 Final estimate

```
  ⑧.5 2
  ①.1 3   THINK: 0.52 + 0.5 is  about 1.
  ⑥.5     THINK: 0.13 + 0.79 is about 1.
+ ⑤.7 9
```
First estimate: ⑳   +   about 2 = 22 Final estimate

Use front-end estimation with adjusting to estimate the sum.

	1.	2.	3.	4.	5.
	1.9	10.8	1.2	4.9	8.52
	2.1	5.3	2.3	10.4	6.5
	3.3	2.4	5.3	6.4	1.13
	+4.7	+ 5.5	+6.2	+ 3.2	+5.79

	6.	7.	8.	9.	10.
	6.31	2.22	20.71	21.62	30.54
	7.8	10.59	30.18	40.2	50.12
	2.27	7.15	9.78	10.39	18.8
	+6.59	+ 4.29	+40.24	+ 5.75	+21.5

	11.	12.	13.	14.	15.
	7.1	3.2	10.1	8.32	4.72
	4.9	5.1	4.4	2.71	2.09
	3.1	2.4	20.5	1.49	2.29
	2.4	1.1	5.5	4.5	5.88
	1.1	2.2	15.6	5.16	7.42
	+6.6	+4.3	+10.2	+1.8	+1.8

Write the money amount in words.

1. $48.75   **2.** $104.50   **3.** $279.30   **4.** $1,483.89

Compute.

5. $63.80 + $58.25 + $124.50   **6.** $293.84 + $53.32 + $127.03

7. $93.53 − $4.24 + $83.18   **8.** $530.49 − $214.96 + $430.51

9. $27.39 + $192.80 − $67.31 − $63.81 − $3.92

10. $1,943.84 − $294.73 − $97.59 − $326.16 − $27.27 + $639.20

Find the answer to the nearest cent.

11. 5% of $293.00

12. $4\frac{1}{2}$% of $374.22

13. $6\frac{1}{2}$% of $93.48

14. $5\frac{3}{4}$% of $1,200

Multiply.

15. $800 × 0.03 × $\frac{1}{4}$

16. $1,500 × 0.09 × $2\frac{1}{2}$

17. $2,200 × 0.055 × 3

18. $840 × 0.0675 × $4\frac{1}{2}$

Multiply. Round to the nearest cent.

19. $280 × 1.3728

20. $1,400 × 2.5182

Solve.

21. How many quarter years are there in 4 y?

22. How many half years are there in $6\frac{1}{2}$ y?

23. How many months are there in $2\frac{1}{4}$ y?

24. How many quarter years are there in $7\frac{1}{2}$ y?

Find the answer.

25. 13 × 25¢ + $4.00

26. 7 × 20¢ + $5.00

27. 19 × 15¢ + $6.00

28. 9 × 30¢ + $7.50

Chapter 7

CHECKING AND SAVINGS ACCOUNTS

Today banks offer many types of accounts to their customers. Why do they do this? Why do the interest rates vary for these accounts?

The most commonly used bank account is a **checking account.**
Checks are a convenient and safe way to make purchases and to pay
bills. Checking accounts also help you to keep records on when and
where you spend your money.

EXAMPLE 1 Suppose you wrote a check for $35.99 to pay the College
Bookstore for some textbooks. Review the parts of the check below
and describe each of your entries.

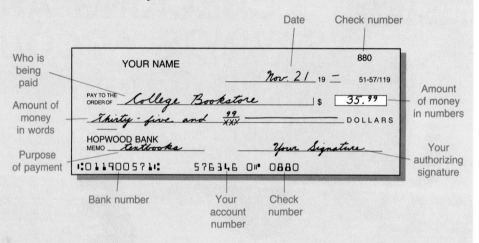

It is important that you have enough money in your checking account
to cover each check that you write.

EXAMPLE 2 You earned $136.00 waiting on tables at the Student Union. You also
had $20.00 in cash from tips. You deposited your paycheck and the
cash in your checking account. Review the **deposit slip** below and
describe each of your entries.

DEPOSIT TICKET		CASH	20	00	
YOUR NAME		LIST CHECKS SINGLY	136	00	
					51-57/119
DATE _November 22_ 19 —					USE OTHER SIDE FOR ADDITIONAL LISTING ◆ ENTER TOTAL HERE
		TOTAL FROM OTHER SIDE			
		TOTAL ITEMS **TOTAL**	156	00	BE SURE EACH ITEM IS PROPERLY ENDORSED
HOPWOOD BANK					
576346ıı●					

CHECKS AND OTHER ITEMS ARE RECEIVED FOR DEPOSIT SUBJECT TO THE PROVISIONS OF THE UNIFORM COMMERCIAL CODE OR ANY APPLICABLE COLLECTION AGREEMENT

All checks and deposits should be recorded in your **check register**, which comes with your checks.

EXAMPLE 3

You completed the check register for your check to the bookstore and for your deposit. What is your new checking account balance?

THINK: The amount of each check must be subtracted from the balance. The amount of each deposit must be added to the balance.

Review the check register below.

		RECORD ALL CHARGES OR CREDITS THAT AFFECT YOUR ACCOUNT			FEE		BALANCE	
NUMBER	DATE	DESCRIPTION OF TRANSACTION	PAYMENT/DEBIT (−)	✔ T	(IF ANY) (−)	DEPOSIT/CREDIT (+)	$ 679	09
877	11/20	Dr. Sandra Stone dog's medicine	$ 15.00	$	$		− 15	00
							664	09
878	11/20	Mike's Sports Shop bowling equipment	42.00				− 42	00
							622	09
879	11/21	Atlantic Electric Co. electric bill	87.42				− 87	42
							534	67
880	11/21	College Bookstore textbooks	35.99				− 35	99
							498	68
	11/22	Deposit				156.00	+ 156	00
							654	68

Your new balance is $654.68.

EXAMPLE 4

Susan's checking account balance was $214.72. She then wrote checks for $45.77, $79.35, and $105.60. She made a deposit of $90.50. Does she have enough money in her account to pay her $78.85 electric bill?

1. Add the deposit to the old balance. $214.72 + $90.50 = $305.22

2. Subtract the checks.
$$\$305.22 - \$45.77 - \$79.35 - \$105.60 = \$74.50$$

Susan's new balance is $74.50. Therefore, she does not have enough money to cover the $78.85 electric bill.

FOR DISCUSSION

1. What does it mean to **bounce** a check? How can you prevent bounced checks?

2. Why should you start writing the amount of the check in numbers and in words as close to the left as possible and add a wavy line after writing the amount in words?

1. Why is it important to save all of your canceled checks?

2. Why do banks often charge customers a monthly service fee on a checking account?

PRACTICE EXERCISES Remember to estimate whenever you use your calculator.

Use the bank statement and the check register below for Exercises 1–6.

CHECK NUMBER	DATE POSTED	AMOUNT	DESCRIPTION OF TRANSACTION	DATE	BALANCE
CHECKING	ACCOUNT	5 7 6 3 4 6 0			
			LAST STATEMENT BALANCE	10-10	2 4 3 2 4
	10-24	3 1 2 00	DEPOSIT	10-24	5 5 5 2 4
				10-27	5 3 7 2 4
683	10-27	1 8 00	PERSONAL CHECK	10-29	4 5 6 8 4
684	10-29	8 0 40	PERSONAL CHECK	11-12	4 1 4 0 9
* 686	11-12	3 8 00	PERSONAL CHECK		
	11-12	4 75	SERVICE CHARGE		

NUMBER	DATE	DESCRIPTION OF TRANSACTION	PAYMENT/DEBT (−)	✓ T	FEE (IF ANY) (−)	DEPOSIT/CREDIT (+)	BALANCE $ 243 24
	10/24	Deposit	$		$	$312 00	+ 312 00
							555 24
683	10/25	Norma's Yarn Shop Sweater yarn	18 00				− 18 00
							537 24
684	10/26	Southwestern Phone Co. telephone bill	80 40				− 80 40
							456 84
685	11/3	Worth's Catalog Sales jeans	19 85				− 19 85
							436 99
686	11/10	Wesley School	38 00				− 38 00
							398 99

What is the:

1. Statement ending balance?

2. Check register balance?

3. Outstanding check number?

4. Amount of the outstanding check?

5. Service charge?

6. Actual reconciled statement balance?

Use the given information to reconcile the bank statement balance with the check register balance. Find the adjusted balance for each.

7. Check register balance: $479.70
   Statement ending balance: $582.43
   Outstanding checks: $76.40, $29.83
   Service charge: $3.50

8. Check register balance: $551.38
   Statement ending balance: $556.63
   Outstanding deposit: $75.00
   Outstanding checks: $62.45, $18.75
   Service charge: $0.95

You earn about $80.00 per wk in a part-time job. You decide to open a **savings account** in order to save enough money for a down payment on a used car.

EXAMPLE 1 You deposited $50.00 in cash from your earnings plus a $25 birthday check in your savings account. Review the **deposit slip** below and describe each of your entries.

SAVINGS DEPOSIT
CITY SAVINGS BANK

	DOLLARS	CENTS
BILLS	50	00
COIN		
CHECK NO.	25	00
TOTAL ▶ $	75	00

OFFICE OF ACCOUNT
Main St.

DATE
1/15/ –

PRINT NAME(S)
YOUR NAME

ACCOUNT NUMBER
073-51203

1-0622 2/89[76616]   DO NOT WRITE BELOW THIS LINE

⑂5040⑈0000⑂

EXAMPLE 2 After several months, you have saved over $900. You withdraw $650.00 to make the down payment on the used car. Review the **withdrawal slip** below and describe each of your entries.

SAVINGS WITHDRAWAL
CITY SAVINGS BANK

DATE
6/11/ –

DOLLARS	CENTS
650	00

OFFICE OF ACCOUNT
Main St.

PAY TO MYSELF OR BEARER $

Six hundred fifty and 00/xxx ———————— DOLLARS

PRINT ACCOUNT NAME
Your Name

ACCOUNT NUMBER
073-51203

SIGNATURE
Your Signature

1-0622 2/89[76616]   DO NOT WRITE BELOW THIS LINE

⑂5050⑈0000⑂

Savings account records are kept in a **passbook.** You need to bring your passbook to the bank each time you make a deposit or a withdrawal. The bank's computer enters each transaction in your passbook.

EXAMPLE 3 You had a balance of $935.00 on June 2. You made a deposit of $62.50 on June 5, a withdrawal of $650.00 on June 11, another deposit of $52.00 on June 18, and had interest of $2.82 posted on July 1. What is your new savings account balance?

THINK: Add deposits and interest. Subtract withdrawals.

OLD BALANCE + DEPOSITS + INTEREST − WITHDRAWALS = NEW BALANCE
$935.00 + $114.50 + $2.82 − $650.00 = $402.32

Your new balance is $402.32. Review the passbook page below.

Name Your Name			Account # 073-51203	
Date	Deposit	Withdrawal	Interest	Balance
6/2	$65.00			$935.00
6/5	$62.50			$997.50
6/11		$650.00		$347.50
6/18	$52.00			$399.50
7/1			$2.82	$402.32

FOR DISCUSSION

1. How are savings accounts different from checking accounts?

2. Why do banks pay interest on savings accounts?

Make up a deposit slip for the deposit. Use today's date and your own name.

1. $85.00 in cash and a check for $43.29

2. $32.00 in cash, $2.75 in coins, and checks for $134.80 and $32.53

3. Checks for $45.89, $187.40, and $14.50 and $25.00 in cash

4. $10.50 in coins, $297.00 in cash, and checks for $135.00 and $273.65

Make up a withdrawal slip for the withdrawal. Use today's date and your own name and signature.

5. $280.00   6. $437.88   7. $47.00   8. $1,350.65

Complete the table.

Old balance	Transaction	New balance
$143.78	Deposit: $44.79	9. ▪
$76.95	Withdrawal: $35.00	10. ▪
$388.39	Deposit: $128.73	11. ▪
$37.51	Interest payment: $5.83	12. ▪
$1,836.68	Deposit: $387.24	13. ▪
$502.31	Withdrawal: $280.00	14. ▪

Compute the running balances for this savings account passbook.

Date	Deposit	Withdrawal	Interest	Balance
10/3				$ 73.98
10/5	$54.87			15. ▪
10/9		$45.00		16. ▪
10/12		$27.50		17. ▪
10/19	$86.36			18. ▪
10/20			$2.56	19. ▪
10/27		$64.00		20. ▪
10/30	$15.84			21. ▪

7.4 SIMPLE AND COMPOUND INTEREST

The **interest** you earn on your checking or savings accounts is determined by:
the interest **rate** expressed as an annual (yearly) percent,
the **principal,** or amount of money in your account, and
the length of **time** (in years) the money is used.

Simple interest is computed by using this formula.

INTEREST = PRINCIPAL $\times$ RATE $\times$ TIME, or $I = p \times r \times t$

EXAMPLE 1
You deposit $400 in a savings account that pays 6% interest per y. How much interest will you earn in 3 mo? How much will then be in your account?

THINK: Principal: $400   **Rate: 6% = 0.06**   **Time: 3 mo = $\frac{1}{4}$ y = 0.25 y**

1. Multiply to find the interest earned.

$$I = p \times r \times t$$
$$I = \$400 \times 0.06 \times 0.25$$
$$I = \$6$$

You will earn $6 in interest.

2. Add to find the new balance. $400 + $6 = $406

At the end of 3 mo, you will have $406 in your account.

For longer periods of time, banks **compound** your interest. They periodically add the interest to your account and compute interest in successive periods on each new higher principal.

EXAMPLE 2
Jeff deposits $750.00 in a savings account that pays 5% interest compounded quarterly. How much will be in the account at the end of 1 y? How much interest will he earn in 1 y?

THINK: Principal: $750   **Rate: 5% = 0.05**   **Time: each $\frac{1}{4}$ y = 0.25 y**

1. Compute 1st-quarter interest and the new balance (principal).

$750.00 $\times$ 0.05 $\times$ 0.25 = $9.38
$750.00 + $9.38 = $759.38

2. Compute 2nd-quarter interest and the new balance (principal).

$759.38 $\times$ 0.05 $\times$ 0.25 = $9.49
$759.38 + $9.49 = $768.87

3. Compute 3rd-quarter interest and the new balance (principal).

$768.87 $\times$ 0.05 $\times$ 0.25 = $9.61
$768.87 + $9.61 = $778.48

4. Compute 4th-quarter interest and the new balance (principal).

$778.48 $\times$ 0.05 $\times$ 0.25 = $9.73
$778.48 + $9.73 = $788.21

At the end of 1 y, Jeff's new savings account balance will be $788.21.

5. Subtract to find the interest. $788.21 − $750.00 = $38.21

Jeff will earn $38.21 in interest.

Banks use a compound interest table to compute compound interest.

EXAMPLE **3** Delia deposits $2,000 in a savings account that pays 8% interest compounded quarterly. How much will she have at the end of 3 y?

THINK: 4 quarters per y means 12 quarters in 3 y.
8% annual interest is equal to 2% interest per quarter.

1. Use the table below to find the compounded value of $1.00.
$1.00 at 2% for 12 periods will grow to $1.2682.

2. Multiply to find the new balance (principal). $2,000 × $1.2682 = $2,536.40

At the end of 3 y, Delia will have $2,536.40.

COMPOUND INTEREST TABLE

No. of Periods	1.5%	2%	2.5%	3%	3.5%	4%	5%
1	1.0150	1.0200	1.0250	1.0300	1.0350	1.0400	1.0500
2	1.0302	1.0404	1.0506	1.0609	1.0712	1.0816	1.1025
3	1.0457	1.0612	1.0769	1.0927	1.1087	1.1248	1.1576
4	1.0614	1.0824	1.1038	1.1255	1.1475	1.1699	1.2155
5	1.0773	1.1041	1.1314	1.1593	1.1877	1.2167	1.2763
6	1.0934	1.1262	1.1597	1.1941	1.2293	1.2653	1.3401
7	1.1098	1.1487	1.1887	1.2299	1.2723	1.3159	1.4071
8	1.1265	1.1717	1.2184	1.2668	1.3168	1.3686	1.4775
9	1.1434	1.1951	1.2489	1.3048	1.3629	1.4233	1.5513
10	1.1605	1.2190	1.2801	1.3439	1.4106	1.4802	1.6289
11	1.1779	1.2434	1.3121	1.3842	1.4600	1.5395	1.7103
12	1.1956	(1.2682)	1.3449	1.4258	1.5111	1.6010	1.7959
13	1.2136	1.2936	1.3785	1.4685	1.5640	1.6651	1.8856
14	1.2318	1.3195	1.4130	1.5126	1.6187	1.7317	1.9799
15	1.2502	1.3459	1.4483	1.5580	1.6753	1.8009	2.0789
16	1.2690	1.3728	1.4845	1.6047	1.7340	1.8730	2.1829
17	1.2880	1.4002	1.5216	1.6528	1.7947	1.9479	2.2920
18	1.3073	1.4282	1.5597	1.7024	1.8575	2.0258	2.4066
19	1.3270	1.4568	1.5987	1.7535	1.9225	2.1068	2.5270
20	1.3469	1.4859	1.6386	1.8061	1.9898	2.1911	2.6533
21	1.3671	1.5157	1.6796	1.8603	2.0594	2.2788	2.7860
22	1.3876	1.5460	1.7216	1.9161	2.1315	2.3699	2.9253
23	1.4084	1.5769	1.7646	1.9736	2.2061	2.4647	3.0715
24	1.4295	1.6084	1.8087	2.0328	2.2833	2.5633	3.2251
25	1.4509	1.6407	1.8539	2.0938	2.3673	2.6658	3.3864

FOR DISCUSSION

1. Which earns more in a year, an account compounded quarterly or the same account compounded daily? Why?

2. Why do banks pay you less interest than they earn on your money?

Remember to estimate whenever you use your calculator.

Compute the simple interest earned and the new balance (principal).

	Principal	Rate	Time
1.	$250	6%	4 y
2.	$500	5%	3 y
3.	$1,250	7%	2 y
4.	$8,020	8%	8 y

	Principal	Rate	Time
5.	$3,500	$5\frac{1}{2}\%$	7 y
6.	$850	$8\frac{1}{2}\%$	10 y
7.	$2,630	$4\frac{3}{4}\%$	3 y
8.	$5,875	$5\frac{3}{4}\%$	5 y

Compute the new balance (principal) and the compound interest earned.

	Principal	Rate	Time
9.	$1,000	5% compounded semiannually	1 y
10.	$5,000	$6\frac{1}{4}\%$ compounded semiannually	2 y
11.	$400	4% compounded quarterly	1 y
12.	$7,500	$7\frac{1}{2}\%$ compounded quarterly	18 mo

Use the compound interest table to find the new balance (principal).

	Principal	Rate	Time
13.	$4,000	6% compounded semiannually	5 y
14.	$6,500	8% compounded semiannually	7 y
15.	$10,000	10% compounded quarterly	4 y
16.	$3,200	6% compounded quarterly	6 y

EXTENSION   Money Market and NOW Accounts

Banks offer special checking accounts that allow you to earn interest.
Most NOW and Money Market accounts require that you keep a
minimum balance of $1,000 or $2,000. Interest is usually compounded
daily and paid monthly on the basis of your average daily balance.

1. How do NOW and Money Market accounts differ from regular checking accounts?

2. If your $5\frac{1}{2}\%$ NOW account has an average daily balance of $2,500
   over the course of a year, about how much interest would you earn?

7.5 WHICH BANK ACCOUNT IS BEST?

When you decide to open a checking account or a savings account, you are often confronted by many different types of accounts. You must examine the features of each and decide which is best for your own particular needs.

PROBLEM A

Victoria has just started a new job and needs to open a checking account in order to deposit her weekly paychecks. So that she can choose which type of account is best for her, the bank's customer service representative gave Victoria a brochure describing the 4 types of checking accounts.

REGULAR CHECKING

Each month, your canceled checks are returned to you with a statement describing your account activity for the month. There is a $5.00 monthly service charge plus 25¢ per check.

NOW CHECKING

This account pays you 5% interest on your checking account balance which is compounded daily and paid monthly. Your NOW account is free if you keep the required minimum daily balance of $1,000 in your account. Below the minimum there is a $7.50 monthly service charge plus 25¢ per check.

VALUE CHECKING

This checking account is ideal for people who do not write many checks. There is no minimum balance and you can write up to 5 checks per month for free. If you write more than 5 checks, there is a monthly service charge of $6.00 plus 20¢ per check.

MONEY MARKET CHECKING

This account pays you about 7% on your checking account balance. Your money market account is free if you keep a minimum daily balance of $2,000 in your account. Below the minimum there is a $7.50 monthly service charge plus 25¢ per check.

DECISION-MAKING FACTORS

Minimum balance requirement
Cost per check

Monthly service charge
Interest paid

DECISION-MAKING COMPARISONS

Compare the 4 options by completing the table.

Factor	Regular	NOW	Value	Money Market
Minimum balance	None	1. ■	2. ■	3. ■
Monthly service charge (if conditions not met)	4. ■	5. ■	$6.00	6. ■
Cost per check (if conditions not met)	7. ■	25¢	8. ■	9. ■
Interest paid	10. ■	11. ■	12. ■	Yes; about 7%

MAKING THE DECISIONS

Which account should Victoria open:

13. If the amount of interest earned were the only factor?

14. If she expects to write about 10 checks per mo and does not expect to have more than $1,000 in her account?

15. If she expects to maintain a low balance and to write only 3 or 4 checks per mo?

16. If she has no problem maintaining a minimum balance of $1,000?

17. What is the monthly service charge if she opens a Regular checking account and writes 12 checks per mo? How much is this per year?

18. What is the monthly service charge if she opens a NOW account and writes 12 checks per mo and maintains a minimum balance of $1,000?

19. What is the monthly service charge on a NOW account if she writes 15 checks per mo and does not maintain a minimum balance of $1,000?

20. Suppose Victoria can earn an average of $5.00 interest per mo on a Money Market account and can maintain a minimum balance of $2,000. What would be her net annual savings over the Regular account in Exercise 17?

21. Do you think that the free checking accounts are worth the minimum balance requirements and the higher service charge penalties?

22. Which account would you choose? Why?

PROBLEM B

After Victoria has worked for several months, her checking account balance has been consistently high enough that she decides to open a savings account. She gets information on the types of savings accounts available so that she can choose which one is best for her.

REGULAR SAVINGS	MONEY MARKET SAVINGS
★ **Can be opened with as little as $5**	★ **Can be opened with $1,500 or more**
★ **Unlimited deposits and withdrawals**	★ **Limit of 5 withdrawals per month**
★ **5½% interest**	★ **Variable interest from 6½% up, adjusted weekly**
★ **No service charge**	★ **$3.00 per month service charge if balance falls below $1,500**

DECISION-MAKING FACTORS

Initial deposit   Access to money   Interest rate   Service charge

DECISION-MAKING COMPARISONS

Compare the 2 options by completing the table.

Factor	Regular savings	Money Market savings
Initial deposit	23. ■	24. ■
Access to money	Any day	25. ■
Interest rate	26. ■	Variable
Service charge	27. ■	28. ■

MAKING THE DECISIONS

Which account should Victoria open:

29. If she only has a small amount of money?

30. If she wants to earn the most interest and she does have $3,000 to deposit?

31. If she expects to make frequent deposits and withdrawals?

32. If she would like to earn 8% interest?

33. If the Money Market savings account averaged $7\frac{1}{2}\%$ interest, how much more could Victoria earn per year over a Regular savings account on a $10,000 deposit?

34. Which account would you open? Why?

CHAPTER REVIEW

Vocabulary   Choose the letter of the word(s) that completes the sentence.

1. Money placed by you into a savings or a checking account is called ■.   [124, 129]

   a. A withdrawal   **b.** A deposit   **c.** Interest

2. Money that is added to your account by the bank is called ■.   [129]

   a. A withdrawal   **b.** A deposit   **c.** Interest

3. When interest is compounded quarterly, it is paid to you ■ times per year.   [132]

   a. One   **b.** Two   **c.** Four

Skills   Find the new bank account balance.

4. Old balance: $387.87
   Check: $37.75
   Deposit: $123.30
   Check: $23.08
   Check: $76.57   [124]

5. Old balance: $1,835.94
   Check: $274.33
   Check: $88.27
   Service charge: $3.50
   Deposit: $385.89   [124]

6. Old balance: $500.00
   Withdrawal: $175.00
   Withdrawal: $60.00
   Deposit: $37.50   [129]

7. Old balance: $675.30
   Deposit: $50.00
   Interest: $2.87
   Withdrawal: $185.00   [129]

Use the given information to reconcile the bank statement balance with the check register balance. Find the adjusted balance for each.   [127]

8. Check register balance: $217.84
   Statement ending balance: $279.50
   Outstanding checks: $15.80, $49.71
   Service charge: $3.85

9. Check register balance: $87.50
   Statement ending balance: $137.90
   Outstanding check: $75.00
   Outstanding deposit: $19.85
   Service charge: $4.75

Find the answer.   [132]

10. How much simple interest will be earned in 3 y on $2,500 in an account that pays 4.5%?

11. What will be the new balance on $800 in an account that earns $6\frac{1}{2}\%$ simple interest for 5 y?

12. Use the compound interest table on page 133. How much interest will be paid on $400 earning 6% compounded quarterly after 4 y?

13. Use the compound interest table on page 133. What will be the new balance on $5,000 earning 4% compounded semiannually after 10 y?

Make up a check for the payment. Use today's date and your own name and signature.

1. Check #136 to Dr. Robin Yeats for $65.00

2. Check #137 to Security Insurance Co. for $258.34

Find the new checking account balance.

3.   Old balance: $783.21
        Check: $73.90
      Check: $182.70
       Check: $57.24
  Service charge: $8.30

4. Old balance: $1,284.89
    Deposit: $231.48
     Check: $83.90
    Check: $374.50
    Check: $214.38

Use the given information to reconcile the bank statement balance with the check register balance. Find the adjusted balance for each.

5. Check register balance: $86.30
Statement ending balance: $171.54
Outstanding checks: $3.90, $87.74
Service charge: $6.40

6. Check register balance: $486.35
Statement ending balance: $500.75
Outstanding checks: $29.40, $165.00
Outstanding deposit: $176.50
Service charge: $3.50

Solve.

7. Jim opened a savings account with a deposit of $250.00. He later deposited $45.00 and then withdrew $120. The bank posted interest of $3.28. What is his new balance?

8. Sarah's savings account balance was $218.00. She withdrew $50 one month and deposited $40 the next. She then withdrew $75. The bank posted interest of $6.83. What is her new balance?

Find the simple interest.

9. $600 at 5% for 10 y

10. $2,300 at $6\frac{1}{4}$% for 4 y

Use the compound interest table on page 133 to find the new balance.

11. $2,500 at 6% compounded semiannually for 4 y

12. $6,000 at 8% compounded quarterly for 5 y

MONEY TIPS

You can save time at the bank by using ATMs (Automated Teller Machines) and save money on transaction fees if the ATMs are owned by the bank.

LET'S LOOK AT THE FACTS

Many banks have **ATMs,** which allow customers to use a special bank card to conduct certain transactions *at any time,* even if the bank itself is closed. Some of these banks do not own their ATMs and may charge up to $1.00 or more for every transaction. With bank-owned ATMs, there is either a much lower transaction fee or no fee at all.

LET'S DISCUSS WHY

1. For what types of transactions might an ATM be used?

2. What are the advantages of dealing with a bank that has ATMs?

3. Why do you think banks which do not own their ATMs charge higher transaction fees?

4. More banks charge an ATM transaction fee for withdrawals than for deposits. What might be the reason for this?

5. If the ABC Bank charges $1.00 per transaction and you use its ATMs 12 times per mo, how much would you pay per year for this service?

6. If you use the XYZ Bank's ATMs and pay only 20¢ per transaction, how much would you save in a year over what you would pay to use the ABC Bank's ATMs in Exercise 5?

7. How could you find out if you are paying ATM transaction fees?

LET'S SEE WHAT YOU WOULD DO

8. Last year, it cost you $90 (75¢ per transaction) to use ATMs at the Capital City Bank, which has 16 locations around the city. The Warshaw County Bank charges no fee but has only 2 ATM locations, one near your office and one at the airport. Discuss the pros and cons of switching your accounts to the Warshaw Bank.

9. The Olympia Federal Bank issues you a special bank card and assigns you a **Personal Identification Number (PIN)** so you can use its ATMs. This is your number exclusively and must be entered into an ATM before any transaction can be conducted. Why should you never give your PIN to someone else?

CALCULATOR FRACTIONS ON A CALCULATOR

You have learned that you can rename fractions and mixed numbers as decimals by dividing the numerator by the denominator. You can also use a calculator to rename a fraction or mixed number as a decimal.

Rename $2\frac{4}{5}$ as a decimal.

Procedure	Calculator Entry	Calculator Display
1. Divide the numerator of the fraction by the denominator.	$\boxed{4}\,\boxed{\div}\,\boxed{5}\,\boxed{=}$	$\boxed{0.8}$
2. Add the whole number.	$\boxed{+}\,\boxed{2}\,\boxed{=}$	$\boxed{2.8}$

So $2\frac{4}{5} = 2.8$.

To rename a fraction or a mixed number as a percent, first use the calculator to rename it as a decimal. Then multiply by 100.

Rename $\frac{3}{8}$ as a percent.

Procedure	Calculator Entry	Calculator Display
1. Divide the numerator by the denominator.	$\boxed{3}\,\boxed{\div}\,\boxed{8}\,\boxed{=}$	$\boxed{0.375}$
2. Multiply by 100.	$\boxed{\times}\,\boxed{1}\,\boxed{0}\,\boxed{0}\,\boxed{=}$	$\boxed{37.5}$

So $\frac{3}{8} = 37.5\%$.

Use a calculator to rename the fraction or mixed number as a decimal. When necessary, round your answer to the nearest thousandth.

1. $\frac{5}{8}$ 2. $\frac{7}{20}$ 3. $\frac{3}{7}$ 4. $4\frac{3}{5}$ 5. $6\frac{1}{6}$

Use a calculator to rename the fraction or mixed number as a percent. When necessary, round your answer to the nearest tenth of a percent.

6. $\frac{3}{4}$ 7. $\frac{9}{20}$ 8. $\frac{11}{25}$ 9. $\frac{5}{7}$ 10. $\frac{1}{6}$

11. $3\frac{3}{5}$ 12. $9\frac{12}{25}$ 13. $6\frac{9}{16}$ 14. $7\frac{5}{6}$ 15. $8\frac{1}{3}$

16. If your calculator has a percent key, $\boxed{\%}$, discover how to rename $\frac{3}{8}$ as a percent.

Round to the nearest cent.

1. $27.868

2. $4.923

3. $30.905

4. $86.2073

5. $0.0753

6. $0.0523

Rename as a decimal.

7. 15%

8. 53%

9. 7%

10. 3%

11. 105%

12. 156%

Rename as a decimal.

13. 1%

14. 1.5%

15. $1\frac{1}{4}$%

16. 0.0405%

17. 0.06308%

18. 0.05506%

Multiply.

19. 0.9 × $40

20. 0.8 × $35

21. 0.7 × $78

22. 0.6 × $835

23. 0.35 × $700

24. 0.46 × $950

25. 0.79 × $748

26. 0.86 × $739

Multiply. Round to the nearest cent.

27. 6 × $5.128

28. 4 × $3.752

29. 40 × $1.499

30. 0.73 × $678.20

31. 0.43 × $809.49

32. 0.74 × $287.51

33. 0.67 × $526.43

34. 0.83 × $1,012.56

35. 0.015 × $2,023.63

36. 0.075 × $59.50

37. 0.0013 × $319.26

38. 0.00046 × $607.43

Find the answer to the nearest cent.

39. What is 13% of $528.20?

40. What is 17% of $832.78?

41. What is 18.6% of $409.86?

42. What is 19.65% of $689.53?

43. What is $1\frac{1}{2}$% of $25.50?

44. What is 1.3% of $62.82?

45. What is 0.04657% of $33?

46. What is 0.02342% of $18.75?

Chapter

8

CREDIT

Many people pay for major purchases with a credit card. What factors should you consider before choosing and applying for a credit card?

Only you can decide whether or not you should get a **credit card.**
Once you get a card, you must accept the responsibility for using it.

You used your credit card to charge a sweater at The Clothing Mart.
The sweater cost $34.97. In the store, you looked over the **charge
receipt** to make sure that all the entries were correct.

EXAMPLE **1** Identify the parts of the charge receipt.

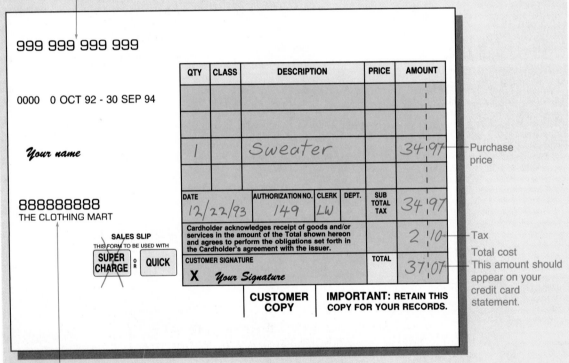

The impression made by
your credit card shows your
account number and the
card's expiration date.

999 999 999 999

0000   0 OCT 92 - 30 SEP 94

Your name

888888888
THE CLOTHING MART

SALES SLIP
THIS FORM TO BE USED WITH
SUPER CHARGE ᵒᴿ QUICK

QTY	CLASS	DESCRIPTION	PRICE	AMOUNT
1		Sweater		34 97

| DATE 12/22/93 | AUTHORIZATION NO. 149 | CLERK LW | DEPT. | SUB TOTAL TAX | 34 97 |

Cardholder acknowledges receipt of goods and/or
services in the amount of the Total shown hereon
and agrees to perform the obligations set forth in
the Cardholder's agreement with the issuer.

| CUSTOMER SIGNATURE X *Your Signature* | | | | | 2 10 |
| | | | | TOTAL | 37 07 |

CUSTOMER COPY

IMPORTANT: RETAIN THIS COPY FOR YOUR RECORDS.

Purchase price

Tax

Total cost
This amount should
appear on your
credit card
statement.

The impression made by
the credit card machine
shows the store's name
and account number.

At the end of the month, you got a statement that showed your
charges, payments, the amount you owe, and other important
information. You compared the statement with your charge receipts.

EXAMPLE 2   Identify the parts of the monthly **credit card statement.**

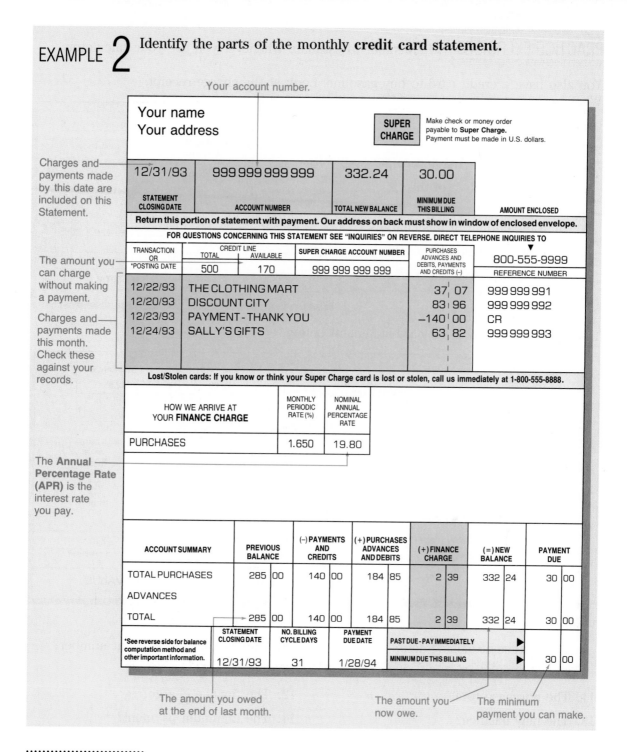

Your account number.

Charges and payments made by this date are included on this Statement.

Your name
Your address

SUPER CHARGE

Make check or money order payable to **Super Charge.** Payment must be made in U.S. dollars.

12/31/93	999 999 999 999	332.24	30.00	
STATEMENT CLOSING DATE	ACCOUNT NUMBER	TOTAL NEW BALANCE	MINIMUM DUE THIS BILLING	AMOUNT ENCLOSED

Return this portion of statement with payment. Our address on back must show in window of enclosed envelope.

FOR QUESTIONS CONCERNING THIS STATEMENT SEE "INQUIRIES" ON REVERSE. DIRECT TELEPHONE INQUIRIES TO

The amount you can charge without making a payment.

Charges and payments made this month. Check these against your records.

TRANSACTION OR *POSTING DATE	CREDIT LINE TOTAL	AVAILABLE	SUPER CHARGE ACCOUNT NUMBER	PURCHASES ADVANCES AND DEBITS, PAYMENTS AND CREDITS (–)	800-555-9999 REFERENCE NUMBER
	500	170	999 999 999 999		
12/22/93	THE CLOTHING MART			37 07	999 999 991
12/20/93	DISCOUNT CITY			83 96	999 999 992
12/23/93	PAYMENT - THANK YOU			–140 00	CR
12/24/93	SALLY'S GIFTS			63 82	999 999 993

Lost/Stolen cards: If you know or think your Super Charge card is lost or stolen, call us immediately at 1-800-555-8888.

HOW WE ARRIVE AT YOUR **FINANCE CHARGE**	MONTHLY PERIODIC RATE (%)	NOMINAL ANNUAL PERCENTAGE RATE
PURCHASES	1.650	19.80

The **Annual Percentage Rate (APR)** is the interest rate you pay.

ACCOUNT SUMMARY	PREVIOUS BALANCE	(–) PAYMENTS AND CREDITS	(+) PURCHASES ADVANCES AND DEBITS	(+) FINANCE CHARGE	(=) NEW BALANCE	PAYMENT DUE
TOTAL PURCHASES	285 00	140 00	184 85	2 39	332 24	30 00
ADVANCES						
TOTAL	285 00	140 00	184 85	2 39	332 24	30 00

*See reverse side for balance computation method and other important information.	STATEMENT CLOSING DATE	NO. BILLING CYCLE DAYS	PAYMENT DUE DATE	PAST DUE - PAY IMMEDIATELY ▶	
	12/31/93	31	1/28/94	MINIMUM DUE THIS BILLING ▶	30 00

The amount you owed at the end of last month.

The amount you now owe.

The minimum payment you can make.

FOR DISCUSSION

How would you check your credit card receipts against a credit card statement?

PRACTICE EXERCISES   Remember to estimate whenever you use your calculator.

You also have a credit card to buy gasoline. Look at the charge receipt.
What is:

1. Your credit card account number?

2. The date of this charge receipt?

3. The expiration date of the credit card?

4. The total amount of this charge?

5. The cost of a gallon of gasoline?

6. The license plate number of the car that got the gasoline?

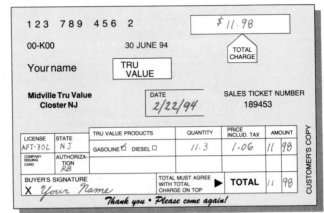

Look at the gasoline credit card statement below.

TRU VALUE		123 789 456 2		MINIMUM PAYMENT	NEW BALANCE
		CREDIT CARD NUMBER		75.00	142.85

FEB. 28, 1994
STATEMENT CLOSING DATE

Your name
Your address

TRANSACTION DATE	SALES TICKET NUMBER	CARD NUMBER			TRANSACTION DESCRIPTION & PURCHASE LOCATION (See Reverse Side For Description of Codes)			AMOUNT
1 03	4368221	001	01	210 KINDRKMCK	WESTWOOD		NJ	10.85
1 12	1527363	001	01	681 PIERMONT	CLOSTER		NJ	9.60
2 19				PAYMENT - THANK YOU				79.39CR
2 20	1523642	001	01	681 PIERMONT	CLOSTER		NJ	9.00
2 22	1196543	001	01	1 MIDVALE	CLOSTER		NJ	10.50
2 22	1894583	001	01	1 MIDVALE	CLOSTER		NJ	11.10
2 23	4365454	001	01	210 KINDRKMCK	WESTWOOD		NJ	11.00

Previous Balance		Payments & Credits		Purchases & Adjustments		FINANCE CHARGES		New Balance
158.88	−	79.39	+	62.05	+	1.39	=	142.93

FINANCE CHARGE INFORMATION			Statement Closing Date	Credit Card Number	Minimum Payment
	PERIODIC RATE	ANNUAL PERCENTAGE RATE	FEB 28 94	123 789 456 2	75.00
To $ 500	1.75%	21%	To Avoid Additional FINANCE CHARGE New Balance Must Be Received By		
Over $ 500	1.50%	18%	MAR 20 94		TRU VALUE

What is:

7. The statement closing date?

8. Your credit card account number?

9. The previous balance?

10. Last month's payment?

11. The purchase total?

12. The finance charge?

13. The new balance?

14. The minimum payment?

15. What is the Annual Percentage Rate (APR) finance charge for amounts up to $500?

16. What is the Annual Percentage Rate (APR) finance charge for amounts over $500?

17. How much was charged on 2/20?

18. How much was charged in January?

8.2 CREDIT FINANCE CHARGES

On your credit card statement, the **finance charge** is the amount you pay if the last balance has not been paid in full. The **unpaid balance** is any of the last balance that was not paid. The **new balance** is the amount you now owe.

NEW BALANCE = UNPAID BALANCE + FINANCE CHARGE + NEW CHARGES

EXAMPLE 1

Last month's balance was $285.00, of which $140.00 has been paid. Your new charges this month totaled $184.85. Your credit card company charges you 1.65% of the unpaid balance as a finance charge. Find the unpaid balance, the finance charge, and the new balance.

1. Subtract to find the unpaid balance. $285 − $140 = $145

The unpaid balance is $145.

2. Multiply to find the finance charge.
   THINK: **1.65% = 0.0165**   0.0165 × $145 = $2.3925

The finance charge is $2.39.

3. Add to find the new balance. $145 + $2.39 + $184.85 = $332.24

The new balance is $332.24.

Some credit cards have variable finance rates as shown below.

$1\frac{1}{2}$% on the first $500 of unpaid balance   1% on the unpaid balance above $500

EXAMPLE 2

The unpaid balance on Myra's account was $1,250. There were no new charges this month. Find the finance charge and the new balance.

1. Multiply to find the finance charge on the first $500.   THINK: $1\frac{1}{2}$% = 0.015   0.015 × $500 = $7.50

2. Multiply to find the finance charge on the amount over $500.
   THINK: $1,250 − $500 = $750   1% = 0.01   0.01 × $750 = $7.50

3. Add to find the total finance charge. $7.50 + $7.50 = $15.00

The total finance charge is $15.00.

4. Add to find the new balance. $1,250 + $15.00 = $1,265

The new balance is $1,265.

FOR DISCUSSION

What are some of the advantages and disadvantages of having a credit card?

Remember to estimate whenever you use your calculator.

Find the unpaid balance, the finance charge, and the new balance to the nearest cent.

1. Last balance: $218.35
   Payments: $0
   Finance rate: 1.5%
   New charges: $35.49

2. Last balance: $80.45
   Payments: $0
   Finance rate: 1%
   New charges: $99.85

3. Last balance: $40.55
   Payments: $0
   Finance rate: 1.3%
   New charges: $88.75

4. Last balance: $143.50
   Payments: $100.00
   Finance rate: 1%
   New charges: $0

5. Last balance: $89.77
   Payments: $19.00
   Finance rate: 1.5%
   New charges: $0

6. Last balance: $530.85
   Payments: $125.00
   Finance rate: 1.2%
   New charges: $0

7. Last balance: $509.65
   Payments: $350.00
   Finance rate: $1\frac{1}{4}\%$
   New charges: $199.89

8. Last balance: $90.85
   Payments: $55.00
   Finance rate: $1\frac{1}{2}\%$
   New charges: $345.90

9. Last balance: $1,025.63
   Payments: $750.00
   Finance rate: $\frac{3}{4}\%$
   New charges: $836.25

Use the variable rates on page 147. Find the total finance charge on the given unpaid balance to the nearest cent.

10. $545.00   11. $718.00   12. $1,465   13. $678.52   14. $2,045.67

Use the variable rates on page 147. Find the unpaid balance, the finance charge, and the new balance to the nearest cent.

	Last balance	Payments	New charges
15.	$234.00	$0	$345.00
16.	$1,089.00	$500.00	$0
17.	$2,534.58	$750.58	$234.00
18.	$345.68	$35.89	$38.34

EXTENSION   Minimum Payments

Some credit card companies require a minimum payment on the new balance. Your new balance is $250. The minimum payment is 15% of the new balance. What is the minimum payment?

Multiply the new balance by 0.15.   0.15 × $250 = $37.50 minimum payment

Find the minimum payment.

1. The minimum payment is 12% of the new balance. The new balance is $456.

2. The minimum payment is 15% of the new balance or $25, whichever is greater. The new balance is $158.

8.3 OVERDRAFT CHECKING

The bank agreed to lend you up to $500 to cover overdrafts. An **overdraft** is a check written for more than the balance in your account.

INTEREST = DAILY INTEREST RATE × SUM OF THE DAILY BALANCES

EXAMPLE 1

The sum of your daily balances for the month was $2,700. The **Annual Percentage Rate (APR)** is 17%. How much interest will you pay?

THINK: Look across from 17% to find the daily interest rate of 0.04657%.

Multiply to find the interest.
THINK: 0.04657% = 0.0004657

0.0004657 × $2,700 = $1.25739

You will pay $1.26 in interest.

Annual percentage rate	Daily interest rate
20%	0.05479%
19%	0.05205%
18%	0.04931%
17%	0.04657%

You can calculate the sum of the daily balances.

EXAMPLE 2

On February 1, the balance in your overdraft account was $245.80.
On February 16, you wrote a $212.50 check.   New balance: $458.30
On February 23, you made a $50 payment.   New balance: $408.30
The APR is 19%. Find the interest and the new balance.

1. Find the sum of the daily balances for February.

Dates	Balance	Number of days	Sum of the balances
Feb. 1–15	$245.80 ×	15	= $3,687.00
Feb. 16–22	$458.30 ×	7	= $3,208.10
Feb. 23–28	$408.30 ×	6	= $2,449.80
Total:		28	$9,344.90

2. Find the daily interest rate for an APR of 19%.   0.05205%

3. Multiply to find the interest.
THINK: 0.05205% = 0.0005205   0.0005205 × $9,344.90 = $4.8640204

The interest is $4.86.

4. Add to find the new balance. $408.30 + $4.86 = $413.16

The new balance is $413.16.

FOR DISCUSSION

The **average daily balance** is the sum of the daily balances divided by the number of days in a month. Your average daily balance for September (30 d) was $126.20. What was the sum of the daily balances?

PRACTICE EXERCISES

Remember to estimate whenever you use your calculator.

Find the interest on the overdraft checking account.

	1.	2.	3.	4.	5.
Sum of daily balances	$2,945	$3,085.60	$4,074	$3,098.45	$2,453.89
Annual percentage rate	19%	20%	17%	18%	17%

Find the interest and the new balance for the account.

6. The sum of the daily balances is $3,845 and the APR is 18%.

7. The sum of the daily balances is $7,086 and the APR is 20%.

8. Sept. 1: Balance $858
   Sept. 5: Made $175 payment
   Sept. 19: Balance changed to $795
   Sept. 20–30: No more activity
   The APR is 20%.

9. March 1: Balance $908
   March 8: Balance changed to $1,035
   March 23: Made $295 payment
   March 24–31: No more activity
   The APR is 18%.

10. June 1: Balance $2,085
    June 5: Made $475 payment
    June 12: Balance changed to $1,985.75
    June 23: Balance changed to $2,135.89
    June 24–30: No more activity
    The APR is 17%.

11. July 1: Balance $75
    July 9: Balance changed to $525
    July 10: Made $175 payment
    July 21: Made $75.89 payment
    July 22–31: No more activity
    The APR is 19%.

8.4 TAKING OUT A LOAN

It is wise to compare different loan rates before you apply for a loan at a certain bank or credit union. The Annual Percentage Rate (APR) is the rate of interest you pay for loans and finance plans.

At a bank or a credit union, a loan officer gives you a loan application to fill out. You usually make monthly payments to pay back a loan.

EXAMPLE 1
You want to borrow $685 to pay off some debts. The loan officer at a bank tells you that the APR is 13.5%. She also tells you that you will pay off the loan in 12 monthly payments of $61.34. How much will you need to repay? What is the interest?

1. Multiply to find the amount you repay. $12 \times \$61.34 = \$736.08$

You will need to repay $736.08.

2. Subtract to find the interest. $\$736.08 - \$685.00 = \$51.08$

The interest is $51.08.

Banks and credit unions use rate tables to find out how much interest you will pay. The interest depends on the amount borrowed, the interest rate, and how long you will take to repay the loan.

EXAMPLE 2
Carlos takes out a $600 loan for a vacation trip. The APR is 14.5%. He will repay the loan in 9 mo. How much interest will he pay? How much will he repay each month?

THINK: Look across from 9 mo to find the interest rate per $100, or $6.138.

INTEREST PER $100

Months	14.5% APR
3	$2.426
6	$4.315
9	$6.138
12	$8.027
15	$9.937

1. Divide to find the number of $100 that Carlos is borrowing. $\$600 \div \$100 = 6$

2. Multiply to find the interest. $6 \times \$6.138 = \$36.828$

Carlos will pay $36.83 in interest.

3. Add to find the total amount he will repay. $\$600 + \$36.83 = \$636.83$

4. Divide to find the monthly payment. $\$636.83 \div 9 = \$70.758888$

Carlos will repay $70.76 per mo for 9 mo.

Banks also use tables to find monthly payments.

EXAMPLE 3 Victoria got a $7,000 loan. How much will she pay each month for a 10-y loan at $12\frac{1}{4}$%? How much interest will she pay?

THINK: Look across from 10 y under $12\frac{1}{4}$% to find the monthly payment for each $100 borrowed, or $1.499.

MONTHLY PAYMENT PER
$100 FINANCED

Years	APR		
	$10\frac{1}{2}$%	$12\frac{1}{4}$%	$13\frac{1}{2}$%
5	2.149	2.237	2.301
10	1.349	1.499	1.523
15	1.105	1.216	1.295

1. Divide to find the number of $100. $7,000 ÷ $100 = 70

2. Multiply to find the payment.   70 × $1.499 = $104.93

Victoria will pay $104.93 per mo.

3. Multiply to find the total amount to be repaid.
   THINK: 10 y = 10 × 12 mo = 120 mo   120 × $104.93 = $12,591.60

4. Subtract to find the interest. $12,591.60 − $7,000 = $5,591.60

Victoria will pay $5,591.60 in interest.

FOR DISCUSSION

A home equity loan is a **secured loan,** since the value of your home guarantees payment. Would the interest rate on a secured loan usually be more or less than the interest rate on an unsecured loan? Why?

PRACTICE EXERCISES   Remember to estimate whenever you use your calculator.

Find the total amount to be repaid and the interest.

	Amount borrowed	Monthly payment	Number of payments
1.	$ 385	$ 67.31	6
2.	$ 809	$ 96.08	9
3.	$ 580	$ 52.27	12
4.	$1,200	$ 75.41	18
5.	$1,385	$104.17	15
6.	$ 239	$ 82.13	3

Find the interest and the monthly payment.

	Amount Borrowed	APR	Months
7.	$ 500	13.5%	6
8.	$ 750	17.6%	9
9.	$ 186	13.5%	3
10.	$ 918	13.5%	12
11.	$1,020	17.6%	12
12.	$1,860	13.5%	18
13.	$1,238	17.6%	15
14.	$908.86	17.6%	18
15.	$1,087.95	13.5%	15
16.	$397.85	17.6%	9

INTEREST PER $100

Months	13.5% APR	17.6% APR
3	2.258	2.945
6	3.974	5.192
9	5.705	7.469
12	7.462	9.788
15	9.235	12.131
18	11.026	14.508

Find the monthly payment and the interest.

	Amount Borrowed	APR	Years
17.	$6,000	$13\frac{1}{4}\%$	5
18.	$8,200	$11\frac{1}{2}\%$	10
19.	$9,350	$15\frac{1}{2}\%$	15
20.	$8,725	$11\frac{1}{2}\%$	10
21.	$11,300	$13\frac{1}{4}\%$	5
22.	$9,890	$11\frac{1}{2}\%$	15
23.	$13,290	$15\frac{1}{2}\%$	15
24.	$6,780	$15\frac{1}{2}\%$	10
25.	$18,535	$13\frac{1}{4}\%$	5
26.	$23,265	$11\frac{1}{2}\%$	15

MONTHLY PAYMENT PER
$100 FINANCED

Years	APR		
	$11\frac{1}{2}\%$	$13\frac{1}{4}\%$	$15\frac{1}{2}\%$
5	2.199	2.288	2.405
10	1.406	1.508	1.644
15	1.168	1.282	1.433

Solve.

27. Kim borrowed $18,565 for 15 y. How much more would her monthly payments have been if the APR were $15\frac{1}{2}\%$ instead of $13\frac{1}{4}\%$?

28. David borrowed $13,675 for 5 y. How much more would he have repaid if the APR were $15\frac{1}{2}\%$ instead of $11\frac{1}{2}\%$?

8.5 INSTALLMENT BUYING

You and your friend Jim saw just the watch you both want. You do not have enough money to buy it. But you think you can afford the **installment plan.** The **installment price** is the total of the installment payments. The **finance charge** is the amount you pay to use the plan.

DESIGNER WATCH $82.50
Installment Plans
$9.15 a month for 12 months
or
$20 down, $6.15 a month for 12 months

FINANCE CHARGE = INSTALLMENT PRICE − REGULAR PRICE

EXAMPLE 1 You choose the installment plan without the down payment. Find the installment price and the finance charge.

1. Multiply to find the total monthly payments (the installment price). $12 \times \$9.15 = \$109.80$

The installment price is $109.80.

2. Subtract to find the finance charge. $\$109.80 - \$82.50 = \$27.30$

The finance charge is $27.30.

You may choose to pay a **down payment** when you get your purchase. In this case, the installment price is the total of the installment payments and the down payment.

EXAMPLE 2 Jim chooses the installment plan with the down payment. Find the installment price and the finance charge.

1. Multiply to find the total monthly payments. $12 \times \$6.15 = \$73.80$

2. Add to find the installment price. $\$73.80 + \$20.00 = \$93.80$

The installment price is $93.80.

3. Subtract to find the finance charge. $\$93.80 - \$82.50 = \$11.30$

The finance charge is $11.30.

FOR DISCUSSION

1. Why did the down payment in Example 2 decrease the finance charge?

2. If the watch were financed for 18 mo instead of 12 mo, would the monthly payments be more or less? Would the installment price be more or less? Why?

Find the installment price and the finance charge.

	1.	2.	3.	4.	5.	6.	7.	8.
Regular price	$85	$102	$198.65	$305.76	$405	$598	$829.85	$932.96
Down payment	$0	$0	$0	$0	$80	$125	$175	$245
Monthly payment	$15	$14	$18	$27.50	$42	$44	$80.76	$64.27
Number of payments	6	9	12	12	9	12	9	12

9. You buy a portable radio on the installment plan. It usually sells for $89.95. You pay $11 per mo for 9 mo.

10. You buy a television on the installment plan. It usually sells for $439.95. You pay $41 per mo for 12 mo.

11. The advertisement for a class ring reads "Nothing down and $17.50 a month for 6 months." The ring usually sells for $89.95.

12. A coat you want is advertised for "$25 down and $35.50 a month for 6 months." The coat usually sells for $220.95.

EXTENSION   Annual Percentage Rate (APR)

A lender should tell you what the APR is. But you should still figure it out for yourself. It might be more than you think. Use this formula to approximate the APR.

$$\text{Approximate APR} = \frac{24 \times \text{Finance charge}}{\text{Amount financed} \times (\text{Number of payments} + 1)}$$

You need to finance $400 for 12 mo toward the cost of a refrigerator. The finance charge is $80. What is the APR?

1. Substitute into the formula. Then solve.

$$\text{APR} = \frac{24 \times \$80}{\$400 \times (12 + 1)} = \frac{\$1,920}{\$400 \times 13} = \frac{\$1,920}{\$5,200} = 0.3692307$$

2. Round to the nearest thousandth and rename as a percent   0.369 = 36.9%

The APR is about 36.9%, much higher than you may have thought.

Find the approximate APR.

	1.	2.	3.	4.	5.	6.	7.	8.
Amount financed	$400	$34.86	$375	$750	$830	$1,010	$99.95	$65.60
Finance charge	$20	$2.64	$21	$78	$96.25	$119.50	$2.80	$8.75
Number of payments	12	6	12	18	15	18	3	9

PROBLEM *Solving* STRATEGY

8.6 FINDING A PATTERN

Situation:

Ketti has a charge account at the Jaycee Department Store. She used her charge account to buy furniture and began paying for it monthly. With her type of charge account, she can pay a different amount each month. Her finance charges for the first 4 mo are shown below.

April	May	June	July
$3.84	$3.68	$3.36	$2.88

Suppose that Ketti makes no other purchases on her charge account and she continues to make payments according to the plan she has been using. What will be the finance charge in August?

Strategy:

Finding a pattern can help you solve some problems.

Applying the Strategy:

The finance charges have been decreasing from one month to the next. Find each difference.

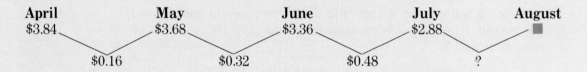

April	May	June	July	August
$3.84	$3.68	$3.36	$2.88	■
$0.16	$0.32	$0.48	?	

Look for a pattern. The differences are increasing by $0.16 each month. The next difference in the pattern will be $0.64, so the finance charge in August will be $2.88 − $0.64, or $2.24.

PRACTICE EXERCISES   Remember to estimate whenever you use your calculator.

Read the problem. Then answer the question.

1. Tony's charge account showed unpaid balances as follows: January—$85; February—$110; and March—$135. How did the increase from February to March compare with the increase from January to February?

2. The finance charges on Beth's charge account were as follows: August—$1.81; September—$1.69; and October—$1.58. If the pattern continues, what will be the finance charge in December?

Solve the problem by finding and using a pattern.

3. Ari used his charge account to buy audio equipment. With his type of charge account, he can pay a different amount each month. His finance charges for the first 4 mo were February—$4.05; March—$3.90; April—$3.60; and May—$3.15. Suppose that Ari makes no other purchases on his charge account and continues to make payments according to the plan he has been using. What will be the finance charge in June?

4. Helga used her charge account to buy a computer. With her type of charge account, she can pay a different amount each month. Her finance charges for the first 4 mo were May—$13.60; June—$11.20; July—$8.80; and August—$6.40. Suppose that Helga makes no other purchases on her charge account and continues to make payments according to the plan she has been using. What will be the finance charge in September?

5. During a 4-mo period, Stan kept a record of the unpaid balances on his charge account. The first month, the unpaid balance was $1,000. In each of the other months, the unpaid balance was 1.1 times as great as the unpaid balance the previous month. What were the unpaid balances for the third and fourth months?

6. Luveen kept a record of all of her charge-account payments for 3 y. The first year, her payments totaled $1,500. In each of the other years, the payments were 80% of those of the previous year. What was the total amount of her payments during the 3 y?

8.7 USING CREDIT WISELY

DECISION MAKING

One of the most important decisions you will make is how and when to use credit. You should never borrow money unless you need it. When you do borrow money, choose the credit plan that is best for you.

PROBLEM

To borrow $2,500 for his tuition, Ron can choose one of these credit plans.
   Charge the tuition on his credit card.
   Get an unsecured bank loan.
   Use the school's tuition plan.
   Ask his parents to get a home equity loan, which he will repay.
Ron listed the features of each plan to help him decide.

Credit Card:
   Finance charge: $1\frac{1}{2}$% of the unpaid balance each month.
   Minimum payment: $100 monthly
   The APR is 19.8%.
   I plan to make the minimum monthly payment. I will not charge anything else on this card. It will take me 31 mo to pay off the loan. The interest will be $597.52.

Unsecured Loan: The APR is 17.6%.
   The bank will only give the loan for 18 mo.
   The loan cannot be paid off any faster.

School's Tuition Plan:
   I can pay the school 12 monthly payments of $220.
   The APR is 10.8%.
   The loan cannot be paid off any faster.

Home Equity Loan:
   The minimum term of the loan is 5 y (60 mo).
   The APR is $11\frac{1}{2}$%.
   Interest paid is tax deductible.
   My parents have the final responsibility for repaying the loan. The loan cannot be paid off any faster.

17.6% APR Interest Per $100
18 mo. $14.508

$11\frac{1}{2}$% APR Monthly Payment Per $100
5 y $2.199

DECISION-MAKING FACTORS

Annual Percentage Rate   Monthly payment   Number of payments
Interest paid   Other factors

DECISION-MAKING COMPARISONS

Complete the table to compare the 4 credit plans.

Factor	Credit card	Unsecured loan	School's tuition plan	Home equity loan
APR	1. ■	17.6%	2. ■	3. ■
Monthly payment	4. ■	5. ■	$220.00	6. ■
Number of payments	31	7. ■	8. ■	60
Interest	$597.52	9. ■	10. ■	11. ■
Other factors	12. ■	Payments are fixed.	13. ■	14. ■

MAKING THE DECISIONS

Which credit plan would Ron choose if the only factor were:

15. Lowest APR?

16. Lowest monthly payment?

17. Least amount of interest?

18. Getting a tax deduction?

19. Which credit plan would allow Ron to adjust his monthly payments?

20. If Ron wants to be totally responsible for repaying the loan, which plan should he eliminate?

21. How much would Ron save in interest by choosing the unsecured loan instead of the home equity loan?

22. How much would Ron save in interest by choosing the school's plan instead of the credit card?

23. Which plans can Ron eliminate if he cannot afford to pay more than $150 per mo? Of the remaining plans, how much can Ron save by choosing the one with the lowest interest?

24. Should you use APR alone to decide which credit plan to choose? Why or why not?

25. Which one of these credit plans would you choose? Why?

CHAPTER REVIEW

Vocabulary   Choose the letter of the word(s) that completes the sentence.

1. On a credit card statement, the ▪ is any of the last balance that was not paid.   [147]

   a. Finance charge   **b.** New balance   **c.** Unpaid balance

2. A check written for more than the balance in your account is called ▪.   [149]

   a. A payment   **b.** The daily interest rate   **c.** An overdraft

3. If you cannot afford the full price of an item, you may be able to use ▪.   [154]

   a. An installment plan   **b.** An APR   **c.** A minimum payment

Skills   Find the unpaid balance, the finance charge, and the new balance.   [144, 147]

4. Last balance: $106.84
   Payments: $75.00
   Finance rate: $1\frac{1}{2}\%$
   New charges: $56.28

5. Last balance: $318.60
   Payments: $80.00
   Finance rate: 1.65%
   New charges: $76.39

6. Last balance: $1,100
   Payments: $100
   Finance rate: $1\frac{1}{2}\%$ on first $500
   1% on over $500
   New charges: $65.40

7. Last balance: $850.68
   Payments: $25.00
   Finance rate: $1\frac{1}{2}\%$ on first $500
   1% on over $500
   New charges: $138.75

Find the interest on the overdraft checking account to the nearest cent.   [149]

8. Sum of daily balances: $525
   Daily interest rate: 0.05205%

9. Sum of daily balances: $2,600
   Daily interest rate: 0.04931%

Use the loan monthly payment table on page 152 for Exercises 10–13.   [151]

10. Sue borrowed $8,000 for 5 y at $10\frac{1}{2}\%$. What is the monthly payment?

11. May borrowed $14,000 for 10 y at $12\frac{1}{4}\%$. What is the monthly payment?

12. Dan borrowed $32,600 for 10 y at $13\frac{1}{2}\%$. How much interest will he pay?

13. Sal borrowed $50,000 for 15 y at $10\frac{1}{2}\%$. How much interest will he pay?

Find the installment price and the finance charge.   [154]

14. Regular price: $130
    Down payment: $0
    Monthly payment: $17.30
    Number of payments: 9

15. Regular price: $950.75
    Down payment: $150
    Monthly payment: $88.10
    Number of payments: 12

CHAPTER TEST

Find the finance charge and the new balance.

1. Last balance: $409.56
   Payments: $160.00
   Finance rate: 1.5%
   New charges: $350.49

2. Last balance: $65.43
   Payments: $20.00
   Finance rate: $1\frac{1}{4}$%
   New charges: $87.60

3. Last balance: $375 Payments: $85
   Finance rate: $1\frac{1}{2}$% on first $500
   1% on over $500
   New charges: $94

Use the daily interest rate table on page 149 to find the interest on the account to the nearest cent.

	4.	5.	6.	7.	8.	9.
Sum of daily balances	$270	$456.90	$509	$810	$3,895.67	$9,007.62
APR	17%	20%	20%	17%	17%	20%

Use the loan payment table on page 152 to find the monthly payment, the total amount to be repaid, and the interest to the nearest cent.

10. Borrow $500 for 5 y at $10\frac{1}{2}$%.

11. Borrow $9,000 for 10 y at $10\frac{1}{2}$%.

12. Borrow $4,675 for 10 y at $12\frac{1}{4}$%.

13. Borrow $12,500 for 5 y at $13\frac{1}{2}$%.

Find the installment price and the finance charge.

	Regular price	Down payment	Monthly payment	Number of payments
14.	$75	$0	$10.42	9
15.	$95.89	$0	$16.75	6
16.	$210	$25	$17.58	12
17.	$273.60	$85	$23.25	9

Your charge account finance charges for the first 4 mo on a single purchase were: Jan.–$8.50, Feb.–$7.55, Mar.–$6.84, and Apr.–$6.37.

18. By how much are the differences in finance charges decreasing each month?

19. What is the total difference over the 4 mo period?

20. What should May's finance charge be?

MONEY TIPS

By calculating how much credit fits into your budget, you can avoid getting into debt.

LET'S LOOK AT THE FACTS

Charging purchases can be very tempting. It can, however, cause you to *spend* far beyond your means. The formula below is an easy way to figure out exactly how much you can buy on credit and pay back without getting deeper into debt. Imagine that the budget shown below is yours.

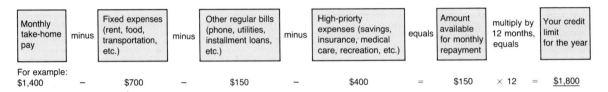

Monthly take-home pay	minus	Fixed expenses (rent, food, transportation, etc.)	minus	Other regular bills (phone, utilities, installment loans, etc.)	minus	High-priorty expenses (savings, insurance, medical care, recreation, etc.)	equals	Amount available for monthly repayment	multiply by 12 months, equals	Your credit limit for the year

For example:
$1,400 — $700 — $150 — $400 = $150 × 12 = $1,800

LET'S DISCUSS WHY

1. If your monthly take-home pay is $1,400, what is your annual take-home pay?

2. What percent of your annual take-home pay does an $1,800 credit limit represent?

3. What percent of your monthly take-home pay is used for fixed expenses? Regular bills? High-priority expenses? Monthly credit repayment?

LET'S SEE WHAT YOU WOULD DO

4. Finance charges (which can range from 12% to 20% or more) are added to the amount you owe on a credit card and are compounded each month. Name some ways to lessen your credit debt.

5. Your rent goes up by $50, raising your fixed expenses to $750. Where could you cut back on spending to make up for this increase?

6. In August, you see a terrific stereo system with a color chamber that changes colors as the music changes. It is on sale for $600 until the end of the year. However, you only have $300 left on your credit limit. Is there any way you could buy it without exceeding your credit limit or borrowing money from anyone?

7. Many experts say that, as a general rule, no more than about 10% to 11% of your take-home pay should be used for buying on credit. If your monthly take-home pay is $1,400, what is your monthly credit range? Your annual credit range?

ESTIMATION SKILLS

FRONT-END ESTIMATION OF DIFFERENCES

One way to estimate differences is by using front-end estimation.

1. Find the greatest number.
2. Identify the place of its leading nonzero digit.
3. Subtract only the digits in that place.

Examples

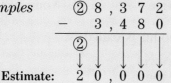

$$\begin{array}{r} ②\ 8\ ,\ 3\ 7\ 2 \\ -\quad 3\ ,\ 4\ 8\ 0 \\ \hline ② \end{array}$$

Estimate: 2 0 , 0 0 0

$$\begin{array}{r} \$\ ⑧\ .\ 7\ 3 \\ -\quad ⑤\ .\ 3\ 9 \\ \hline ③ \end{array}$$

Estimate: $ 3 . 0 0

$$\begin{array}{r} 0\ .\ ⑧\ 1\ 7 \\ -\ 0\ .\ ⑥\ 6\ 8 \\ \hline ② \end{array}$$

Estimate: 0 . 2

To get a more precise estimate, front-end estimation can be adjusted upward or downward by *also* using the next greatest place. With subtraction, you will need to think of either a *plus* or a *minus* of your first estimate.

Examples

$$\begin{array}{r} ②\ \boxed{8}\ ,\ 3\ 7\ 2 \\ -\quad \boxed{3}\ ,\ 4\ 8\ 0 \end{array}$$

First estimate: ② 0 , 0 0 0
    + about   ⑤ , 0 0 0
Final estimate: 2 5 , 0 0 0

$$\begin{array}{r} \$\ ⑧\ .\ \boxed{7}\ 3 \\ -\quad ⑤\ .\ \boxed{3}\ 9 \end{array}$$

First estimate: $ ③ . 0 0
    + about   0 . ④ 0
Final estimate: $ 3 . 4 0

$$\begin{array}{r} 0\ .\ ⑧\ \boxed{1}\ 7 \\ -\ 0\ .\ ⑥\ \boxed{6}\ 8 \end{array}$$

First estimate: 0 . ② 0
    − about   0 . 0 ⑤
Final estimate: 0 . 1 5

Use front-end estimation with adjusting to estimate the difference.

1. 573 −128	2. 4,309 − 186	3. 86,245 − 5,017	4. 33,432 −18,507	5. 95,880 − 8,141
6. 35,081 − 6,327	7. 24,973 − 8,789	8. $4.52 − 3.27	9. $27.50 − 2.89	10. $9.93 − 0.50
11. $62.85 − 37.44	12. $53.75 − 47.36	13. $47.23 − 9.72	14. $8.75 − 0.29	15. $2.09 − 0.45
16. 6.583 −4.471	17. 0.489 −0.273	18. 0.892 −0.049	19. 0.607 −0.152	20. 0.322 −0.076
21. 0.873 − 0.425	22. 0.982 −0.079	23. 0.902 −0.353	24. 0.513 −0.36	25. 0.73 −0.472

Choose the letter of the word(s) that completes the sentence.

1. The sum of a group of numbers divided by the number of addends is called the ■.

    a. Mean   **b.** Median   **c.** Mode   **d.** None of these

2. The sale price of an item is found by subtracting the ■ from the regular price.

    a. Mark up   **b.** Sales tax   **c.** Sale price   **d.** None of these

3. Money placed by you into a savings or a checking account is called ■.

    a. A deposit   **b.** A withdrawal
    c. Interest   **d.** None of these

4. When interest is compounded quarterly, it is paid to you ■ times per year.

    a. One   **b.** Two   **c.** Four   **d.** None of these

5. On a credit card statement, the ■ is any of the last balance that was not paid.

    a. Finance charge   **b.** New balance
    c. Unpaid balance   **d.** None of these

Select the best estimated answer.

6. $4.89 + 0.4 + 1.39$ **a.** 3   **b.** 4   **c.** 5.4   **d.** 6.4

7. $289.7 - 35.2$ **a.** 200   **b.** 240   **c.** 260   **d.** 340

8. 6×3.7 **a.** 2.4   **b.** 10   **c.** 24   **d.** 30

9. $\$63.84 \div 19$ **a.** $2.00   **b.** $2.50   **c.** $3.00   **d.** $4.00

Compute.

10. $9.3 + 6.3 + 5.4$

    a. 20   **b.** 21   **c.** 21.1   **d.** None of these

11. $5,700 - 923$

    a. 4,777   **b.** 4,823   **c.** 5,200   **d.** None of these

12. 6×7.3

    a. 42   **b.** 42.8   **c.** 43.8   **d.** None of these

13. $3\overline{)9{,}270}$

    a. 309   **b.** 3,090   **c.** 3,090 R 1   **d.** None of these

14. $4\overline{)6.8}$

    a. 1.2   **b.** 1.4   **c.** 2   **d.** None of these

Solve.

15. This week, Rose worked 3 h on Monday, $5\frac{1}{2}$ h on Wednesday, and $4\frac{3}{4}$ h on Friday. Her hourly wage is $15. How much did she earn this week?

    a. $127.50   **b.** $198.75   **c.** $205   **d.** None of these

16. Jean bought a tee-shirt for $7.98, a tape for $6.95, a sweatshirt for $11.50, and a card for $0.85. Find the total cost of her purchases.

    a. $26.43   **b.** $27.25   **c.** $30   **d.** None of these

17. The regular price of a clock radio is $17.90. This week it is on sale for 20% off. Find the sale price.

    a. $14.32   **b.** $15.32   **c.** $17   **d.** None of these

18. Frank's savings account balance was $450. He withdrew $75 one week and deposited $100 the next week. He then withdrew $25. Then the bank posted interest of $8.36. What is his new balance?

    a. $400   **b.** $450   **c.** $458.36   **d.** None of these

19. The regular price of a sofa is $575. Leon bought it on an installment plan. With no down payment, he agreed to pay $55 per mo for 12 mo. What was his finance charge?

    a. $75   **b.** $85   **c.** $660   **d.** None of these

20. A package of pencils contains 12 pencils. There are 175 students taking a test. If each student gets 1 pencil, how many packages are needed?

    a. 10   **b.** 14   **c.** 15   **d.** None of these

THINKING ABOUT MATH

1. It costs $5.50 to rent golf clubs and $3.75 to rent a cart at the golf course. The pro shop is selling a set of used clubs with bag for $50. If you plan to play golf at least 6 times this season, should you buy the used set of clubs?

2. Town A has a 6% sales tax on clothing. Town B in another state has no sales tax on clothing. If you plan to buy a jacket for $50, is it better to buy it in Town B? Explain why or why not.

Add or subtract.

1. $145 + $567　　**2.** $116.85 + $203.97　　**3.** $409.87 + $90.16

4. $746 − $219　　**5.** $378.26 − $45.13　　**6.** $906.47 − $514.53

Multiply.

7. 6 × $225　　**8.** 15 × $204　　**9.** 9 × $213.05

10. 16 × $305.56　　**11.** 27 × $209.83　　**12.** 51 × $519.76

Find the answer to the nearest cent.

13. 7% of $95

14. 15% of $140.60

15. 8.5% of $219

16. 16.4% of $319.65

Divide. Round to the nearest tenth.

17. 214 ÷ 5　　　　**18.** 317 ÷ 6　　　　**19.** 403 ÷ 7

20. 347 ÷ 12　　　**21.** 518 ÷ 16　　　**22.** 607 ÷ 23

23. 287 ÷ 2.8　　　**24.** 417 ÷ 3.6　　　**25.** 235 ÷ 9.7

26. 2,087 ÷ 4.6　　**27.** 1,897 ÷ 10.8　　**28.** 4,387 ÷ 19.6

Use the price list. Find the cost.

29. 1 mirror

30. 1 set of bumper guards

31. 2 tail lights

32. 5 car deodorizers

33. 2 headlights and 1 set of floor mats

34. 4 seat cushions, 1 tail light, and 3 car deodorizers

AUTO SUPPLY SHOP - PRICE LIST	
Bumper guards	$89.^{95}
Headlight	$47.^{85}
Floor mats	$40.^{59}
Mirror	$28.^{50}
Tail light	$29.^{75}
Seat cushion	$18.^{95}
Car deodorizer	$ 3.^{75}

Chapter 9

AUTOMOBILE EXPENSES

When buying a car, some people look at new as well as used cars. What information is needed before deciding which to buy?

An **automobile loan** is a secured loan. A bank or other lender actually holds **title** to the car until the loan is repaid. When you buy a car, you need to determine how much you need to finance (borrow).

EXAMPLE 1

The cost of a car, with sales tax and registration fees, is $12,036.47. You get a trade-in allowance of $1,250 for your old car and you put $2,000 down in cash. How much do you need to finance?

1. Add to find the down payment. $1,250 + $2,000 = $3,250

2. Subtract to find the amount to be financed. $12,036.47 − $3,250 = $8,786.47

You need to finance $8,786.47.

You need to include the finance charge when determining the total cost of the car.

EXAMPLE 2

You borrow $8,786.47 at $10\frac{1}{4}$% for 5 y.

Find the finance charge (interest) and the total cost of the car.

THINK: Use the chart to find the monthly payments.

$10\frac{1}{4}$% APR	Monthly payments per $100
5 y (60 mo) $2.14	

1. Find the finance charge.
   - Find the number of $100 to be financed. $8,786.47 ÷ $100 = 87.8647
   - Multiply to find the monthly payment.   87.8647 × $2.14 = $188.03045 ≈ $188.03
   - Multiply to find the total amount to be repaid over 60 mo.   60 × $188.03 = $11,281.80
   - Subtract to find the finance charge. $11,281.80 − $8,786.47 = $2,495.33

The finance charge is $2,495.33.

2. Add to find the total cost of the car.

THINK: Cost from Example 1 was $12,036.47. $12,036.47 + $2,495.33 = $14,531.80

The total cost of the car is $14,531.80.

FOR DISCUSSION

Most new-car dealers also arrange car loans. Suppose that a car dealer
offers a very low interest rate. Does that necessarily mean that
the total cost of the car will be less than if the interest rate were higher? Explain.

PRACTICE EXERCISES   Remember to estimate whenever you use your calculator.

Complete the table.

Cost of car	Down payment	Amount to be financed	Monthly payment	No. of months	Amount to be repaid	Finance charge	Total cost
$12,090	$3,400	$8,690	$187.86	60	$11,271.60	$2,581.60	$14,671.60
$13,789	$2,600	1. ■	$286.48	48	2. ■	3. ■	4. ■
$10,908	$5,650	5. ■	$171.64	36	6. ■	7. ■	8. ■
$11,678	$4,270	9. ■	$190.74	48	10. ■	11. ■	12. ■
$9,624	$700	13. ■	$193.84	60	14. ■	15. ■	16. ■
$12,476	$3,075	17. ■	$242.06	48	18. ■	19. ■	20. ■
$14,980	$5,690	21. ■	$303.26	36	22. ■	23. ■	24. ■
$13,678	$4,875	25. ■	$226.66	48	26. ■	27. ■	28. ■
$15,823	$6,950	29. ■	$289.65	60	30. ■	31. ■	32. ■

Use the monthly payment table. Find the finance charge and the total cost.

33. Price: $12,876
    Down payment: $2,855
    Loan rate: $10\frac{1}{2}\%$ for 4 y

34. Price: $10,098
    Down payment: $4,980
    Loan rate: 7.9% for 3 y

35. Price: $15,708
    Down payment: $1,800
    Loan rate: 12.6% for 5 y

36. Price: $18,500
    Down payment: $6,000
    Loan rate: 10.5% for 4 y

MONTHLY PAYMENT PER $100

APR	3 y	4 y	5 y
7.9%	$3.13	$2.44	$2.02
$10\frac{1}{2}\%$	$3.25	$2.56	$2.15
12.6%	$3.35	$2.66	$2.25

The **Environmental Protection Agency (EPA)** does tests to find out how many miles a car can go on a gallon of gasoline (mi per gal, or **mpg**). The estimated highway and city mileage ratings are shown on a new-car sticker. The actual gasoline mileage may be different from the EPA estimates. You can compute a car's mpg.

MPG = MILES DRIVEN ÷ GALLONS OF GASOLINE USED

EXAMPLE 1

Your odometer read 12,386 mi. You drove your car until the odometer read 16,282 mi and the car used 203 gal of gasoline. About how many miles per gallon has your car been getting?

1. Subtract to find how far you drove.

$$16,282 \text{ mi} - 12,386 \text{ mi} = 3,896 \text{ mi}$$

2. Estimate the mpg.

THINK: 3,896 mi is about 4,000 mi.
203 gal is about 200 gal. $4,000 \text{ mi} \div 200 \text{ gal} = 20 \text{ mpg}$

Your car has been getting about 20 mpg.

You can compute the approximate cost of gasoline for a trip. Cost per gallon can be written as **cpg**.

COST = (MILES DRIVEN ÷ MPG) × CPG

EXAMPLE 2

You are planning to drive 672 mi on a trip. Your car gets about 20 mpg. Gasoline costs $1.129 per gal (cpg = $1.129). About how much will gasoline for the trip cost?

1. Divide to find number of gallons.

$$672 \text{ mi} \div 20 \text{ mpg} = 33.6 \text{ gal}$$

2. Multiply to find the cost of the gasoline. Then round up to the nearest ten dollars.

$$33.6 \text{ gal} \times \$1.129 \text{ cpg} = \$37.9344 \approx \$40.00$$

The gasoline for a 672-mi trip will cost about $40.00.

You will have to pay for preventive maintenance and repairs for your car. **Preventive maintenance** is periodic servicing to prevent more-costly repairs. **Repairs** are made when something goes wrong. The table on page 173 shows the approximate costs of preventive maintenance and some common repairs for 5 cars during the first 3 y of driving.

ESTIMATED MAINTENANCE AND REPAIR COSTS—FIRST 3 YEARS

	Arrow	Boltan	Decade	Elice	Van
Preventive maintenance	$620	$926	$745	$713	$978
Water pump	$196	$277	$103	$207	$236
Alternator	$248	$416	$309	$298	$497
Brake pads	$113	$89	$94	$87	$143
Starter	$318	$228	$239	$258	$209

EXAMPLE 3 Steve wants to compare the maintenance and repair costs of cars before he buys. He computes the total cost of maintenance and one of each repair for the Arrow and the Decade. Which car has the lower maintenance and repair cost?

1. Add the Arrow costs. $620 + $196 + $248 + $113 + $318 = $1,495

2. Add the Decade costs. $745 + $103 + $309 + $94 + $239 = $1,490

Because $1,490 < $1,495, the Decade has the lower cost.

FOR DISCUSSION

1. Lighter cars and smaller engines usually mean better gas mileage. How else could the gas mileage of a car be improved?

2. Why is it important to get a written estimate before any repair work is done? What other steps could you take to ensure that maintenance and repairs are done correctly?

Remember to estimate whenever you use your calculator.

Find the mileage. Estimate the mpg.

	Car A	Car B	Car C	Car D	Car E	Car F
1st Odometer reading	2,367	10,567	18,972	34,502	68,087	106,587
2nd Odometer reading	2,566	12,923	22,028	40,100	76,594	120,688
Miles driven	1. ■	2. ■	3. ■	4. ■	5. ■	6. ■
Gallons of gasoline used	11	97	223	272	509	921
Mpg	7. ■	8. ■	9. ■	10. ■	11. ■	12. ■

Find the approximate cost of gasoline for an 800-mi trip. Round up to
the nearest ten dollars. Use the estimated mpg from the table above.

	Car A	Car B	Car C	Car D	Car E	Car F
Brand Y $0.939/gal	13. ■	14. ■	15. ■	16. ■	17. ■	18. ■
Brand Z $1.102/gal	19. ■	20. ■	21. ■	22. ■	23. ■	24. ■

Use the maintenance and repair table on page 173. Solve.

25. Which car has the highest combined cost of maintenance and repairs?

26. Which car has the lowest combined cost of maintenance and repairs?

27. Barbara takes her Van in to have the water pump and the brake pads fixed. There is a 7% sales tax on the cost of repairs. What is the total cost?

28. Roy has the alternator and the starter fixed on his Decade. There is a 9% sales tax on the cost of repairs. What is the total cost?

EXTENSION   Depreciation

Cars lose some of their value every month. This loss in value is called
depreciation. The average car depreciates about 45% after 4 y.

A car originally cost $12,000. About what will it be worth after 4 y?

$0.45 \times \$12,000 = \$5,400$ estimated amount of depreciation

$\$12,000 - \$5,400 = \$6,600$ estimated value in 4 y

Find the estimated amount of depreciation and the depreciated value in 4 y.

1. Original cost: $14,500

2. Original cost: $12,380

3. Original cost: $18,087

4. Original cost: $10,666

5. Original cost: $15,075

6. Original cost: $24,840

For your own protection, you should not drive a car unless you have **automobile insurance.** Many states require that you be insured. An insurance company will pay, within limits, for the costs of an accident.

Liability insurance covers you for injury to others or for damage to their property. Liability insurance is identified by the amounts of coverage.

LIABILITY INSURANCE

Type	Amount	Yearly base premium
Bodily injury	25/50	$144.50
	50/100	$161.25
	100/300	$176.80
Property damage	25	$78.60
	50	$89.90
	100	$103.45

```
100/300/50          Property damage
    |              →$50,000 for damage
    |                 to other's property
    ↓
Bodily injury
$100,000 maximum   →$300,000 maximum
to each person       for all injuries
you injure           in 1 accident
```

The **yearly base premium** depends on the coverage you choose.

EXAMPLE 1

You buy 100/300/50 liability insurance. What is the yearly base premium?

THINK: Locate the premiums in the table.

Add to find the total base premium. $176.80 + $89.90 = $266.70

The yearly base liability premium is $266.70.

Collision insurance pays for damage to your car caused by an accident. **Comprehensive insurance** pays for damage to or losses from your car caused by fire, theft, vandalism, and weather. Both types of insurance have **deductibles.** The premiums depend on the deductibles.

EXAMPLE 2

You buy $200-deductible collision insurance and $100-deductible comprehensive insurance. What is the total yearly premium?

THINK: Locate the premiums in the table.

Add to find the total base premium.

$141.71 + $56.90 = $198.61

The total yearly base premium is $198.61.

COLLISION/COMPREHENSIVE YEARLY BASE PREMIUMS

Deductible	Collision	Comprehensive
$50	$197.38	$72.65
$100	$183.42	$56.90
$200	$141.71	Not available

Insurance policies are **rated** on a number of factors that can increase the cost of the base premium. These factors are your age, gender, driving record, and purpose for driving.

The graphs below show the ratings, by age and gender, for unmarried drivers under age 25.

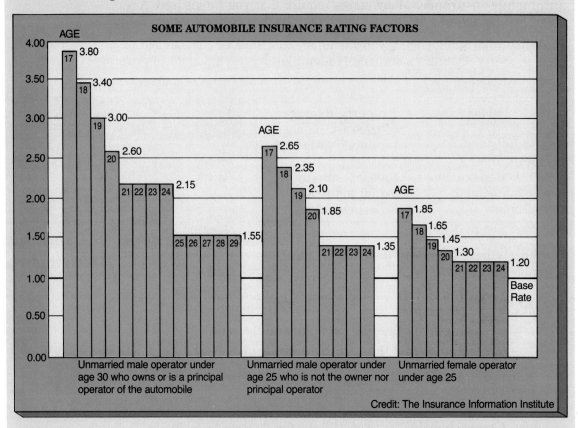

SOME AUTOMOBILE INSURANCE RATING FACTORS

Credit: The Insurance Information Institute

To find the total premium, multiply the base premium by the rating factor.

EXAMPLE 3   George purchased 50/100/25 liability insurance, $100-deductible collision insurance, and $50-deductible comprehensive insurance. George is a 17-year-old male who drives his parents' car. What is his total premium for those coverages?

1. Add to find the total base premium.
   THINK: Find the premiums in the tables on page 175.

$$\$161.25 + \$78.60 + \$183.42 + \$72.65 = \$495.92$$

2. Multiply the base premium by the rating factor.
   THINK: Find the rating factor on the graph. (2.65)

$$2.65 \times \$495.92 = \$1,314.188$$

George's total yearly premium is $1,314.19.

1. How would you decide whether to get a higher or a lower deductible for collision and comprehensive insurance?

2. Why do you think younger people and men have higher rating factors?

PRACTICE EXERCISES   Remember to estimate whenever you use your calculator.

Use the rate tables on page 175. Find the total yearly base premium.

1. Liability: 25/50/25
   Collision: $100 deductible
   Comprehensive: $50 deductible

2. Liability: 50/100/50
   Collision: $200 deductible
   Comprehensive: $50 deductible

3. Liability: 100/300/100
   Collision: $50 deductible
   Comprehensive: $100 deductible

4. Liability: 50/100/25
   Collision: $100 deductible
   Comprehensive: $100 deductible

Use the rating factors graph on page 176. Find the rating factor.

5. Unmarried male, 18
   Drives his own car

6. Unmarried male, 19
   Drives parents' car

7. Unmarried female, 17

8. Unmarried female, 19

9. Unmarried male, 24
   Drives his own car

10. Unmarried male, 24
    Drives parents' car

Complete the table.

Driver	Liability	Yearly base premium	Collision deductible	Yearly base premium	Compre-hensive deductible	Yearly base premium	Total base premium	Rating factor	Total premium
Male, 18, owns car	25/50/25	11. ■	$100	12. ■	$50	13. ■	14. ■	15. ■	16. ■
Female, 17	100/300/100	17. ■	$50	18. ■	$100	19. ■	20. ■	21. ■	22. ■
Male, 19, not owner	50/100/50	23. ■	$200	24. ■	$50	25. ■	26. ■	27. ■	28. ■
Female, 18	25/50/50	29. ■	$50	30. ■	$50	31. ■	32. ■	33. ■	34. ■
Male, 18, not owner	100/300/50	35. ■	$200	36. ■	$100	37. ■	38. ■	39. ■	40. ■
Female, 20	25/50/50	41. ■	$100	42. ■	$50	43. ■	44. ■	45. ■	46. ■

One of your teachers rented a car for 1 d.

The cost of a car rental often includes a **daily rate** and a **mileage charge.**

DO DRIVE CAR RENTAL		
Car	Daily rate	Cost per mile
Compact	$29	$0.26
Midsize	$36	$0.31
Luxury	$41	$0.35
Van	$48	$0.41
100 FREE MILES EACH DAY		

EXAMPLE 1 The teacher rented a midsize car. The odometer read 38,546 mi when the car was taken and 38,724 mi when the car was brought back. What did the rental car cost?

THINK: Find the daily rate and the mileage charge for a midsize car.

1. Find the mileage charge.
   - Subtract to find the number of miles.
   - Subtract to find the number of chargeable miles.
   - Multiply to find the mileage charge.

2. Add to find the total cost.

$$38,724\,\text{mi} - 38,546\,\text{mi} = 178\,\text{mi}$$

$$178\,\text{mi} - 100\,\text{mi} = 78\,\text{mi}$$

$$78 \times \$0.31 = \$24.18$$

$$\$36 + \$24.18 = \$60.18$$

The rental car cost $60.18.

To find approximate rental-car costs, estimate the number of miles you will travel.

EXAMPLE 2 The coach of the high-school debating team plans to rent a van for 4 d to take the team from Houston to Dallas and back. The estimated one-way mileage is 270 mi. About how much will it cost to rent the van?

1. Find the mileage charge.
   - Find the total mileage.
   - Subtract to find the chargeable mileage.
     THINK: 4 d × 100 mi = 400 mi free
   - Multiply to find the mileage charge.

2. Multiply to find the total daily-rate charge.

3. Add to find the total cost. Then round up.

$$2 \times 270\,\text{mi} = 540\,\text{mi}$$

$$540\,\text{mi} - 400\,\text{mi} = 140\,\text{mi}$$

$$140 \times \$0.41 = \$57.40$$

$$4 \times \$48 = \$192$$

$$\$192 + \$57.40 = \$249.40 \approx \$300.00$$

It will cost about $300.00 to rent the van.

1. Why do rental-car companies usually refuse to rent cars to people under age 25?

2. Why do rental-car companies require a cash deposit or a blank, signed credit card slip when a car is rented?

PRACTICE EXERCISES   Remember to estimate whenever you use your calculator.

Use the rate table on page 178. Find the rental cost.

1. Car: Compact
   Days: 1
   Mileage: 207

2. Car: Midsize
   Days: 2
   Mileage: 623

3. Car: Van
   Days: 6
   Mileage: 1,023

4. Car: Luxury
   Days: 3
   Mileage: 678

Complete the table.

Car	Odometer		Days	Total daily-rate charge	Chargeable mileage	Mileage charge	Total cost
	Begin	End					
Midsize	29,036	29,236	1	5. ■	6. ■	7. ■	8. ■
Compact	40,208	41,140	4	9. ■	10. ■	11. ■	12. ■
Van	51,208	53,040	2	13. ■	14. ■	15. ■	16. ■
Luxury	18,907	19,345	7	17. ■	18. ■	19. ■	20. ■
Van	9,308	10,506	5	21. ■	22. ■	23. ■	24. ■
Midsize	29,938	30,501	3	25. ■	26. ■	27. ■	28. ■

Use the rate table on page 178. Approximate the rental cost.

29. Liz plans to rent a compact car to travel from Los Angeles to San Francisco and back. The estimated one-way mileage is 500 mi. The trip will take 6 d.

30. Eric is going to rent a midsize car to travel from Cincinnati to St. Louis and back. The estimated one-way mileage is 450 mi. The trip will take 5 d.

31. Lou wants to rent a luxury car to drive from Atlanta to Dallas and back. The estimated one-way mileage is 1,000 mi. The trip will take 7 d.

32. The athletic director needs to rent 2 vans to travel from Washington DC, to St. Louis and back. The estimated one-way mileage is 1,800 mi. The trip will take 5 d.

9.6 CHOOSING A NEW CAR

DECISION
MAKING

Comparison shopping can help you make sure that the car you buy fits within your budget and provides you with the level of safety you want and can afford.

PROBLEM

Theresa had been looking at new cars for several weeks. She found 3 cars that she liked. She listed the features of each car to help her decide which one to buy. Each car has comparable optional equipment.

> **CAR A**
> Price: $14,509.86
> mpg: 19   Uses economy unleaded at $1.019 per gal
> Estimated preventive maintenance and repair costs for 3 y: $2,180
> Insurance costs: $1,653 per y
> Safety: Good driver protection
>   Good passenger protection
>
> **CAR B**
> Price: $12,804.60
> mpg: 22   Uses super unleaded at $1.149 per gal
> Estimated preventive maintenance and repair costs for 3 y: $2,320
> Insurance costs: $1,708 per y
> Safety: Good driver protection
>   Moderate passenger protection
>
> **CAR C**
> Price: $10,987.00
> mpg: 18.5   Uses regular unleaded at $1.039 per gal
> Estimated preventive maintenance and repair costs for 3 y: $1,978
> Insurance costs: $2,018 per y
> Safety: Moderate driver protection
>   Moderate passenger protection

DECISION-MAKING FACTORS

Price	Monthly loan payment	Gasoline costs
Maintenance/repair costs	Cost per mile	Safety

DECISION-MAKING COMPARISONS

Compare the 3 cars by completing the table.

- Assume that Theresa will drive 15,000 mi per y.
- Theresa will put $2,000 down and finance the rest with a 4-y loan at $10\frac{1}{2}\%$. Use the monthly payment table on page 171.
- To find the total annual car expenses:
  Add one year's car payments, gasoline costs, insurance costs, and $\frac{1}{3}$ of the maintenance and repair costs.
- To find the cost per mile, divide the annual expenses by 15,000.

Factors	Car A	Car B	Car C
Price	1. ■	$12,804.60	2. ■
Monthly loan payment	$320.25	3. ■	4. ■
Gas costs for 1 y	5. ■	6. ■	$842.43
Maintenance/repair costs for 1 y	7. ■	$773.33	8. ■
Total annual expense	$7,027.14	9. ■	10. ■
Cost per mile	$0.47	11. ■	12. ■
Safety	13. ■	14. ■	Driver: Moderate Passenger: Moderate

MAKING THE DECISIONS

Which car should Theresa buy if the only factor were:

15. Price?

16. Monthly loan payment?

17. Gasoline costs?

18. Maintenance/repair costs?

19. Cost per mile?

20. Safety?

21. How much lower would Theresa's annual maintenance/repair costs be if she bought Car C instead of Car A?

22. How much would she save each year by choosing the car with the lowest annual expense over the car with the highest annual expense?

23. How much lower would her monthly payments be if she bought Car C instead of Car B?

24. How much would she save on gasoline each year if she bought Car B instead of Car A?

25. Should Theresa base her decision on the price of the car alone? Why or why not?

26. Which car would you buy? Why?

CHAPTER REVIEW

Vocabulary   Choose the letter of the word(s) that completes the sentence.

1. The price you pay for a car after making a deal with the car dealer is the ▪. [168]

   a. Negotiated price   **b.** Sticker price   **c.** Trade-in allowance

2. The amount of money you can subtract from the price of a new car by turning in your old car is the ▪. [168]

   a. Negotiated price   **b.** Sticker price   **c.** Trade-in allowance

3. The type of automobile insurance that covers you for injury to others or for damage to their property is called ▪. [175]

   a. Liability   **b.** Collision   **c.** Comprehensive

Skills   Find the amount owed for the car.   [168]

4. Negotiated price: $12,750
   Sales tax: 8.5%
   Registration fee: $45

5. Negotiated price: $14,879
   Trade-in allowance: $985
   Sales tax: 7%
   Registration fee: $38.75

Find the answer.

6. Rafael drove 783 mi on 45 gal of gasoline. What is his estimated mpg?   [172]

7. Mary drove 1,853 mi on 80 gal of gasoline. What is her estimated mpg?   [172]

8. Louise spent $125 for a new water pump and $98 for new brake pads. There is a 6% sales tax on the cost of repairs. What was her total cost?   [172]

9. Use the insurance rate tables on page 175. Abe purchased 25/50/100 liability insurance, $200 deductible collision insurance, and $100 deductible comprehensive insurance. What is his total yearly base premium?   [175]

10. Use the insurance rate table on page 175 and the rating factors graph on page 176. How much would 100/300/100 liability insurance cost an 18-year-old who drives his parents' car?   [175]

11. Use the car rental table on page 178. How much would it cost Dara to rent a compact car for 2 d and drive 800 mi?   [178]

12. Use the car rental table on page 178. How much would it cost Victoria to rent a luxury car for 6 d and drive 1,256 mi?   [178]

13. Use the car rental table on page 178. How much would it cost Paul to rent a van for 3 d and drive 709 mi?   [178]

Find the amount owed for the car.

1. Negotiated price: $14,806.00
   Sales tax: 7%
   Registration fee: $55.00

2. Negotiated price: $10,937.00
   Trade-in allowance: $950.00
   Sales tax: 6.7%
   Registration fee: $87.50

Estimate the mpg.

3. Miles driven: 883.2
   Gallons of gasoline used: 28

4. Miles driven: 963.6
   Gallons of gasoline used: 46.5

Use the insurance rate tables on page 175. Find the total yearly base premium.

5. Liability: 50/100/50
   Collision: $100 deductible
   Comprehensive: $50 deductible

6. Liability: 100/300/100
   Collision: $50 deductible
   Comprehensive: $100 deductible

Use the insurance rate tables on page 175 and the rating factors graph
on page 176. Find the yearly total premium.

7. How much would 25/50/50 liability
   insurance cost a 20-year-old female
   driver?

8. How much would $100-deductible
   collision insurance cost an 18-year-old
   male driver who drives his parents'
   car?

Use the car rental rate table at the right.
Find the car rental cost.

9. Car: Luxury
   Days: 4
   Mileage: 916

10. Car: Midsize
    Days: 7
    Mileage: 1,308

EASY DRIVE CAR RENTAL

Car	Daily rate	Cost per mile
Compact	$25	$0.28
Midsize	$34	$0.35
Luxury	$40	$0.40
50 FREE MILES EACH DAY		

Solve.

11. Brenda drives a car that gets about
    20 mpg. Gas costs $1.079 per gal.
    About how much will gas cost to
    drive 5,000 mi? Round the cost up.

12. Enrico bought a car for $16,489. He
    put down $2,800 and financed the
    rest. He will make a car payment of
    $307.20 each month for 48 mo. What
    is the total cost of the car?

MONEY TIPS

Renting a car can cost less if you take advantage of mid-week rates and package rates.

LET'S LOOK AT THE FACTS

You can save money by renting a car on certain days or for longer periods of time with special **packages.** Study the rates given below.

AMERICANA RENT-A-CAR COMPANY

Category	Days	Rate
Regular	Mon-Tues-Wed-Thurs	$48 a day
Regular	Fri-Sat-Sun	$75 a day
Weekender Special	Fri through Sun	$150
Week O' Wheels	Mon through Sun	$308

LET'S DISCUSS WHY

1. Which days are considered mid-week days? Weekend days?

2. Why do people rent cars on weekdays? Why do they rent cars on weekends?

3. At regular rates, would it cost more to rent a car from Monday through Thursday or from Friday through Sunday? How much more?

4. Compare the cost of renting a car for 7 d by using all of the rates and packages shown above. Which package or combination of rates would cost the most? The least?

5. How much would you save by using the Weekender Special package instead of regular weekend day rates to rent a car for Friday, Saturday, and Sunday?

6. Rental rates cover basic rental only. What other considerations might increase or decrease your total rental cost?

LET'S SEE WHAT YOU WOULD DO

7. You have $150 and want to rent a car for the weekend. Which rate would give you the most rental time for your money?

8. You need to rent a car to transport your belongings to the college dormitory. The move could take either 3 or 4 d. You need to reserve the car in advance. What is the least expensive way to rent the car for 3 d? For 4 d?

CALCULATOR THE CONSTANT FEATURE

Many calculators have a **constant arithmetic feature.** This feature allows you to repeatedly add, subtract, multiply, or divide a certain number each time you press the is-equal-to key, $\boxed{=}$.

In addition, subtraction, and division, the number entered *after* the operation symbol becomes the constant.

Procedure	Calculator Entry	Calculator Display
Add: 7 + 4 + 4 + 4	$\boxed{7}\boxed{+}\boxed{4}\boxed{=}\boxed{=}\boxed{=}$	19.
Subtract: 72 − 9 − 9	$\boxed{7}\boxed{2}\boxed{-}\boxed{9}\boxed{=}\boxed{=}$	54.
Divide: 450 ÷ 5 ÷ 5 ÷ 5	$\boxed{4}\boxed{5}\boxed{0}\boxed{÷}\boxed{5}\boxed{=}\boxed{=}\boxed{=}$	3.6

Try each of the above examples on your calculator. In each case, do you get the same answer as shown?

In multiplication, the calculator works differently. The number entered *before* the operation symbol becomes the constant.

Procedure	Calculator Entry	Calculator Display
Multiply: 6 × 2 × 6 × 6	$\boxed{6}\boxed{×}\boxed{2}\boxed{=}\boxed{=}\boxed{=}$	432.
Multiply: 5 × 5 × 5 × 5 × 5	$\boxed{5}\boxed{×}\boxed{=}\boxed{=}\boxed{=}\boxed{=}$	3125.

Try each of the above multiplication examples on your calculator. In each case, do you get the same answer as shown?

Write the final display answer.

1. $\boxed{3}\boxed{9}\boxed{+}\boxed{8}\boxed{=}\boxed{=}$

2. $\boxed{8}\boxed{.}\boxed{6}\boxed{-}\boxed{.}\boxed{5}\boxed{=}\boxed{=}\boxed{=}$

3. $\boxed{3}\boxed{×}\boxed{2}\boxed{.}\boxed{5}\boxed{=}\boxed{=}\boxed{=}\boxed{=}$

4. $\boxed{6}\boxed{4}\boxed{0}\boxed{÷}\boxed{4}\boxed{=}\boxed{=}\boxed{=}$

5. $\boxed{4}\boxed{.}\boxed{8}\boxed{3}\boxed{+}\boxed{.}\boxed{5}\boxed{=}\boxed{=}\boxed{=}\boxed{=}$

6. $\boxed{7}\boxed{-}\boxed{.}\boxed{3}\boxed{2}\boxed{=}\boxed{=}\boxed{=}\boxed{=}\boxed{=}$

7. $\boxed{8}\boxed{.}\boxed{6}\boxed{2}\boxed{÷}\boxed{.}\boxed{2}\boxed{=}\boxed{=}\boxed{=}$

8. $\boxed{1}\boxed{.}\boxed{7}\boxed{×}\boxed{2}\boxed{.}\boxed{5}\boxed{=}\boxed{=}\boxed{=}\boxed{=}$

Use your calculator's constant feature to complete each pattern.

9. 15, 21, 27, ■, ■, ■

10. 59, 48, 37, ■, ■, ■

11. 3, 6, 18, ■, ■, ■

12. 729, 243, 81, ■, ■, ■

Estimate the sum or difference.

1. 593 + 435
2. 1,495 + 2,187
3. 3,288 + 1,788
4. 424 − 285
5. 3,832 − 675
6. 4,248 − 2,765

Find the answer.

7. How much greater is 1,754 + 854 than 2,487?

8. How much greater is 2,395 + 1,734 than 3,639?

Estimate the quotient.

9. 447 ÷ 50
10. 2,857 ÷ 50
11. 1,845 ÷ 60
12. 4,189 ÷ 52

Multiply or divide.

13. 4 × $379
14. 3 × $758
15. 15 × 80¢
16. 7 × 75¢

17. 800 ÷ 25
18. 750 ÷ 30
19. 1,500 ÷ 25
20. 480 ÷ 15

Find the elapsed time.

21. From 10:30 A.M. to 4:45 P.M.
22. From 7:43 A.M. to 11:07 A.M.

23. From 9:41 A.M. to 7:15 P.M.
24. From 1:15 P.M. to 9:10 P.M.

Complete. Use the Time Zones table at the right.

25. At 10 A.M. MST, it is ▩ CST.
26. At 6 P.M. CST, it is ▩ PST.
27. At 12 noon PST, it is ▩ EST.
28. At 12 noon EST, it is ▩ PST.

TIME ZONES			
Pacific Standard Time (PST)	Mountain Standard Time (MST)	Central Standard Time (CST)	Eastern Standard Time (EST)
11 A.M.	12 noon	1 P.M.	2 P.M.

Find the answer to the nearest cent.

29. 15% of $11.75
30. 20% of $15.35

31. 5% of $82.60
32. 15% of $23.89

33. 10% of $39.50
34. 20% of $52.50

35. 5% of $39.00
36. 25% of $36.40

10
TRANSPORTATION

When planning a vacation, you need to think about transportation, meals, lodging, and entertainment. Suppose you have a limited budget. How could you keep your travel expenses down?

10.1 ESTIMATING DISTANCES AND TRAVEL TIMES

Mileage charts are very useful for planning trips. Suppose you are planning a trip from Detroit to Washington, DC, with a stop in Cincinnati.

EXAMPLE 1 How many miles will you need to drive?

		Estimate	**Actual**
1. Use the chart to find each distance.			
Detroit to Cincinnati: 259 mi		300 mi	259 mi
Cincinnati to Washington: 481 mi		+500 mi	+481 mi
2. Add to find the total mileage.		800 mi	740 mi

You will drive about 800 mi, or exactly 740 mi.

EXAMPLE 2 How much longer is the trip with the stop in Cincinnati than the direct route to Washington, DC?

		Estimate	**Actual**
1. Use the chart to find each distance.			
Detroit to Cincinnati to Washington: 740 mi		700 mi	740 mi
Detroit to Washington: 506 mi		−500 mi	−506 mi
2. Subtract to find the difference.		200 mi	234 mi

The trip is about 200 mi longer, or exactly 234 mi longer.

EXAMPLE 3 If you plan to drive at an average speed of 50 mi per h, about how long will it take to make the trip with the stop in Cincinnati?

THINK: DISTANCE = RATE × TIME, SO TIME = DISTANCE ÷ RATE

Round and divide to find the time.   700 ÷ 50 = 14

The trip should take about 14 h of driving time.

DRIVING MILEAGE CHART

	ATLANTA, GA	BOSTON, MA	CHICAGO, IL	CINCINNATI, OH	DALLAS, TX	DENVER, CO	DETROIT, MI	HOUSTON, TX	LOS ANGELES, CA	MIAMI, FL	NEW YORK, NY	PITTSBURGH, PA	ST. LOUIS, MO	SAN FRANCISCO, CA	SEATTLE, WA
ATLANTA, GA															
BOSTON, MA	1087														
CHICAGO, IL	674	963													
CINCINNATI, OH	440	840	287												
DALLAS, TX	795	1748	917	920											
DENVER, CO	1398	1949	996	1164	781										
DETROIT, MI	699	695	266	259	1143	1253									
HOUSTON, TX	788	1804	1067	1029	243	1019	1265								
LOS ANGELES, CA	2182	2978	2054	2179	1387	1059	2311	1538							
MIAMI, FL	655	1504	1329	1095	1300	2037	1352	1190	2687						
NEW YORK, NY	841	206	802	647	1552	1771	637	1608	2786	1308					
PITTSBURGH, PA	687	561	452	287	1204	1411	287	1313	2426	1200	368				
ST. LOUIS, MO	541	1141	289	340	630	857	513	779	1845	1196	948	588			
SAN FRANCISCO, CA	2496	3095	2142	2362	1753	1235	2399	1912	379	3053	2934	2578	2089		
SEATTLE, WA	2616	2976	2013	2300	2078	1307	2279	2274	1131	3273	2815	2465	2081	808	
WASHINGTON, DC	608	429	671	481	1319	1616	506	1375	2631	1075	233	221	793	2799	2684

Why is the highway distance between 2 cities usually more than the air distance?

PRACTICE EXERCISES   Remember to estimate whenever you use your calculator.

Use the mileage chart to find the driving distance for the trip.

1. Los Angeles to Dallas

2. Denver to St. Louis

3. Detroit to Pittsburgh to Washington, DC

4. Seattle to San Francisco to Los Angeles

Use the mileage chart to estimate the driving distance for the trip.

5. New York to Pittsburgh to St. Louis

6. Houston to Denver to San Francisco

7. Boston to Cincinnati to Atlanta

8. Washington, DC, to Dallas to Los Angeles

Solve.

9. How much shorter is a direct trip from Boston to Chicago than one with a stop in New York?

10. How much longer is a trip from St. Louis to San Francisco with a stop in Denver than a direct trip?

11. How much shorter is a direct trip from Miami to Los Angeles than one with a stop in Houston?

12. How much longer is a trip from Detroit to Seattle with a stop in Cincinnati than a direct trip?

If you average 50 mi per h, estimate how long the trip will take.

13. Los Angeles to Dallas

14. Denver to St. Louis

15. New York to Pittsburgh to St. Louis

16. Boston to Cincinnati to Atlanta

17. Detroit to Pittsburgh to Washington, DC

18. Seattle to San Francisco to Los Angeles

19. Houston to Denver to San Francisco

20. Washington, DC, to Dallas to Los Angeles

Solve.

21. It took $5\frac{1}{4}$ h to drive to another city while averaging 52 mi per h. About how far did you drive?

22. At 60 mi per h, which city is most likely to be reached driving for 11 h from Washington, DC?

PROBLEM Solving STRATEGY

10.2 USING A MAP

Situation:

Paula is driving from Kearns to Granite Park using Route 173, Interstate 15, and Route 171. How far does she need to travel? Is there an alternate route?

Strategy:

Reading a map can help you to solve a problem.

KEY	
🛡15	Interstate Highway
🛡89	U.S. Highway
🛡181	State Highway
•	Town
→□	Highway Exit Number
•	Places to Visit

Applying the Strategy:

A. About how many miles is it from Kearns to Granite Park?

> **THINK:** Copy the *Miles* **map scale** on the edge of an index card. Use the card like a ruler. Place the card along the highways to be measured.

East from Kearns along (173) to (15) → about 5.0 mi

North on (15) to (171) → about 3.0 mi

East on (171) to Granite Park → +about 0.5 mi
about 8.5 mi

It is about 8.5 mi from Kearns to Granite Park.

B. Paula hears on the radio that Exit 301 on (173) is closed for repairs. What other way could she travel to Granite Park?

THINK: Look for an alternate route.

1. Which other highway is near Granite Park?

   (89)

2. In which direction would Paula travel on (89)?

   North

3. When (89) meets (171), which way should she turn to get to Granite Park?

   Left, or West

PRACTICE EXERCISES

Read the map to solve the problem.

Tony traveled from Murray to Millcreek. He used (89), (80), and (195).

1. About how far did he travel on (89)?

2. About how far did he travel on (80)?

3. About how far did he travel on (195)?

4. About how far did he travel all together?

Alice traveled from South Salt Lake directly south for about 3.5 mi. She then traveled directly east for about 5 mi.

5. Which highway that runs north and south runs through South Salt Lake?

6. Which highway crosses (89) at about 3.5 mi south of South Salt Lake?

7. Which town is located about 5 mi east of (89) on (266)?

8. Which town was Alice in?

About how far is it from:

9. Millcreek to Holladay using (195)?

10. Exit 15 to Exit 18 on (215)?

11. West Valley City to Granite Park using (171)?

12. Cottonwood to (181) along Highland Drive?

Solve.

13. Which highways would you use to travel from Granite Park to Taylorsville?

14. Bill wants to travel from West Jordan to West Valley City. He cannot use (15) because of an accident. Name 2 other ways he could get there.

10.3 BUS AND TRAIN TRAVEL

Buses and trains are convenient means of transportation that are used by many people to commute to work as well as to travel comfortably from city to city. Bus and train **schedules** provide information on routes, arrival and departure times, and frequency of service.

EXAMPLE 1

If you are in Atlanta and want to be in Greensboro before 6:00 P.M., which bus should you take? When does it depart?

Check the schedule by reading up:

    Bus #145 leaves Atlanta at 9:15 A.M. and arrives in Greensboro at 4:55 P.M.

    Bus #204 leaves Atlanta at 10:20 A.M. but does not arrive in Greensboro until 8:35 P.M.

You should take Bus #145, departing from Atlanta at 9:15 A.M.

EXAMPLE 2

How long does it take Bus #106 to get from Washington, DC, to Atlanta?

1. Check the schedule by reading down:

    The bus leaves at 7:10 A.M. and arrives at 5:30 P.M.

2. **THINK:** 7:10 A.M. is 4 h and 50 min before noon, and 5:30 P.M. is 5 h and 30 min after noon.

3. Add the times.   9 h and 80 min = 10 h and 20 min

It will take 10 h and 20 min to get to Atlanta.

BUS SCHEDULE				
Bus #	#106 Express	#145 Express	#167 Local	#204 Local
	Read Down	Read Up	Read Down	Read Up
Washington, DC	7:10a	7:05p	11:30a	11:55p
Manassas, VA			12:10p	11:10p
Culpepper, VA		6:10p	12:45p	10:50p
Monroe, VA	8:20a		1:05p	10:25p
Danville, VA			1:40p	9:45p
Greensboro, NC		4:55p	2:35p	8:35p
Salisbury, NC			4:10p	7:00p
Charlotte, NC	11:55a	3:05p	5:50p	5:15p
Spartanburg, SC			8:15p	3:00p
Greenville, SC	2:35p		9:10p	2:05p
Clemson, GA		11:10a	10:25p	12:45p
Toccoa, GA			11:05p	11:55a
Atlanta, GA	5:30p	9:15a	12:45a	10:20a

Train and bus schedules are usually printed in similar ways.

EXAMPLE 3 You are in Philadelphia on a Friday. The earliest you can catch a train to Washington, DC, is noon. What is the earliest you can arrive in Washington?

Check the schedule:

Look across from Philadelphia to find the first train after noon. This is Train #222. Read down to find when this train arrives in Washington.

The #222 arrives in Washington at 1:55 P.M.

EXAMPLE 4 How long does it take Train #179 to get from New Haven to Philadelphia?

1. Check the schedule:

Train #179 leaves New Haven at 9:25 A.M. and arrives in Philadelphia at 12:59 P.M.

2. THINK: 9:25 A.M. is 2 h and 35 min before noon and 12:59 P.M. is 1 min less than an hour after noon.

3. Add mentally. 2 h and 35 min plus 1 h less 1 min = 3 h and 34 min

The #179 will take 3 h and 34 min to get to Philadelphia.

TRAIN SCHEDULE

Train Number ▶		451	122	102	173	634	222	135	179	110	214	465
Days of Operation ▶		Ex Sa Su	Sa Su only	Ex Sa Su	Ex Sa Su	Sa Su only	Ex Sa Su	Sa only	Ex Su	Su only	Ex Sa	Ex Su
New Haven, CT	Dp	7 32A			8 28A	8 28A		9 25A	9 25A			10 30A
Bridgeport, CT					8 51A	8 51A						10 53A
Stamford, CT		8 20A			9 16A	9 16A		10 11A	10 11A			11 18A
Rye, NY					9 33A	9 27A						
New York, NY	Ar	9 15A			10 17A	10 13A		11 08A	11 08A			12 15P
New York, NY	Dp	9 30A	9 30A	10 00A	10 30A	10 30A	11 00A	11 30A	11 30A	11 30A	12 00N	12 30P
Newark, NJ		9 43A	9 45A	10 13A	10 43A	10 43A	11 13A	11 44A	11 44A	11 44A	12 13P	12 43P
Metropark, NJ		9 57A	9 59A	10 27A				11 58A	11 58A	11 58A		
New Brunswick, NJ												
Princeton Jct., NJ												
Trenton, NJ		10 23A	10 25A		11 18A	11 19A		12 23P	12 23P	12 23P		1 22P
N. Philadelphia, PA								12 48P	12 48P	12 48P		
Philadelphia, PA		10 54A	10 56A	11 16A	11 49A	11 50A	12 11P	12 59P	12 59P	12 59P	1 10P	1 55P
Wilmington, DE		11 18A	11 21A	11 37A	12 12P	12 14P	12 32P	1 23P	1 23P	1 23P	1 31P	2 19P
Newark, DE												
Aberdeen, MD												
Baltimore, MD		12 08P	12 09P	12 23P	1 02P	1 04P	1 20P	2 19P	2 19P	2 19P	2 17P	3 11P
BWI Airport Rail Sta., MD					1 14P	1 16P						
New Carrollton, MD		12 32P	12 42P		1 29P	1 31P	1 44P	2 41P	2 41P	2 41P		3 35P
Washington, DC EST	Ar	12 44P	12 54P	12 55P	1 41P	1 43P	1 55P	2 56P	2 56P	2 56P	2 49P	3 48P

1. Why do many commuters purchase **monthly passes** for bus or train travel?

2. Why do many buses and trains run different schedules on weekends?

PRACTICE EXERCISES

Remember to estimate whenever you use your calculator.

Use the bus schedule to solve.

1. If you take Bus #106, what time will you arrive in Greenville?

2. If you take Bus #204, what time will you arrive in Danville?

3. If you leave Clemson at 11:10 A.M., what time does the bus get you into Culpepper?

4. If you leave Salisbury at 4:10 P.M., what time does the bus get you into Toccoa?

5. Which bus should you take from Washington, DC, if you need to arrive in Atlanta for an early meeting?

6. Which bus should you take from Charlotte if you want to arrive in Washington, DC, by 8:00 P.M.?

7. What time does the local to Washington, DC, leave Spartanburg?

8. How long does it take Bus #204 to get from Spartanburg to Manassas?

9. How long does it take Bus #167 to get from Washington, DC, to Atlanta?

10. How much faster does Bus #106 get from Monroe to Charlotte than Bus #167?

Use the train schedule to solve.

11. If you take Train #122, what time will you arrive in Trenton?

12. If you take Train #110, what time will you arrive in Wilmington?

13. If you leave Stamford at 9:16 A.M. on a Saturday, what time will you arrive in Baltimore?

14. If you leave Newark at 10:13 A.M., what time will you arrive in Washington, DC?

15. What is the latest train you can take from New York on a Tuesday to arrive in Washington, DC, by 3:00 P.M.?

16. Which train should you take from New Haven in order to arrive in New York by 10:00 A.M.?

17. How long does it take Train #122 to get from New York to Washington, DC?

18. How long does it take Train #179 to get from Metropark to Baltimore?

19. How much faster does Train #222 get from New York to Washington, DC, than Train #179?

20. Which train and bus route gets you from New York to Washington, DC, to Atlanta in the shortest time? How long will the trip take?

Pam Robbins lives in Dallas. She and her parents are planning a 1-wk vacation trip to Los Angeles.

FLIGHT SCHEDULE

From Dallas/Fort Worth (CST)

Leave	Arrive	Flight	Freq.
TO: Chicago, IL (CST)			
7:05 a	9:15 a	Central 580	Daily
8:30 a	10:33 a	Hemisphere 542	Daily
11:06 a	1:15 p	Central 180	x7
1:00 p	2:51 p	Sierra 272	Daily
4:10 p	6:21 p	Hemisphere 716	x6
TO: Los Angeles, CA (PST)			
8:40 a	9:35 a	Sierra 389	Daily
10:50 a	11:54 a	Central 651	Daily
12:01 p	12:45 p	Hemisphere 247	x7
4:08 p	4:55 p	Central 533	Daily
6:42 p	7:29 p	Central 217	Daily
TO: New York, NY (EST)			
7:00 a	10:58 a	Central 244	Daily
10:19 a	2:25 p	Sierra 224	x5
1:00 p	5:18 p	Central 164	Daily
4:20 p	8:40 p	Hemisphere 281	Daily
7:51 p	11:59 p	Sierra 466	Daily

EXAMPLE 1

If the Robbinses want to arrive in Los Angeles by noon, which flight should they take? When does it depart?

Check the flight schedule:

The last flight between Dallas and Los Angeles to arrive before noon is Central Airlines Flight #651. It departs from Dallas at 10:50 A.M. and arrives at 11:54 A.M.

They should take Flight #651, departing from Dallas at 10:50 A.M.

EXAMPLE 2

How long will the flight take?

THINK: Departs: 10:50 A.M. Dallas   Arrives: 11:54 A.M. Los Angeles
11:54 A.M. Los Angeles time is 1:54 P.M. Dallas time.

10:50 A.M. to 1:54 P.M. is 3 h and 4 min.

So the flight will take just over 3 h.

EXAMPLE 3

How much will it cost for airfare if they get the SuperSaver rates?

1. Check the Fare Schedule.   The round-trip SuperSaver fare is $239.

2. Multiply to find the fare for 3 people. $3 \times \$239 = \$717$

The Robbinses will pay $717 for SuperSaver airfare.

FROM: Dallas / Fort Worth, TX		ROUND-TRIP FARE SCHEDULE	
TO:	Regular Coach	First Class	SuperSaver*
Chicago	$475	$625	$188
Los Angeles	$550	$675	$239
New York	$595	$725	$259
* SuperSaver fares — must stay over Saturday night			

1. Why do people flying long distances try to arrive several hours before a scheduled meeting?

2. Why are Coach, First Class, and SuperSaver fares so different?

PRACTICE EXERCISES

Remember to estimate whenever you use your calculator.

Use the Flight Schedule to identify the best flight to take from Dallas in order to arrive in:

1. Chicago by 4:00 P.M.

2. New York by noon.

3. Los Angeles after 6:00 P.M.

4. Chicago by 10:00 A.M.

5. Los Angeles by 5:00 P.M.

6. New York by 9:00 P.M.

Find the actual flight time for the flight. Refer to the Time Zones table on page 186 of this book.

7. Leave 11:15 A.M. EST   Arrive 1:30 P.M. CST

8. Leave 2:15 P.M. CST   Arrive 4:45 P.M. PST

9. Leave 3:00 P.M. PST   Arrive 5:15 P.M. MST

10. Leave 10:00 A.M. MST   Arrive 4:40 P.M. EST

11. Leave 1:25 P.M. CST   Arrive 3:15 P.M. PST

Use the Flight Schedule to find the actual flight time for the flight.

12. Central #180

13. Hemisphere #247

14. Sierra #224

Use the Fare Schedule to find the round-trip airfare for the trip.

15. Dallas to New York, First Class

16. Dallas to Los Angeles, Regular Coach

17. Dallas to Chicago, SuperSaver

18. Dallas to Los Angeles, First Class

Solve.

19. How much more expensive is a First Class round-trip ticket from Dallas to New York than a Regular Coach ticket?

20. How much can you save by flying round trip from Dallas to Chicago at SuperSaver rates rather than Regular Coach?

21. Jim and Phyllis flew from Dallas to Los Angeles and back at SuperSaver rates. How much over the Regular Coach rates did they save on the 2 tickets?

22. Richard flew round trip on business from Dallas to New York one week and from Dallas to Chicago the next week. If he flew First Class, how much did he spend on airfare?

10.5 USING SUBWAYS

One of the most convenient forms of transportation in many large cities is the subway. Subway systems usually have route maps in each station and in each car to help you find your way. Washington, DC, has one of the nation's newest subway systems.

Washington, DC Partial Subway Map

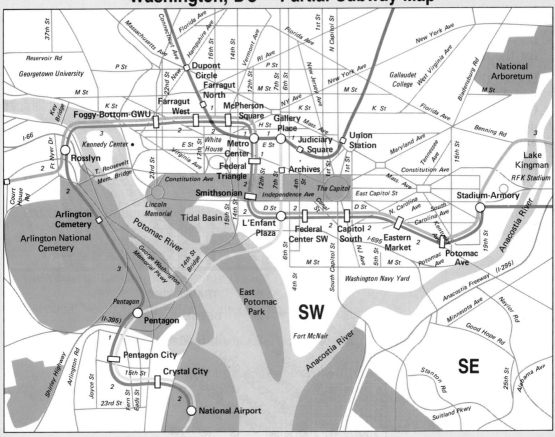

Add.

1. $329 + $981 + $523.18   2. $1,089 + $104 + $161

3. $4,092.67 + $234.81 + $3,009.61

4. $2,068.41 + $90.38 + $18.42

5. $109.57 + $1,037.62 + $73.56

6. $32,087 + $56.78 + $345.91

Subtract.

7. $947 − $186   8. $2,098 − $1,076

9. $372.41 − $186.37   10. $2,376.51 − $1,341.29

11. $913.07 − $568.71   12. $3,076.41 − $1,356.78

Rename as a decimal.

13. 2%   14. 5%   15. 3.5%

16. 6.5%   17. 7.5%   18. 2.75%

Multiply. Round to the nearest cent.

19. 0.02 × $5,000   20. 0.05 × $3,000   21. 0.075 × $7,000

22. 0.05 × $486.34   23. 0.065 × $4,520.38   24. 0.035 × $28,962.41

Find the answer.

25. 2% of $8,500   26. 2.75% of $19,500   27. 7.5% of $28,762.41

Use the Taxable Income table at the right. In which interval does the taxable income lie?

28. $13,240   29. $13,012.50

30. $13,347.89   31. $13,428.99

32. $25,658   33. $25,799.45

34. $25,812.35   35. $25,942.75

TAXABLE INCOME

At least	But less than	At least	But less than
13,000	13,050	25,600	25,650
13,050	13,100	25,650	25,700
13,100	13,150	25,700	25,750
13,200	13,250	25,750	25,800
13,250	13,000	25,800	25,850
13,300	13,350	25,850	25,900
13,350	13,400	25,900	25,950
13,400	13,450	25,950	26,000

A combination of local, state, and federal taxes pays for our public schools. How would education be affected if taxes were not used to provide public schools?

During the past year, you worked at Namca Industries. At the end of the year, the company sent you a **W-2 form.** The form shows how much you earned and how much was withheld for federal taxes, Social Security, and state and local taxes. The company sent copies of the W-2 form to federal and local tax agencies.

EXAMPLE 1 Read and interpret this W-2 form.

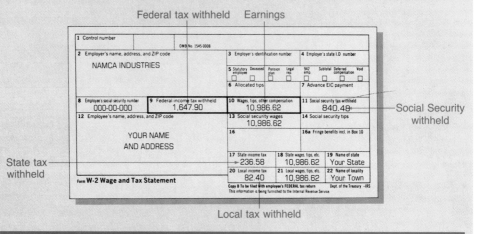

Federal tax withheld   Earnings

Social Security withheld

State tax withheld

Local tax withheld

Last year, you also earned interest from your bank account. The bank sent a **1099 form** to show how much interest you earned.

EXAMPLE 2 Read and interpret this 1099 form.

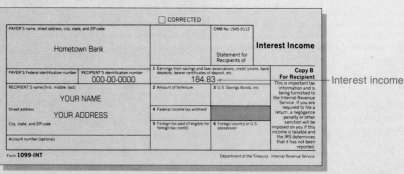

Interest income

Your **gross income** is the total of earnings, interest, and dividends.

EXAMPLE 3 What was your gross income last year?

Add. $10,986.62 + $184.83 = $11,171.45

Your gross income was $11,171.45.

FOR DISCUSSION

1. Why are copies of the W-2 and 1099 forms sent to federal, state, and local tax agencies?

2. How could you check your W-2 form to be sure it is correct?

PRACTICE EXERCISES   Remember to estimate whenever you use your calculator.

Use the W-2 form on page 212 for Exercises 1–4. How much was withheld for:

1. Federal income tax?

2. Social Security tax?

3. State income tax?

4. Local income tax?

Find the gross income.

5. Wages: $17,435
   Interest: $296

6. Wages: $23,672
   Interest: $408

7. Wages: $12,009
   Interest: $96

8. Wages: $13,098
   Wages: $18,456
   Interest: $308

9. Wages: $7,892
   Tips: $8,623
   Interest: $129

10. Wages: $34,709
    Interest: $728
    Interest: $1,203

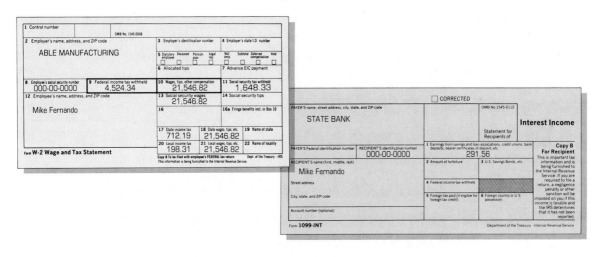

Use Mike Fernando's W-2 and 1099 forms. Find these amounts.

11. Wages

12. Federal tax withheld

13. Social Security withheld

14. State tax withheld

15. Local tax withheld

16. Interest income

17. Gross income

The **Internal Revenue Service (IRS)** collects **federal income taxes.** Tax receipts are used primarily for social and defense programs, and to pay interest on the national debt.

Tax deductions and **tax exemptions** reduce the amounts of income to be taxed. **Adjusted Gross Income (AGI)** is gross income less any adjustments to income. **Taxable income** is AGI less any exemptions or deductions. Your federal taxes are based on your taxable income.

EXAMPLE 1

Last year, your gross income was $11,171.45. You had no adjustments to income and you are entitled to 1 exemption of $2,150. You had a standard deduction of $3,400. What is your AGI and your taxable income?

THINK: There were no adjustments. Your Adjusted Gross Income (AGI) is the same as your gross income.

1. Add to find the total of exemptions and deductions. $2,150 + $3,400 = $5,550

2. Subtract to find your taxable income. $11,171.45 − $5,550 = $5,621.45

Your taxable income is $5,621.45

You use tax tables to find the tax due. You use your **filing status** to find your tax.

EXAMPLE 2

If you are single, how much tax do you owe on $5,621.45?

THINK: Find your taxable income in the table. $5,621.45 is between $5,600 and $5,650.

Look down the "Single" column to find your tax.

Your tax is $844.

If taxable income is—		And you are—			
At least	But less than	Single	Married filing jointly	Married filing sepa-rately	Head of a house-hold
				Your tax is—	
5,000					
5,000	5,050	754	754	754	754
5,050	5,100	761	761	761	761
5,100	5,150	769	769	769	769
5,150	5,200	776	776	776	776
5,200	5,250	784	784	784	784
5,250	5,300	791	791	791	791
5,300	5,350	799	799	799	799
5,350	5,400	806	806	806	806
5,400	5,450	814	814	814	814
5,450	5,500	821	821	821	821
5,500	5,550	829	829	829	829
5,550	5,600	836	836	836	836
5,600	5,650	844	844	844	844
5,650	5,700	851	851	851	851
5,700	5,750	859	859	859	859
5,750	5,800	866	866	866	866
5,800	5,850	874	874	874	874
5,850	5,900	881	881	881	881
5,900	5,950	889	889	889	889
5,950	6,000	896	896	896	896

If too much tax was withheld, you will get a **refund.** If not enough tax was withheld, you will owe more taxes.

EXAMPLE **3** You had $752.15 withheld in federal taxes. Your federal tax is actually $937. How much do you owe or how much of a refund can you expect?

THINK: The tax withheld is less than the tax. You will owe money.

Subtract. $937 − $752.15 = $184.85

You owe $184.85.

FOR DISCUSSION

How can 2 people with the same taxable income pay different taxes?

PRACTICE EXERCISES   Remember to estimate whenever you use your calculator.

Find the Adjusted Gross Income (AGI) and taxable income.

1. Gross income: $20,876
   Adjustments: $1,500
   1 Exemption: $2,150
   Deduction: $3,400

2. Gross income: $23,190
   Adjustments: $1,970
   2 Exemptions: $4,300
   Deduction: $3,400

3. Gross income: $32,098
   Adjustments: $0
   2 Exemptions: $4,300
   Deduction: $5,700

Use the tax tables on pages 475–479. Find the taxable income and the tax owed.

4. Single
   Gross income: $25,374
   Adjustments: $750
   1 Exemption: $2,150
   Deduction: $3,400

5. Married, filing separately
   Gross income: $43,092
   Adjustments: $3,762
   2 Exemptions: $4,300
   Deduction: $2,850

6. Married, filing joint return
   Gross income: $30,926
   Adjustments: $1,500
   3 Exemptions: $6,450
   Deduction: $5,700

7. Single
   Gross income: $19,723
   Adjustments: $0
   1 Exemption: $2,150
   Deduction: $3,400

How much tax is owed or how much of a refund can be expected?

8. Tax withheld: $2,110.35
   Actual tax: $2,407

9. Tax withheld: $5,817.89
   Actual tax: $4,829

10. Tax withheld: $8,324.13
   Actual tax: $7,899

11. Tax withheld: $4,976.54
   Actual tax: $5,080

Tax Form 1040EZ is often called the **short form.** This form can only be used if your filing status is single and you have no dependents. You use the information from the W-2 and 1099 forms to complete Form 1040EZ.

EXAMPLE   Read and interpret Chad Blaire's Tax Form 1040EZ.

Department of the Treasury—Internal Revenue Service	
Form 1040EZ	**Income Tax Return for Single Filers With No Dependents** (o)
	OMB No. 1545-0675

Name & address

Use the IRS label (see page 10). If you don't have one, please print.

Please print your numbers like this:

9876543210

L A B E L	Chad Blaire
	Print your name (first, initial, last)
	33 Robin Lane
H E R E	Home address (number and street). (If you have a P.O. box, see page 11.) Apt. no.
	Hometown, USA 00000
	City, town or post office, state, and ZIP code. (If you have a foreign address, see page 11.)

Your social security number

000 00 0000

Please see instructions on the back. Also, see the Form 1040EZ booklet.

Presidential Election Campaign (see page 11)
Do you want $1 to go to this fund? ▶

Note: *Checking "Yes" will not change your tax or reduce your refund.*

[X]

		Dollars	Cents

Report your income

Attach Copy B of Form(s) W-2 here. Attach tax payment on top of Form(s) W-2.

Note: *You must check Yes or No.*

1   Total wages, salaries, and tips. This should be shown in Box 10 of your W-2 form(s). (Attach your W-2 form(s).)   1 | 21 | 050 | 37 |

2   Taxable interest income of $400 or less. If the total is more than $400, you cannot use Form 1040EZ.   2 | | 241 | 68 |

3   Add line 1 and line 2. This is your **adjusted gross income.**   3 | 21 | 292 | 05 |

4   Can your parents (or someone else) claim you on their return?
☐ **Yes.** Do worksheet on back; enter amount from line E here.
☒ **No.** Enter 5,550.00. This is the total of your standard deduction and personal exemption.   4 | 5 | 550 | 00 |

5   Subtract line 4 from line 3. If line 4 is larger than line 3, enter 0. This is your **taxable income.**   5 | 15 | 742 | 05 |

Figure your tax

6   Enter your Federal income tax withheld from Box 9 of your W-2 form(s).   6 | 2 | 699 | 37 |

7   **Tax.** Use the amount on **line 5** to find your tax in the tax table on pages 16-18 of the booklet. Enter the tax from the table on this line.   7 | 2 | 359 | 00 |

Refund or amount you owe

8   If line 6 is larger than line 7, subtract line 7 from line 6. This is your **refund.**   8 | | 340 | 37 |

9   If line 7 is larger than line 6, subtract line 6 from line 7. This is the **amount you owe.** Attach your payment for full amount payable to the "Internal Revenue Service." Write your name, address, social security number, daytime phone number, and "1991 Form 1040EZ" on it.   9 | | | |

Sign your return

Keep a copy of this form for your records.

I have read this return. Under penalties of perjury, I declare that to the best of my knowledge and belief, the return is true, correct, and complete.

Your signature	Date 4/12/-
X Chad Blaire	Your occupation Secretary

For IRS Use Only — Please do not write in boxes below.

For Privacy Act and Paperwork Reduction Act Notice, see page 4 in the booklet.   Cat. No. 11329W   **Form 1040EZ**

How to complete Form 1040EZ:

- Chad entered his name, address, and Social Security number. The form cannot be processed without the Social Security number.

- The IRS would prefer that you use the label they provide.

- Notice that dollar signs are not used on tax forms.

Line 1 Remember to attach a copy of your W-2 form(s). You must report earnings even if you don't get a W-2 Form.

Line 2 Do *not* attach a copy of Form 1099. Do not use Form 1040EZ if your interest income is over $400.

Line 4 Chad did not check the yes–box, since he is not taken as an exemption on his parents' tax form.

Line 4 Chad did not check the yes–box on Line 4, so he is entitled to the standard deduction (3,400.00) and the personal exemption (2,150.00).

Line 6 Chad used information from the W-2 form(s) to enter the tax withheld.

Line 7 Chad used the amount from Line 5 to find his tax in the tax table. His taxable income falls between $15,700 and $15,750. He finds his tax in the tax table for single persons.

If line 5 is at least—	But less than—	Your tax is—
15,000		
15,600	15,650	2,344
15,650	15,700	2,351
15,700	15,750	2,359
15,750	15,800	2,366

Line 8 If Chad is due a refund, the IRS will mail him a check a few months after his tax form is processed.

Line 9 If Chad still owed money, he would write his Social Security number on the check he sends to the IRS.

- Chad signed and dated his return.

How to complete Schedule A—Itemized Deductions:

Line 1 Liz could not include health expenses paid for by insurance.

Line 3 Liz multiplied 0.075 × $31,580 (the AGI) to get $2,369.00. She rounded to the nearest dollar to make computation easier.

Line 4 Since Line 3 is greater than Line 1, Liz cannot take a deduction for medical and dental expenses.

Line 5 These amounts are from Liz's W-2 form, plus any additional taxes she paid. Federal income taxes are *not* deductible.

Line 6 Liz owns her house and pays real estate taxes.

Line 8 Shows the total deduction for taxes.

Line 9a The bank sent Liz a statement showing how much interest she had paid.

Line 12 Shows the total deduction for paid interest.

Line 14 This deduction is the value of books Liz donated to the library.

Line 16 Shows the total deduction for contributions.

Line 23 Liz multiplied 0.02 × $31,580 to get $632.

Line 24 Liz subtracted to find her total miscellaneous deductions.

Line 26 Shows the total of Liz's itemized deductions.

Everyone is entitled to a **standard deduction.** Only use itemized deductions if the total is more than the standard deduction. The standard deduction depends on filing status.

EXAMPLE 2 Liz is single. Should she itemize deductions or use the standard deduction?

Liz compared the total of her itemized deductions ($4,567) with her standard deduction ($3,400). The total itemized deductions are greater than the standard deduction.

Liz will itemize deductions.

STANDARD DEDUCTIONS

Single	$3,400
Married, filing joint return or widow(er) with dependent child	$5,700
Married, filing separate return	$2,850
Head of household	$5,000

FOR DISCUSSION

1. Why are homeowners likely to have more deductions than renters?

2. Why is it important to keep records of expenses you want to deduct on your tax return?

Remember to estimate whenever you use your calculator.

Use the Schedule A on page 219 for Exercises 1–6.

1. What was Liz's deduction for real estate taxes?

2. What was Liz's deduction for contributions other than cash?

3. What was the total of Liz's unreimbursed business expenses?

4. How much of Liz's unreimbursed business expenses could be deducted?

5. What is the total of Liz's itemized deductions?

6. How much more than the standard deduction are Liz's itemized deductions?

Find the difference between the itemized and the standard deduction. Which should the person use?

7. Single
Total itemized deductions: $2,304

8. Married, joint return
Total itemized deductions: $3,256

9. Married, separate return
Itemized deductions: $3,409

10. Head of household
Itemized deductions: $6,958

Find the total itemized deductions. Should the person(s) use the itemized or standard deduction?

11. Lester Jefferson
Single
Adjusted Gross Income
(Form 1040—Line 31): $27,500

Allowable Medical Expenses
(Line 1): $780

State and Local Taxes
(Line 5): $1,090

Other Taxes
(Line 7): $205

Cash Contributions
(Line 13): $550

Casualty Loss
(Line 17): $600

12. Jim and Marge Cochran
Married, Filing a Joint Return
Adjusted Gross Income
(Form 1040—Line 31): $57,300

Allowable Medical Expenses
(Line 1): $2,456

State and Local Taxes
(Line 5): $2,035

Real Estate Taxes
(Line 6): $1,653

Mortgage Interest
(Line 9a): $3,025

Cash Contributions
(Line 13): $1,200

11.5 STATE AND CITY INCOME TAXES

Some **state and city income taxes** are a percent of a person's
Adjusted Gross Income from their federal tax Form 1040.

STATE TAX

Adjusted Gross Income	Tax rate
First $8,000	2%
Next $7,000	3.5%
Next $5,000	5%
Over $20,000	6.5%

EXAMPLE 1

Bob's Adjusted Gross Income was $22,250.
How much state tax does he owe?

1. Multiply to find the tax.

First $8,000	→	0.02 × $8,000 = $160
Next $7,000	→	0.035 × $7,000 = $245
Next $5,000	→	0.05 × $5,000 = $250
Over $20,000	→	0.065 × $2,250 = $146.25

2. Add to find the total tax. $801.25

Bob's state tax is $801.25.

Some states and cities have tax rates that include personal exemptions.

EXEMPTIONS

Single	$1,750
Married	$3,400
Each Dependent	$ 750

CITY TAX

Adjusted Gross Income	Tax rate
First $9,000	1.5%
Next $6,000	2.75%
Over $15,000	3.5%

EXAMPLE 2

Kathy and Harry have a combined Adjusted Gross Income of $29,540.
They have 1 child. How much city income tax do they pay?

1. Add to find their total exemption. $3,400 + $750 = $4,150

2. Subtract to find the taxable income. $29,540 − $4,150 = $25,390

3. Multiply to find the tax.

First $9,000	→	0.015 × $9,000 = $135
Next $6,000	→	0.0275 × $6,000 = $165
Over $15,000	→	0.035 × $10,390 = $363.65

4. Add to find the total tax. $663.65

Kathy and Harry's city tax is $663.65.

1. What taxes other than income taxes might a state or city have?

2. Why would a city or state need to raise money through income taxes?

PRACTICE EXERCISES   Remember to estimate whenever you use your calculator.

Use the state tax table on page 222 to find the state tax on the Adjusted Gross Income.

1. $6,872

2. $13,581

3. $20,615

4. $19,762

5. $43,181

6. $12,924

Use the city tax table and exemptions on page 222 to find the city tax.

7. Single, 0 dependents
Adjusted Gross
Income: $9,324

8. Married, 1 dependent
Adjusted Gross
Income: $12,618

9. Married, 3 dependents
Adjusted Gross
Income: $37,861

Complete the table to find the amount each person owes, or the refund they should get for state and city taxes. Use the tables on page 222.

	Mike, single	Teresa, married, 1 dependent
Adjusted Gross Income	$19,468.12	$32,812.41
State tax withheld	$698.13	$1,214.41
State tax	10. ■	16. ■
State tax owed or refund	11. ■	17. ■
Exemptions (dollar value)	12. ■	18. ■
City taxable income	13. ■	19. ■
City tax withheld	$418.32	$709.21
City tax	14. ■	20. ■
City tax owed or refund	15. ■	21. ■

11.6 PROJECTING ESTIMATES

Situation:

Jake is a freelance writer. His paychecks have no taxes withheld from them. He must submit his own estimated tax payments quarterly to the federal, state, and local governments.

Quarterly Estimated
Taxes Due

April 15	June 15
September 15	January 15

Strategy:

Projecting estimates can sometimes help you to solve a problem.

Applying the Strategy:

A. Last year, Jake paid $4,956 in federal taxes. If Jake expects to earn about the same income this year as last year, how much estimated federal tax should Jake pay on April 15?

THINK: Last year, Jake paid about $5,000 in federal taxes. This year, he expects to earn about the same amount of income. Therefore, he expects to pay about the same amount of taxes.

Divide by 4 to find the quarterly amount.
$5,000 ÷ 4 = $1,250

Jake should pay $1,250 of estimated federal tax on April 15.

B. Suppose that in August, Jake realized that his income would be greater than he had expected for the year. He estimated that he should pay an additional $1,500 to the federal government, for a total of $6,500. He had already made the April 15 and June 15 payments of $1,250 each. How much will Jake pay on September 15 and January 15?

1. Multiply to find the amount already paid.
   2 × $1,250 = $2,500

2. Subtract to find the amount still owed.
   $6,500 − $2,500 = $4,000

3. Divide by 2 to find the amount for each of the last 2 payments.
   $4,000 ÷ 2 = $2,000

Jake will pay $2,000 for each of the last 2 payments.

Remember to estimate whenever you use your calculator.

Betty estimated that she will need to pay $3,200 in state taxes this year.
She divided that amount by 4 and found that she should make four $800
payments during the year. In July, Betty realized that her income would
be lower than she had expected. She estimated that she should pay $600
less to the state. She had already made the April 15 and June 15
payments.

1. In July, how much did Betty estimate her state taxes to be?

2. How much money had Betty already paid?

3. How much money did Betty have left to pay?

4. How many payments were left for Betty to make?

5. How much estimated state tax was due on September 15 and on
   January 15 if both payments were equal?

This table shows estimated taxes
3 freelance writers estimated they
should pay this year.

	Estimated Taxes		
Name	**Federal**	**State**	**City**
Jed	$2,000	$ 850	$180
Irene	$8,000	$3,000	$600
Burt	$7,000	$2,400	$600

Use the facts in the table to solve the problem.

6. Jed will make 4 equal estimated tax
   payments to the state. How much
   should each payment be?

7. Jed will make 4 equal estimated tax
   payments to the city. How much
   should each payment be?

8. Irene had planned to make four
   $2,000 payments for her federal
   taxes. After 2 payments, she reduced
   her estimated federal tax due by
   $1,500. How much were each of
   Irene's last 2 payments?

9. Jed had planned to make four $500
   payments for his federal taxes. After
   one payment, he increased his
   estimated federal tax due by $900.
   How much were each of Jed's last 3
   payments?

10. Irene had planned to make 4 equal
    payments for her city taxes. After 2
    payments, she lowered her estimated
    city taxes due by $100. How much
    were each of Irene's last 2 payments?

11. Burt planned to make 4 equal
    payments on his federal, state, and
    city taxes. He now wants to increase
    each estimated tax by 20%. How
    much money will Burt have to spend
    each quarter to pay all 3 estimated
    taxes?

11.7 CHOOSING THE CORRECT TAX FORM

You can use one of 3 tax forms to file your income taxes: FORM 1040EZ, FORM 1040A, or FORM 1040.

FORM 1040EZ can only be used by single people with no dependents, no adjustments, no itemized deductions, and taxable income less than $50,000. Taxable interest cannot exceed $400.

FORM 1040A can be used by anyone with taxable income less than $50,000. Adjustments are allowable only for Individual Retirement Accounts (IRAs). No itemized deductions are allowed.

FORM 1040 can be used by anyone. All adjustments are allowed and deductions can be itemized.

You want to use the simplest form and still pay the lowest allowable tax.

PROBLEM

You are a community tax consultant. Three different people come to you for advice on which tax form to use and how much tax to pay.

	PERSON A	PERSON B	PERSON C
Filing status	Single	Married, joint return	Single
Exemptions	1 person, not claimed on another return	2 adults 1 child	1 person, claimed on another return
Wages	$25,062	$19,390 and $27,430	$18,093 and $7,642 in tips
Interest	Bank A: $237 Bank B: $95	Bank: $319 Fund: $116	Bank: $302
Adjustments	IRA: $275	IRA: $2,500	None
Allowable deductions			
Medical	$627	$1,079	$295
Taxes	$935	$618	$308
Interest	$239	$920	$0
Contributions	$285	$570	$185
Miscellaneous	$628	$315	$216

DECISION-MAKING FACTORS

Filing status	Wages	Interest income	Adjustments to income
Exemptions	AGI	Itemized deductions	Standard deduction

DECISION-MAKING COMPARISONS

Complete the table to compare the 3 people. Use the table on page 220 for Exercises 15–16.

Factors	Person A	Person B	Person C
Filing status	Single	1. ▪	2. ▪
Wages	$25,062	3. ▪	4. ▪
Interest income	5. ▪	6. ▪	$302
Adjustments to income	7. ▪	IRA: $2,500	8. ▪
Adjusted Gross Income	9. ▪	10. ▪	$26,037
Exemptions ($2,150 per each allowable exemption)	11. ▪	12. ▪	$0—No exemptions
Itemized deductions	13. ▪	14. ▪	$1,004
Standard deduction	15. ▪	16. ▪	$3,400

17. Which form should each person use if filing status were the only factor?

18. Which form should each person use if filing status and interest income were the only factors?

19. Which form should each person use if filing status, interest income, and adjustments to income were the only factors?

20. Should each person use itemized deductions or the standard deduction?

21. Which tax form should each person use? Explain.

22. What is the amount of the deduction for each person?

23. What is the total of exemptions and deductions for each person?

24. What is the taxable income for each person?

25. What is the federal income tax for each person? Use the tax tables on pages 475–479.

CHAPTER REVIEW

Vocabulary   Choose the letter of the word(s) that completes the sentence.

1. The W-2 form is used to report ■.   [212]

   a. Interest   **b.** Wages   **c.** Deductions

2. Gross income, less any adjustments, is called ■.   [214]

   a. Taxable Income   **b.** Adjusted Gross Income   **c.** Exemptions

3. Amounts that reduce the income to be taxed are called ■.   [214]

   a. Deductions   **b.** Taxable income   **c.** AGIs

Skills   Find the answer.

Use the W-2 and the 1099 forms
to find the amount.   [212]

4. Wages

5. Federal tax withheld

6. State tax withheld

7. City tax withheld

8. Social Security tax withheld

9. Interest

10. Gross income

Solve.

11. Sarah's gross income is $27,345. She
    has $789 in adjustments to income.
    What is her Adjusted Gross Income?
    [214]

12. Martin's AGI is $19,456, with a $3,400
    deduction and no exemptions.
    What is his taxable income?   [214]

13. Lee Ann's taxable income is $18,932
    and she is single. What is her federal
    tax?   [214]

14. Ira files Form 1040EZ and is not
    claimed on another form. How much
    is his personal exemption?   [216]

15. The Martinez's joint return has
    itemized deductions of $2,780. Should
    they take the itemized or the
    standard deduction?   [219]

16. Diana's Adjusted Gross Income was
    $19,874 last year. How much state tax
    did she pay? (Use the tax table on
    page 222.)   [222]

Ron and Beth are married and filing a joint return. They have 1 child and will take the standard deduction.

Use the W-2 forms to find the amount.

1. Total gross income

2. Total federal tax withheld

3. Total state tax withheld

4. Total city tax withheld

5. Total Social Security tax withheld

W-2 Form (Ron Showard) — SMITH INDUSTRIES

1 Control number	
OMB No. 1545-0008	
2 Employer's name, address, and ZIP code	SMITH INDUSTRIES
3 Employer's identification number	
4 Employer's state I.D. number	
8 Employee's social security number	000-00-0000
9 Federal income tax withheld	1,215.63
10 Wages, tips, other compensation	17,462.87
11 Social security tax withheld	1,335.91
12 Employee's name, address, and ZIP code	Ron Showard
17 State income tax	219.41
18 State wages, tips, etc.	17,462.87
20 Local income tax	83.16
21 Local wages, tips, etc.	17,462.87

Form W-2 Wage and Tax Statement
Copy B To be filed with employee's FEDERAL tax return   Dept. of the Treasury—IRS
This information is being furnished to the Internal Revenue Service.

W-2 Form (Beth Showard)

8 Employee's social security number	000-00-0000
9 Federal income tax withheld	416.29
10 Wages, tips, other compensation	6,471.32
11 Social security tax withheld	495.06
12 Employee's name, address, and ZIP code	Beth Showard
17 State income tax	119.62
18 State wages, tips, etc.	6,471.32
20 Local income tax	32.11
21 Local wages, tips, etc.	6,471.32

Form W-2 Wage and Tax Statement
Copy B To be filed with employee's FEDERAL tax return   Dept. of the Treasury—IRS
This information is being furnished to the Internal Revenue Service.

Find the Adjusted Gross Income, taxable income, and federal tax. Use the federal tax tables on pages 475–479.

6. Single, 1 exemption
   Gross income: $27,456
   Adjustments: $569
   Standard deduction: $3,400

7. Married, filing jointly, 3 exemptions
   Gross income: $32,709
   Adjustments: $1,750
   Standard deduction: $5,700

Use the W-2 forms at the top of the page. Use the federal tax tables on pages 475–479. Use the state and city tax tables on page 222.

8. What is the Showards' federal tax?

9. How much federal tax do the Showards owe, or what is their refund?

10. What is the Showards' state tax?

11. How much state tax do the Showards owe, or what is their refund?

12. What is the Showards' city tax?

13. How much city tax do the Showards owe, or what is their refund?

Howard's estimated taxes for the year were: Federal: $4,000; State: $1,670; and City: $420.

14. Howard will make 4 equal payments to each this year. How much should each payment to each agency be?

15. After 2 payments, Howard lowered his estimated federal taxes due by $300. How much were each of his last 2 federal tax payments?

You will have more money in each paycheck if you claim 1 tax deduction instead of 0.

LET'S LOOK AT THE FACTS

1 or 0 are personal deductions that refer only to you *as an individual.* If you claim 1 deduction, the amount of your weekly paycheck will be greater, since less tax will be taken out. If you claim 0 deductions, your weekly paycheck will be lower, since more tax will be taken out.

LET'S DISCUSS WHY

1. Some people claim 1 deduction because they prefer to get more money in each paycheck. Why might they prefer this?

2. If you claim 0 deductions, more tax will be taken out of your paycheck each week and you might be entitled to a refund. When would you receive this refund?

3. On January 1, you declared 1 deduction on your employment form. On July 1, you change jobs. You will earn the same salary but you change your deduction claim to 0. Next April, at tax time, are you likely to owe money? Get a refund? Neither?

4. Many people claim deductions for their spouse, their children, and their home mortgage payments. Tax experts warn that declaring too many deductions may require a large payment plus penalties in April. How can this be avoided?

5. Declaring too few deductions may result in a large refund. While this sounds appealing, you could be losing money by doing this. How is this possible?

LET'S SEE WHAT YOU WOULD DO

6. You must make car, student loan, and credit card payments every month. Would you prefer to receive more money in your weekly paycheck or receive a large refund later? Explain your decision.

7. By claiming 1 deduction instead of 0, you receive $65 more in each weekly paycheck. What could you do with that extra money that might earn you even more money?

8. You are single and have no debts or financial obligations. Your accountant tells you that you will be getting a $5,200 refund this year. Make a list of all the things you might do with that money.

 **CALCULATOR** THE MEMORY KEYS

You can use calculators with **memory keys** to solve multi-step problems. These are the memory keys.

M+	M–	MR or RM	MC or CM
Adds a number to memory.	Subtracts a number from memory.	Recalls a number from memory.	Clears memory.

Using memory keys, compute: $(15 + 12) + (8 \times 5)$.

Procedure	Calculator Entry	Calculator Display
1. Perform the operation within the first set of parentheses.	⒈⑤ ➕ ① ② ⩵	27.
2. Add the result to memory.	M+	M 27.
3. Perform the operation within the second set of parentheses.	⑧ ✕ ⑤ ⩵	M 40.
4. Add the result to memory.	M+	M 40.
5. Recall the total in memory.	MR	M 67.

So $(15 + 12) + (8 \times 5) = 67$.

Always make sure you clear the memory before you use it.

Use a calculator to compute.

1. $(5 \times 6) + (3 \times 2)$
2. $(8 \times 6) - (9 + 2)$
3. $(11 + 5) + (7 - 3)$

4. $(14.9 + 6) + (15.6 - 5.2)$
5. $(9.2 \times 8.3) + (16.2 - 4.5)$
6. $(248 \times 2.5) - (14.5 + 108)$

7. $(4.6 \div 2) - (0.4 + 1.3)$
8. $(0.7 \times 3) + (8 \div 0.2)$
9. $(0.36 \div 0.3) + (0.8 \div 0.2)$

Use a calculator to solve.

10. Zelda must pay a 16% tax on her taxable income of $18,000. Her husband must pay a 19% tax on $23,000. How much tax must Zelda and her husband pay?

11. A state income tax is 1% on the first $4,000 and 1.5% on the next $4,000. What would be the total state tax for an income of $7,800?

Add.

1. $24,850 + $18,920

2. $57,350 + $9,840

3. $125,050 + $78,360

4. $225,100 + $83,692

Subtract.

5. $93,450 − $71,130

6. $70,545 − $48,670

7. $91,800 − $56,072

8. $130,985 − $87,987

Multiply.

9. 9 × $24,000

10. 4 × $34,850

11. 6 × $108,762

12. 0.6 × $123,050

13. 0.4 × $90,765

14. 0.8 × $86,098

Find the answer.

15. 6% of $20,000

16. 9% of $34,500

17. $5\frac{1}{2}$% of $58,050

18. $7\frac{1}{2}$% of $102,085

Divide. Round the answer to the nearest cent.

19. $45,000 ÷ 0.3

20. $38,975 ÷ 0.28

21. $58,975 ÷ 0.28

22. $108,764 ÷ 0.28

Solve the proportion.

23. $\frac{1}{2} = \frac{n}{10}$

24. $\frac{2}{5} = \frac{n}{10}$

25. $\frac{1}{5} = \frac{n}{20}$

26. $\frac{1}{4} = \frac{n}{12}$

27. $\frac{1}{1.5} = \frac{n}{12}$

28. $\frac{1}{1.5} = \frac{n}{18}$

Use the diagram of the room.

29. What is the width?

30. What is the length?

31. Find the perimeter in feet.

32. Find the area in square feet.

33. Find the area in square yards.

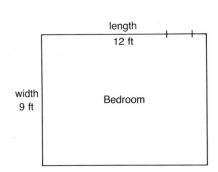

Chapter
12

HOUSING

Housing costs include a mortgage or rent, utilities, and the decoration or remodeling of the house or apartment. What costs were involved in furnishing this room?

Before you look for an apartment, you should know the maximum amount you can afford to spend on **rent.** In general, you should be able to spend a maximum of 28% of your gross monthly pay on rent.

EXAMPLE 1   Your annual gross salary is $16,980. What is the maximum amount you should be able to spend on rent?

1. Divide to find your monthly gross pay. $16,980 ÷ 12 = $1,415

2. Multiply to find the maximum rent.

   THINK: 28% = 0.28   0.28 × $1,415 = $396.20

You should be able to spend a maximum of $396.20 on rent.

Utilities such as gas and electricity are usually not included in the rent.

EXAMPLE 2   You want to rent a 1-bedroom apartment in the Knickerbocker Square Apartments. *Plus Utilities* means that you must pay separately for electricity and gas. About how much will you pay each month for both rent and utilities?

> **KNICKERBOCKER SQUARE APARTMENTS**
> $375 1 bedroom
> $460 2 bedrooms
> $525 3 bedrooms
> Plus Utilities

THINK: Rent for a 1-bedroom apartment: $375
Average monthly utility costs:
Electricity—$65   Gas—$43

1. Add to find cost of utilities. $65 + $43 = $108

2. Add to find the total cost. $375 + $108 = $483

You will pay about $483 per mo for both rent and utilities.

You may need to pay a **security deposit** and a **fee** to a rental agent when you move into your apartment. These payments are **move-in costs.**

EXAMPLE 3   Your rent is $375 per mo. You paid 60% of that as a rental fee and you paid twice that as a security deposit. What were your move-in costs?

1. Multiply to find the rental fee.

   THINK: 60% = 0.6   0.6 × $375 = $225

2. Multiply to find the security deposit.   2 × $375 = $750

3. Add to find the total move-in costs. $225 + $750 = $975

Your move-in costs were $975.

FOR DISCUSSION

1. What other costs might a person have when moving into his or her first apartment?

2. What other costs might a person have when he or she moves from one apartment to another one?

PRACTICE EXERCISES

Remember to estimate whenever you use your calculator.

Find the maximum monthly rent for the gross monthly pay.

1. $828 per mo
2. $2,110 per mo
3. $1,665 per mo

Find the gross monthly pay and the maximum monthly rent. For Exercises 7–9, the work week is 40 h, 50 wk per y.

4. $11,208 per y
5. $14,940 per y
6. $21,708 per y

7. $7.30 per h
8. $8.15 per h
9. $11.80 per h

Use the advertisements for Exercises 10–20.
Find the total monthly cost for rent, utilities, and extras.
Use these amounts for utilities.
Electricity—$49 per mo Gas—$37 per mo

10. THE OVERLOOK
    Studio

11. THE OVERLOOK
    1 bedroom

12. HASTINGS HOUSE
    1 bedroom

13. ECKERSON APTS.
    2 bedrooms

14. ECKERSON APTS.
    1 bedroom

15. THE OVERLOOK
    2 bedrooms

16. HASTINGS HOUSE
    3 bedrooms
    Parking

17. ECKERSON APTS.
    2 bedrooms
    Health Club

THE OVERLOOK
Studio $285
1 bdrm $360
2 bdrm $415
Plus Utilities

ECKERSON APTS.
1 bdrm $495
2 bdrm $660
Plus elec.
Health Club —
$35 per month extra

HASTINGS HOUSE
1 bdrm $375
2 bdrm $485
3 bdrm $520
(utilities included)
Parking —
$40 per month

Find the move-in costs.

Building	18. THE OVERLOOK	19. HASTINGS HOUSE	20. ECKERSON APTS.
Apartment type	1 bedroom	2 bedrooms	2 bedrooms
Rental agent fee	75% of 1 month's rent	10% of annual rent	1 month's rent
Security deposit	2 months' rent	1 month's rent	$1\frac{1}{2}$ month's rent

You know you will need to borrow money to buy a house. Before you look at houses, you should know the maximum you should be able to borrow and the maximum you should be able to spend for a house. In general, you should borrow no more than 2 times your annual gross income.

EXAMPLE 1

You have saved $31,000 to buy a house. Your annual gross income is $28,600. What is the maximum you should be able to borrow? What is the maximum you should be able to spend for a house?

1. Multiply to find the maximum you should borrow.

$$2 \times \$28,600 = \$57,200$$

The maximum you should be able to borrow is $57,200.

2. Add to find the maximum you can spend.

$$\$57,200 + \$31,000 = \$88,200$$

The maximum you should be able to spend on a house is $88,200.

You would like to buy a house that **appreciates** (increases in value) each year. The more the appreciation, the higher the future value of the house.

EXAMPLE 2

Fran bought a house for $85,000. Her house appreciated 5% each year. What was the value of the house after 2 y? How much had it appreciated?

1. Multiply to find the first year's appreciation. **THINK: 5% = 0.05**

$$0.05 \times \$85,000 = \$4,250$$

2. Add to find the value after 1 y.

$$\$85,000 + \$4,250 = \$89,250$$

3. Multiply to find the second year's appreciation.
THINK: Use the value after 1 y.

$$0.05 \times \$89,250 = \$4,462.50$$

4. Add to find the value after 2 y.

$$\$89,250 + \$4,462.50 = \$93,712.50$$

Fran's house was valued at $93,712.50 after 2 y.

5. Subtract to find the amount of appreciation.

$$\$93,712.50 - \$85,000 = \$8,712.50$$

Fran's house was worth $8,712.50 more than she paid for it.

What factors do you think make a house appreciate in value?

PRACTICE EXERCISES

Remember to estimate whenever you use your calculator.

The person(s) want to buy a house. What is the maximum they can afford to borrow? What is the maximum they should be able to spend?

1. Fred Henderson's savings: $18,000
   Gross salary: $41,000 per y

2. Denise Chin's savings: $41,600
   Gross salary: $36,500 per y

3. Marge LaBeau's savings: $27,620
   Gross salary: $785 per wk

4. Rafael Rodriguez's savings: $41,600
   Gross salary: $2,850 per mo

5. Karen Goldblum's savings: $0
   Gross salary: $3,760 per mo

6. The Militano's savings: $17,085
   Gross salaries: Terri $37,200 per y
                   Frank $1,975 per mo

Complete the table to find the appreciation and the value of the house.

Value	Yearly rate of appreciation	Appreciation in 1 y	Value after 1 y
$50,000	10%	7. ■	8. ■
$94,500	5%	9. ■	10. ■
$76,845	8%	11. ■	12. ■
$80,395	9%	13. ■	14. ■
$88,340	7.5%	15. ■	16. ■

Solve.

17. Greg's house was valued at $45,500. The house appreciated 15% each year. What was the value after 2 y?

18. Lillian's house was valued at $70,500. The house appreciated 6.5% each year. What was the value after 2 y?

EXTENSION   Appreciation

Just because a house costs more than another does not mean that it will be more valuable in the future. Ed bought a house for $53,900. It appreciated 13% each year. Eileen bought a house for $61,000. It appreciated 6% each year.

1. Which house was worth more after 2 y?

2. If the houses keep appreciating in the same way, what will the difference in value be in 5 y?

A **condominium** is a building in which apartments are owned. You purchase an apartment just as you would purchase a house. As the owner of an individual condo, or apartment, you pay an additional monthly **maintenance fee** for the care of the building and the grounds. The maintenance fee may include utilities.

> **LUXURY CONDO**
> **1 BR $67,000**
> **Maint. $150/mo**
> **Util. & Taxes**
> Magnificent View
>
> Financing Available
> 10% down
> $551/mo
>
> Parking
> Shopping on premises
>
> Sales office on site
> Call for appt.

EXAMPLE 1
You bought the luxury condo advertised in the newspaper. How much did you put down? How much will you pay each month?

THINK: Price: $67,000
Down payment: 10% = 0.1
Loan payment: $551 per mo
Maintenance fee: $150 per mo

1. Find the down payment. $0.1 \times \$67,000 = \$6,700$

You put down $6,700.

2. Add to find the total monthly payment. $\$551 + \$150 = \$701$

You will pay $701 per mo.

Remember that you should be able to spend 28% of your gross monthly pay for housing. When buying a condominium, that 28% includes maintenance, mortgage payment, taxes, and insurance.

You can "roughly" estimate the gross monthly pay you will need to afford the condominium by just using the loan payment and the maintenance fee.

EXAMPLE 2
The monthly payments for the condominium in Example 1 are $701. Roughly estimate the least you could earn each month to afford the condominium.

THINK: $701 is about $700.   0.28 is about 0.3

If MONTHLY HOUSING COST $= 0.28 \times$ GROSS MONTHLY PAY,
then GROSS MONTHLY PAY $=$ MONTHLY HOUSING COST $\div 0.28$
$=$ $\$700$ $\div 0.3$
$= \$2,333.33$

To afford the condominium, your gross monthly pay would need to be at least $2,340. It would definitely need to be more to cover taxes and insurance.

FOR DISCUSSION

1. Why might someone choose to buy a condominium instead of a house?

2. Condominium maintenance fees are not fixed; they go up as expenses go up. What problems could this cause for the condominium owner?

PRACTICE EXERCISES   Remember to estimate whenever you use your calculator.

Find the down payment and the total monthly payment for the condominium.

1.
PRESTIGE CONDOMINIUMS
$178,000
Maint. $400/mo
Financing: 20% down
$1,260/mo

2.
CLIFFSIDE CONDOS
$90,840
Maint. $125/mo
Financing: 10% down
$714/mo

3.
SCHOOLHOUSE CONDOMINIUMS
$68,755
Maint. $115/mo
Financing: 5% down
$582/mo

Roughly estimate the minimum gross monthly pay needed to afford the condominium's total loan and maintenance payments.

4. $550   5. $948   6. $685   7. $535   8. $1,050

Solve.

9. Pete bought a condominium for $87,600. He put 10% down and pays $705 per mo. The maintenance fee is $105 per mo. Find the down payment and the total monthly payment.

10. Lorraine's condo cost $63,400. She put 15% down and pays $573 per mo. The monthly maintenance fee is $95. Find the down payment and the total monthly payment.

11. Colleen wants to buy a condominium with monthly payments of $1,010. Roughly estimate the minimum gross monthly pay she needs to afford it.

12. Miguel wants to buy a condominium with monthly payments of $643. His current gross pay is $1,875 per mo. About how much more would he need to earn per month to afford the condominium?

EXTENSION   Planning Ahead for Maintenance Fees

CLOVERLEAF CONDOS
$87,450
Maint. $115/mo
Financing:
10% down $689/mo

Brian wants to buy the condominium described in the advertisement. He thinks that the maintenance fee will go up 40% over the next 2 y. He wants to plan ahead. If Brian is right, what will his total monthly payments be in 2 y?

The loan you get to buy a house or a condominium is called a **mortgage.** Your monthly mortgage payment depends on the amount you borrow, the interest rate, and the number of payments.

EXAMPLE 1

You bought a house for $82,750. You put 20% down. You borrowed the remainder at 10.5% for 30 y. What was the down payment and the mortgage amount? How much will you pay each month?

MORTGAGE PAYMENTS PER $1,000			
	Monthly payment		
Interest rate	20-y loan	25-y loan	30-y loan
9.0%	$9.00	$8.40	$8.05
9.5%	$9.33	$8.74	$8.41
10.0%	$9.66	$9.09	$8.78
10.5%	$9.99	$9.45	$9.15
11.0%	$10.33	$9.81	$9.53
11.5%	$10.66	$10.16	$9.90
12.0%	$11.01	$10.53	$10.29
12.5%	$11.36	$10.90	$10.67
13.0%	$11.72	$11.28	$11.06
13.5%	$12.07	$11.66	$11.45
14.0%	$12.44	$12.04	$11.85
14.5%	$12.80	$12.42	$12.25
15.0%	$13.17	$12.81	$12.64
15.5%	$13.54	$13.20	$13.05
16.0%	$13.92	$13.59	$13.45
16.5%	$14.29	$13.99	$13.86
17.0%	$14.67	$14.38	$14.26
17.5%	$15.05	$14.78	$14.67
18.0%	$15.44	$15.18	$15.08

1. Multiply to find the down payment.
   THINK: 20% = 0.2
   $0.2 \times \$82,750 = \$16,550$

The down payment was $16,550.

2. Subtract to find the mortgage amount.
   $\$82,750 - \$16,550 = \$66,200$

The mortgage amount was $66,200.

3. Divide to find how many $1,000 you are borrowing.
   $\$66,200 \div \$1,000 = 66.2$

4. Multiply to find the monthly payment.
   THINK: Use the loan payment table. Find the monthly payment per $1,000, or $9.15.

   $66.2 \times \$9.15 = \$605.73$

You will pay $605.73 per mo.

The **closing** is the day on which you sign the mortgage papers and the contract. You will have to pay **closing costs** to the bank and others who helped process the mortgage. These closing costs may include **points.** Each point is 1% of the mortgage amount.

EXAMPLE 2

The mortgage amount was $66,200. Your closing costs were $2\frac{1}{2}$ points, $250 for the bank's attorney, and a $185 title fee. How much were your closing costs?

THINK: $2\frac{1}{2}$ points = $2\frac{1}{2}\% = 0.025$

1. Multiply to find the points. $0.025 \times \$66,200 = \$1,655$

2. Add to find the closing costs. $\$1,655 + \$250 + \$185 = \$2,090$

Your closing costs were $2,090.

FOR DISCUSSION

1. How could you estimate the extra cost per month of borrowing $50,000 for 30 y at 11% instead of 10%?

2. Some people get an **adjustable rate mortgage (ARM).** As interest rates go up and down, the mortgage rates go up and down. What are the advantages and disadvantages of this type of mortgage?

PRACTICE EXERCISES   Remember to estimate whenever you use your calculator.

Find the monthly payment to the nearest cent.

Mortgage amount	Interest rate	Term	Monthly payment
$45,000	11.5%	30 y	1. ■
$89,000	10.5%	25 y	2. ■
$76,500	9.5%	30 y	3. ■
$67,300	10.0%	20 y	4. ■
$98,700	10.5%	30 y	5. ■

Complete the table to find the down payment, the mortgage amount, and the monthly payment.

Purchase price	Percent down	Down payment	Mortgage amount	Interest rate	Term	Monthly payment
$124,000	20%	6. ■	7. ■	10.5%	30 y	8. ■
$89,700	10%	9. ■	10. ■	10.0%	20 y	11. ■
$93,620	30%	12. ■	13. ■	11.0%	25 y	14. ■
$79,840	15%	15. ■	16. ■	9.5%	30 y	17. ■

Find the closing costs.

Mortgage amount	Points	Attorney's fees	Title fees	Closing costs
$37,000	3	$750	$300	18. ■
$57,000	1	$900	$250	19. ■
$109,500	4	$840	$175	20. ■
$96,450	$2\frac{1}{2}$	$575	$375	21. ■
$88,750	$3\frac{1}{2}$	$465	$305	22. ■

12.5 REAL ESTATE TAXES

Local governments collect **real estate taxes.** The taxes are used to pay for municipal services and schools. The real estate tax is based on the **assessed valuation** of a property. The assessed valuation is a percent of the property's **market value.** The tax rate is an amount per $100 of assessed valuation.

EXAMPLE 1   The market value of your property is $88,700. The assessment rate is 70%. What is the assessed valuation? If the real estate tax rate is $4.29 per $100, what is your annual real estate tax?

ASSESSED VALUATION = ASSESSMENT RATE × MARKET VALUE

1. Multiply to find the assessed valuation.
   THINK: 70% = 0.7 $0.7 × \$88,700 = \$62,090$

The assessed valuation of your property is $62,090.

2. Divide to find the number of $100 of
   assessed valuation. $\$62,090 ÷ \$100 = 620.9$

3. Multiply to find the real estate tax. $620.9 × \$4.29 = \$2,663.661$

Your annual real estate tax is $2,663.66.

You usually pay $\frac{1}{12}$ of your annual real estate tax with your monthly mortgage payment. The bank then pays the taxes when they are due.

EXAMPLE 2   Your monthly mortgage payment is $487. Your annual real estate tax is $2,663.66. What is your combined monthy payment to the bank?

1. Divide to find the monthly
   tax payment. $\$2,663.66 ÷ 12 = \$221.97166 ≈ \$221.97$

2. Add to find the combined.
   payment. $\$221.97 + \$487 = \$708.97$

Your combined payment is $708.97.

1. Why might the tax rate in a town increase?

2. How could a bank earn money for itself by collecting $\frac{1}{12}$ of the real estate taxes each month and holding them until the tax payment is due?

PRACTICE EXERCISES   Remember to estimate whenever you use your calculator.

Find the assessed valuation.

	1.	2.	3.	4.	5.
Market value	$95,000	$118,000	$72,900	$87,300	$98,450
Assessment rate	80%	75%	100%	45%	78%

Find the annual real estate tax.

	6.	7.	8.	9.	10.
Assessed valuation	$64,300	$51,700	$39,200	$80,400	$107,650
Tax rate per $100	$3.72	$4.06	$5.04	$2.89	$4.87

Find the combined monthly payment to the bank.

	11.	12.	13.	14.	15.
Monthly mortgage payment	$413	$397	$516	$471	$507
Annual real estate tax	$3,696	$5,124	$4,344	$3,708	$5,256

Solve.

16. The market value of Serita's house is $125,000. The assessment rate is 70%. What is the assessed valuation?

17. The market value of Tony's house is $95,000. The assessment rate is 55%. What is the assessed valuation?

18. The market value of Ruben's house is $135,000. The assessment rate is 65%. The real estate tax rate is $3.29 per $100. What is the assessed valuation and his annual real estate tax?

19. The market value of Kathy's house is $89,900. The assessment rate is 80%. The real estate tax rate is $4.23 per $100. What is the assessed valuation and her annual real estate tax?

20. Ruben's monthly mortgage payment is $564. Use your answer to Exercise 18 to find his combined monthly payment to the bank.

21. Kathy's monthly mortgage payment is $459. Use your answer to Exercise 19 to find her combined monthly payment to the bank.

12.6 HOMEOWNER'S INSURANCE

If you own a house or condominium or rent an apartment, you need **homeowner's insurance.** Homeowner's insurance pays for damage to your property and belongings and provides liability coverage in case someone is injured on your property. Most homeowner's policies cover loss or damage from all perils except flood, earthquake, and nuclear accident.

You should insure a home or condominium for its full **replacement value,** or the amount it would cost to reconstruct it if destroyed. If you insure for 100% replacement value, then your insurance company will provide these additional coverages.

Other structure (garage, etc.)	10% of house-replacement value
Personal property	50% of house-replacement value
Additional living expenses while house is being repaired or replaced	20% of house-replacement value
Trees, shrubs, plants	5% of house-replacement value

EXAMPLE 1

Your house is fully insured for its replacement value of $98,500. What other coverage would homeowner's insurance provide for losses or damages?

Multiply to find the amounts.

Other structures	(10%)	$0.1 \times \$98,500 = \$9,850$
Personal property	(50%)	$0.5 \times \$98,500 = \$49,250$
Living expenses	(20%)	$0.2 \times \$98,500 = \$19,700$
Trees, shrubs, plants	(5%)	$0.05 \times \$98,500 = \$4,925$

If you rent, you should get homeowner's insurance to cover the full replacement value of your personal property against losses due to fire or theft. Then the insurance company will provide these additional coverages.

Alterations to the apartment	10% of property-replacement value
Additional living expenses while apartment is being repaired	20% of property-replacement value

EXAMPLE 2

Gail rents and fully insures her personal property for $19,250. What other coverage would homeowner's insurance provide for losses or damage?

Multiply to find the amounts.

Alterations	(10%)	$0.1 \times \$19,250 = \$1,925$
Living expenses	(20%)	$0.2 \times \$19,250 = \$3,850$

FOR DISCUSSION

1. Statistics show that 96% of homeowners, but only 32% of renters, have insurance. Why is that?

2. What are the dangers of not having homeowner's insurance?

PRACTICE EXERCISES   Remember to estimate whenever you use your calculator.

Complete the table to show the coverages provided for the homeowner.
The home is insured for its full replacement value.

Home-replacement value	Other structures	Personal property	Additional living expenses	Trees, shrubs, plants
$78,000	1. ■	2. ■	3. ■	4. ■
$109,500	5. ■	6. ■	7. ■	8. ■
$87,645	9. ■	10. ■	11. ■	12. ■

Complete the table to show the coverages provided for the renter.
Personal property is insured for its full replacement value.

Personal property-replacement value	Alterations to apartment	Additional living expenses
$7,600	13. ■	14. ■
$18,250	15. ■	16. ■
$31,118	17. ■	18. ■

EXTENSION   Fire Prevention

This circle graph shows the leading causes of fires in the United States.

There were 868,000 fires in 1 y. About how many of them were caused by:

1. Heating equipment?   **2.** Cooking?

3. Children playing?   **4.** Smoking?

5. Based on these statistics, what steps could you take to reduce fire hazards in your home?

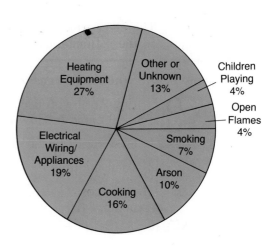

The cost of **utilities** such as electricity, water, natural gas, or heating oil are part of your living costs. **Meters** keep track of how much electricity, water, and natural gas are used.

An electric meter shows the number of **kilowatt-hours (kWh).**

1 kWh is 1,000 watts of electricity used for 1 h.

EXAMPLE 1   Read the electric meter. When the pointer is between 2 numbers, read the lower number.

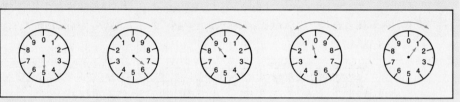

The meter reads 56,901 kWh.

You pay for electricity by the kWh.

EXAMPLE 2   On April 1, your electric meter read 54,095 kWh. On May 1, the meter read 56,901 kWh. A kWh costs $0.0528. How much did it cost you for the electricity used from April 1 to May 1?

COST OF ELECTRICITY = COST PER KWH × KWH

1. Subtract to find the number of kWh used. $56,901 - 54,095 = 2,806$

2. First estimate the cost. $3,000 × \$0.05 = \$150$

3. Then multiply to find the exact cost. $2,806 × \$0.0528 = \$148.1568$

The electricity cost $148.16. The answer is reasonable since it is close to the estimate, $150.

You usually pay for the natural gas you use in units of 100 cubic ft.

EXAMPLE 3   During April, you used 184 hundred cubic ft of gas. Gas costs $0.6133 per 100 cubic ft. How much did it cost you for gas during April?

1. First estimate the cost. $200 × \$0.60 = \$120$

2. Then multiply to find the exact cost. $184 × \$0.6133 = \$112.8472$

The gas cost $112.85. The answer is reasonable since it is close to the estimate, $120.

You usually pay for the water you use in units of 1,000 cubic ft.

EXAMPLE 4 From July through August, you used 2,890 cubic ft of water. Water costs $14.38 per 1,000 cubic ft. How much did it cost you for water?

1. Divide to find the number of 1,000 cubic ft. $2,890 \div 1,000 = 2.89$

2. First estimate the cost. $3 \times \$14 = \$42$

3. Then multiply to find the exact cost. $2.89 \times \$14.38 = \$41.5582$

The water cost $41.56. The answer is reasonable since it is close to the estimate, $42.

FOR DISCUSSION

1. How could you estimate the savings that would result from using less electricity?

2. Is more electricity used in summer or in winter? Why?

PRACTICE EXERCISES
Remember to estimate whenever you use your calculator.

Read the electric meter.

1.
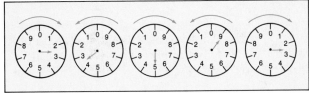

2.
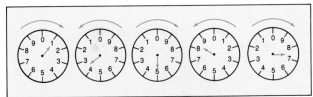

3.
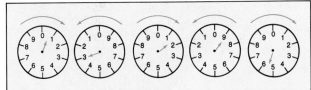

Complete the table to find the kWh used and the cost of the electricity.

Second reading	First reading	kWh used	Cost per kWh	Total cost
52,038 kWh	49,165 kWh	4. ■	$0.0493	5. ■
9,607 kWh	8,406 kWh	6. ■	$0.0603	7. ■
60,831 kWh	43,194 kWh	8. ■	$0.0238	9. ■
19,743 kWh	12,162 kWh	10. ■	$0.0537	11. ■

Find the cost of the gas.

	12.	13.	14.	15.
100 Cubic ft used	141	159	933	222
Cost per 100 cubic ft	$0.5879	$0.9482	$0.0328	$0.6934

Complete the table to find the number of 1,000 cubic ft and the cost of the water.

Cubic ft used	1,000 Cubic ft used	Cost per 1,000 cubic ft	Total cost
3,051	16. ■	$14.38	17. ■
2,134	18. ■	$13.50	19. ■
4,892	20. ■	$11.23	21. ■
4,809	22. ■	$15.85	23. ■

Solve.

24. Gas costs $0.8523 per 100 cubic ft. How much is that per cubic ft?

25. Water costs $13.87 per 1,000 cubic ft. How much is that per cubic ft?

EXTENSION   Monthly Costs of Owning a Home

This circle graph shows the percents of monthly payments the average homeowner spends on mortgage, taxes, utilities, and insurance. A homeowner spends about $1,450 per mo on expenses. About how much is spent on:

1. Mortgage?

2. Utilities?

3. Taxes?

4. Insurance?

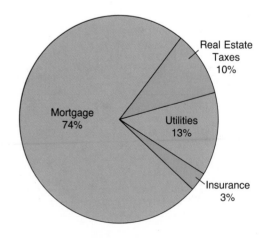

Real Estate Taxes 10%

Mortgage 74%

Utilities 13%

Insurance 3%

You decide to paint the living room walls. You want to make only 1 trip to the paint store to get the paint, so you use the accepted guideline: 1 gal of paint covers about 400 square ft (including spaces for windows and doors).

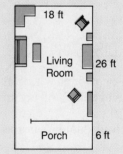
14 ft
18 ft
Living Room

EXAMPLE 1

The ceiling in the room is 8 ft high. How many gallons of paint will you need to paint the walls? How much will the paint cost at $16.85 per gal (including tax)?

THINK: Identify the dimensions of the room.

Length = 18 ft   Width = 14 ft   Height = 8 ft

1. Add to find the perimeter. $14 + 18 + 14 + 18 = 64$ ft

2. Multiply to find the area of the 4 walls. $8 \times 64 = 512$ square ft

3. Divide to find the number of gallons. $512 \div 400 = 1.28$ gal

Since 1.28 gal > 1 gal, you will need 2 gal of paint.

4. Multiply to find the cost. $2 \times \$16.85 = \$33.70$

The paint will cost $33.70.

Denise hired a contractor to remodel her living room and porch. **Remodeling** means entirely rebuilding 1 or more rooms. **Contractors** often quote remodeling costs by the square foot.

18 ft
Living Room   26 ft
Porch   6 ft

EXAMPLE 2

The contractor charged $18 per square ft to remodel the living room and $8 per square ft to remodel the porch. How much did the remodeling cost?

THINK: Identify the dimensions of the rooms.

Living room: 26 ft by 18 ft   Porch: 18 ft by 6 ft

1. Multiply to find the area of each room.
Living room: $26 \times 18 = 468$ square ft
Porch: $18 \times 6 = 108$ square ft

2. Multiply to find the cost of remodeling each room.
Living room: $468 \times \$18 = \$8,424$
Porch: $108 \times \$8 = \$864$

3. Add to find the total cost. $\$8,424 + \$864 = \$9,288$

It cost $9,288 to remodel the living room and the porch.

Scale drawings help people decide where to place furniture in a room. You can use a proportion to find scale dimensions.

EXAMPLE **3** A room is 12 ft long by 9 ft wide. You use a scale of 1 in. = 1.5 ft. What is the scale width of the room?

    1. Write a proportion. $\frac{1}{1.5} = \frac{w}{9}$ ← scale ← actual

    2. Cross multiply. $\frac{1}{1.5} = \frac{w}{9}$

$$1.5w = 9$$

    3. Solve for n. $w = 9 \div 1.5$

$$w = 6$$

    The scale width is 6 in.

FOR DISCUSSION

1. For rooms with 8-ft ceilings, why could you buy 1 gal of paint for every 50 ft of perimeter?

2. How could you use a scale drawing to decide where to put furniture?

PRACTICE EXERCISES   Remember to estimate whenever you use your calculator.

Find the perimeter of the room.

1. 14 ft by 15 ft   **2.** 9 ft by 12 ft   **3.** 13 ft by 15 ft   **4.** 12 ft by 18 ft

How many gallons of paint are needed to paint the walls? How much will the paint cost?

5. Room: 14 ft by 15 ft
    Ceiling: 8 ft
      Paint: $13.95/gal

6. Room: 16 ft by 20 ft
    Ceiling: 8 ft
      Paint: $17.05/gal

7. Room: 24 ft by 38 ft
    Ceiling: 8 ft
      Paint: $10.65/gal

How much will the remodeling cost?

8. Room: 9 ft by 12 ft
   Cost: $14/square ft

9. Garage: 14 ft by 16 ft
   Cost: $9/square ft

10. Basement: 12 ft by 24 ft
    Cost: $10.50/square ft

Find the scale dimensions of the room.

11. Room: 12 ft by 15 ft
    Scale: 1 in. = 1.5 ft

12. Room: 15 ft by 20 ft
    Scale: 2 in = 5 ft

13. Room: 12 ft by 15 ft
    Scale: 5 cm = 2 ft

Use the scale drawing below for Exercises 14–19.

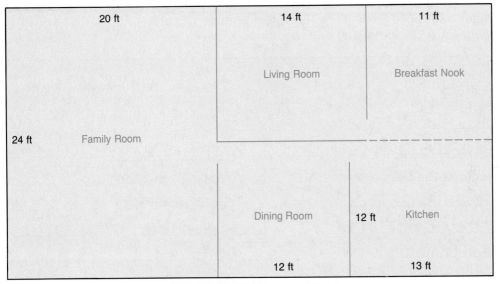

FIRST FLOOR All ceilings are 8 ft high.

14. How many gallons of paint should be bought to paint the living room walls? How much would the paint cost at $17.85 per gal?

15. How many gallons of paint should be bought to paint the walls of all of the rooms? How much would the paint cost at $16.35 per gal?

16. How much would it cost to remodel the dining room at $11.50 per square ft?

17. How much would it cost to remodel the entire first floor at $9.20 per square ft?

18. What would be the scale dimensions of the family room if the scale were 1 in. = 1.5 ft?

19. What would be the scale dimensions of the entire first floor if the scale were 5 cm = 2 ft?

Solve.

20. Alan wants to buy a rug for a 6 yd by 4 yd room. The rug costs $20.50 per square yd. How many square yards does he need? How much will the rug cost?

21. Charlene wants to put a rug in her 12 ft by 15 ft bedroom. The rug costs $18.00 per square yd. How many square yards does she need? How much will the rug cost?

12.9 CHOOSING A MORTGAGE

Banks and other lending institutions provide many different kinds of home mortgages. Listing the features of several mortgages can help you to decide which one to choose.

PROBLEM

Noel and Dave are buying a home. They need a $65,000 mortgage. They have 3 mortgages to choose from. They listed the features of each mortgage to help them decide which one to choose.

PEOPLES BANK

Amount: $65,000

Type: Fixed rate

Interest rate: 11.5%

Points: 1

Term: 30y

Other closing costs: $960

NATIONAL BANK

Amount: $65,000

Type: Fixed rate

Interest rate: 11%

Points: 2

Term: 25y

Other closing costs: $1,425

INTOWN BANK

Amount: $65,000

Type: Adjustable rate

(Interest can go up or down)

Interest rate: 10.5%

Points: 3

Term: 20y

Other closing costs: $640

DECISION-MAKING FACTORS

Annual Percentage Rate (APR)   Type of mortgage   Monthly payment
Closing costs (incl. points)   Term   Amount to be repaid

DECISION-MAKING COMPARISONS

Complete the table to compare the 3 mortgages. Use the table on page 240 to find the monthly payment.

Factors	Peoples Bank	National Bank	Intown Bank
APR	11.5%	1. ■	2. ■
Type	Fixed	3. ■	4. ■
Monthly payment	5. ■	6. ■	$649.35 (may vary)
Closing costs (incl. points)	7. ■	$2,725	8. ■
Term	9. ■	10. ■	11. ■
Amount to be repaid	12. ■	13. ■	$155,844 (may vary)

MAKING THE DECISIONS

Which mortgage should Noel and David choose if they wanted

14. The lowest APR?

15. The lowest monthly payment?

16. The shortest term?

17. To pay the least in closing costs?

18. Why might they choose an adjustable rate mortgage?

19. What are the dangers of choosing an adjustable rate mortgage?

20. How much less would they repay if they got their mortgage from the National Bank instead of the Peoples Bank?

What would their monthly payments be if the adjustable rate mortgage:

21. Rose to $12\frac{1}{2}\%$?

22. Fell to $9\frac{1}{2}\%$?

23. Which mortgage would you choose? Why?

CHAPTER

REVIEW

Vocabulary Choose the letter of the word(s) that completes the sentence.

1. A building in which apartments are owned is called a ■. [238]

    a. Rental **b.** House **c.** Condominium

2. The percent of the mortgage amount paid at the closing is called ■. [240]

    a. Interest **b.** Points **c.** Appreciation

3. Utility companies sell electricity by the ■. [246]

    a. Kilowatt hour **b.** Cubic foot **c.** Hour

Skills Find the answer.

4. Ed earns $1,500 per mo. What is the maximum monthly rent he should be able to afford? [234]

5. Maria's rent is $405 per mo. Utilities are $109. What is her total monthly cost? [234]

6. Lucy earns $26,500 per y. How much should she be able to borrow to buy a house? [236]

7. Martin's $55,000 house appreciated 15% over the last year. What is it now worth? [236]

8. Ron put 20% down on a $37,000 condo. How much was that? [238]

9. Liz put 20% down on a $75,000 house. What is her mortgage amount? [240]

Use the Mortgage Payments table on page 240 for Exercises 10–11.

10. Fran got a $56,000 mortgage for 25 y at 11%. How much will she pay each month? [240]

11. Carlos put 15% down on a $90,000 house. What is the mortgage amount and his monthly payment for a 30-y loan at 11.5%? [240]

12. Sam's mortgage was $63,000. The closing costs were 2 points and $405 in fees. What were his closing costs? [240]

13. The market value of Monica's property is $88,000. The assessment rate is 80%. What is the assessed valuation? [242]

14. The assessed valuation of Jack's house is $45,000. The tax rate is $4.85 per $100. What is his annual real estate tax? [242]

15. Dawn's house used 2,093 kWh of electricity. How much did the electricity cost at $0.0427 per kWh? [246]

16. Diana used 172 hundred cubic ft of gas. How much did the gas cost at $0.7215 per 100 cubic ft? [246]

17. Carl's rectangular living room measures 18 ft by 21 ft by 8 ft high. How many gallons of paint are needed to paint the walls? [249]

254 CHAPTER 12

Find the maximum monthly rent for the gross pay.

1. Gross monthly pay: $520

2. Gross annual salary: $20,900

Find the maximum to borrow for a house.

3. Gross annual income: $24,090

4. Gross monthly income: $1,620

Find the appreciation and the appreciated value of the house.

5. Initial value: $53,000
   Appreciation: 15% per y for 1 y

6. Initial value: $60,900
   Appreciation: 10% per y for 2 y

7. Find the total monthly cost.
   Rent: $585 per mo
   Electricity: $59 per mo
   Gas: $42 per mo
   Health club: $30 per mo

8. Find the down payment and the total monthly payment.
   Condo price: $100,980
   Maintenance: $225 per mo
   Financing: 15% down, $832 per mo

Use the Mortgage Payments table on page 240.

9. What is the monthly payment on a 25-y, $95,000 mortgage at 12%?

10. The closing costs for an $83,000 mortgage were $1\frac{1}{2}$ points and $98 in fees. How much was that?

Find the assessed valuation and the annual real estate tax.

11. Market value: $230,000
    Assessment rate: 80%
    Tax rate: $3.29 per $100

12. Market value: $198,900
    Assessment rate: 75%
    Tax rate: $4.09 per $100

Use the homeowner's insurance information on page 244.

13. A house is insured for its full replacement value of $137,000. What is the coverage for personal property?

14. A renter's personal property is insured for its full replacement value of $23,500. What is the coverage for additional living expenses?

Find the cost of the utility.

15. Electricity used: 3,905 kWh
    Cost per kWh: $0.0398

16. Water used: 4,287 cubic ft
    Cost per 1,000 cubic ft: $12.97

Find the answer.

17. A room measures 18 ft by 15 ft by 8 ft high. How many gallons of paint are needed to paint the walls?

18. How much would it cost to remodel a 22 ft by 16 ft room at $8.50 per square ft?

By calling at certain times on certain days, you can save money on local telephone calls.

LET'S LOOK AT THE FACTS

Many cities offer discount rates for local calls (when the caller and the person being called are in the same area). In some places, calls between nearby communities or counties are also considered local.

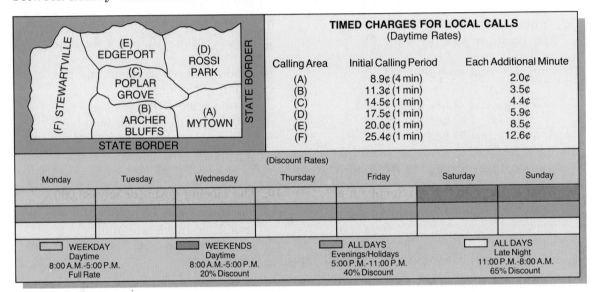

TIMED CHARGES FOR LOCAL CALLS
(Daytime Rates)

Calling Area	Initial Calling Period	Each Additional Minute
(A)	8.9¢ (4 min)	2.0¢
(B)	11.3¢ (1 min)	3.5¢
(C)	14.5¢ (1 min)	4.4¢
(D)	17.5¢ (1 min)	5.9¢
(E)	20.0¢ (1 min)	8.5¢
(F)	25.4¢ (1 min)	12.6¢

(Discount Rates)

Monday	Tuesday	Wednesday	Thursday	Friday	Saturday	Sunday

WEEKDAY Daytime 8:00 A.M.-5:00 P.M. Full Rate	WEEKENDS Daytime 8:00 A.M.-5:00 P.M. 20% Discount	ALL DAYS Evenings/Holidays 5:00 P.M.-11:00 P.M. 40% Discount	ALL DAYS Late Night 11:00 P.M.-8:00 A.M. 65% Discount

LET'S DISCUSS WHY

1. Why do you think telephone companies give discounts on local calls?

2. Which would cost more: a 10-min call from Poplar Grove to Rossi Park on Saturday at 4:00 P.M. or a 10-min call from Rossi Park to Poplar Grove on Sunday at 8:00 P.M.?

LET'S SEE WHAT YOU WOULD DO

3. You live in Mytown and have your own consulting business at home. You have 1 telephone for business, as well as personal, calls. Most of your business calls are made on weekdays between 9:00 A.M. and 5:00 P.M. Should you use *timed service* or *untimed service*, which charges a flat monthly fee for a specific number of hours' calling time?

4. Your office is in south Edgeport. You live in Stewartville near the state border, which is 26 mi from work, so you decide to move. There is 1 apartment near your office in Edgeport and 1 just over the county line in Mytown. You make many personal phone calls. Considering this factor alone, which apartment would you take? Why?

ESTIMATION SKILLS

ESTIMATION OF QUOTIENTS USING COMPATIBLE NUMBERS

If one number can be divided by another with a remainder of 0, the numbers are called **compatible numbers.** You can estimate quotients using compatible numbers.

1. Find compatible numbers that are close in value to the given divisor and dividend.

2. Divide, using the compatible numbers.

Sometimes only the dividend needs to be changed.

Examples $4,695 \div 4$
          $\downarrow$
THINK: $4,800 \div 4 = 1,200$
Estimate: $1,200$

$\$93.68 \div 30$
          $\downarrow$
THINK: $\$90 \div 30 = \$3$
Estimate: $\$3$

At other times, it is necessary to change both the divisor and the dividend.

Examples $372,568 \div 232$
          $\downarrow$ $\downarrow$
THINK: $400,000 \div 200 = 2,000$
Estimate: $2,000$

$762.84 \div 9.35$
          $\downarrow$ $\downarrow$
THINK: $720 \div 9 = 80$
Estimate: 80

Use compatible numbers to estimate the quotient.

1. $55 \div 3$

2. $641 \div 2$

3. $413 \div 4$

4. $902 \div 32$

5. $537 \div 61$

6. $873 \div 22$

7. $3,892 \div 16$

8. $85,376 \div 416$

9. $652,400 \div 822$

10. $\$274.62 \div 5$

11. $\$31.45 \div 6$

12. $\$86.38 \div 3$

13. $\$912.98 \div 45$

14. $\$652.30 \div 72$

15. $\$4,362.00 \div 89$

16. $\$185.75 \div 12$

17. $\$172.30 \div 28$

18. $\$4,313.00 \div 22$

19. $45.2 \div 9$

20. $203.4 \div 7$

21. $131.35 \div 4$

22. $23 \div 4.2$

23. $492.6 \div 8.1$

24. $30.2 \div 7.5$

25. $0.461 \div 0.23$

26. $28.474 \div 3.16$

27. $29.06 \div 5.47$

CUMULATIVE REVIEW

Choose the letter of the word(s) that completes the sentence.

1. To determine which package of food is the better buy, compare the ■.

   a. Unit prices   **b.** Package prices   **c.** Sizes   **d.** None of these

2. You multiply rate (in miles per hour) by time (in hours) to find ■.

   a. Average speed   **b.** Mpg   **c.** Distance   **d.** None of these

3. Gross income, less any adjustments, is called ■.

   a. Taxable income   **b.** Adjusted gross income (AGI)
   c. A deduction   **d.** None of these

4. The W-2 form is used to report ■.

   a. Wages   **b.** Deductions   **c.** Interest   **d.** None of these

5. Utility companies sell electricity by the ■.

   a. Hour   **b.** Kilowatt-hour   **c.** Cubic foot   **d.** None of these

Select the best estimated answer.

6. $5,672 + 6,154 + 705$ **a.** 10,000   **b.** 11,000   **c.** 11,700   **d.** 12,700

7. $9,763 - 3,099$ **a.** 5,000   **b.** 6,000   **c.** 7,000   **d.** 13,000

8. 61×398 **a.** 2,400   **b.** 18,000   **c.** 24,000   **d.** 240,000

9. $39,765 \div 21$ **a.** 200   **b.** 2,000   **c.** 2,500   **d.** 3,000

Compute.

10. $6,437 + 9,804 + 351$

    a. 15,592   **b.** 16,582   **c.** 16,592   **d.** None of these

11. $40.08 - 6.75$

    a. 3.33   **b.** 33   **c.** 33.33   **d.** None of these

12. 8×679

    a. 4,879   **b.** 5,432   **c.** 5,600   **d.** None of these

13. $7\overline{)4.76}$

    a. 0.68   **b.** 0.71   **c.** 0.8   **d.** None of these

14. 75% of 36

    a. 24   **b.** 28   **c.** 32   **d.** None of these

Solve.

15. You buy milk for $2.09 and 2.2 lb of meat at 85¢ per lb. You also have a "25¢ off" coupon for the milk. What is the total cost?

    a. $1.62   **b.** $3.71   **c.** $3.96   **d.** None of these

16. On the first day of vacation, Monica drove 428.7 mi. She used 11 gal of gas. Estimate the mpg.

    a. 20 mpg   **b.** 40 mpg   **c.** 44 mpg   **d.** None of these

17. A train leaves New York City at 9:17 A.M. (EST) and arrives in Fayetteville at 6:07 P.M. (EST). Find the traveling time.

    a. 8 h 47 min   **b.** 8 h 50 min   **c.** 9 h 50 min   **d.** None of these

18. A room measures 23 ft × 16 ft × 8-ft high. If 1 gal of paint covers about 400 square ft, about how many gallons of paint are needed to paint the walls?

    a. 1 gal   **b.** 2 gal   **c.** 3 gal   **d.** None of these

19. Jean has a part-time job. In 2 wk, she earned a total of $120. During the first week, she earned $20 more than the second week. How much did she earn in each of the 2 wk?

    a. $70 and $50   **b.** $50 and $70
    c. $80 and $40   **d.** None of these

20. Enrico had planned to make four $700 payments for his estimated federal taxes. After one payment, he increased his estimated federal tax due by $1,200. How much were each of Enrico's last 3 payments?

    a. $300   **b.** $700   **c.** $1,100   **d.** None of these

THINKING ABOUT MATH

1. List some of the factors to consider before you buy a car. How can these factors help you decide which car to buy?

2. Pretend you are a salesperson who must travel from Orlando, Florida, to Austin, Texas. Which method of transportation should you use—plane, bus, or car? List some of the factors considered in your decision.

3. Why do people usually prefer to buy a home rather than to rent?

Multiply.

1. $145 \times \$50$

2. $1{,}500 \times \$75$

3. $180 \times 36¢$

4. $225 \times 56¢$

5. $20 \times 5\frac{1}{2}$

6. $8 \times 6\frac{2}{3}$

7. $150 \times 4\frac{2}{5}$

8. $80 \times 5\frac{3}{4}$

9. $2 \times \frac{2}{3} \times 16$

10. $2 \times \frac{1}{3} \times 8$

11. $4 \times \frac{1}{2} \times 14$

Estimate the quotient.

12. $3{,}326 \div 400$

13. $1{,}807 \div 290$

14. $2{,}680 \div 300$

Divide and round to the nearest tenth.

15. $750 \div 9$

16. $3{,}873 \div 15$

17. $2{,}580 \div 27$

18. $1{,}900 \div 12$

Add or subtract.

19. $4\frac{1}{2} + \frac{3}{8}$

20. $\frac{5}{8} + 5\frac{3}{4}$

21. $3\frac{1}{3} - \frac{2}{3}$

22. $4\frac{5}{8} - \frac{3}{4}$

Convert to feet.

23. 15 yd

24. $5\frac{1}{3} \text{ yd}$

25. $24 \text{ yd } 2 \text{ ft}$

26. $17 \text{ yd } 8 \text{ ft}$

Convert to yards.

27. 18 ft

28. 288 ft

29. 100 ft

30. 85 ft

Find the perimeter.

31.
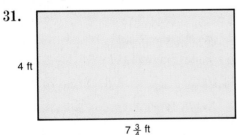
4 ft

$7\frac{3}{4}$ ft

32.
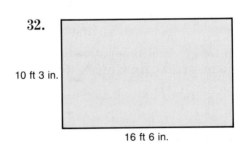
10 ft 3 in.

16 ft 6 in.

Find the area.

33.
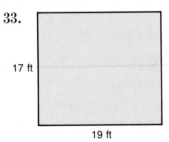
17 ft

19 ft

34.
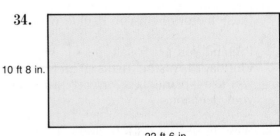
10 ft 8 in.

22 ft 6 in.

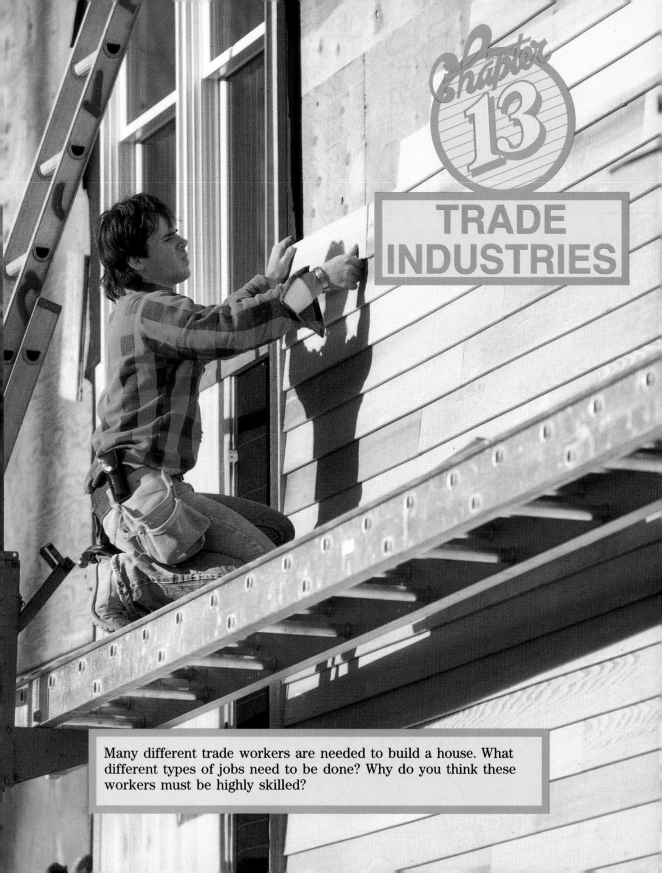

TRADE INDUSTRIES

Many different trade workers are needed to build a house. What different types of jobs need to be done? Why do you think these workers must be highly skilled?

13.1 CARPENTRY

Carpenters usually estimate the cost of a job on a square-foot basis. New residential construction is estimated at about $50 per square ft and renovation work is estimated at about $75 per square ft.

EXAMPLE 1 Charles Atamian is a carpenter who submits an estimate to build a 24 ft by 30 ft addition to a house. At $50 per square ft, how much does he estimate the job will cost?

1. Find the number of square ft (area).   24 ft × 30 ft = 720 square ft

2. Multiply to estimate the cost.   720 × $50 = $36,000

Charles estimates the addition will cost $36,000.

Carpenters usually buy lumber by the **board foot.** A board foot is the amount of wood in a board 1-in. thick by 1-ft wide by 1-ft long.

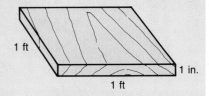

1 ft   1 in.   1 ft

EXAMPLE 2 How many board feet are in 1 16-ft-long piece of 2 in. by 4 in. lumber?

THINK: Thickness: 2 in.   **Width: 4 in.**   **Length: 16 ft**

Since 4 in. = $\frac{1}{3}$ ft, the board is 2 in. by $\frac{1}{3}$ ft by 16 ft.

Multiply to find the board feet.   2 in. × $\frac{1}{3}$ ft × 16 ft = $\frac{32}{3}$ = $10\frac{2}{3}$ board ft

The board contains $10\frac{2}{3}$ board ft.

EXAMPLE 3 Charles needs 36 16-ft-long 2 in. by 8 in. boards for the rafters and 60 8-ft-long 2 in. by 4 in. boards for the wall studs. At 36¢ per board ft, how much will the lumber cost?

1. Find the number of board feet in each size of lumber.

2 in. × 8 in. × 16 ft = 2 in. × $\frac{2}{3}$ ft × 16 ft = $\frac{64}{3}$ = $21\frac{1}{3}$ board ft

2 in. × 4 in. × 8 ft = 2 in. × $\frac{1}{3}$ ft × 8 ft = $\frac{16}{3}$ = $5\frac{1}{3}$ board ft

2. Multiply by the number of boards.

36 boards × $21\frac{1}{3}$ board ft =   768 board ft

60 boards × $5\frac{1}{3}$ board ft =   <u> 320 board ft</u>

3. Add.   Total = 1,088 board ft

4. Multiply by the cost per board foot.

1,088 board ft × $0.36 = $391.68

The lumber will cost $391.68.

FOR DISCUSSION

1. Why is the cost of renovation work often higher than the cost of new construction?

2. What is the difference between 1 board foot and 1 linear, or straight-measured, foot of lumber?

PRACTICE EXERCISES   Remember to estimate whenever you use your calculator.

Find the estimated cost. Estimate new construction at $50 per square ft and renovation work at $75 per square ft.

1. New: 9 ft by 12 ft

2. New: 20 ft by 24 ft

3. New: 28 ft by 40 ft

4. Renovation: 10 ft by 15 ft

5. Renovation: 18 ft by 30 ft

6. Renovation: 20 ft by 45 ft

7. Renovation: 50 ft by 64 ft

Complete the table.

Board size	Length of board	Number of boards	Number of board feet	Cost per board foot	Total cost
1 in. by 6 in.	12 ft	2	8. ▓	37.5¢	9. ▓
2 in. by 4 in.	10 ft	24	10. ▓	27¢	11. ▓
2 in. by 6 in.	16 ft	15	12. ▓	32.5¢	13. ▓
1 in. by 10 in.	6 ft	8	14. ▓	40¢	15. ▓
2 in. by 8 in.	14 ft	30	16. ▓	29.5¢	17. ▓

Complete to find the total cost of the purchase.

Qty.	Item	Unit Cost	Total
10	2 in. by 6 in. by 12 ft board	30¢/board foot	18. ▓
18	2 in. by 4 in. by 12 ft board	30¢/board foot	19. ▓
6	4 ft by 8 ft plywood	$14.95/sheet	20. ▓
4 pkg.	gray shingles	$19.75/pkg.	21. ▓
5 lb	common nails	62¢/lb	22. ▓
		Total	23. ▓

RAY'S LUMBER COMPANY

Rachel O'Neal is a **plumber.** She installs and repairs sinks, showers, bath tubs, and toilets.

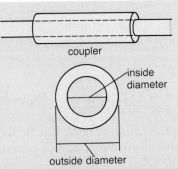

coupler

inside diameter

outside diameter

EXAMPLE 1 Rachel needs to connect 2 pieces of plastic drain pipe with a plastic coupler. The pipe has an inside diameter of $1\frac{5}{8}$ in. and a thickness of $\frac{1}{4}$ in. Find the required inside diameter of the coupler.

THINK: Inside diameter of the coupler = Outside diameter of the pipe = Inside diameter of the pipe plus twice the pipe's thickness

Add to find the diameter of the coupler.

$$1\tfrac{5}{8}\text{ in.} + \tfrac{1}{4}\text{ in.} + \tfrac{1}{4}\text{ in.} = 1\tfrac{5}{8}\text{ in.} + \tfrac{2}{8}\text{ in.} + \tfrac{2}{8}\text{ in.} = 1\tfrac{9}{8}\text{ in.} = 2\tfrac{1}{8}\text{ in.}$$

The inside diameter of the coupler must be $2\frac{1}{8}$ in.

EXAMPLE 2 To install an underground sprinkler system, Rachel needs fifteen $18\frac{1}{2}$-ft-long sections of plastic pipe. If the pipe comes in 100-ft coils, about how many coils will Rachel need?

THINK: $18\frac{1}{2}$ ft is about 20 ft.

$100 \div 20 = 5$, so Rachel can get about 5 sections per coil.

5 sections per coil means about 15 sections from 3 coils.
Rachel will need three 100-ft coils of pipe.

EXAMPLE 3 Rachel needs twelve 20-ft lengths of copper pipe, 20 copper couplers, and 8 elbow joints to install plumbing in a new house. Pipe costs 35¢ per ft, couplers cost 55¢ each, and elbows cost 85¢ each. She charges $30 per h for labor. How much will the 48-h job cost?

1. Multiply to find the cost of materials.

$$12 \times 20\text{ ft} \times \$0.35/\text{ft} = \$84.00$$
$$20 \times \$0.55 = \$11.00$$
$$8 \times \$0.85 = \$\ 6.80$$
$$\$101.80$$

2. Add to find the total cost of materials.

3. Multiply to find the labor charges. $\qquad 48 \times \$30.00 = \$1,440$

4. Add to find the total cost. $\qquad \$101.80 + \$1,440 = \$1,541.80$

The total cost of the job will be $1,541.80.

1. Why does a 10-ft piece of $\frac{3}{4}$-in. copper tubing cost more than a 10-ft piece of $\frac{1}{2}$-in. copper tubing?

2. Why does doubling the diameter of a pipe quadruple the pipe's capacity?

PRACTICE EXERCISES   Remember to estimate whenever you use your calculator.

Complete the table of pipe measurements.

Inside diameter	Thickness of pipe	Outside diameter
$1\frac{1}{4}$ in.	$\frac{1}{16}$ in.	1. ■
$2\frac{1}{8}$ in.	$\frac{3}{16}$ in.	2. ■
$3\frac{3}{4}$ in.	$\frac{3}{8}$ in.	3. ■

Inside diameter	Thickness of pipe	Outside diameter
4. ■	$\frac{1}{8}$ in.	$2\frac{1}{4}$ in.
5. ■	$\frac{5}{16}$ in.	$3\frac{11}{16}$ in.
$\frac{3}{4}$ in.	6. ■	$1\frac{1}{8}$ in.

Complete the table to estimate the coils of pipe needed.

Number of pieces needed	Length of each piece	Total length	Number of 20-ft sections needed	Number of 100-ft coils needed
12	$8\frac{1}{2}$ ft	7. ■	8. ■	9. ■
26	16 ft 9 in.	10. ■	11. ■	12. ■
15	26 ft 4 in.	13. ■	14. ■	15. ■

Find the total cost of the job. Assume labor charges of $24.00 per h.

16. Materials: 50 ft copper pipe at 27¢/ft; 6 couplers at 59¢ each; 4 elbows at 79¢ each; 3 valves at $4.99 each
    Labor: $3\frac{1}{2}$ h

17. Materials: 250 ft plastic pipe at 12¢/ft; 80 ft copper pipe at 32¢/ft; 2 toilets at $120 each; 3 sinks at $85.50 each; 3 faucets at $27.50 each
    Labor: 18 h

EXTENSION   Leaky Faucets

The kitchen faucet in the Powells' house drips once every 5 s. If there are 100 drops per oz, how many gallons of water can be wasted in 1 wk? In 1 y?

Tom Williams is an **electrical contractor.** He wires houses and buildings to distribute the flow of electricity. Electricians estimate the materials they will need to complete a job.

EXAMPLE 1

If Tom averages 75 ft of wire per room when wiring a new home, how many 100-ft coils of wire should be purchased for a 9-room house?

1. Multiply to estimate the total amount of wire.

$9 \times 75 \text{ ft} = 675 \text{ ft}$

2. Divide to find the number of coils. Round up to be sure there is enough.

$675 \div 100 = 6.75 \text{ coils}$
$6.75 \approx 7 \text{ coils}$

Tom should purchase 7 coils of wire.

EXAMPLE 2

For an addition to a house, Tom ordered 200 ft of #14 electrical-cable wire, 9 outlet boxes, 3 switches, and 6 3-prong receptacles. Find the total cost of the materials if the wire costs $39.50 per 100 ft, the outlet boxes are $4.65 each, the switches are $3.75 each, and the receptacles are $3.25 each.

1. Multiply to find the total cost of each item.

wire	$2 \times \$39.50 =$	$79.00
outlet boxes	$9 \times \$4.65 =$	$41.85
switches	$3 \times \$3.75 =$	$11.25
receptacles	$6 \times \$3.25 =$	$19.50

2. Add to find the total cost. $151.60

The materials will cost $151.60.

EXAMPLE 3

For most jobs, Tom charges $24.75 per h for labor for himself and $15.45 per h for his assistant. What is the labor charge for a job on which they work together for $7\frac{1}{2}$ h?

1. Multiply to find the total charges.

electrician $7.5 \text{ h} \times \$24.75/\text{h} = \$185.625 \approx \$185.63$

assistant $7.5 \text{ h} \times \$15.45/\text{h} = \$115.875 \approx \$115.88$

2. Add to find the total. $301.51

The total labor charge is $301.51.

1. Why do most building codes require that electrical work be done by licensed electricians?

2. What purpose do fuses and circuit breakers play in a building's electrical system?

PRACTICE EXERCISES   Remember to estimate whenever you use your calculator.

Complete the table.

Average number of feet of wire per room	Number of rooms	Number of 100-ft coils needed	Cost per 100 ft	Total cost
75	3	1. ▦	$29.95	2. ▦
65	5	3. ▦	$32.50	4. ▦
90	6	5. ▦	$39.65	6. ▦
120	8	7. ▦	$45.25	8. ▦
80	11	9. ▦	$37.80	10. ▦

Complete the table. Assume that 1 d = 8 h.

Time worked	Number of electricians	Hourly labor rates	Total labor charge
$6\frac{1}{2}$ h	1; 1 assistant	$21.00; $15.00	11. ▦
15 h	1; 2 assistants	$18.73; $12.00	12. ▦
$12\frac{3}{4}$ h	1; 2 assistants	$37.25; $25.85	13. ▦
5 d	2; 2 assistants	$27.45; $18.50	14. ▦
2 d 3 h	2; 2 assistants	$38.35; $27.50	15. ▦

Find the total cost of the job. Assume labor charges of $28.50 per h for 1 electrician.

16. Parts: 800 ft #12 wire at $26.79 per 100 ft; 400 ft #8 wire at $19.85 per 100 ft; 12 outlet boxes at $7.45 each; 6 receptacles at $5.35 each; 6 outlet covers at $1.19 each

    Labor: $7\frac{3}{4}$ h

17. Parts: 300 ft #14 wire at $31.95 per 100 ft; 5 junction boxes at $9.50 each; 12 switches at $4.87 each; 2 dimmers at $3.95 each; 25 insulators at 16¢ each

    Labor: $5\frac{1}{2}$ h

Sam and Rick Owens are professional **painting contractors.** They need to order the correct amount of paint and to estimate the costs of jobs.

One gallon of most interior paint covers about 400 square ft with 1 coat.

EXAMPLE 1

Sam and Rick have been contracted to paint two 11 ft by 30 ft walls. Each wall contains two 3 ft by 5 ft windows and a 3 ft by 7 ft door. Sam and Rick will use 2 coats of paint. How many gallons of paint will they need? At $12.75 per gal, how much will the paint cost?

1. Find the area to be painted.

- Find the total area. $2 \times 11 \text{ ft} \times 30 \text{ ft} = 660 \text{ square ft}$
- Find the unpainted area. $4 \times 3 \text{ ft} \times 5 \text{ ft} = 60 \text{ square ft}$
  $\underline{2 \times 3 \text{ ft} \times 7 \text{ ft} = 42 \text{ square ft}}$
  102 square ft
- Subtract to find the painted area. $660 - 102 = 558 \text{ square ft}$
- Multiply to find the area for 2 coats of paint. $2 \times 558 = 1{,}116 \text{ square ft}$

2. Divide to find the number of gallons needed. $1{,}116 \div 400 = 2.79 \text{ gal}$

Sam and Rick will need to buy 3 gal of paint.

3. Multiply to find the cost. $3 \times \$12.75 = \$38.25$

The paint will cost $38.25.

EXAMPLE 2

Sam and Rick usually work together and charge $20.00 per h each for their labor. It took them $3\frac{1}{2}$ h to paint the 2 walls. What was the labor cost?

THINK: 2 people $\times$ $3\frac{1}{2}$ $\times$ $20.00 per h

Multiply. $2 \times 3\frac{1}{2} \times \$20 = \$140.00$

Their labor charge was $140.00.

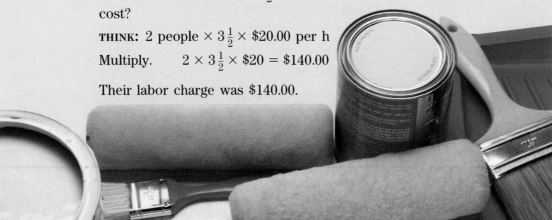

Why does a gallon of interior paint usually cover more area than a
gallon of exterior paint?

PRACTICE EXERCISES   Remember to estimate whenever you use your calculator.

Complete the table. Assume that each wall contains two 3 ft by 5 ft
windows and a 3 ft by 7 ft door. Assume that paint costs $16.50 per gal.

Dimensions of wall(s)	Total area	Unpainted area	Painted area	Number of coats	Number of gallons needed	Cost of paint
one 9 ft by 12 ft	1. ■	2. ■	3. ■	1	4. ■	5. ■
one 15 ft by 25 ft	6. ■	7. ■	8. ■	1	9. ■	10. ■
one 8 ft by 16 ft	11. ■	12. ■	13. ■	2	14. ■	15. ■
two 24 ft by 40 ft	16. ■	17. ■	18. ■	2	19. ■	20. ■
two 40 ft by 70 ft	21. ■	22. ■	23. ■	2	24. ■	25. ■

Complete the table. Assume that 1 d = 8 h.

Number of painters	Time worked per painter	Cost per hour per painter	Total labor cost
2	12 h	$14.00	26. ■
5	$2\frac{1}{2}$ d	$16.50	27. ■
3	4 d 3 h	$21.15	28. ■
12	5 d	$18.75	29. ■

Use the diagram of the barn for Exercises 30–34.
What is the area of:

30. the longer side?   **31.** the shorter side?

32. the triangular rise?

33. 2 longer sides, 1 shorter side, and the
triangular rise?

34. One gallon of exterior paint covers about
250 square ft. How many gallons of paint
will be needed to cover the area in
Exercise 33?

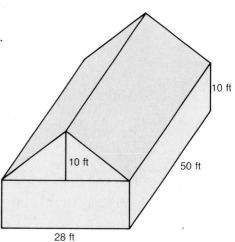

10 ft

10 ft

50 ft

28 ft

13.5 MASONRY

Carla Mendez is a **mason.** She uses bricks, cement blocks, and mortar to construct walls and fireplaces. Masons use mathematics to order materials, to compute the cost of jobs, and to complete projects accurately and according to plans.

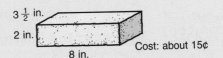

Cost: about 15¢

Masons use standard-sized bricks that measure 8 in. by 2 in. by $3\frac{1}{2}$ in. They use standard-sized concrete blocks that measure 16 in. by 8 in. by 8 in.

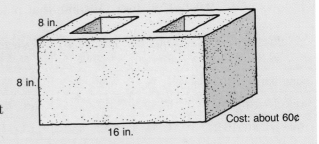

Cost: about 60¢

EXAMPLE 1

Carla is contracted to construct a 249-square-ft brick facade on the front of a new house. If Carla uses 9 bricks per square ft, how many bricks should she order? At 15¢ per brick, how much will the bricks cost?

1. Multiply to find the number of bricks.

$$249 \text{ square ft} \times 9 \text{ bricks/square ft} = 2{,}241 \text{ bricks}$$

Carla should order 2,241 bricks.

2. Multiply to find the cost. $2{,}241 \times \$0.15 = \$336.15$

The bricks will cost $336.15.

EXAMPLE 2

Carla has found that mixing 2 bags of cement with 5 cubic ft of sand makes enough mortar for about 100 square ft of brickwork. How many bags of cement will she need for the 249-square-ft job in Example 1? At $6.75 per bag, how much will the cement cost?

1. Use a proportion to find the number of bags. Round the answer up.

THINK: 2 bags is to 100 square ft as n bags is to 249 square ft.

$$\frac{2 \text{ bags}}{100 \text{ square ft}} = \frac{n \text{ bags}}{249 \text{ square ft}}$$
$$100n = 2 \times 249$$
$$100n = 498$$
$$n = 498 \div 100 = 4.98 \approx 5$$

Carla will need 5 bags of cement.

2. Multiply to find the cost. $5 \times \$6.75 = \$33.75$

The cement will cost $33.75.

FOR DISCUSSION

1. Why do masons usually order more bricks than their computations indicate?

2. Why are many fireplaces constructed primarily of cement blocks with bricks placed only on the visible parts?

PRACTICE EXERCISES   Remember to estimate whenever you use your calculator.

Complete the table. Assume that concrete blocks cost 60¢ each and that you use 10 blocks per square yd.

Total area	Number of blocks needed	Cost of blocks
12 square yd	1. ▨	2. ▨
38 square yd	3. ▨	4. ▨
327 square yd	5. ▨	6. ▨
1,624 square yd	7. ▨	8. ▨

Complete the table. Assume that bricks cost 15¢ each and that you use 9 bricks per square ft. Assume that you need 2 bags of cement for 100 square ft and that cement costs $7.25 per bag.

Total area	Number of bricks needed	Cost of bricks	Number of bags of cement needed	Cost of cement
120 square ft	9. ▨	10. ▨	11. ▨	12. ▨
375 square ft	13. ▨	14. ▨	15. ▨	16. ▨
2,120 square ft	17. ▨	18. ▨	19. ▨	20. ▨
11,250 square ft	21. ▨	22. ▨	23. ▨	24. ▨

Use the diagram of the house for Exercises 25–27.

25. What is the area of the longer side of the house, excluding windows and doors? The shorter side?

26. At 9 bricks per square ft, how many bricks will be needed to face the 2 visible sides?

27. At 2 bags of cement per 100 square ft, how many bags of cement will be needed for the job in Exercise 26?

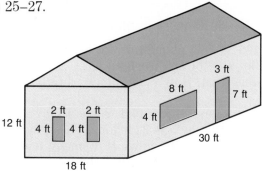

13.6 DRAWING A DIAGRAM

Situation:

Mike owns a landscape-contracting company. Mike's crew built a fence around a square piece of land that measured 4 yd on each side. The fence posts were placed 1 yd apart. How many posts did Mike need?

Strategy:

Drawing a diagram can help you to solve a problem.

Applying the Strategy:

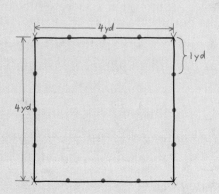

1. Draw a square.

2. Mark the 4 corner posts.

3. Mark posts 1 yd apart.

4. Count the number of posts needed.

Mike needed 16 posts.

FOR DISCUSSION

Mike designed a flower bed for a customer. The first row of flowers was red. The second row of flowers was yellow. This pattern was repeated.

1. What would you draw to help you see the flower bed?

2. What color were the flowers in the ninth row?

PRACTICE EXERCISES

Copy the diagram. Then fill in the missing numbers to solve the problem.

1. Mike's crew planted a row of pine trees on the 60-ft side of Mr. Wesley's yard. A pine was planted every 10 ft. How many pines were planted?

2. A 12-ft-long flower bed was cut into a rectangular lawn. The lawn is 32 ft long. The flower bed is in the center of the lawn. How many feet of lawn are on each side of the flower bed?

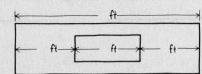

Solve the problem by drawing a diagram.

3. Mike's crew built a fence around a square piece of land. The land was 9 yd on each side. The fence posts were placed 3 yd apart. How many posts were used?

4. Mike planned a garden with 15 rows of flowers. The first row was blue, the second was white, the third was pink. How many times was this pattern repeated?

5. An azalea garden contains 49 azaleas, 7 in each row. The center and end azaleas in each row are pink. How many pink azaleas are there in all?

6. A row of trees was planted along Maple Drive. The length of the row was 148 ft. A tree was planted every $18\frac{1}{2}$ ft. How many trees were planted?

7. Mike built a fence around a rectangular garden that was 16 yd long and 12 yd wide. The posts were placed 2 yd apart. How many posts did he need?

8. A rectangular lawn contains three 7-ft-square flower beds. There is a border of 3 ft between each flower bed and the perimeter of the plot. How long is the plot?

13.7 QUALITY AND QUANTITY VS. PRICE

DECISION MAKING

Many goods are produced and sold in a variety of qualities. It is common to see items advertised as "Good" or "Everyday Grade" at lower prices and "Deluxe" or "Our Best" at higher prices.

PROBLEM A

Sandra's flooring contractor showed her samples of 3 grades of vinyl flooring for her 3 yd by 4 yd kitchen. She needs to decide which grade to order.

GOOD VINYL FLOORING $8.99/square yd	STYLISH VINYL FLOORING $10.99/square yd No-Wax Finish	DELUXE VINYL FLOORING $12.99/square yd Never needs waxing 10-year guarantee

DECISION-MAKING FACTORS

Cost
Maintenance/upkeep

Quality
Guarantees

DECISION-MAKING COMPARISONS

Compare the 3 options by completing the table.

Factor	Good flooring	Stylish flooring	Deluxe flooring
Total cost	1. ■	$131.88	2. ■
Quality	Average	3. ■	4. ■
Maintenance	Needs waxing	5. ■	6. ■
Guarantees	7. ■	None	8. ■

MAKING THE DECISIONS

Which flooring should Sandra order:

9. If cost were the only factor?

10. If quality were the only factor?

11. If ease of maintenance *and* cost were important factors?

12. Which flooring could she expect to last the longest? Why?

13. How much could Sandra save by using the Good flooring instead of the Deluxe flooring to do the kitchen? What could cause her not really to save this much over the next 10 y?

14. Which type of flooring would you order? Why?

PROBLEM B

Many contractors have the opportunity to save money by **buying in bulk.** A mason might find brick available at 3 different rates, depending on the quantity he orders. He must decide the best way to order the bricks based on the following pricing information.

LOOSE BRICKS—16¢ each	BRICKS ON A PALLET—$49.00 (400 bricks/pallet)	TRUCKLOAD OF BRICKS—$430.00 (10 pallets/truckload)

DECISION-MAKING FACTORS

Cost

Availability of storage space

Minimum purchase/number needed

Ease of transport

DECISION-MAKING COMPARISONS

Compare the 3 options by completing the table.

Factor	Loose	Pallet	Truckload
Cost per brick	16¢	15. ■	16. ■
Minimum purchase of bricks	None	17. ■	18. ■
Need for storage	19. ■	Moderate	20. ■
Ease of transport	21. ■	22. ■	Low

MAKING THE DECISIONS

Which way should the mason order the bricks:

23. If cost were the only factor?

24. If he only needs 150 bricks?

25. If transportation is not a factor and he needs 500 bricks?

26. How much can the mason save by ordering a pallet instead of 400 loose bricks?

27. How much can the mason save by ordering a truckload instead of 10 pallets?

28. What is the least expensive way to order 2,000 bricks? How much will they cost?

29. Suppose the mason needs 3,600 bricks for a job. What is the best way to order the bricks? How much will they cost?

30. What hidden costs might be involved before assuming that buying bricks by the truckload is least expensive?

31. Which way would you order the bricks if you needed 300? 3,000? 5,000? Why?

CHAPTER REVIEW

Vocabulary   Choose the letter of the word(s) that completes the sentence.

1. Carpenters usually pay for lumber by the ▪.   [262]

   a. Piece   **b.** Board foot   **c.** Ton

2. The amount of paint needed is most dependent on ▪.   [268]

   a. Length   **b.** Area   **c.** Volume

3. A skilled person who works with bricks, cement blocks, and mortar
   is called a(n) ▪.   [270]

   a. Plumber   **b.** Electrical contractor   **c.** Mason

Skills   Find the answer.

4. At $55 per square ft, how much will it
   cost to add a 16 ft by 24 ft playroom
   to a house?   [262]

5. At $75 per square ft, how much will it
   cost to renovate 35,000 square ft of
   abandoned factory space?   [262]

6. At 32¢ per board ft, what will be the
   cost of 25 16-ft-long pieces of 2 in. by
   10 in. lumber?   [262]

7. How thick is a pipe with an inside
   diameter of $2\frac{3}{8}$ in. and an outside
   diameter of $2\frac{3}{4}$ in.?   [264]

8. If you need 25 12-ft sections of pipe,
   how many 100-ft coils do you need to
   buy?   [264]

9. A plumber charges $28 per h for
   labor. How much will a 24-h job
   cost?   [264]

10. An electrician averages 75 ft of wire
    per room when wiring a new home.
    How many 100-ft coils of wire should
    be purchased for a 6-room
    house?   [266]

11. An electrician charges $29.75 per h
    for his own labor and $18.75 per h
    for his assistant's. What is the total
    labor charge for a $6\frac{1}{2}$-h job?   [266]

12. What is the area to be painted on two
    16 ft by 30 ft walls that each contain
    one 3 ft by 5 ft window and a 3 ft by
    7 ft door?   [268]

13. If a gallon of paint covers about 350
    square ft, how much paint is needed
    to put 2 coats on the walls in
    Exercise 12?   [268]

14. At 9 bricks per square ft, how many
    bricks are needed to construct a
    brick facade on a $9\frac{1}{2}$ ft by 27 ft
    wall?   [270]

15. At 15¢ per brick, how much will it
    cost to construct the wall in Exercise
    14?   [270]

Find the cost.

1. 2,200 square ft of construction at $50 per square ft

2. 600 square ft of renovation at $75 per square ft

3. Ten 18-ft-long pieces of 2 in. by 4 in. lumber at 47¢ per board ft

4. Fifteen 20-ft sections of pipe at 15¢ per ft

5. 400 ft of electrical cable wire at $42.75 per 100 ft

6. 18 gal of paint at $13.99 per gal

Solve.

7. What is the inside diameter of a sewer pipe with a $6\frac{1}{4}$-in. outside diameter and a $\frac{5}{16}$-in. thickness?

8. How many 100-ft coils of wire are needed for a 7-room house if an electrician uses an average of 75 ft per room?

9. An electrician charges $32.50 per h for her labor and $24.75 per h for her assistant's labor. What is the labor charge for a $9\frac{1}{2}$-job?

10. What is the area to be painted on two 9 ft by 20 ft walls that each contain two 3 ft by 5 ft windows and a 3 ft by 7 ft door?

11. Paint costs $15.99 per gal, and 1 gal covers about 400 square ft. How much will it cost to put 2 coats on the walls in Exercise 10?

12. At 9 bricks per square ft and 18¢ per brick, what will it cost to add a brick facade to the 15 ft by 36 ft side of a house?

Find the cost of the materials.

13. Twelve 8-ft-long pieces of 2 in. by 4 in. lumber at 29.5¢ per board foot; 8 sheets paneling at $8.99 per sheet; 2 lb nails at 85¢ per lb

14. 175 ft copper pipe at 18¢ per ft; 100 ft plastic pipe at 26¢ per ft; 8 plastic elbows at 69¢ each; 10 couplers at 49¢ each

Solve the problem by drawing a diagram.

15. Fencing was built around a 6 yd by 6 yd piece of land. The posts were 1 yd apart. How many posts were there?

16. There are 18 rows in a garden. The first row is white, the second is pink, and the third is red. This pattern is repeated. What color is the 15th row?

MONEY TIPS

Service contracts on many items can save you money on repairs and maintenance.

LET'S LOOK AT THE FACTS

Many new items include a **warranty** that covers defects and repairs during the first 90 d, the first year, and so forth. After the warranty expires, paying 1 annual **service contract** fee on a computer, for example, could save you money.

APT-4F WORD PROCESSOR/COMPUTER SYSTEM	
(Service Contract—$350 per year)	
Parts Replacement Charges:	**Service & Labor Charges:**
Brightness control knob . . . . $ 12	Service call. . . . . $ 75
Disc drive on/off switch . . . . $ 15	Labor (repair time, per hour). . . . . $ 35
Printer cable . . . . $ 40	Maintenance check and
Keyboard adjustment . . . . $ 55	system cleaning. $100
Printer carriage . . . . $ 60	Pickup & delivery for
Interface unit. . . . . $ 90	in-shop repairs. . . . . $ 50
Disc drive. $200	Reinstallation of repaired system. . . . . . $ 45

LET'S DISCUSS WHY

1. When would you be more likely to have ongoing or increasing problems with your computer?

2. For every call to your home or office, you pay a service charge regardless of whether any work is done or not. How much would it cost just to call in a repair person 5 times in 1 y?

3. Your computer needs an overall cleaning twice a year. Each call requires $1\frac{1}{2}$ h of labor. What would this cost per year?

4. Your computer was repaired 10 times last year. You had bought a service contract for last year. Therefore, what was the most that each service call actually cost you?

LET'S SEE WHAT YOU WOULD DO

5. You bought a service contract on your computer for 2 y. In the first year, no repairs were needed. In the second year, all major parts were replaced, and the computer was cleaned twice and taken into the shop twice. Four service calls were made, requiring 12 h of labor. Compare the total cost with the cost of the service contract.

6. Look around your home, school, or office. On how many items could you take out a service contract?

CALCULATOR DISCOUNTS AND ADD-ONS

You can use a calculator to find the total cost of an item selling at a discount or one that includes an add-on such as sales tax.

A drill that regularly sells for $64 is being sold at a 15% discount. What is the sale price?

Procedure	Calculator Entry	Calculator Display
1. Enter the regular price.	6 4	64.
2. Enter the − key.	−	64.
3. Enter the discount rate.	1 5 %	54.4

The sale price is $54.40.

Try this on your calculator. On some calculators, you may need to enter the = key after the % key. If your calculator does not have a % key, multiply 64 by the decimal equivalent of 15% (.15) and subtract this amount from the original price.

What is the total cost of a $325 lamp on which a 6% sales tax must be paid?

Procedure	Calculator Entry	Calculator Display
1. Enter the regular price.	3 2 5	325.
2. Enter the + key.	+	325.
3. Enter the sales tax rate.	6 %	344.5

The total price is $344.50.

Try this on your calculator. On some calculators, you may need to enter the = key after the % key. If your calculator does not have a % key, multiply 325 by the decimal equivalent of 6% (.06) and add this to the original amount.

Use a calculator to compute.

1. Regular price: $300
   Discount rate: 12%
   Sale price: ■

2. Regular price: $50
   Discount rate: 21.5%
   Sale price: ■

3. Regular price: $175
   Sales tax rate: 6.5%
   Total cost: ■

Use a calculator to solve.

4. A power saw that lists for $85 is on sale at a 25% discount. What is the sale price?

5. What is the total price of a $480 air conditioner in a state with a 7.5% sales tax?

Compute.

1. $8\frac{1}{2} \times \$12.20$ **2.** $17\frac{3}{4} \times \$18.50$ **3.** $56\frac{1}{2} \times \$25.74$

4. $(4 \times \$56.80) + (5 \times \$284.50)$ **5.** $(15 \times \$14.80) + (8 \times \$37.60)$

Divide. Round to the nearest whole number.

6. $\$1,000 \div \$63.49$ **7.** $\$250 \div \$7.65$ **8.** $\$750 \div \$85.60$

9. $8\frac{3}{4} \div 1\frac{3}{4}$ **10.** $15 \div 1\frac{1}{2}$ **11.** $13\frac{1}{2} \div 2\frac{1}{4}$

Solve for n.

12. $\frac{15}{120} = \frac{n}{800}$ **13.** $\frac{24}{90} = \frac{300}{n}$ **14.** $\frac{2}{125} = \frac{n}{5,000}$

Find the answer.

15. 1% of 2,400   **16.** 2% of 360   **17.** 5% of 6,700

18. 3% of 175   **19.** 15% of 4,000   **20.** $1\frac{1}{2}$% of 500

Copy and complete.

21. 1 liter = ▥ milliliters   **22.** 500 milliliters = ▥ liters

23. 50 cubic centimeters = ▥ milliliters   **24.** 1,000 milligrams = ▥ grams

25. 3 grams = ▥ milligrams   **26.** 1,000 cubic centimeters = ▥ liters

Add or subtract.

27. 3 min 37 s + 8 min 51 s   **28.** 17 min 28 s + 4 min 43 s

29. 30 min − 14 min 23 s   **30.** 45 min − 8 min 12 s

Use the line graph for Exercises 31–37. How many bathing suits were bought during the month?

31. April   **32.** May

33. June   **34.** July

35. August   **36.** September

37. During which period of time was there the greatest increase in sales?

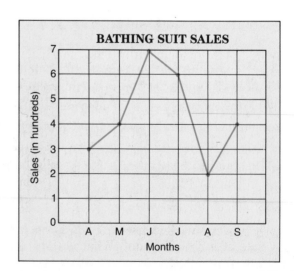

Chapter 14

OTHER PROFESSIONS

Many different people are needed to run an office. What types of jobs are done in an office? Why do you think some jobs pay more than others?

Mathematics is used extensively in the advertising industry in designing ads and computing the cost of placing ads in newspapers and magazines.

The cost of display ads in newspapers is usually computed based on **column-inches,** or the number of columns wide the ad is by the number of inches long the ad runs.

EXAMPLE 1

Fits-Well Shoe Store placed an ad for a sale in the local newspaper. The ad was 3 columns wide and ran $5\frac{1}{2}$ in. The newspaper charged $11.34 per column-inch. How much did it cost to run the ad for 1 d?

1. Multiply to find the column-inches. $3 \times 5\frac{1}{2}$ in. $= 16\frac{1}{2}$
2. Multiply to find the cost.

   THINK: $16\frac{1}{2} = 16.5$ $16.5 \times \$11.34 = \$187.11$

The ad cost $187.11.

EXAMPLE 2

The Hoyt Agency designed an ad $8\frac{1}{2}$ in. wide by 11 in. long. How much did it cost to run the ad for 5 d if each column was $2\frac{1}{8}$ in. wide?

THINK: If each column was $2\frac{1}{8}$ in. wide, then 2 columns were $4\frac{1}{4}$ in. wide and 4 columns were $8\frac{1}{2}$ in. wide.

So an $8\frac{1}{2}$ in. $\times$ 11 in. ad used 4 columns.

1. Multiply to find the column-inches. 4×11 in. $= 44$
2. Multiply to find the cost. $44 \times \$11.34 \times 5$ d $= \$2,494.80$

It cost $2,494.80 to run the ad for 5 d.

Many newspapers have set rates for quarter-, half-, and full-page ads.

EXAMPLE 3

An ad agency has a $1,500 budget for a client. For how many days can they run a half-page ad? If the ad were reduced in size, for how many days could they run a quarter-page ad?

AD RATES	
Full page –	$1,326.12
Half page –	$667.53
Quarter page –	$341.86

1. Divide to find the half-page time. $\$1,500 \div \$667.53 = 2.24709$

They could run the half-page ad for 2 d.

2. Divide to find the quarter-page time. $\$1,500 \div \$341.86 = 4.387761$

They could run the quarter-page ad for 4 d.

Why is the cost of a full-page ad often so much greater in one newspaper than in another?

PRACTICE EXERCISES

Remember to estimate whenever you use your calculator.

Complete the table. Assume the cost per column-inch is $16.87.

Number of columns	Number of inches	Number of column-inches	Cost to place ad
1	$3\frac{1}{2}$	1. ■	2. ■
3	$7\frac{1}{4}$	3. ■	4. ■
2	$10\frac{3}{4}$	5. ■	6. ■
5	$14\frac{1}{4}$	7. ■	8. ■

Complete the table. Assume that each column is $1\frac{3}{4}$ in. wide and that the cost per column-inch is $23.48.

Ad size (width by length)	Number of column-inches	Cost to place ad
$3\frac{1}{2}$ in. by 8 in.	9. ■	10. ■
$1\frac{3}{4}$ in. by $4\frac{1}{2}$ in.	11. ■	12. ■
$5\frac{1}{4}$ in. by $10\frac{3}{4}$ in.	13. ■	14. ■
$8\frac{3}{4}$ in. by $8\frac{3}{4}$ in.	15. ■	16. ■

Use the ad rates on page 282 to solve.

17. With a $2,500 budget, for how many days could you run a half-page ad?

18. With a $4,000 budget, for how many days could you run a quarter-page ad?

19. Each page in a newspaper is 6 columns wide by 20 in. long. How many column-inches are there in a quarter-page ad? At $14.87 per column-inch, how much will the ad cost?

20. Each page in a local newspaper is 8 columns wide by 14 in. long. How many column-inches are in a half-page ad? At $8.31 per column-inch, how much will the ad cost?

Salespeople in all industries frequently use graphs to display important sales data. These graphs provide information quickly and in a visually pleasing way. Graphs of sales data are often used to evaluate the success of past activities and to plan future activities.

Line graphs are very useful for showing trends over time.

A large discount appliance chain graphed the sales of 2 major brands of televisions during each month of the past year.

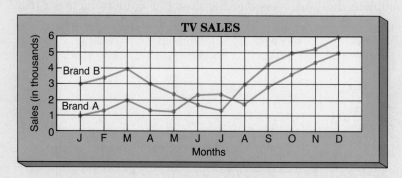

EXAMPLE 1
For which months were sales of Brand A greater than those of Brand B?

The Brand A line is higher than the Brand B line in only June and July.

EXAMPLE 2
The store ran a major advertising campaign for Brand A during May and June. Did the campaign appear to have been successful?

Since sales for Brand A surpassed those of Brand B following the campaign, it looks like the campaign was successful in promoting sales.

EXAMPLE 3
How would you explain the higher sales of both brands during November and December?

It is likely that many televisions were purchased as gifts during the holiday season, when many stores make 30% to 50% of their annual sales.

1. What are some advantages of using a graph rather than a table with the same data?

2. Given the TV sales trends shown in the graph, when might you best schedule a major ad campaign to boost sales of Brand A? Brand B?

PRACTICE EXERCISES

Write 3 conclusions that can be drawn from the data in the graph.

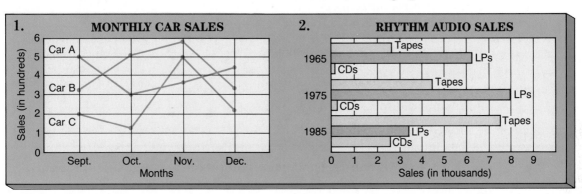

1. MONTHLY CAR SALES

Sales (in hundreds): Car A, Car B, Car C — Months: Sept., Oct., Nov., Dec.

2. RHYTHM AUDIO SALES

1965: Tapes, LPs, CDs; 1975: Tapes, LPs, CDs; 1985: Tapes, LPs, CDs — Sales (in thousands): 0 1 2 3 4 5 6 7 8 9

Suggest 1 action, including its timing, that you would use to boost sales in:

3. Cars.

4. Tapes, LPs, or CDs.

Use graph paper. Make a line graph for the data in the table.

5. SALES

Week	Shoes	Sneakers
1	543	389
2	390	137
3	817	580
4	645	244
5	287	256

(Hint: Label the vertical scale in hundreds to 900.)

6. PURCHASES

Year	Hotdogs	Burgers
1985	4,385	3,189
1986	6,408	4,890
1987	5,724	5,836
1988	4,233	7,492
1989	4,879	8,943

(Hint: Label the vertical scale in thousands to 9,000.)

Write 3 conclusions that can be drawn from the data in:

7. Exercise 5.   8. Exercise 6.

Suggest 1 action, including its timing, that you would use to boost sales in:

9. Shoes.   10. Hot dogs.

International travelers and travel agents frequently turn to mathematics when they use **exchange rates** to convert dollars to other currencies, or other currencies to dollars. Travelers also use exchange rates to compute the equivalent value of an item in 2 different currencies.

EXAMPLE 1

Before leaving for France, you converted $600 in U.S. currency to francs. How many francs did you receive?

THINK: **$1 U.S. = 6.076 francs**

1. Use a proportion.

THINK: **$1 is to 6.076 francs as $600 is to *n* francs.**

$$\frac{\$1}{6.076 \text{ francs}} = \frac{\$600}{n \text{ francs}}$$

$$n = 600 \times 6.076 = 3{,}645.6$$

2. Round down. $3{,}645.6 \approx 3{,}645$

You received 3,645 francs.

Exchange rates		
$1 U.S. =	1.344	Canadian dollars
	6.076	French francs
	143.7	Japanese yen
	0.620	British pounds
	1.817	German marks

EXAMPLE 2

When you were in England, your hotel room was billed at a rate of 47 British pounds per night. How much was this in U.S. dollars?

THINK: **$1 U.S. = 0.620 pounds**

1. Use a proportion.

THINK: **$1 is to 0.620 pounds as *n* dollars is to 47 pounds.**

$$\frac{\$1}{0.620 \text{ pounds}} = \frac{n}{47 \text{ pounds}}$$

$$0.620n = 47$$

$$n = 47 \div 0.620 = 75.806451$$

2. Round up. $75.806451 \approx 75.81$

In U.S. dollars, the room was $75.81 per night.

FOR DISCUSSION

The dollar/yen exchange rate once fluctuated widely between 120 yen to the dollar and 160 yen to the dollar. When would have been the worst time to buy a Japanese import car? Why?

PRACTICE EXERCISES Remember to estimate whenever you use your calculator.

What is the value of $750 U.S. in:

1. Francs?

2. Canadian dollars?

3. Yen?

4. Marks?

5. Pounds?

Complete the table.

Item	Value in U.S. dollars	Value in other currency
Watch	$75	6. ■ pounds
Dress	$260	7. ■ francs
Camera	$195	8. ■ yen
Jewelry	$39.95	9. ■ Canadian dollars
Clarinet	$550	10. ■ marks

Convert to dollars.

11. Perfume for 125 francs

12. Clothes for 79 Canadian dollars

13. An umbrella for 10 pounds

14. A television for 45,000 yen

15. A car for 23,000 marks

16. Furniture for 12,000 francs

17. Souvenirs for 101 Canadian dollars

18. A painting for 455 marks

EXTENSION The Effects of Changing Exchange Rates

An Army corporal stationed in West Germany is paid $320 per wk. What is the impact on the corporal's wages when the exchange rate decreases from 1.872 marks to 1.714 marks to the dollar?

Procedure: 1. Convert the wages to marks at the old rate.

2. Convert the wages to marks at the new rate.

3. Convert the decrease in marks to dollars at the old rate, that is, the loss in buying power expressed in dollars.

A key component of all assembly lines and all manufacturing industries is **quality control**—that is, assuring the same high quality and consistency in each manufactured item. Quality control inspectors use **sampling techniques** and proportions in their ongoing efforts to assure quality goods for the buyer.

EXAMPLE 1

A quality-control inspector pulls 1 out of every 150 light bulbs from the production line for testing. If the line produces 27,000 bulbs per d, how many are pulled for testing?

Use a proportion.

THINK: 1 is to 150 as n is to 27,000.

$$\frac{1}{150} = \frac{n}{27,000}$$

$$150n = 27,000$$

$$n = 27,000 \div 150 = 180$$

The inspector pulls 180 light bulbs for testing.

Inspectors use sampling to predict the number of defective items.

EXAMPLE 2

On a given day, a quality-control inspector found 2 defective bulbs out of 115 that were tested. If the day's total production was 22,500 bulbs, predict how many were defective.

Use a proportion.

THINK: 2 is to 115 as n is to 22,500.

$$\frac{2 \text{ defective}}{115 \text{ tested}} = \frac{n \text{ defective}}{22,500 \text{ produced}}$$

$$115n = 2 \times 22,500 = 45,000$$

$$n = 45,000 \div 115 = 391.30434$$

You would predict that about 391 bulbs were defective.

EXAMPLE 3

A company that produces toaster ovens tries to inspect 5% of the 2,500 units produced each day. If the company can tolerate a defective rate of no more than 1%, how many toaster ovens can acceptably be found to be defective during a given day?

1. Multiply to find how many are tested.

   THINK: 5% = 0.05 $0.05 \times 2,500 = 125$

2. Multiply to find acceptable defects.

   THINK: 1% = 0.01 $0.01 \times 125 = 1.25$

So 1 defective toaster oven among every 125 tested would be acceptable. A second defective unit would suggest an unacceptably high defective rate.

FOR DISCUSSION

Company A tests 10% of the radios it produces. Company B tests 20% of the radios it produces. Can you conclude that Company B will have a higher likelihood of greater quality? Why?

PRACTICE EXERCISES   Remember to estimate whenever you use your calculator.

Complete the table.

Sampling criteria for inspection	Number of items produced	Number of items inspected
1 in 10	370	1.
Every 8th item	1,280	2.
3%	800	3.
1 in 50	3,750	4.
3 out of every 20	140	5.
Every 30th item	15,000	6.
$\frac{1}{2}\%$	5,400	7.
2 out of every 15	780	8.

Complete the table.

Number of items found defective	Number sampled	Number produced	Predicted number of defective items
8	275	2,000	9.
1	60	150	10.
13	850	7,400	11.
3	200	18,000	12.
2	185	1,500	13.
22	5,800	97,000	14.

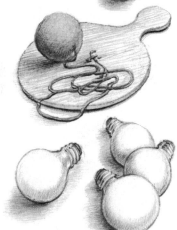

Solve.

15. No more than $\frac{1}{2}\%$ of the rotor blades manufactured can be found to be defective. If 2% of the 13,500 blades are tested, how many defective blades can be acceptably found?

16. A toy manufacturer inspects 5% of its monthly production of 4,350 toys. If the company can tolerate a 1% defective rate, how many defective toys can be acceptably found?

Nurses and other health-care professionals use mathematics when prescribing and administering medicine. **Standard dosages** must often be adjusted to fit a patient's age and condition.

EXAMPLE 1

A particular drug comes in an 8 mg per 1 mL solution. How many milliliters should be injected to provide a 20-mg dose?

Use a proportion.

THINK: 8 mg is to 1 mL as 20 mg is to n mL.

$$\frac{8\text{ mg}}{1\text{ mL}} = \frac{20\text{ mg}}{n\text{ mL}}$$

$$8n = 20$$

$$n = 20 \div 8 = 2.5$$

2.5 mL should be injected to provide a 20-mg dose.

Mathematics and measurement also play a critical role in an activity such as setting lifesaving **intravenous solution flow rates.**

EXAMPLE 2

A patient is prescribed a 1-L intravenous bottle of lactate solution every 8 h. How many drops per minute should be flowing if there are 12 drops per cc (cubic centimeter)?

1. Find the number of cc per minute.
   • Divide to find the number of milliliters per minute.
     THINK: 1 L = 1,000 mL
     8 h = 8 × 60 = 480 min   1,000 ÷ 480 = 2.0833333 ≈ 2.08 mL

   • Find the number of cc per minute.
     THINK: 1 mL = 1 cc   2.08 mL per min = 2.08 cc per min

2. Multiply to find the number of drops per minute.   2.08 × 12 = 24.96 ≈ 25

The drop rate should be 25 drops per min.

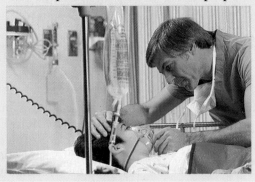

FOR DISCUSSION

1. A drug comes in 10 mg per 1 mL strength and 25 mg per 1 mL strength. To provide a 50-mg dose, why might a nurse inject 2 mL of the stronger solution rather than 5 mL of the weaker solution?

2. Why is it critical that intravenous drop rates be closely monitored?

PRACTICE EXERCISES   Remember to estimate whenever you use your calculator.

Complete the table.

Available medication	Prescribed dose	Quantity to be administered
10 mg per 1 mL	30 mg	1. ▩ mL
4 mg per 1 mL	10 mg	2. ▩ mL
250 mg per 1 mL	150 mg	3. ▩ mL
30 mg per 1 mL	200 mg	4. ▩ mL
12 mg per 1 mL	20 mg	5. ▩ mL
10 mg per 1 tablet	40 mg	6. ▩ tablets
5 mg per 1 tablet	12.5 mg	7. ▩ tablets
25 mg per 2 tablets	75 mg	8. ▩ tablets
8 mg per 1 tablet	10 mg	9. ▩ tablets
100 mg per 1 tablet	250 mg	10. ▩ tablets

Solve.

11. A patient is prescribed 1 L of intravenous solution every 6 h. How many drops per minute should be administered if there are 10 drops per cc?

12. A patient is prescribed 500 mL of intravenous solution every 2 h. How many drops per minute should be administered if there are 50 drops per cc?

13. At 20 drops per cc, how many milliliters are being administered each hour if the drop rate is 30 drops per min?

14. At 12 drops per cc, how many milliliters are being administered each hour if the drop rate is 20 drops per min?

Radio and television programmers use mathematics to do scheduling of programs, music, and advertising. Radio and television advertising executives use mathematics when they sell ad time on their stations.

EXAMPLE 1

A radio program schedule calls for 4 songs between 10:05 and 10:30 A.M. The songs run (in minutes and seconds) 2:53, 3:21, 2:47, and 4:06, respectively. If the schedule allows 30 s for the disc jockey to introduce each song, how much time is left for advertising?

THINK: 10:05 A.M. to 10:30 A.M. = 25 min available.

1. Add to find the time for music.
   Minutes: $2 + 3 + 2 + 4 = 11$ min
   Seconds: $53 + 21 + 47 + 6 = 127$ s $= 2$ min 7 s
   11 min + 2 min 7 s = 13 min 7 s

2. Multiply to find the DJ time. 4×30 s $= 120$ s $= 2$ min

3. Add to find the total music
   and DJ time.   13 min 7 s + 2 min = 15 min 7 s

4. Subtract to find the time   25 min   24 min 60 s
   left for advertising. $\underline{-15 \text{ min } 7 \text{ s}}$ → $\underline{-15 \text{ min } 7 \text{ s}}$
                                                      9 min 53 s

9 min and 53 s remain for advertising.

EXAMPLE 2

A radio station averages one 30-s advertisement every 5 min. If the station charges $239.50 for each 30-s spot, how much is its hourly advertising income?

THINK: 1 ad per 5 min = 60 ÷ 5, or 12 ads per h

Multiply to find the income. 12 × $239.50 = $2,874.00

The hourly advertising income is $2,874.

FOR DISCUSSION

1. Why are audience ratings so important to radio and television stations?

2. About what percent of a prime-time TV hour is devoted to commercials? Why?

PRACTICE EXERCISES   Remember to estimate whenever you use your calculator.

Find the total time scheduled. (Remember: 4:30 means 4 min 30 s.)

1.   News: 4:30
     Weather: 0:45
     Song 1: 3:13
     Song 2: 4:27
     Song 3: 2:51
     3 60-s ads
     6 30-s ads
     3 15-s ads

2.   Song 1: 5:35
     Song 2: 4:38
     Song 3: 4:08
     Song 4: 3:49
     20-s intro for
     each song
     7 30-s ads

3.   News: 7:45
     Sports: 4:15
     Weather: 3:20
     Traffic: 2:15
     5 15-s ads
     9 30-s ads

How much time remains to fill a half-hour in:

4. Exercise 1?

5. Exercise 2?

6. Exercise 3?

Use the rate table to find the advertising income.

7. 5 15-s ads

8. 6 60-s ads

9. 4 15-s and 7 30-s ads 10. 6 60-s and 4 30-s ads

AD RATES	
15-s spots	$35.75
30-s spots	$63.40
60-s spots	$121.70

Use the rate table to solve.

11. How many 30-s spots can run for $1,000?

12. How many 60-s spots can be aired on a $2,000 ad budget?

13. How much income will a radio station earn by running 10 15-s ads, 9 30-s ads, and 5 60-s ads?

14. How much more will a radio station earn if it runs 20 15-s ads instead of 5 60-s ads?

14.7 EVALUATING RAISES AND PROMOTIONS

DECISION
MAKING

Many jobs are advertised at a particular starting pay but promise periodic **raises** for good performance. Sometimes a job with a lower starting pay eventually can provide a higher pay.

PROBLEM A

Bess has been offered 2 similar jobs with different pay structures.

Job 1: Offers $200 per wk plus $20 increases every 6 mo for the next 3 y.
Job 2: Offers $215 per wk plus $30 increases every year for the next 3 y.

Bess needs to decide which job to take.

DECISION-MAKING FACTORS

Starting pay   Pay in 3 y   Total income over 3 y

DECISION-MAKING COMPARISONS

Compare the 2 jobs by completing the table.

	JOB 1		JOB 2	
	Weekly pay	Total income	Weekly pay	Total income
1st 6 months	$200	$5,200	$215	1. ▧
2nd 6 months	2. ▧	3. ▧	$215	4. ▧
3rd 6 months	5. ▧	6. ▧	7. ▧	8. ▧
4th 6 months	$260	9. ▧	10. ▧	11. ▧
5th 6 months	12. ▧	13. ▧	$275	14. ▧
6th 6 months	15. ▧	16. ▧	17. ▧	18. ▧
Total income		19. ▧		20. ▧

MAKING THE DECISIONS

Which job should Bess take:

21. If starting pay were the only factor?

22. If pay after 3 y were the only factor?

23. If total income over 3 y were the only factor?

24. Which job would you choose? Why?

25. If Bess were offered a third job at $240 per wk with no promised raises, should she take it over Job 1 and Job 2? Why?

294 CHAPTER 14

A common form of **promotion** is from a job that pays an hourly wage to a more professional job that pays an annual salary.

PROBLEM B

You have been working a 35-h week in a job that pays $6.38 per h. You average 5 h per wk overtime at time and a half. You are offered a promotion to a 40-h per wk job that pays $12,900 per y with no overtime provision. Should you accept the promotion?

DECISION-MAKING FACTORS

Annual pay   Hours per week   Prestige   Responsibility

DECISION-MAKING COMPARISONS

Compare the present job and the promotion by completing the table.

	Present job	Promotion
Annual pay, excluding overtime	26. ■	27. ■
Annual pay, including overtime	28. ■	$12,900
Hours per week, excluding overtime	35 h	29. ■
Hours per week, including overtime	30. ■	31. ■
Regular hourly wage	32. ■	33. ■
Overtime hourly wage	34. ■	35. ■

MAKING THE DECISIONS

Would you take the promotion:

36. If annual pay excluding overtime were the only factor?

37. If annual pay including overtime were the only factor?

38. If regular hourly wage were the only factor?

39. If overtime hourly wage were the only factor?

40. Would you take the promotion if it were offered to you? Why?

41. Would you take the promotion if it paid $15,000 per y? Why?

CHAPTER REVIEW

Vocabulary   Choose the letter of the word(s) that completes the sentence.

1. Newspaper advertising is sold by the ▪.   [282]

   a. Square inch   **b.** Inch   **c.** Column-inch

2. Trends over time can be easily seen on a ▪ graph.   [284]

   a. Bar   **b.** Line   **c.** Circle

3. Currency is converted by means of the ▪.   [286]

   a. Bank's formula   **b.** Exchange rate   **c.** Denomination factor

4. The manufacturing function that assures product consistency is
   called ▪.   [288]

   a. Quality control   **b.** Uniformity monitoring   **c.** Variation inspection

Skills   Find the answer.

5. What is the cost of a 3-column by
   7-in. ad in a newspaper that charges
   $19.73 per column-inch?   [282]

6. What is the cost of a $4\frac{1}{2}$-in. by 10-in.
   ad in a newspaper with $1\frac{1}{2}$-in.
   columns that charges $14.86 per
   column-inch?   [282]

7. If $1 U.S. is equal to 6.147 francs,
   what is the value of $450 in francs?
   [286]

8. If $1 U.S. is equal to 142.9 yen, what
   is the value in dollars of an item
   priced at 3,895 yen?   [286]

9. How many televisions will be tested
   if a quality-control inspector samples
   1 out of every 25 televisions during a
   week when 1,575 were produced?
   [288]

10. If a product inspector finds 3
    defective items out of 80 that are
    tested, how many defective items are
    likely to be defective in a production
    run of 800?   [288]

11. A drug comes in a 12 mg per 1 mL
    solution. How much should be
    injected to provide a 30-mg dose?
    [290]

12. A medication comes in 5-mg tablets.
    How many tablets should be
    administered to provide a $7\frac{1}{2}$-mg
    dose?   [290]

13. A radio schedule calls for songs that
    run 3:14, 5:24, and 4:48. How much
    time does this leave for ads during a
    20-min segment?   [292]

14. At $29.75 for a 15-s spot and $54.35
    for a 30-s spot, how much income
    will be earned by five 15-s spots and
    eight 30-s spots?   [292]

Find the cost.

1. A 3-column by $10\frac{1}{2}$-in. ad in a newspaper that charges $19.47 per column-inch

2. A 6-in. by 8-in. ad in a newspaper with 2-in. columns and a $15.38 per column-inch charge

3. Fifteen 30-s and six 15-s radio spots on a station that charges $6.75 per 15-s ad and $10.35 per 30-s ad

4. 10 60-s and 12 30-s radio spots on a station that has a flat charge of $29.38 per min

Solve.

5. If $1 U.S. is equal to 0.637 pounds, what is the value of $1,500 in pounds?

6. If $1 U.S. is equal to 1.793 marks, what is the value in dollars of an item priced at 735 marks?

7. If 2% of each production run is pulled for inspection, how many items will be inspected in a production run of 900 items?

8. If an inspector finds 3 defective items out of 400 checked, how many defective items are likely to be found in a production run of 5,000 items?

9. How many 8-mg tablets should be administered to provide a 20-mg dose?

10. A drug comes in a 3 mg per 1 mL solution. How much should be injected to provide a 12-mg dose?

Use the chart for Exercises 11–14. How much time is scheduled:

11. For music?   12. All together?

RADIO XYZ 9:00 A.M.–9:30 A.M.
Music: 12:35
News: 5:15
Weather: 3:40

13. How much time is left for advertising?

14. All of the ad spots run for 30 s and cost $55.30 each. How much income will the radio station earn?

15. Use graph paper. Make a line graph for the data in the table. (Hint: Label the vertical scale in fifties—0, 50, 100, and so on to 550.)

16. Write 3 conclusions that can be drawn from the graph in Exercise 15.

SALES

Week	Brand A	Brand B
1	375	505
2	253	425
3	520	371
4	408	287

MONEY TIPS

Your level of education can affect the amount of money you earn.

LET'S LOOK AT THE FACTS

Your academic degree can greatly influence your degree of financial success in today's sophisticated workplace. Look over the figures in the bar graph shown here. Remember that these are median figures.

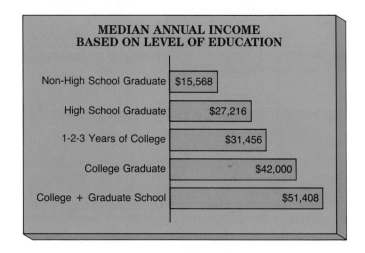

MEDIAN ANNUAL INCOME BASED ON LEVEL OF EDUCATION

Non-High School Graduate	$15,568
High School Graduate	$27,216
1-2-3 Years of College	$31,456
College Graduate	$42,000
College + Graduate School	$51,408

LET'S DISCUSS WHY

1. How much more can a college graduate earn than a high school graduate? Than a non–high school graduate? Why?

2. How much more can a college graduate earn than someone with 3 y of college? What might be the reasons for this?

3. What might be some reasons for not completing high school? College? Could some of these problems be resolved? How?

4. Why do you think education affects how much you can earn?

5. Are there any alternatives to taking out a loan in order to further your education? Are there any ways to cut expenses so you would have more money for your education?

LET'S SEE WHAT YOU WOULD DO

6. You did not complete high school, are now 21 y old, and live with your aunt and uncle. You would like to have an apartment of your own, but the only place you can find costs $675 per mo. What steps could you take to improve your economic status?

7. It will take 3 y to complete your Masters Degree. You work and earn a net pay of $31,500 per y (gross pay is $42,000). To attend graduate school, you would have to pay $420 per mo for a loan. Would the loan be worth it? Why? Keep in mind your current income and what your income might be in 3 y.

ESTIMATION OF PRODUCTS OF DECIMALS

If one of two factors is close to 1, the other factor is a good estimate of the product.

Examples 0.976×4.32
                        ↓

THINK: $1 \times 4.32 = 4.32$
Estimate: 4.32

$9,180 \times 1.03$
                    ↓

THINK: $9,180 \times 1 = 9,180$
Estimate: 9,180

Here is an estimation procedure to use when one of two factors is close to 0.5.

1. Use $\frac{1}{2}$ for the factor close to 0.5.

2. If the other factor is not an even number, round it up 1.

3. Multiply.

Examples 0.463×5.6
                         ↓

THINK: $\frac{1}{2} \times 5.6$
              $5.6 \div 2 = 2.8$
Estimate: 2.8

375×0.53
       ↓   ↓

THINK: $376 \times \frac{1}{2}$
            $376 \div 2 = 188$
Estimate: 188

Estimate the product. Look for factors close to 1 or close to $\frac{1}{2}$.

1. 1.1×78

2. 84×0.52

3. 0.94×150

4. 6.7×1.072

5. 0.483×39

6. 6.2×0.509

7. 1.117×24.25

8. 0.048×0.899

9. 0.395×12.3

10. 0.996×0.06

11. 0.558×1.98

12. 0.471×18.9

13. 3.07×0.606

14. 0.002×0.9847

15. 0.498×0.008

16. 0.8743×0.0102

17. 0.268×0.499

18. 12.317×0.9243

19. 0.50137×0.0106

20. 1.299×0.8201

21. 0.469×0.00010

Add or subtract.

1. $475 + $819

2. $631.18 + $47.52

3. $789.56 + $123.48

4. $827 − $351

5. $303.50 − $126.40

6. $838.51 − $629.48

7. $134,097 + $238,692

8. $256,240 + $109,378

9. $309,472 − $168,341

10. $260,480 − $48,396

Rename as a percent.

11. 0.78

12. 0.06

13. 0.1924

14. 0.5379321

15. 0.0824877

16. 0.9106025

Multiply.

17. 0.9 × $146

18. 0.8 × $150

19. 0.7 × $436

20. 0.85 × $936

21. 0.73 × $816

22. 0.62 × $735

Estimate.

23. $6,400 ÷ 3

24. $19,201 ÷ 5

25. $37,200 ÷ 4

26. $197,600 ÷ 4

27. $41,830 ÷ 5

28. $76,921 ÷ 4

Divide. Round to the nearest dollar.

29. $316 ÷ 7

30. $407 ÷ 3

31. $723 ÷ 8

32. $573 ÷ 4

33. $825 ÷ 7

34. $999 ÷ 8

35. $1,200 ÷ 6

36. $2,600 ÷ 6

37. $5,100 ÷ 6

38. $7,800 ÷ 12

39. $9,400 ÷ 12

40. $16,000 ÷ 12

Chapter

15

PERSONAL FINANCE

Prices for most items have changed drastically over the years! What would it cost you today to buy similar items? Why are the prices so different?

It seems that you pay more for things each year. Indeed, most prices have risen steadily during the past decades. The **Consumer Price Index (CPI)** has gone up over 200% since it was first used in 1967. This steady increase in prices is called **inflation.** The **inflation rate** is the percent that prices increase.

EXAMPLE 1

Suppose that, in January, the average cost of food for your family was $143 per wk. At the end of the year, the average cost of food was $159 per wk. What was the inflation rate for your food costs?

INFLATION RATE = PRICE INCREASE ÷ ORIGINAL PRICE

1. Subtract to find the price increase. $159 − $143 = $16

2. Divide to find the inflation rate. $16 ÷ $143 = 0.1118881

3. Rename as a percent.   11.2%

The inflation rate was about 11.2%.

As the inflation rate goes up, the **purchasing power** goes down.

EXAMPLE 2

Your net income was $17,000 per y. During the year, the inflation rate was 8%. What was the purchasing power of your income after inflation?

1. Multiply to find the decrease in purchasing power.

   THINK: 8% = 0.08   0.08 × $17,000 = $1,360

2. Subtract to find the purchasing power after inflation. $17,000 − $1,360 = $15,640

Your $17,000 salary had the purchasing power of $15,640 after inflation.

FOR DISCUSSION

1. How could you be sure that your income was keeping up with inflation?

2. Why is inflation particularly difficult for people with fixed incomes?

Remember to estimate whenever you use your calculator.

Complete the table to find the inflation rate to the nearest tenth of a percent.

Item	Sports tickets	Weekly food	Monthly rent	Car rental	Gallon of gasoline	Slacks	Paper clips
Current price	$12.00	$183.00	$262.00	$104.00	$1.24	$33.89	$0.89
Original price	$10.00	$167.00	$257.00	$89.00	$0.98	$31.95	$0.63
Price increase	1. ■	2. ■	3. ■	4. ■	5. ■	6. ■	7. ■
Inflation rate	8. ■	9. ■	10. ■	11. ■	12. ■	13. ■	14. ■

Complete the table to find the purchasing power after inflation.

Net income	$19,000	$22,500	$24,600	$28,750	$30,325	$34,875
Inflation rate	10%	8%	4%	11%	6.5%	7.5%
Decrease in purchasing power	15. ■	16. ■	17. ■	18. ■	19. ■	20. ■
Purchasing power after inflation	21. ■	22. ■	23. ■	24. ■	25. ■	26. ■

Solve.

27. Originally, a box of your favorite cereal cost $1.29. Now the price is $1.47. What was the inflation rate to the nearest tenth of a percent?

28. During the year when Andy's income was $26,480, the inflation rate was 7.5%. What was the purchasing power of his income after inflation?

EXTENSION   Deflation

A steady decrease in prices is called **deflation.** The prices of some goods and services have deflated during the past decades. Originally, a certain computer cost $1,900. A few years later, the same computer cost $1,100. What was the rate of deflation?

1. Subtract to find the price decrease. $1,900 − $1,100 = $800

2. Divide to find the deflation rate. $800 ÷ $1,900 = 0.4210526

The deflation rate was about 42.1%.

Find the deflation rate to the nearest tenth of a percent.

1. Current price: $350
   Original price: $420

2. Current price: $1,165
   Original price: $1,830

3. Current price: $0.99
   Original price: $1.29

Maria and Roberto were trying to determine their **net worth.** They got out records that showed all they owned (**assets**) and all they owed (**liabilities**).

EXAMPLE 1

Maria and Roberto's assets are listed below. What is the total value of their assets?

ASSETS	*Maria and Roberto Sanchez*	
Checking and Savings Account(s)		$ 6,432
Cash		$ 312
Stocks and Bonds		—
Car		$ 7,200
House		$ 93,000
Contents of House		$ 19,600
Collections, etc.	*Baseball Cards*	$ 289
	TOTAL ASSETS	$126,833

EXAMPLE 2

Maria and Roberto's liabilities are listed below. What is the total value of their liabilities?

LIABILITIES	*Maria and Robert Sanchez*
Balance on Mortgage	$46,830
Balance on Auto Loan	$14,800
Balance on Other Loans	$ 2,630
Balance on Credit Cards	$ 890
TOTAL LIABILITIES	$65,150

To determine net worth, you subtract liabilities from assets.

EXAMPLE 3

Find Maria and Roberto's net worth.

Subtract. $126,833 − $65,150 = $61,683

Maria and Roberto's net worth is $61,683.

FOR DISCUSSION

1. How would the net worth of a homeowner be different from the net worth of a renter?

2. Why is a person's net worth not a good indication of the amount of money he or she has available?

PRACTICE EXERCISES

Remember to estimate whenever you use your calculator.

Use the assets and liabilities listed below for Exercises 1–12.

ASSETS	Bill and Sally Jefferson
Checking/Savings/Cash	$ 3,892
Stocks/Bonds	$ 1,150
Car	$ 6,750
House	$63,900
House Contents	$12,850
Collections, etc.	$ 932
TOTAL ASSETS	

LIABILITIES	Bill and Sally Jefferson
Balance on Mortgage	$38,433
Balance on Auto Loan	$ 1,830
Balance on Other Loans	$ 2,850
Balance on Credit Cards	$ 1,263
TOTAL LIABILITIES	

1. How much do Bill and Sally have in checking, savings, and cash?

2. What is the balance on Bill and Sally's mortgage?

3. What is the total value of Bill and Sally's house and contents?

4. What is the total of Bill and Sally's assets?

5. What is the total of Bill and Sally's liabilities?

6. What is Bill and Sally's net worth?

Suppose Bill and Sally got a second mortgage of $45,000 to put an addition on their house. The value of the house increased by $47,600. The value of the house contents increased by $2,800. Their checking, savings, and cash dropped to $513. All their other assets and liabilities remained the same.

7. What is the value of their house with the addition?

8. What is the new value of the contents of the house?

9. What is the mortgage balance, including the second mortgage?

10. What is the new total of Bill and Sally's assets?

11. What is the new total of Bill and Sally's liabilities?

12. What is Bill and Sally's new net worth?

15.6 ADJUSTING A BUDGET

DECISION MAKING

A **balanced budget** has enough income to meet expenses. It is important to have a balanced budget. You cannot continue to spend more than you earn.

PROBLEM

The Nampo family has a decision to make. Their income is $512 less than their expenses. They listed these 3 plans to help them decide which one to use.

PLAN A The Nampos could try to bring home $512 more per mo. They would need to earn about $750 to bring home $512.

PLAN B The Nampos could *cut* $512 from their budget. They would cut the $75 savings from fixed costs. The other cuts would have to come from living expenses.

PLAN C The Nampos could try to bring home $260 more per mo. They would need to earn about $380 to bring home $260. They would cut the other $252 from the budget. They would make all their cuts from living expenses.

BUDGET SHEET FOR THE MONTH OF _April_		
FOR _The Nampo Family_		

LIVING EXPENSES		FIXED EXPENSES	
Food	$446	Rent	—
		Mortgage	$516
HOUSEHOLD		Car Payment	$120
		Savings	$75
Electricity	$93	Contingency	$40
Natural Gas	$61		
Telephone	$72	TOTAL	$751
Water	$11		
Other	—	**ANNUAL EXPENSES**	
		INSURANCE	
TRANSPORTATION		Life	$215
		Home	$308
Gas/Oil	$118	Car	$925
Parking/Tolls	$28		
Repairs	$60	Medical/Dental	$670
Bus/Train/Cab	$35	Vacation	$900
Other	—	Property Taxes	$1,855
		Home Repairs	$110
PERSONAL			
		TOTAL	$4,983
Clothing	$90		
Expenses	$150	MONTHLY SHARE	$415
Credit Card	—	**MONTHLY SUMMARY**	
		NET INCOME	$2,002
ENTERTAINMENT			
		TOTALS	
Movies/Sports	$30	Living	$1,348
Eating Out	$154	Fixed	$751
		Annual	$415
TOTAL (LIVING EXPENSES)	$1,348	TOTAL EXPENSES	$2,514
		BALANCE	−$512

DECISION-MAKING FACTORS

Living expenses   Fixed expenses   Total expenses
Net income   Balance   Extra hours worked   Other factors

DECISION-MAKING COMPARISONS

Compare the 3 plans by completing the table.

Factors	Plan A	Plan B	Plan C
Living expenses	$1,348	1. ■	2. ■
Fixed expenses	3. ■	4. ■	$751
Total expenses (including share of annual expenses)	5. ■	$2,002	6. ■
Net income	$2,514	7. ■	8. ■
Balance	9. ■	10. ■	0
Extra hours worked each month at $9.50 per h	79 h	11. ■	12. ■
Other factors	Away from home 20 h more per wk	13. ■	14. ■

MAKING THE DECISIONS

Which plan should the Nampos choose if the only factor were

15. Having a higher net salary?

16. Not reducing living costs?

17. Having a balance of 0?

18. Not working additional hours?

19. How much lower would the Nampos' fixed expenses be if they choose Plan B instead of Plan C?

20. How much lower would the Nampos' fixed expenses be if they choose Plan B instead of Plan A?

21. How much higher would the Nampos' living expenses be if they choose Plan A instead of Plan C?

22. About how many fewer hours would the Nampos work if they choose Plan C instead of Plan A?

23. How would you advise the Nampos to cut living expenses if they choose Plan C?

24. How would you advise the Nampos to cut living expenses if they choose Plan B?

25. Which of these plans would you choose? Why?

CHAPTER

REVIEW

Vocabulary   Choose the letter of the word(s) that completes the sentence.

1. The percent that prices increase is called the ■.   [302]

   a. Inflation rate   **b.** CPI   **c.** Price difference

2. The expenses that vary from month to month are called ■.   [304]

   a. Living expenses   **b.** Annual expenses   **c.** Net pay

3. An organized plan for spending money is called a ■.   [304, 306]

   a. Charge account   **b.** Annual expense   **c.** Budget

Skills   Find the answer.

4. A price went from $87 to $93. What was the inflation rate?   [302]

5. A price went from $7.39 to $7.99. What was the inflation rate?   [302]

6. What is the purchasing power of $17,800 after 8% inflation?   [302]

7. What is the purchasing power of $30,296 after 9% inflation?   [302]

8. What should be budgeted for food if past expenses have been $396, $408, and $472?   [304]

9. What should be budgeted for gas if past expenses have been $93, $72, and $86?   [304]

10. What is the monthly share of an annual $2,088 expense?   [304]

11. What is the monthly share of an annual $5,832 expense?   [304]

Use the table of estimated costs for raising a family on page 309 for Exercises 12–13.

12. What will it cost to raise a child that will be born 3 y from now, from birth to age 18?   [308]

13. What will it cost to raise a child that will be born 2 y from now, from age 5 to age 18 and pay for 4 y of private college tuition?   [308]

Don's house and its contents are worth $156,300. He has $8,362 in checking/savings/cash, and his car is worth $8,364. Don has balances of $64,382 on his mortgage; $5,380 on his auto loan; and $3,172 on his credit card.

Find Don's: [310]

14. Total assets.   15. Total liabilities.   16. Net worth.

CHAPTER TEST

Find the inflation rate.

1. Original price: $153
Price now: $167

2. Original price: $2.39
Price now: $2.89

3. Original price: $1,500
Price now: $1,785

Find the purchasing power after inflation.

4. Amount: $19,300
Inflation rate: 9%

5. Amount: $27,078
Inflation rate: 7%

6. Amount: $52,800
Inflation rate: 5%

Find the amount to budget for May.

7. Past transportation expenses:
Feb., $48; March, $52; April, $71

8. Past food expenses:
Feb., $432; March, $416; April, $427

Use the monthly budget for Exercises 9–11.

9. Find the monthly share of the annual expenses.

10. Find the total monthly expenses.

11. Find the balance.

MONTHLY BUDGET	
Living expenses	$ 894
Fixed expenses	$ 739
Annual expenses	$7,092
Net pay	$2,309

Use the table of estimated costs for raising a family on page 309 for Exercises 12–13.

12. A child will be born next year. About how much will it cost to raise the child from birth to age 18?

13. A child will be born next year. About how much will it cost to raise the child from age 5 to 18 and pay 4 y tuition at a public college?

Use the assets and liabilities listed below for Exercises 14–16.

ASSETS	Hal and Carol Roberts
Checking/Savings/Cash	$ 7,309
Stocks/Bonds	$ 2,360
Car	$ 12,980
House/House Contents	$ 138,900
TOTAL ASSETS	

LIABILITIES	Hal and Carol Roberts
Balance on Mortgage	$78,976
Balance on Auto Loan	$ 4,670
Balance on Other Loans	$ 9,456
Balance on Credit Cards	$ 2,098
TOTAL LIABILITIES	

Find the Roberts':

14. Total assets.

15. Total liabilities.

16. Net worth.

MONEY TIPS

Investing in collectibles may help you fight inflation and realize a profit.

LET'S LOOK AT THE FACTS

Many people collect things, not simply as a hobby, but because certain things tend to increase in value over time. Following is a list of categories that could include **collectible items.**

1. Coins	2. Stamps	3. Records 4. Fine Art 5. Comic Books
6. Autographs	7. Old Flags	8. Film Props 9. Rare Books 10. Classic Cars
11. Tiffany Glass	12. Foreign Currency	13. Disney Memorabilia
14. Ancient Porcelain	15. Diamonds/Gemstones	16. Historical Photos
17. Original Manuscripts	18. Items Belonging to Celebrities	

LET'S DISCUSS WHY

1. There is only 1 1856 British Guinea one penny stamp remaining in the entire world. In 1962, it was valued at $55,000. In 1987, it was valued at $1,250,000. What is the percent of increase?

2. A drawing done by a famous artist was certified authentic by an art expert. What else might make it even more valuable?

3. Why would some items increase in value while others would not?

4. Think of examples for categories 8, 9, 16, 17, and 18. What do you think determines the value of each?

LET'S SEE WHAT YOU WOULD DO

5. You inherit a large wooden chest from your aunt. Inside is a Mickey Mouse watch; movie posters; buttons; porcelain Disney figurines marked *limited edition;* a *Fantasia* record album; 2 ticket stubs from Disneyland dated July 17, 1955; and a complete Mouseketeer outfit. How would you find out their value? If they are valuable but you do not want to sell them yet, what would you do with them?

6. In the early 1980s, some people thought that original Coca-Cola cans, Geraldine Ferraro campaign buttons, Cabbage Patch Kids, and toy robots would be big collectibles in the next 10–15 y. Have you heard of these items? If not, ask friends and family what they know about them.

# CALCULATOR FIND WHAT PERCENT ONE NUMBER IS OF ANOTHER

You can use a calculator to find what percent one number is of another. Remember, on some calculators you may need to enter the $=$ key after the $\%$ key.

60 is what percent of 75?

Procedure	Calculator Entry	Calculator Display
1. Enter 60.	6 0	60.
2. Enter the ÷ key.	÷	60.
3. Enter 75 and the % key.	7 5 %	80.

So 60 is 80% of 75.

If your calculator does not have a $\%$ key, multiply by 100 instead.

90 is what percent of 40?

Procedure	Calculator Entry	Calculator Display
1. Divide 90 by 40.	9 0 ÷ 4 0 =	2.25
2. Multiply by 100.	× 1 0 0 =	225.

So 90 is 225% of 40.

Use a calculator to find the answers.

1. 45 is what percent of 90?

2. 5 is what percent of 20?

3. 250 is what percent of 50?

4. 110 is what percent of 550?

5. 27 is what percent of 0.45?

6. $68.40 is what percent of $22.80?

7. $3.25 is what percent of $125?

8. $18.60 is what percent of $2.50?

Use a calculator to solve.

9. Julio earns $1,200 per mo. He pays $300 rent. What percent of his monthly pay goes for rent?

10. Sally has budgeted $480 for travel expenses. She has already spent $60. What percent has she spent?

11. Frank saved $2.25 of each $25 he earned. What percent of his income did he save?

12. Of 25 students enrolled in a course, 4 transferred out. What percent of the students remained in the course?

Subtract.

1. $1,287.50 − $1,000

2. $87.23 − $50

3. $564.32 − $500

4. $7,384.24 − $5,000

5. $39\frac{1}{8} − 28\frac{5}{8}$

6. $84\frac{1}{2} − 68\frac{3}{4}$

7. $7\frac{7}{8} − 3\frac{3}{4}$

8. $74\frac{1}{4} − \frac{5}{8}$

Rename as a decimal.

9. $43\frac{1}{4}$

10. $27\frac{5}{8}$

11. $14\frac{3}{4}$

12. $8\frac{7}{8}$

Multiply.

13. $80 × 17\frac{3}{8}$

14. $150 × 50\frac{1}{2}$

15. $250 × 24.62$

16. $450 × 3.875$

Divide. Round down to the nearest whole number.

17. $1,000 ÷ $7\frac{3}{4}$

18. $5,000 ÷ $24\frac{7}{8}$

19. $300 ÷ $5\frac{5}{8}$

20. $500 ÷ $28\frac{1}{2}$

21. $2,000 ÷ $63\frac{1}{8}$

22. $7,500 ÷ $13\frac{1}{4}$

Find the answer to the nearest cent.

23. 8.75% of $2,500

24. 7.739% of $459.50

25. 5.438% of $9,873.50

26. 6.75% of $5,000

27. $5\frac{3}{4}$% of $4,000

28. $6\frac{1}{2}$% of $7,420.80

Find the answer to the nearest tenth of a percent.

29. $43.85 is what percent of $250?

30. $983.50 is what percent of $1,000?

31. $135.38 is what percent of $500?

32. $1,218.49 is what percent of $1,000?

Millions of shares of stock are traded each day on the New York Stock Exchange. Why do people invest their money in stocks? How do stockbrokers help them?

A popular form of investing money is through the purchase of **Series EE United States Savings Bonds.** Many employers offer payroll deduction plans to purchase savings bonds, and many people give bonds as gifts. Series EE Savings Bonds are available with **face values** of $50; $75; $100; $200; $500; $1,000; $5,000; and $10,000. They can be purchased for $\frac{1}{2}$ of their face value.

EXAMPLE 1

What is the cost of a $500 Series EE Savings Bond?

THINK: The purchase price is $\frac{1}{2}$ of the face value.

Multiply. $\qquad \frac{1}{2} \times \$500 = \$250$

A $500 savings bond will cost $250.

Savings bonds earn variable rates of interest but guarantee 5.5% compounded semiannually for the first year, increasing by $\frac{1}{4}$% each half year to a maximum of 7.5% after 5 y. Savings bonds can be redeemed or cashed in at any time after 6 mo at values derived from the table at the right.

GUARANTEED REDEMPTION VALUES ON $50 BONDS

Years held	Value	Years held	Value
0.5	$25.69	5.5	37.48
1.0	26.40	6.0	38.89
1.5	27.22	6.5	40.34
2.0	28.14	7.0	41.86
2.5	29.16	7.5	43.43
3.0	30.29	8.0	45.06
3.5	31.54	8.5	46.75
4.0	32.92	9.0	48.50
4.5	34.44	9.5	50.32
5.0	36.14	10.0	52.20

EXAMPLE 2

How much will you receive if you redeem a $200 savings bond after 6 y?

1. Use the table. After 6 y, a $50 bond can be redeemed for $38.89.

2. Divide to find how many $50 are in $200.

   $200 ÷ $50 = 4

3. Multiply.

   $4 \times \$38.89 = \$155.56$

The $200 bond can be redeemed for $155.56.

EXAMPLE **3** How much interest was earned on the $200 savings bond redeemed after 6 y?

THINK: INTEREST EARNED = REDEMPTION VALUE − PURCHASE PRICE

Subtract. $155.56   − $100   = $55.56

You earned $55.56 interest.

FOR DISCUSSION

1. Who pays the interest on U.S. Savings Bonds?

2. Why are U.S. Savings Bonds considered to be "patriotic" investments?

PRACTICE EXERCISES   Remember to estimate whenever you use your calculator.

Find the cost of buying the bonds.

	1.	2.	3.	4.	5.	6.
Face value of bond	$100	$75	$50	$500	$1,000	$5,000
Number of bonds	1	1	4	2	3	5

Find the redemption value of the bond.

	7.	8.	9.	10.	11.	12.
Face value of bond	$500	$500	$5,000	$1,000	$100	$75
Years held	3.0	4.5	5.0	8.0	2.5	9.0

Complete the table.

Bonds held	Years held	Redemption value	Interest earned
3 $500 bonds	$3\frac{1}{2}$	13. ■	14. ■
2 $100 bonds	8	15. ■	16. ■
2 $1,000 bonds	$5\frac{1}{2}$	17. ■	18. ■
5 $50 bonds	$7\frac{1}{2}$	19. ■	20. ■
8 $5,000 bonds	6	21. ■	22. ■
6 $75 bonds	1	23. ■	24. ■
7 $10,000 bonds	$4\frac{1}{2}$	25. ■	26. ■

You can purchase another investment called a **certificate of deposit,** or **CD,** at your bank. Since money invested in a CD must be left on deposit for a set period of time to avoid a penalty charge, CDs earn higher interest than regular savings accounts.

CDs can usually be purchased for $500 or more at terms of 30 d, 90 d, 6 mo, 1 y, and 5 y. The longer the term, the higher the interest rate, but the longer you do not have ready access to your money.

The table shows how 1 bank advertises its CDs. Since interest is compounded daily, you can use the **annual effective yield** to find the actual interest earned in a year. The annual effective yield can also be used to compare CDs with the returns on other investments.

CERTIFICATES OF DEPOSIT

Term	Annual rate	Annual effective yield
30 d	6%	6%
90 d	7.15%	7.38%
6 mo	7.30%	7.54%
1 y	7.65%	7.92%
5 y	7.75%	8.03%

EXAMPLE 1

How much interest will you earn on a 1-y $5,000 CD?

1. Use the table.

   The annual effective yield for a 1-y CD is 7.92%.

2. Multiply to find the interest.

   THINK: 7.92% = 0.0792 $0.0792 \times \$5,000 = \$396.00$

You will earn $396 interest on the CD.

The annual effective yield must be divided by 2 for 6-mo terms, by 4 for 90-d terms, and by 12 for 30-d terms.

EXAMPLE 2

How much interest will you earn on a 90-d $2,000 CD?

1. Use the table.

   The annual effective yield for a 90-d CD is 7.38%.

2. Multiply to find the annual interest.

   THINK: 7.38% = 0.0738 $0.0738 \times \$2,000 = \$147.60$

3. Divide to find the 90-d interest.

   THINK: 90 d is $\frac{1}{4}$ of a year. $\$147.60 \div 4 = \$36.90$

The CD will earn $36.90 interest.

1. Why do CDs earn higher interest than regular savings accounts?
2. Why are some people hesitant to purchase longer-term CDs?

PRACTICE EXERCISES

Remember to estimate whenever you use your calculator.

Use the table on page 322. What is the annual effective yield for the CD?

1. 1-y CD   **2.** 90-d CD   **3.** 30-d CD   **4.** 5-y CD   **5.** 6-mo CD

Find the interest earned over the term.

	6.	7.	8.	9.	10.	11.
Amount invested	$2,500	$1,000	$7,500	$5,000	$1,500	$10,000
Term of CD	1 y	1 y	6 mo	30 d	90 d	6 mo

Solve.

12. Michael invested $15,000 in a 6-mo CD. After 6 mo, he took his interest and reinvested the $15,000 in another 6-mo CD. How much interest did he earn in all?

13. Nancy invested $15,000 in a 1-y CD. How much interest did she earn? Did the 1-y CD earn more or less than the 2 6-mo CDs in Exercise 12? How much more or less?

14. Sonya invested $5,000 in a 90-d CD. After 90 d, she took her interest and reinvested the $5,000 in another 90-d CD. How much interest did she earn in all?

15. Manuel invested $5,000 in a 6-mo CD. How much interest did he earn? Did the 6-mo CD earn more or less than the 2 90-d CDs in Exercise 14? How much more or less?

EXTENSION   Investment Yield

The annual yield of any investment is calculated by dividing the interest earned in 1 y by the amount invested. For example, if you earned $163.85 interest on an investment of $2,000, your annual yield was $163.85 ÷ $2,000, or 0.081925, or 8.2%.

You earned $397.37 interest on a $5,000 CD and $203.75 interest on a $3,000 savings account. Which investment provided the greater yield?

16.3 CORPORATE STOCKS

Another form of investment is buying **corporate stocks** that are traded on a stock exchange. A **share** of stock is a piece of ownership in a corporation. Owners of stocks are paid **dividends** on their shares when the corporation makes a profit.

Investors also make or lose money when they sell their stocks, depending on whether the price has gone up or down. Stocks can be purchased or sold through stockbrokers and you can keep track of how your stocks are doing by reading the stock tables in the financial sections of most newspapers.

EXAMPLE 1

Part of a stock exchange listing is shown below. Identify the column headings.

Highest and lowest prices over past year

Annual dividend per share in dollars and cents

Yield = Dividend ÷ Price

Number of shares sold in 100s

Increase (+) or decrease (–) in closing price from the previous day

Closing price on previous day

Highest and lowest prices of the day

52-week High	52-week Low	Stock	Div	Yld	Sales 100s	High	Low	Last	Chg.
37⅜	27⅝	EGH	.56	1.6	683	34⅞	34⅛	34¾	+ ½
11¾	9¾	EQT N	1.05	10.2	97	10⅜	10¼	10¼	– ⅛
17½	13⅝	EQT P	1.66	12.1	115	14	13¾	13¾	– ¼
16½	9½	ERN		--	108	14	13½	13½	– ⅜
39⅝	29½	ER Syst	.50	1.6	1142	32	31¼	31¾	– ½
53	29¾	EagleT	1.12	2.4	109	45¾	45	45¾	+ ½
33¼	24½	EastProd	1.30	4.9	318	26½	26	26½	+ ⅜
40½	30¼	East Util	2.30	7.2	213	32¼	31¾	31⅞	– ⅛
85⅛	52⅛	EGadw	2.52	2.9	1286	87	84¼	87	+ 2⅛
94	63	Eatone	2.00	2.1	742	94	92¾	93⅛	– ⅜
25⅜	14⅞	Echmer	.56	3.3	1532	17	16¾	17	---
31½	20¾	Ecotab	.58	2.0	212	29⅜	28⅞	28⅞	– ⅝
44	33	EdisWr	1.80	4.8	60	37¼	36¾	37¼	+ ¾
19⅞	14⅜	EDA	.28	1.8	141	15½	15¼	15⅜	+ ⅛
14¼	9⅛	EdMat	.16	1.3	71	12	11¾	12	+ ¼
38⅞	21⅝	Edmond	.68	2.1	130	32⅜	31¾	32	– ⅜
13¾	6⅛	Eldar	.22	1.6	124	13½	13¼	13½	---
13⅛	4	ElecDr		--	30	4⅜	4¼	4¼	– ⅛
31¾	13⅝	Elctspt	.08	.3	479	30⅝	30¼	30⅝	– ⅛
18	12½	Elgon		--	70	14⅜	14	14¼	– ¼
3	1⅜	Elsant		--	166	2¼	2⅛	2¼	---
10⅞	8⅞	Emrit	1.20	12.0	83	10	9⅞	10	+ ⅛
110¼	78½	EmrsAl	2.88	2.7	1450	107¾	105¼	107¾	+ 1¼
12¾	6¼	ERan		--	955	7⅛	6⅞	7	– ⅛
18	10½	EmprA		--	971	16	15⅝	15⅞	– ⅜
43¼	30¾	Enhart	1.40	3.2	594	43¾	42⅝	43⅜	+ ¾
29¼	17¼	EnglF	.52	2.1	1085	25	24½	24⅝	– ¾
22⅝	14⅜	EntB		--	287	22	21	22	+ 1⅝
50⅝	37⅞	Enrin	2.48	5.5	630	45	44¾	45	+ ¼
26	13⅛	Encrsh	.80	3.3	922	24½	24	24¼	– ¼
18½	10⅛	EnsExt	1.20	8.1	194	15	14½	14¾	– ⅛
8⅞	4½	Entora		--	271	8½	8⅛	8½	+ ¼
6⅛	3⅛	EntexB	.60	14.5	66	4¼	4⅛	4⅛	– ⅛
19⅝	12⅜	EntexTr	.35	2.4	1020	15	14⅛	14⅞	+ ¼
24½	14¾	EnwSys		--	368	20⅛	19¾	20	+ ¼
26	18	EnwSy	1.75	7.3	29	24⅛	24	24⅛	+ ⅛
28½	19½	Equipax	.68	3.0	105	23	22¾	22¾	– ¼
6⅝	4⅛	EquiMk		--	435	4⅝	4½	4⅝	---
10⅞	8¾	EqtBl	.50	5.3	134	9½	9⅜	9⅜	– ¼
46⅞	28	EqtBs	1.20	2.8	101	44	43½	43½	– ⅜
10	6	Equitax	.16	2.0	33	8	7⅞	7⅞	– ¼
35	19	ErbSys	.52	1.8	71	29¼	29	29	– ⅜
42⅜	29	EssWt	.72	1.7	41	42½	42	42½	+ ⅝
35	20½	EsxTh	.60	2.4	205	28	25	25	– 3¼
20¼	10¼	Estren		--	41	16½	16¼	16¼	– ½
32¼	16	EthyPr	.40	1.3	1081	29⅞	29⅜	29¾	---
92	57½	ExetRf	3.60	4.0	6132	89⅝	89⅛	89½	+ ⅛

EXAMPLE 2 You decide to buy 50 shares of Empire Airfreight (EmprA). How much will the shares cost?

1. Use the stock listing to find that the last price for EmprA was $15\frac{7}{8}$.

2. Rename the price as a decimal. $15\frac{7}{8} = \$15.875$

3. Multiply to find the cost. $50 \times \$15.875 = \$793.75$

The stock will cost $793.75.

EXAMPLE 3 You purchased 40 shares of Ethyl Products (EthyPr) at $16\frac{7}{8}$. How much profit will you make if you sell the shares today?

1. Use the stock listing to find that the last price for Ethyl was $29\frac{3}{4}$.

2. Subtract to find the increase $\$29\frac{3}{4} \ - \$16\frac{7}{8}$
   for each share.
   $$\downarrow \qquad\quad \downarrow$$
   $$\$29.75 - \$16.875 = \$12.875$$

3. Multiply to find the profit. $40 \times \$12.875 = \$515$

You will make a profit of $515.00.

EXAMPLE 4 How much did you receive in dividends over the past year from your 250 shares of Exeter Refining (ExetRf)? What was your rate of return (yield) on your investment over the past year?

1. Use the stock listing to find that Exeter paid a dividend of $3.60 per share and that the last price was $89\frac{1}{2}$.

2. Multiply to find your earnings. $250 \times \$3.60 = \$900$

3. Multiply to find the value of $250 \times \$89\frac{1}{2}$
   your investment.
   $$\downarrow$$
   $$250 \times \$89.50 = \$22,375$$

4. Divide to find your return. $\$900 \div \$22,375 = 0.0402234 = 4\%$

You received $900 in dividends, representing a 4% return on your investment.

FOR DISCUSSION

1. What causes stocks to go up or down in price?

2. What is meant by a "bull" market and a "bear" market?

Remember to estimate whenever you use your calculator.

Use the stock listing to answer.

1. What was the highest price Elgon was traded at over the past year?

2. What was the lowest price Enhart was traded at over the past year?

3. How many shares of ERN were traded on this particular day?

4. By how much did a share of Equitax decline from its 52-wk high?

5. How much did Eastern Gadwick (EGadw) pay per share in dividends?

6. What was the day's high price for Enrin?

7. Which 3 stocks closed at their highest prices in a year?

Find the current cost of the shares.

	8.	9.	10.	11.	12.	13.
Stock	Eldar	EntB	East Util	EDA	Estren	EagleT
Number of shares held	75	30	125	65	250	2,300

Complete the table.

Purchase price	Last price	Number of shares	Amount of Profit (P) or loss (L)
$14\frac{1}{2}$	$21\frac{3}{4}$	30	14. ■
$25\frac{7}{8}$	$19\frac{1}{4}$	80	15. ■
$84\frac{3}{8}$	$125\frac{1}{2}$	50	16. ■
64	$42\frac{7}{8}$	250	17. ■

Complete the table.

Stock owned	Dividend per share	Total annual dividend	Rate of return
10 shares of EGH	18. ■	19. ■	20. ■
40 shares of EdisWr	21. ■	22. ■	23. ■
75 shares of EssWt	24. ■	25. ■	26. ■
500 shares of EDA	27. ■	28. ■	29. ■

Another form of investment is buying **corporate bonds** or **municipal bonds.** When corporations need to raise large sums of money for such things as plant expansions or when states and cities need money for such things as roads or schools, they issue bonds. When you buy a bond, you are really lending the corporation or the government your money, based on an agreement that you will be paid interest over the life of the bond and repaid the full amount when the bond matures.

The face value of a bond, often $1,000, is called the **par value.** The **maturity date** of the bond, often 5, 10, or 20 y, is when the bond can be redeemed at par value. However, many investors buy and sell bonds on the bond market before they reach maturity at the bond's **market price,** which may be higher or lower than the par value.

BONDS			
Bond	**Maturity date**	**Interest rate**	**Market price**
Excelsior Corporation	1994	$5\frac{1}{2}\%$	$825
Roadway Company	1997	$7\frac{1}{4}\%$	$1,075
State of Ohio	1992	$6\frac{3}{4}\%$	$937

EXAMPLE 1

At what percent of par are the Excelsior Corporation bonds currently selling?

THINK: $1,000 par value bonds are selling for $825.

Divide to find the percent. $825 ÷ $1,000 = 0.825 = 82.5\%$

The bonds are currently selling at 82.5% of par.

EXAMPLE 2

How much interest would you receive per year if you owned 8 State of Ohio $1,000 bonds?

THINK: Interest is paid on the par value, not on the market price.

1. Multiply to find the interest on 1 bond.
$$6\tfrac{3}{4}\% \text{ of } \$1,000 = 0.0675 \times \$1,000 = \$67.50$$

2. Multiply to find the interest on 8 bonds.
$$8 \times \$67.50 = \$540$$

You would earn $540 annually in interest.

EXAMPLE 3

What is the current yield on a $1,000 Roadway Company bond?

THINK: CURRENT YIELD = ANNUAL INTEREST ÷ MARKET PRICE

1. Multiply to find the annual interest.
$$7\tfrac{1}{4}\% \times \$1,000 = 0.0725 \times \$1,000 = \$72.50$$

2. Divide to find the current yield.
$$\$72.50 \div \$1,075 = 0.0674418 = 6.7\%$$

The current yield is 6.7%.

FOR DISCUSSION

1. How are bonds different from stocks?

2. How are municipal bonds different from corporate bonds?

Remember to estimate whenever you use your calculator.

BONDS			
Chapman International	1994	$8\frac{3}{4}\%$	$975
City of Yuma	1995	$5\frac{3}{8}\%$	$950
Dover Products	1998	$7\frac{3}{4}\%$	$1,050
Eastern Metals	1997	$9\frac{1}{2}\%$	$837.50
Finch Township	1996	$6\frac{5}{8}\%$	$1,087.50

Use the bond listing above.
Which bond(s):

1. Has the earliest maturity?

2. Is currently the most expensive?

3. Has the lowest interest rate?

4. Has the highest interest rate?

5. Are selling below par?

6. Are selling above par?

Find the current cost of the bonds.

7. 4 Dover bonds

8. 8 Finch bonds

9. 20 Eastern Metals bonds

10. 15 City of Yuma bonds

At what percent of par is the $1,000 bond currently selling?

11. Market price: $950

12. Market price: $875

13. Market price: $837.50

14. Market price: $1,500

15. Market price: $1,050

16. Market price: $1,125

Find the annual interest you would earn each year from the bonds.

17. 6 Chapman $1,000 bonds

18. 10 City of Yuma $1,000 bonds

19. 30 Eastern $1,000 bonds

20. 50 Finch $1,000 bonds

Find the current yield on the bond.

21. Chapman

22. City of Yuma

23. Dover

24. Finch

Rather than selecting your own mixture of stocks and other investments, you can pool your money with other investors and buy shares in a **mutual fund.** When the fund earns money on its investments, the profits are paid to investors in the fund in the form of **dividends.**

Most mutual funds have a **sell price** that represents the value of a share and a **buy price** that is usually higher than the sell price, since it includes a sales charge.

According to the mutual fund listing, a share of the Corvette Fund can be sold for $23.17, it can be purchased for $24.76, and its value increased by 6¢ a share from the previous day.

MUTUAL FUNDS

Fund	Sell	Buy	Chg.
Allegiance	10.31	10.74	+.09
Americana	15.07	NL	+.07
Cornell	13.98	15.28	−.04
Corvette	23.17	24.76	−.06
Criteria	17.18	NL	+.14
Dayton	6.95	7.24	−.03
Forecast	7.38	7.85	+.07
Future	24.12	NL	−.11
Generation	10.25	11.01	+.02
Guard	36.54	38.12	+.16
Hanover	16.45	NL	−.03
International	12.83	14.12	+.08
Keymark	9.56	NL	−.14

NL means No Load
(Buy price is equal to sell price.)

EXAMPLE 1 What will it cost to buy 80 shares of the Hanover Fund?

THINK: Since the fund is NL, the buy price is the same as the sell price.

Multiply to find the price.

$$80 \times \$16.45 = \$1,316$$

80 shares will cost $1,316.00.

EXAMPLE 2 An investor sells 250 shares of the Forecast Fund. What is the current value of these shares?

THINK: The sell price for a share of the fund is $7.38.

Multiply to find the value. $250 \times \$7.38 = \$1,845$

The 250 shares are currently worth $1,845.00.

FOR DISCUSSION

What are the advantages of investing in a mutual fund rather than buying individual stocks or bonds?

PRACTICE EXERCISES

Remember to estimate whenever you use your calculator.

Use the mutual funds listing on page 330. Complete the table.

Fund	Cost to buy 1 share	Cost to buy 50 shares	Cost to buy 250 shares
Guard	1. ■	2. ■	3. ■
Criteria	4. ■	5. ■	6. ■
Cornell	7. ■	8. ■	9. ■
Future	10. ■	11. ■	12. ■

Find the current value of the mutual fund shares.

13. 400 shares of Allegiance

14. 1,500 shares of Keymark

15. 550 shares of Generation

16. 40 shares of Dayton

17. 2,200 shares of Americana

18. 750 shares of International

Solve.

19. An investor has $4,000 to invest in a mutual fund. How many shares of the Forecast Fund can be bought?

20. An investor has $12,000 to invest in a mutual fund. How many shares of the Hanover Fund can be bought?

21. An investor bought 400 shares of the Generation Fund at $8.17 per share. If the shares are sold at today's price, how much profit will be made?

22. An investor bought 650 shares of the Criteria Fund at $21.74 per share. If the shares are sold at today's price, how much of a loss will there be?

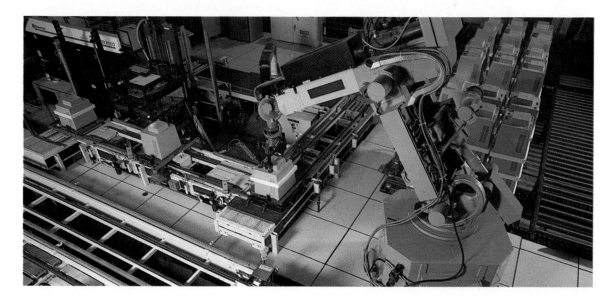

Many employees are automatically enrolled in a **pension plan** that provides them with a **pension** after they retire. Most pension plans combine employee payroll deductions with employer contributions that are invested in stocks, bonds, or mutual funds.

Many pension benefits can be calculated using the formula and the benefit percent table below.

$$\begin{matrix} \text{ANNUAL PENSION} \\ \text{BENEFIT} \end{matrix} = \begin{matrix} \text{BENEFIT} \\ \text{PERCENT} \end{matrix} \times \begin{matrix} \text{YEARS OF} \\ \text{SERVICE} \end{matrix} \times \begin{matrix} \text{AVERAGE ANNUAL} \\ \text{EARNINGS} \end{matrix}$$

BENEFIT PERCENT FOR EACH YEAR OF SERVICE

Years of Service	Age 55	56	57	58	59	60	61	62	63	64	65+
5 to 9	0	0	0								
10	1.00	1.06	1.12	1.20	1.30	1.40	1.52	1.64	1.76	1.88	2.00
11	1.07	1.12	1.18	1.25	1.35	1.44	1.55	1.66	1.78	1.89	2.00
12	1.13	1.18	1.24	1.31	1.39	1.48	1.58	1.69	1.79	1.90	2.00
13	1.20	1.25	1.29	1.36	1.44	1.52	1.62	1.71	1.81	1.90	2.00
14	1.26	1.31	1.35	1.41	1.48	1.56	1.65	1.74	1.82	1.91	2.00
15	1.33	1.37	1.41	1.47	1.53	1.60	1.68	1.76	1.84	1.92	2.00
16	1.40	1.43	1.47	1.52	1.58	1.64	1.71	1.78	1.86	1.93	2.00
17	1.46	1.49	1.53	1.57	1.62	1.68	1.74	1.81	1.87	1.94	2.00
18	1.53	1.56	1.58	1.62	1.67	1.72	1.78	1.83	1.89	1.94	2.00
19	1.59	1.62	1.64	1.68	1.71	1.76	1.81	1.86	1.90	1.95	2.00
20	1.66	1.68	1.70	1.73	1.76	1.80	1.84	1.88	1.92	1.96	2.00
21	1.73	1.74	1.76	1.78	1.81	1.84	1.87	1.90	1.94	1.97	2.00
22	1.79	1.80	1.82	1.84	1.85	1.88	1.90	1.93	1.95	1.98	2.00
23	1.86	1.87	1.87	1.89	1.90	1.92	1.94	1.95	1.97	1.98	2.00
24	1.93	1.93	1.93	1.94	1.94	1.96	1.97	1.98	1.98	1.99	2.00
25 or over	2.00	2.00	2.00	2.00	2.00	2.00	2.00	2.00	2.00	2.00	2.00

EXAMPLE

A worker retires at age 59 with 18 y of service in the company. If her average annual earnings were $35,000, what is her annual pension benefit? How much will she receive per month?

1. Use the table. The benefit percent for a 59-year-old with 18 y of service is 1.67.

2. Use the formula to find the annual benefit. $1.67\% \times 18 \times \$35,000 = \$10,521$

3. Divide to find the monthly benefit. $\$10,521 \div 12 = \$876.75$

This worker will receive a pension of $10,521 per y, or $876.75 per mo.

Why does an employee's contributions to his or her pension fund represent only a small part of the eventual pension benefits?

PRACTICE EXERCISES   Remember to estimate whenever you use your calculator.

Use the benefit percent table on page 332. Complete the table.

Age at retirement	Years of service	Average annual earnings	Benefit percent	Annual pension	Monthly pension
65	20	$24,000	1. ■	2. ■	3. ■
57	15	$18,900	4. ■	5. ■	6. ■
58	23	$12,400	7. ■	8. ■	9. ■
63	12	$39,850	10. ■	11. ■	12. ■
69	34	$24,375	13. ■	14. ■	15. ■

EXTENSION   IRAs

IRAs, or **Individual Retirement Accounts,** allow many people who are not covered by company pension plans to save for their retirement on their own.

Person(s)	Adjusted Gross Income	Full annual tax deduction	Tax-deferred investment income
Single	below $25,000	Yes; $2,000	All
Single	above $25,000	No	All
Married couple; 1 earner	below $40,000	Yes; $2,250	All
Married couple; 2 earners	below $40,000	Yes; $4,000	All
Married couple	above $40,000	No	All

1. Why are people not covered by company pension plans allowed to deduct their annual IRA contributions from their taxes?

At what income level do the person(s) lose their ability to deduct their entire IRA contributions from their taxes?

2. Single person   3. Married couple

4. How are IRAs beneficial to all of the persons listed in the table?

16.7 WORKING BACKWARD

Situation:

Edie wants to make 1 investment now so that she will have $24,000 to take a luxury cruise when she retires in 18 y. She invests in a mutual fund in which her money is expected to double every 9 y. How much money should Edie initially invest in order to have $24,000 in 18 y?

Strategy:

Working backward can help you find a solution.

Applying the Strategy:

1. What amount should be in Edie's fund at the end of the 9th y so it would double to be $24,000 by the end of the 18th y?

   THINK: $\frac{1}{2}$ of $24,000 = $\frac{1}{2} \times$24,000 = $12,000

2. What amount should Edie invest initially so that at the end of the 9th y it would double to be $12,000?

   THINK: $\frac{1}{2}$ of $12,000 = $\frac{1}{2} \times$12,000 = $6,000

   Edie should initially invest $6,000.

FOR DISCUSSION

Roy invests money once in a real-estate partnership. It is expected that his money will triple every 7 y. He wants to have $108,000 in 21 years to set up his own business.

1. Explain how you can work backward to determine how much money Roy should initially invest.

2. What is the solution?

Remember to estimate whenever you use your calculator.

Solve by working backward.

Alice wants to have $40,000 saved to help pay for her daughter's college education 18 y from now. She invests in a corporate bond fund in which her money is expected to double every 9 y.

1. What amount should be in Alice's fund at the end of the 9th y so it would double to be $40,000 by the end of the 18th y?

2. What amount should Alice initially invest so that at the end of the 9th y it would double to be $20,000?

Ben invests money once in a stock income fund. It is expected that the money in his account will triple every 8 y. Ben wants to have $81,000 in 24 y to supplement his retirement income.

3. What amount should be in Ben's account at the end of the 16th y so it would triple to be $81,000 by the end of the 24th y?

4. What amount should be in Ben's account at the end of the 8th y so it would triple to be $27,000 by the end of the 16th y?

5. What amount should Ben initially invest so that at the end of the 8th y it would triple to be $9,000?

6. Susan wants to have $100,000 saved to begin investing in real estate 20 y from now. She invests in a fund she expects to double her money every 10 y. How much money should Susan invest in the fund?

7. Beth wants to have $36,000 saved to start her own business 12 y from now. She invests money once in a bond fund. She expects her money to double every 6 y. How much money should Beth initially invest?

8. Roberto buys a zero coupon bond for his newborn grandson. It is expected that the money will double every 12 y. How much should Roberto spend on the bond so that his grandson will have $75,000 in 36 y?

9. Alicia wants to have $35,000 saved to help pay for some property in 15 y. Her mutual funds are expected to double her money every $7\frac{1}{2}$ y. How much should Alicia initially invest in the funds?

10. Helga invests money in a fund in which her money is expected to double every 7.5 y. How much money should Helga invest now if she wants to have $200,000 for retirement in 30 y?

11. Martin wants to have $270,000 saved for his retirement $37\frac{1}{2}$ y from now. He invests in a stock and bond portfolio in which his money is expected to triple every $12\frac{1}{2}$ y. What should Martin initially invest in the portfolio?

16.8 BUYING STOCKS

Louis and Rebecca O'Rourke decide it would be fun, and perhaps profitable, to invest some of their money in the stock market.

PROBLEM

Louis and Rebecca decide to start with a $3,000 investment. They visit a stockbroker and ask for the names of a variety of "high-tech" companies. They take the list and use the stock listings from their newspaper and information from their broker to prepare the following table. In which stock or stocks should they invest?

New Era	$37.50/share	20¢ dividend	Up $5/share in past year	High risk
Geoparts	$87.37/share	$2.75 dividend	Down $20/share in past year	Moderate risk
Technics	$3.87/share	No dividend	Up 50¢/share in past year	Moderate risk
Laserpert	$15.25/share	$1.75 dividend	Up $4.50/share in past year	Low risk
Jetstorm	$117.75/share	$4.50 dividend	Down $2/share in past year	Low risk
Phantom	$21.50/share	$1.00 dividend	Up $3.00/share in past year	High risk

DECISION-MAKING FACTORS

Yield (Dividends ÷ Price)   Growth prospects   Risk

DECISION-MAKING COMPARISONS

Compare the 6 stocks by completing the table.

Stock	Price per share	Dividend per share	Yield	Percent Increase (I) or decrease (D) in price over past year	Risk
New Era	1. ■	$0.20	2. ■	3. ■	4. ■
Geoparts	5. ■	6. ■	7. ■	8. ■	Moderate
Technics	$3.87	9. ■	10. ■	11. ■	12. ■
Laserpert	13. ■	14. ■	11.5%	15. ■	16. ■
Jetstorm	17. ■	18. ■	19. ■	1.7% (D)	20. ■
Phantom	21. ■	22. ■	23. ■	24. ■	25. ■

Which stock should Louis and Rebecca buy if the only factor were:

26. Lowest price?

27. Highest dividend?

28. Highest yield?

29. Greatest recent percent growth?

30. Which stock should be purchased if Louis and Rebecca wish to minimize risk and maximize yield?

31. Which stock should be purchased if Louis and Rebecca are willing to take high risks and wish to maximize the yield?

32. Which stock(s) are probably the safest investments? Why?

33. Louis and Rebecca decide to place $\frac{1}{2}$ of their investment in a low-risk, low-yield investment and half of their investment in a high-risk, high-yield investment. How many shares of which stocks should they buy?

34. How would you invest the $3,000? Why?

CHAPTER

REVIEW

Vocabulary   Choose the letter of the word(s) that completes the sentence.

1. Investments that allow you to pool your money and invest in a variety of investments are called ▦.   [330]

    a. Stocks   **b.** Mutual funds   **c.** Corporate bonds

2. Investments that are really loans to the federal government are called ▦.   [320]

    a. Savings bonds   **b.** Government stocks   **c.** Certificates of deposit

3. Investments are best compared based on their ▦.   [322, 336]

    a. Dividends   **b.** Interest rate   **c.** Yield

Skills   Find the answer.

4. Warren redeemed a $500 U.S. savings Bond for $389.67. How much interest did he earn on the bond?   [320]

5. How much interest will Jennifer earn on a 6-mo $2,000 CD that has an annual effective yield of 7.784%?   [322]

6. What is the cost of 60 shares of a stock selling at $35\frac{5}{8}$?   [324]

7. What is the value of 500 shares of a stock trading at $56\frac{1}{8}$?   [324]

8. How much profit did Myra make when she bought 30 shares of a stock at $17\frac{3}{4}$ and sold than at $31\frac{3}{8}$?   [324]

9. What was the loss when Kevin was forced to sell 150 shares of stock at $27\frac{1}{2}$ that he purchased at $41\frac{3}{4}$?   [324]

10. What is the yield on a stock that sells for $46\frac{1}{2}$ and pays $2.75 in dividends?   [324]

11. What is the yield on a bond that costs $953 and pays $68.93 in interest annually?   [327]

12. How much interest is earned on a $1,000 bond that pays 6.492%?   [327]

13. How much will Chita earn on 240 shares of a mutual fund that pays $5.90 per share in dividends?   [330]

14. A pension plan pays 2% per y for each year of service. How much will the annual pension benefit be for a woman with 24 y of service and average annual earnings of $37,500?   [332]

15. A pension plan pays 1.5% per y for each year of service. How much will the annual pension benefit be for a man with 17 y of service and average annual earnings of $26,000?   [332]

CHAPTER TEST

Complete the table.

Type of investment	Purchase price	Interest or dividend	Yield
A share of stock	$27.50	$1.15 dividend	1. ■
A corporate bond	$935.00	$89.47 interest	2. ■
A share of a mutual fund	$17.50	42¢ dividend	3. ■
A municipal bond	$1,000	$57.90 interest	4. ■

Solve.

5. If a $50 U.S. Savings Bond can be redeemed for $38.89 after 6 y, how much will a $1,000 bond be worth after 6 y?

6. How much interest is earned on a $3,000 6-mo CD that offers an effective annual yield of 6.86%?

7. What is the cost of 125 shares of a stock selling at $59\frac{3}{8}$?

8. How much profit did you make when you bought 750 shares of a stock at $12\frac{1}{2}$ and sold them at $19\frac{3}{4}$?

9. How much was lost when you sold 25 shares of stock at $25\frac{1}{8}$ that you purchased at $34\frac{3}{4}$?

10. How much interest is earned on a $1,000 bond that pays 5.831%?

11. A pension plan pays 2% per y for each year of service. How much will the annual pension benefit be for a worker with 28 y of service and average annual earnings of $18,000?

12. You want to have $48,000 saved in 18 y. The fund you invest in expects to double your money after 9 y. How much should you initially invest in the fund?

You decide to invest $1,000 in either:
   a. A stock selling for $14.50 that pays $1.00 in dividends.
   b. A corporate bond that pays 8.52%.
   c. A mutual fund selling for $28.75 that pays 25¢ in dividends.
   d. A 1-y CD with an effective annual yield of 7.41%.

13. What are the annual dividends paid on $1,000 of the stock?

14. What are the annual dividends paid on $1,000 of the mutual fund?

15. Which offers the higher return, the stock or the mutual fund?

16. How much more interest will the corporate bond pay per year than the CD?

Self-employed persons can invest in and manage their own retirement plans.

LET'S LOOK AT THE FACTS

Most companies have retirement plans for their employees. Self-employed persons can establish similar plans for themselves. One type is called a **Keogh profit-sharing plan,** which allows you to invest varying amounts up to 15% of your Net Earned Income (NEI). The formulas shown below can be used to calculate your NEI and your contribution amounts.

$$\text{NET EARNED INCOME} = \frac{\text{NET PROFITS (GROSS INCOME MINUS EXPENSES)}^*}{1 + \% \text{ OF CONTRIBUTION}}$$

$$\text{PLAN CONTRIBUTION} = \text{NET EARNED INCOME (NEI)} \times \% \text{ OF CONTRIBUTION}$$

*Gross income minus expenses, shown on Schedule C of your 1040 tax return.

LET'S DISCUSS WHY

1. Why do you think it would be a good idea for self-employed persons to invest in a retirement plan?

2. You can invest as much as 15% of your NEI but no more than $30,000 in any one year. If $30,000 was 15% of your NEI, what would your total annual NEI be?

3. If your annual NEI is $40,000, what would your plan contribution be if you invest 5% of it? 8% of it? 12% of it?

4. You are not required to contribute to a retirement plan every year. What might be some reasons for not contributing in some years?

5. Contributions to a Keogh profit-sharing plan are considered business expense deductions. How would this affect the taxes you pay now?

LET'S SEE WHAT YOU WOULD DO

6. You are a freelance artist. Last year, you earned $35,000 and you invested 5% of it in a Keogh profit-sharing plan. This year you will earn about the same amount of money but would like to invest 10% of it. Your expenses this year, however, are higher. What are your options, and which do you think would be the most financially sound option to choose?

7. You have been investing in a tax-deferred Keogh profit-sharing plan since age 38. You are now age 64, healthy, and able to continue working productively. Discuss the financial pros and cons of retiring.

ESTIMATION SKILLS

OVERESTIMATES AND UNDERESTIMATES OF PRODUCTS AND QUOTIENTS

The symbols $^+$ and $^-$ may be used to show that an actual product is greater than or less than an estimate.

Examples

38×295
↓   ↓
$40 \times 300 = 12,000$
First estimate: 12,000

THINK: Each factor was rounded up, so the actual product is less than 12,000.

Final estimate: $12,000^-$

9.2×5.327
↓   ↓
$9 \times 5 = 45$
First estimate: 45

THINK: Each factor was rounded down, so the actual product is greater than 45.

Final estimate: 45^+

$18 \times \$74.45$
↓   ↓
$20 \times \$70 = \$1,400$
First estimate: $1,400

THINK: One factor was rounded up and one was rounded down. It is not immediately clear whether $1,400 is high or low. Keep the first estimate.

Final estimate: $1,400

Estimated quotients can be adjusted in a similar way.

Examples

$822 \div 21$
↓   ↓
$800 \div 20 = 40$
First estimate: 40

THINK: $21 \times 40 = 840$ Since $840 > 822$, the actual quotient is less than 40.

Final estimate: 40^-

$\$142.98 \div 28$
↓   ↓
$\$150 \div 30 = \$5$
First estimate: $5

THINK: $28 \times \$5 = \$140$ Since $\$140 < \$142.98$, the actual quotient is greater than $5.

Final estimate: $\$5^+$

Estimate the product or quotient. Where appropriate, use the symbol $^+$ or $^-$ to indicate whether the actual answer is greater than or less than the estimate.

1. 49×66

2. 32×325

3. 58×315

4. $27 \times \$2.98$

5. $18 \times \$2.29$

6. $31 \times \$21.50$

7. 4.2×9.3

8. 6.7×19.38

9. 5.25×7.854

10. $616 \div 32$

11. $855 \div 42$

12. $4,316 \div 81$

13. $\$38.60 \div 20$

14. $\$74.16 \div 25$

15. $\$560.98 \div 72$

16. $9.15 \div 2.8$

CUMULATIVE REVIEW

Choose the letter of the word(s) that completes the sentence.

1. The ■ calculator key can be used when you have entered the wrong number into the calculator.

   a. Clear   **b.** Clear entry   **c.** Memory   **d.** None of these

2. A check written for more than the balance in your account is called ■.

   a. New balance   **b.** A payment   **c.** An overdraft   **d.** None of these

3. The percent of the mortgage amount paid at the closing is called ■.

   a. Points   **b.** Mortgage rate   **c.** Appreciation   **d.** None of these

4. An organized plan for spending money is called ■.

   a. An annual expense   **b.** A charge account
   c. A budget   **d.** None of these

5. Investments that are really loans to the federal government are called ■.

   a. Stocks   **b.** Savings bonds   **c.** Mutual funds   **d.** None of these

Select the best estimated answer.

6. 85¢ + $3.18 + $4.96   **a.** $7.00   **b.** $7.50   **c.** $8.00   **d.** $8.90

7. 0.42 − 0.089   **a.** 0.2   **b.** 0.3   **c.** 0.4   **d.** 0.5

8. 82 × $0.36   **a.** $2.40   **b.** $3.20   **c.** $32   **d.** $320

9. 416.3 ÷ 7.89   **a.** 5   **b.** 6   **c.** 50   **d.** $500

Compute.

10. 38.7 + 42.9 + 16.34

    a. 96.94   **b.** 97.9   **c.** 97.94   **d.** None of these

11. 6,504 − 4,397

    a. 2,107   **b.** 2,297   **c.** 10,901   **d.** None of these

12. 9 × 5.73

    a. 45.37   **b.** 51.57   **c.** 54   **d.** None of these

13. 8)7.76

    a. 0.9   **b.** 0.97   **c.** 97   **d.** None of these

14. $33\frac{1}{3}$% of 54

    a. 5.4   **b.** 18   **c.** 27   **d.** None of these

Solve.

15. Sandy works a 40-h week at an hourly rate of $7.45. Her deductions total $93.50. What is her net pay?

    a. $167.25   **b.** $204.50   **c.** $391.50   **d.** None of these

16. During the billing period, you used 4,236 kWh of electricity. The utility company charges $0.0375 per kWh. What was the total cost of electricity during this period?

    a. $127.08   **b.** $158.85   **c.** $168.85   **d.** None of these

17. If 3% of each production run is pulled for inspection, how many items will be inspected in a production run of 800 items?

    a. 24   **b.** 30   **c.** 80   **d.** None of these

18. The average price of a house was $70,000. The average price is now $77,000. Find the inflation rate.

    a. 1%   **b.** 7%   **c.** 10%   **d.** None of these

19. Fencing was installed to enclose a yard that measures 6 yd by 3 yd. The fence posts are 1 yd apart. How many posts are there?

    a. 18   **b.** 20   **c.** 162   **d.** None of these

20. You want to have $63,000 saved in 18 y. The fund you invest in expects to triple your money every 9 y. How much should you initially invest in the fund to reach your goal?

    a. $6,000   **b.** $8,000   **c.** $10,000   **d.** None of these

THINKING ABOUT MATH

1. Why do masons usually order more bricks than their computations indicate?

2. Why is inflation particularly difficult for people with fixed incomes?

3. How would the budget for a single person differ from the budget for a family?

4. Why are some people hesitant to purchase long-term certificates of deposit?

Write in lowest terms.

1. $\frac{5}{10}$ 2. $\frac{8}{12}$ 3. $\frac{36}{100}$ 4. $\frac{24}{72}$

Multiply. Write the answer in lowest terms.

5. $\frac{1}{4} \times \frac{3}{4}$ 6. $\frac{2}{3} \times \frac{5}{8}$ 7. $\frac{3}{10} \times \frac{4}{9}$ 8. $\frac{2}{5} \times \frac{3}{7}$

Rename as a percent.

9. $\frac{1}{5}$ 10. $\frac{34}{50}$ 11. $\frac{6}{20}$ 12. $\frac{12}{30}$

Round to the nearest whole number.

13. 14.86   14. 3.1242   15. 837.9284   16. 25.395

Find the answer.

17. 20% of 350   18. 10% of 283

19. $33\frac{1}{3}$% of 660   20. 60% of 750

Look at a standard number cube.

21. How many possible numbers can come up for 1 roll?

22. How many numbers are greater than 2?

23. How many numbers are less than 3?

24. How many numbers are even?

25. How many numbers are odd?

Look at a standard deck of playing cards.

26. How many cards are there in the deck?

27. How many spades are there in the deck?

28. How many 6s are there in the deck?

29. How many queens are there in the deck?

Chapter 17

PROBABILITY

Meteorologists study climate and weather conditions. Weather predictions are made on the basis of past weather patterns. How reliable are the daily predictions of a 5-day weather forecast?

Add.

1. $0.2 + 0.9$ **2.** $4.3 + 0.7$ **3.** $9.7 + 5.6$

4. $0.8 + 19.3$ **5.** $16.2 + 9.03$ **6.** $7.08 + 9.93$

Subtract.

7. $0.6 - 0.3$ **8.** $8.2 - 0.4$ **9.** $4.3 - 2.7$

10. $17.3 - 12.1$ **11.** $20.8 - 7.9$ **12.** $9.07 - 3.8$

Multiply.

13. $\frac{1}{5} \times 5$ **14.** $\frac{1}{7} \times 7$ **15.** $\frac{1}{2} \times 2$ **16.** $\frac{1}{4} \times 4$

17. $\frac{1}{6} \times 6$ **18.** $\frac{1}{3} \times 3$ **19.** $\frac{1}{10} \times 10$ **20.** $\frac{1}{12} \times 12$

Divide.

21. $9 \div 9$ **22.** $22 \div 22$ **23.** $16 \div 16$ **24.** $53 \div 53$

25. $0.2 \div 0.2$ **26.** $0.7 \div 0.7$ **27.** $1.25 \div 1.25$ **28.** $0.65 \div 0.65$

Rename as a decimal.

29. 80% **30.** 16% **31.** 9% **32.** 12.5%

Find the answer.

33. 80% of 25 **34.** 16% of 30 **35.** 9% of 70 **36.** 12.5% of 90

37. 2^2 **38.** 3^2 **39.** 6^2 **40.** 8^2

Find the missing number.

41. $n + 3 = 9$ **42.** $n - 4 = 11$ **43.** $n + 6 = 22$ **44.** $n - 10 = 33$

45. $3 \times n = 21$ **46.** $n \div 2 = 8$ **47.** $8 \times n = 72$ **48.** $n \div 10 = 7$

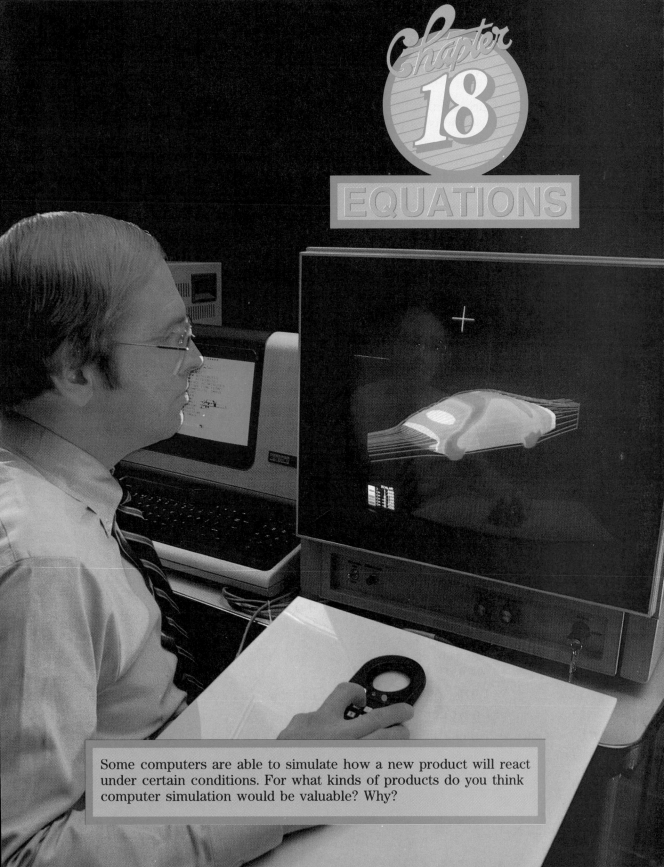

Chapter 18

EQUATIONS

Some computers are able to simulate how a new product will react under certain conditions. For what kinds of products do you think computer simulation would be valuable? Why?

To **simplify the expression** to the right, you need to use the correct **order of operations.**

$$3^2 + 6 \cdot 4$$
$$\downarrow$$

The raised dot means multiply.

Order of Operations
- Raise to a power.
- Multiply or divide in order from left to right.
- Add or subtract in order from left to right.

EXAMPLE 1

Simplify.

1. Raise to a power.

2. Multiply.

3. Add.

$3^2 + 6 \cdot 4$

$9 + 6 \cdot 4$

$9 + \quad 24$

33

So $3^2 + 6 \cdot 4 = 33$.

To simplify expressions with **parentheses,** do the work within the parentheses first.

EXAMPLE 2

Simplify.

1. Work within parentheses.

   THINK: Divide first,
   then subtract.

2. Multiply.

   THINK: $4(1.6)$ means $4 \cdot 1.6$.

3. Add.

$5 + 4(1.8 - 0.6 \div 3)$

$5 + 4(1.8 - 0.2)$
$5 + 4(1.6)$

$5 + \quad 6.4$

11.4

So $5 + 4(1.8 - 0.6 \div 3) = 11.4$.

To simplify expressions with a **division bar,** do the work first above the bar, then below the bar.

EXAMPLE 3

Simplify.

1. Do work above bar.

   THINK: Add.

2. Do work below bar.

   THINK: Divide, then subtract.

3. Divide.

$\dfrac{3 + 2}{30 \div 5 - 1}$

$\dfrac{5}{30 \div 5 - 1}$

$\dfrac{5}{6 - 1} = \dfrac{5}{5}$

1

So $\dfrac{3 + 2}{30 \div 5 - 1} = 1$.

How do different calculators use the rules for order of operations?

 Remember to estimate whenever you use your calculator.

Simplify the expression mentally.

1. $3 + 8 - 6$

2. $4 \cdot 7 - 7$

3. $8 - 3 + 5$

4. $2^2 + 12 \div 3$

5. $7(3 + 2)$

6. $3(3^2 + 2)$

7. $6 \cdot 2^3 + 3$

8. $(3 \cdot 4 - 6) + 7$

9. $(17 - 5 \cdot 3) + 2^2$

Simplify the expression.

10. $40 - 10 - 19$

11. $47 - 19 \cdot 2$

12. $28 \div 7 \cdot 8$

13. $21 - 24 \div 8$

14. $4^2 + 3 \cdot 2$

15. $5^2 - 16 \div 4$

16. $3(14 - 2) + 6$

17. $19 + (6 \cdot 3 + 2)$

18. $3 + 2(1.8 - 0.4)$

19. $7 - 5(0.8 - 0.4)$

20. $\frac{8}{2} + 12 - 7$

21. $\frac{6 - 3 + 5}{8 - 6}$

22. $\frac{8 - 3 \cdot 2 + 3}{10}$

23. $\frac{6}{15 - 4 \cdot 3}$

24. $\frac{12 - 3(4) + 6}{3(18 - 16)}$

25. $\frac{2^2 \div 2 - 3(0.5)}{0.6 - 0.5}$

26. $\frac{6 + 6 - 3^2}{4(9.5 - 6 \div 3)}$

27. $\frac{2^5 \div (7 - 5 + 6)}{8 + 3(2^2)}$

 Computers and Order of Operations

Computers use different symbols to stand for some operations. **Computer-programming languages** use the rules for order of operations.

Arithmetic symbol	Computer symbol
$6 + 2$	$6 + 2$
$6 - 2$	$6 - 2$
6×2	$6 * 2$
$6 \div 2$	$6/2$
6^2	$6 \wedge 2$

Find the computer's answer.

1. $4 * 3 + 6$

2. $(5 - 2) * 7$

3. $6/3 + 4$

4. $5 + 8/2$

5. $4 \wedge 2 + 1$

6. $7 + 3 \wedge 2$

7. $4 * 5 \wedge 2$

8. $27/3 \wedge 2$

9. $(6 - 2) \wedge 2$

10. $(7 + 5)/(4 * 3)$

11. $4 + 3 \wedge 2 * 5$

12. $(3 * 12)/3 \wedge 2$

18.2 EXPRESSIONS AND EQUATIONS

An **algebraic expression** consists of 1 or more variables with or without operational signs. A **variable** is a letter used to stand for a number.

You can translate word phrases into algebraic expressions. The table below lists some words commonly used to describe operations.

> Add (+): sum of, total, and, increased by, more than
>
> Subtract (−): difference of, decreased by, fewer, less
>
> Multiply (·): of, product of, at, times
>
> Divide (÷): quotient of, for each, shared equally, ratio

EXAMPLE 1 Write algebraic expressions for these word phrases.

a. 9 less than w

b. 7 times y plus 3

c. $\frac{2}{5}$ of y

$w - 9$

$7 \cdot y + 3$, or

$\frac{2}{5} \cdot y$

$7y + 3$

$\frac{2}{5}y$

An **equation** is a mathematical sentence that states that 2 expressions are equal.

EXAMPLE 2 Write equations for these statements.

a. 2 times the sum of 5 and n is 34.

$2 \cdot (5 + n) = 34$, or $2(5 + n) = 34$

b. Your age is 6 more than $\frac{1}{2}$ of 22.

$a = \frac{1}{2} \cdot 22 + 6$, or $a = \frac{1}{2}(22) + 6$

You can write an equation for a word problem.

EXAMPLE 3 Write an equation for this problem.

Chad bought a computer for $10 more than $\frac{1}{2}$ of its regular price. Chad paid $304. What was the regular price of the computer?

THINK: $10 more than $\frac{1}{2}$ the regular price is $304.

Write. $10 $+$ $\frac{1}{2}r$ $= \$304$

FOR DISCUSSION

Describe the equation in words.

1. $4 + n = 13$
2. $16(5 - 3) = x$
3. $\frac{8 - 2y}{2} = 3$

PRACTICE EXERCISES

Write an algebraic expression for the word phrase.

1. The sum of x and 9
2. 15 divided by x

3. 19 less than y
4. The product of 3 and x

5. 8 more than y
6. 12% of y

7. 8 fewer than y
8. 6 more than the difference of x and 5

9. 6 more than the product of y and 9
10. 10 increased by 3 less than y

Write an equation for the statement.

11. 10 increased by 6 is equal to y.
12. The product of 6 and 3 is x.

13. 10% of y is 42.
14. 16 is 11 more than y.

15. 4 times the sum of 6 and y is 19.
16. 40 is the sum of x and 16.

17. 6 less than the product of x and 2 is 42.
18. Your test score is 23 divided by 25.

Write the letter of the equation that matches the word problem.

19. Claire bought 9 pads for $0.64 each. How much did she spend?

20. Eight students shared the cost of a $20 gift. How much did each pay?

21. The $20 model less the discount costs $8. What is the discount?

a. $a = 9 + \$0.64$

b. $\frac{\$20}{8} = p$

c. $9(\$0.64) = s$

d. $\$20 - d = \$8$

e. $\frac{\$20}{d} = \$8$

Write an equation for the problem.

22. The $40 cost of a taxi ride was shared equally by 5 people. How much did each person pay?

23. Ryan increased the 9 models in his collection by 13. How many models are there in his collection now?

24. Sandy bought a dress for 60% of its regular price. She paid $42. What was the regular price?

25. Six friends each paid $12 as their share of a meal. They added a $15 tip to the cost of the meal. How much did the meal cost the group all together?

18.3 EVALUATING EXPRESSIONS AND FORMULAS

To **evaluate an expression,** first replace the variable with a given value. Then simplify the resulting expression.

EXAMPLE 1 Evaluate: $7y + 3$ for $y = 6$.

1. Replace y with 6. $7y + 3 = 7(6) + 3$

2. Simplify. $42 \quad + 3$

45

There may be more than 1 variable in the expression.

EXAMPLE 2 Evaluate: $\frac{bh}{2}$ for $b = 3$ and $h = 12$.

1. Replace b with 3 and h with 12. $\frac{bh}{2} = \frac{3(12)}{2}$

2. Simplify. $\frac{36}{2}$

18

Remember to follow the rules for order of operations.

EXAMPLE 3 Evaluate: $\frac{a(x-4)}{y}$ for $a = 3$, $x = 12$, and $y = 6$.

1. Replace the variables with the given values. $\frac{a(x-4)}{y} = \frac{3(12-4)}{6}$

2. Simplify. $\frac{3(8)}{6} = \frac{24}{6}$

4

You can also evaluate formulas. A **formula** is an equation that expresses a relationship between 2 or more quantities involving more than 1 variable. This formula shows how to convert from Celsius to Fahrenheit temperature readings. $F = \frac{9}{5}C + 32$

EXAMPLE 4 Evaluate the formula to solve this problem. The temperature is 25° Celsius. What is the reading in degrees Fahrenheit?

1. Replace C with 25. $F = \frac{9}{5}C + 32 = \frac{9}{5}(25) + 32$

2. Simplify. $F = \frac{9}{\overset{1}{\cancel{5}}}(\overset{5}{\cancel{25}}) + 32 = 45 + 32 = 77$

A temperature reading of 25°C is 77°F.

What formula would you use to:

1. Find the area of a wall in your classroom?

2. Find the distance you can drive in a given time?

PRACTICE EXERCISES

Remember to estimate whenever you use your calculator.

Evaluate for $x = 8$.

1. $x + 3$
2. $10 - x$
3. $11x$
4. $\frac{x}{2}$

5. $3x - 2$
6. $\frac{x}{4} + 2$
7. $19 - 2x$
8. $23 + \frac{x}{8}$

Evaluate for $a = 2$ and $b = 4$.

9. $a + b$
10. $b - a$
11. ab
12. $\frac{b}{a}$

13. $2b + a$
14. $(12 - b) + a$
15. $6 - \frac{b}{a}$
16. $4a - 2b$

Evaluate.

17. $3(x - 4)$ for $x = 7$
18. $\frac{12}{x} - 2$ for $x = 3$

19. $(x + 2)6$ for $x = 4$
20. $\frac{24}{x} + 5$ for $x = 12$

21. $x(y - 5)$ for $x = 2$, $y = 7$
22. $x\left(\frac{y}{8}\right)$ for $x = 6$, $y = 56$

23. $x - y + z$ for $x = 7$, $y = 2$, $z = 4$
24. $x(y - z)$ for $x = 3$, $y = 9$, $z = 2$

25. $x + \frac{y}{z} - 2$ for $x = 12$, $y = 21$, $z = 3$
26. $\frac{x(y + 3)}{(3 + y)z}$ for $x = 12$, $y = 1$, $z = 6$

Evaluate the formula to solve the problem.

27. The temperature is 30° Celsius. What is the Fahrenheit reading?
    (Use $F = \frac{9}{5}C + 32$.)

28. The temperature is 86° Fahrenheit. What is the Celsius reading?
    [Use $C = \frac{5}{9}(F - 32)$.]

29. A car traveled at a rate of 45 mph for $2\frac{1}{2}$ h. What distance was that?
    (Use $d = rt$.)

30. You painted a square wall 13 ft on a side. How many square feet was that? (Use $A = s^2$.)

Addition and subtraction are **inverse operations.** One undoes the other. To solve an equation, use an inverse operation to get the variable by itself.

When a number is attached to a variable by subtraction, you can unattach it by adding that number to both sides of the equation.

EXAMPLE 1   The price of your weekly train ticket has been decreased by $9 to $15. What was the original cost of the ticket?

1. Write an equation.

   THINK: Original cost less $9 is $15. $c - \$9 = \$15$

2. Solve the equation.

   THINK: $9 is attached by $c - \$9 + \$9 = \$15 + \$9$
   subtraction. Add
   $9 to both sides. $c = \$24$

3. Check the solution.

   THINK: Substitute the value $\$24 - \$9 \stackrel{?}{=} \$15$
   of c into the
   original equation. $\$15 = \$15$ It checks.

The original cost of the ticket was $24.

When a number is attached to a variable by addition, you can unattach it by subtracting that number from both sides of the equation.

EXAMPLE 2   You increased your weekly pay by $3.80 to $73.30. How much had you been earning?

1. Write an equation.

   THINK: Weekly pay plus $3.80 $p + \$3.80 = \$73.30$
   is $73.30.

2. Solve the equation.

   THINK: $3.80 is attached by $p + \$3.80 - \$3.80 = \$73.30 - \$3.80$
   addition. Subtract
   $3.80 from both sides. $p = \$69.50$

3. Check the solution.

   THINK: Substitute the value $\$69.50 + \$3.80 \stackrel{?}{=} \$73.30$
   of p into the
   original equation. $\$73.30 = \$73.30$ It checks.

You had been earning $69.50 per wk.

Why is "− 9.5" called the **additive inverse** of "+ 9.5"?

PRACTICE EXERCISES

Remember to estimate whenever you use your calculator.

Solve. Check your solution.

1. $x - 15 = 45$ **2.** $x - 2.8 = 1.6$ **3.** $x - 7 = 0$ **4.** $2.8 = x - 3.7$

5. $405 = x - 35$ **6.** $5 + x = 92$ **7.** $x + 23 = 50$ **8.** $x + 4.7 = 7.2$

9. $x - 6 = 0$ **10.** $31 = x + 18$ **11.** $12.9 = x + 7.1$ **12.** $29 = x + 12$

13. $23 = a + 18$ **14.** $b - 4.3 = 7.8$ **15.** $24 + c = 90$ **16.** $3.2 = d - 1.5$

17. $23.6 = m - 28$ **18.** $3.6 + n = 8.9$ **19.** $p + 6 = 504$ **20.** $7.8 + r = 9.3$

21. $-(7) + n = 21$ **22.** $n - 7 = -3$ **23.** $-(9) + a = 6$ **24.** $-(3.5) - d = 2$

Write an equation and solve.

25. The store manager reduced the price by \$6 to \$38. What was the original price?

26. Ron improved his test score by 8 points to 89 points. What was his original test score?

27. The price of a share of Zeno stock increased from $34\frac{1}{4}$ to $37\frac{1}{2}$. By how much did the stock increase?

28. The price of a share of Naman stock decreased from 19 to $17\frac{1}{4}$. By how much did the stock decrease?

29. Your \$128 regular pay, plus commission, was \$237. How much was your commission?

30. Your \$983 monthly pay, less expenses, was \$47. What were your expenses?

Multiplication and division are inverse operations.

When a number is attached to a variable by division, you can unattach it by multiplying both sides of the equation by that number.

EXAMPLE 1

You prepaid $92, which was $\frac{1}{2}$ of the cost of your trip. How much will the trip cost?

1. Write an equation.

   THINK: $\frac{1}{2}$ of the cost is $92. $\qquad \frac{c}{2} = \$92$

2. Solve the equation.

   THINK: 2 is attached by division. Multiply both sides by 2.

   $2\left(\frac{c}{2}\right) = 2(\$92)$

   $c = \$184$

3. Check the solution.

   THINK: Substitute the value of c into the original equation.

   $\frac{\$184}{2} \stackrel{?}{=} \$92$

   $\$92 = \$92$ It checks.

The trip will cost $184.

When a number is attached to a variable by multiplication, you can unattach it by dividing both sides of the equation by that number.

EXAMPLE 2

You are trying to guess a number your friend is thinking of. You know that 0.8 times the number is 24. What is the number?

1. Write an equation.

   THINK: 0.8 times the number is 24. $\qquad 0.8n = 24$

2. Solve the equation.

   THINK: 0.8 is attached by multiplication. Divide both sides by 0.8.

   $\frac{0.8n}{0.8} = \frac{24}{0.8}$

   $n = 30$

3. Check the solution.

   THINK: Substitute the value of n into the original equation.

   $0.8(30) \stackrel{?}{=} 24$

   $24 = 24$ It checks.

Your friend is thinking of the number 30.

Why does $\frac{x}{7}$ mean the same as $\frac{1}{7}(x)$?

PRACTICE EXERCISES   Remember to estimate whenever you use your calculator.

Solve. Check your solution.

1. $\frac{x}{4} = 8$

2. $\frac{x}{4} = 12$

3. $\frac{x}{7} = 6$

4. $7 = \frac{x}{0.2}$

5. $34 = \frac{x}{1.5}$

6. $\frac{x}{3} = 42$

7. $4x = 16$

8. $0.5x = 12$

9. $42 = 1.2x$

10. $3x = 7.5$

11. $1.25x = 15$

12. $32 = 0.02x$

13. $3a = 12$

14. $8b = 56$

15. $\frac{c}{5} = 12$

16. $21 = \frac{d}{3}$

17. $14 = 0.1p$

18. $\frac{n}{7} = 12$

19. $2 = \frac{y}{9}$

20. $0.7r = 21$

21. $2.5s = 55$

22. $32 = \frac{t}{0.04}$

23. $3.2 = 1.25n$

24. $160 = \frac{n}{0.7}$

Write an equation and solve.

25. One-fifth of a number is 9. What is the number?

26. Seven times a number is 56. What is the number?

27. Ralph paid $55, $\frac{1}{5}$ of the cost of the car rental. How much did it cost to rent the car?

28. The profits of a sale were shared equally by 3 partners. Each one received $305. What were the profits?

29. Profits in December were 4 times the profits in November. December's profits were $2,492. What were November's profits?

30. Lynne bought her plane ticket for $432, which was 90% of the original price. What was the original price?

Sometimes you need to use 2 steps to solve an equation.

EXAMPLE 1 You bought 7 boxes of cassette tapes and 5 individual tapes for a total of 89 tapes. How many tapes were in each box?

1. Write an equation.

   THINK: 7 boxes plus 5 tapes is 89 tapes.

   $$7b + 5 = 89$$

2. Solve the equation.

   THINK: Unattach first by subtraction, then by division.

   $$7b + 5 - 5 = 89 - 5$$
   $$7b = 84$$
   $$\frac{7b}{7} = \frac{84}{7}$$
   $$b = 12$$

3. Check the solution.

   THINK: Substitute the value of b into the original equation.

   $$7(12) + 5 \overset{?}{=} 89$$
   $$89 = 89 \quad \text{It checks.}$$

There were 12 tapes in each box.

Sometimes you may need to simplify before you solve.

EXAMPLE 2 You earned $40, plus $\frac{1}{5}$ of your sales, less $15 for withholding, to equal a net pay of $130. What were your sales?

1. Write an equation.

   THINK: $40 plus $\frac{1}{5}$ of sales minus $15

   $$\$40 + \frac{s}{5} - \$15 = \$130$$

2. Simplify the equation.

   THINK: $40 − $15 = $25

   $$\$25 + \frac{s}{5} = \$130$$

3. Solve the equation.

   THINK: Unattach first by subtraction, then by multiplication.

   $$\$25 - \$25 + \frac{s}{5} = \$130 - \$25$$
   $$\frac{s}{5} = \$105$$
   $$5\left(\frac{s}{5}\right) = 5(\$105)$$
   $$s = \$525$$

4. Check the solution.

   THINK: Substitute the value of s into the original equation.

   $$\$40 + \frac{\$525}{5} - \$15 \overset{?}{=} \$130$$
   $$\$40 + \$105 - \$15 \overset{?}{=} \$130$$
   $$\$130 = \$130 \quad \text{It checks.}$$

Your sales were $525.

Why do we add or subtract first when solving a 2-step equation?

PRACTICE EXERCISES   Remember to estimate whenever you use your calculator.

Simplify the equation.

1. $13 + \frac{n}{2} - 9 = 54$

2. $3 + 5x + 7 = 70$

3. $18 + 3t - 7 = 51$

Solve. Check your solution.

4. $9s + 8 = 71$

5. $4y - 6 = 42$

6. $54 = 7x + 12$

7. $38 = \frac{t}{4} + 8$

8. $4z - 0.8 = 4$

9. $19 + 8s = 91$

10. $70 = \frac{a}{6} - 10$

11. $\frac{b}{8} - 2.6 = 15.2$

12. $87 = 15 + \frac{z}{10}$

13. $19 + \frac{x}{3} - 3 = 17$

14. $15 + 6y - 2 = 31$

15. $31 = 0.08c - 21$

16. $34 + \frac{d}{5} - 19 = 42$

17. $1.2a - 79 = 17$

18. $14 + 2z - 23 = 43$

19. $-(80) + 0.4b = 92$

20. $-(27) + 3z + 51 = 42$

21. $-(4) + \frac{y}{8} + 23 = 36$

Write an equation and solve.

22. Five more than three times a number is 32. What is the number?

23. Six less than $\frac{2}{5}$ of a number is 49. What is the number?

24. A number divided by 7, plus 6, is 18. What is the number?

25. Thirty percent of a number, minus 8, is 4. What is the number?

26. Angelo bought 3 boxes of erasers, plus 3 more erasers, for a total of 57. How many erasers were in a box?

27. Julie bought $\frac{1}{3}$ case of granola bars. She gave away 3 of the bars and had 15 left. How many granola bars were in a case?

28. Manuel drove the same distance on each of 5 d. Then he drove 35 mi more for a total of 675 mi. How many miles did he drive on each of the 5 d?

29. Claire delivered 28 papers, 4 less than 80% of the papers she needs to deliver. How many papers does Claire usually deliver?

30. Sally earned $80, plus $\frac{1}{8}$ of her sales, less $20 withholding, for a total net of $192. What were her sales?

31. Enrico earned $70, plus 15% of his sales, less $42 withholding, for a total net of $166.45. What were his sales?

18.7 SOLVING A SIMPLER PROBLEM

Situation:

Bernard invests in stocks. Last year, his income from investments was $4,176.85. This year, his income from investments was $643.25 less than it was last year. What was the total income from his investments for the 2 y?

Strategy:

Sometimes it helps to solve a simpler problem. Using **rounded numbers** can make the situation seem easier. Often, you can also "break" a problem into subproblems and write an equation for each subproblem.

Applying the Strategy:

You do not know this year's income from investments. So, first you need to find that income. Then you can find the total income for the 2 y.

Subproblem 1: Let x represent the investment income this year.

THINK: $643.25 is about $600. $4,176.85 is about $4,000.

INCOME LAST YEAR − $600 = INCOME THIS YEAR
$$\$4,000 - \$600 = x$$
$$\$3,400 = x$$

Bernard's income this year was about $3,400.

Subproblem 2: Let t represent the total income from investments.

INCOME LAST YEAR + INCOME THIS YEAR = TOTAL INCOME
$$\$4,000 \quad + \quad \$3,400 \quad = t$$
$$\$7,400 \quad = t$$

Bernard's total investment income
for the 2 y was about $7,400.

Now solve the problem using the actual numbers.

Subproblem 1: $4,176.85 - 643.25 = x$
$3,533.60 = x$

Subproblem 2: $4,176.85 + 3,533.60 = t$
$7,710.45 = t$

Bernard's total investment income for the 2 y was $7,710.45.

PRACTICE EXERCISES   Remember to estimate whenever you use your calculator.

Write the letter of the better choice for simplifying the problem.

1. Don invests in stocks. Last year, his income from investments was $2,630.50. This year, his income from investments was $792.25 more than it was last year. What was the total income from his investments in the 2 y?

   a. $2,600 - 800 = x$
   $1,800 = x$

   $2,600 + 1,800 = t$
   $4,400 = t$

   b. $2,600 + 800 = x$
   $3,400 = x$

   $2,600 + 3,400 = t$
   $6,000 = t$

2. Stella earns $21,216 per y. This is 2.6 times as much as her younger sister, Tina, earns. What is the difference between their incomes?

   a. $21,000 = 3t$
   $7,000 = t$

   $21,000 - 7,000 = d$
   $14,000 = d$

   b. $t = 3 \times 21,000$
   $t = 63,000$

   $63,000 - 21,000 = d$
   $42,000 = d$

Solve by writing a simpler problem.

3. Al and Ben are brothers. They are saving to buy a stereo. Al saves $13.75 per wk. Ben saves $2.75 less per wk than Al saves. In all, how much money do the 2 brothers save each week?

4. Winona invests in stocks. Last year, her income from investments was $2,750. This year, her income from investments was 2.1 times as great as it was last year. What was the total income from her investments in the 2 y?

5. Karen Ching earns $50,232 per y. This is 4.6 times as much as her son earns. What is the difference between their incomes?

6. For 3 y, Marianne has been depositing money in a special bank account. During the third year, she deposited $3,960. This amount was $935 more than she deposited during the second year. The third-year amount was 2.4 times as much as she deposited during the first year. What was the total amount that she deposited during the 3 y?

CHAPTER REVIEW

Vocabulary   Choose the letter of the word(s) that completes the sentence.

1. A variable is a letter used to stand for ■.   [366]

   a. Addition   **b.** A number   **c.** An expression

2. A statement with an = sign is called ■.   [366]

   a. A translation   **b.** An expression   **c.** An equation

3. To solve the equation $3x - 7 = 20$, you would ■ first.   [374]

   a. Add   **b.** Subtract   **c.** Multiply

Skills   Simplify the expression.   [364]

4. $37 - 6 \cdot 4$ 5. $24 \div 2 - 3^2 - 1$ 6. $\frac{4(6 - 3)}{2(20 - 2)}$

Write an equation for the statement.   [366]

7. 15 fewer than y is 6.   8. 12% of x is 20.

9. 32 divided by y is 8.   10. 4 times the sum of 2 and x is 44.

Evaluate.   [368]

11. $3x + 9$ for $x = 7$ 12. $A = lw$ for $l = 6$, $w = 9$

Solve.

13. $x - 8 = 32$ [370]   14. $x + 4.7 = 7.9$ [370]

15. $3x = 18$ [372]   16. $\frac{y}{5} = 6$ [372]

17. $7y + 9 = 44$ [374]   18. $0.8x - 10 = 30$ [374]

Write an equation and solve.

19. The temperature decreased 9° from 76°. What is the new temperature? [370]

20. Your hourly wage increased $1.50 to $6.35. What was your original wage? [370]

21. A number multiplied by 9 is 36. What is the number?   [372]

22. Ed answered 60% of the questions correctly for a score of 15. How many questions were on the test?   [372]

23. Rex bought 6 boxes of erasers and 7 additional erasers for a total of 151. How many erasers were in a box? [374]

24. Sandra earned $80, plus 20% of her sales, less $28 withholding, for a total net of $128. What were Sandra's sales?   [374]

378   CHAPTER 18

Simplify the expression.

1. $29 - 6 \cdot 3$

2. $2(6 - 3)$

3. $20 \div (3 + 2^3 - 1)$

4. $\frac{2(3 + 7) - 4}{4(7 - 5)}$

Write an expression or an equation.

5. 10 increased by x

6. 3 more than the product of 7 and x

7. 8 less 5 is equal to x.

8. 5 times the difference of x and 3 is 42.

Evaluate.

9. $4(y + 3)$ for $y = 9$

10. $2x + (3 - y) + z$ for $x = 9$, $y = 2$, $z = 7$

Solve.

11. $x - 15 = 7$

12. $17 + y = 32$

13. $5y = 30$

14. $\frac{x}{2} = 38$

15. $0.6z = 4.8$

16. $9x - 3 = 24$

17. $5 + 4x = 29$

18. $23 + 6y - 15 = 62$

Write an equation and solve.

19. The temperature increased from $3°$ to $12°$. How much did the temperature rise?

20. Lori decreased her number of work hours by 7 to 29. How many hours had Lori been working?

21. One-third of a number is 16. What is the number?

22. Les read 42 pages, which is 60% of the pages he has to read. How many pages does he have to read in all?

23. Six buses left the terminal. Five buses had all the seats taken, and 1 bus had 18 seats taken, for a total of 253. How many seats were on each bus?

24. Joanne earned $95, plus 15% of her sales, less $72 withholding, for a total of $398. What were her sales?

25. Ira invests in stocks. Last year, his income from investments was $2,385.75. This year, his income from investments was $757.95 more than it was last year. What was the total income from his investments for the 2 y?

CALCULATOR — SOLVE EQUATIONS

You can use a calculator to solve equations.

Solve for n: $n + 1.8 = 3.4$.

THINK: Subtract 1.8 from both sides of the equation.

Procedure	Calculator Entry	Calculator Display
$n + 1.8 = 3.4$		
$n + 1.8 - 1.8 = 3.4 - 1.8$		
$n = 3.4 - 1.8$	$\boxed{3}\,\boxed{.}\,\boxed{4}\,\boxed{-}\,\boxed{1}\,\boxed{.}\,\boxed{8}\,\boxed{=}$	$\boxed{1.6}$
$n = 1.6$		

You can also solve 2-step equations on a calculator.

Solve for n: $6n + 8.4 = 36$.

THINK: First subtract, and then divide.

Procedure	Calculator Entry	Calculator Display
$6n + 8.4 = 36$		
$6n + 8.4 - 8.4 = 36 - 8.4$		
$6n = 36 - 8.4$	$\boxed{3}\,\boxed{6}\,\boxed{-}\,\boxed{8}\,\boxed{.}\,\boxed{4}\,\boxed{=}$	$\boxed{27.6}$
$6n = 27.6$		
$6n \div 6 = 27.6 \div 6$	$\boxed{\div}\,\boxed{6}\,\boxed{=}$	$\boxed{4.6}$
$n = 4.6$		

Use a calculator to solve for n.

1. $n + 14.7 = 33.9$

2. $n - 18 = 2.6$

3. $n + 0.06 = 1.29$

4. $6n = 33$

5. $9.3n = 0.2418$

6. $4.5n = 37.35$

7. $\frac{n}{12} = 2.6$

8. $\frac{n}{3.2} = 4.7$

9. $\frac{n}{0.04} = 800$

10. $4n + 8 = 22$

11. $6n + 3.2 = 26$

12. $2.5n - 12.5 = 17.5$

Write an equation and then use your calculator to solve.

13. A bookkeeper worked 35 h and earned $367.50. What did he earn per hour?

14. The Jacksons ordered a bed priced at $692.95 and 2 matching chairs. The bill came to $1,213.95. What did each chair cost?

ESTIMATING PRODUCTS AND QUOTIENTS OF FRACTIONS AND MIXED NUMBERS

Here is one way to estimate the product of a mixed number and a fraction close to $\frac{1}{2}$.

1. Round the fraction to $\frac{1}{2}$.

2. Round the mixed number to the nearest even number.

3. Multiply.

Examples

$$8\frac{3}{4} \times \frac{2}{5}$$
$$\downarrow \quad \downarrow$$
THINK: $\quad 8 \times \frac{1}{2}$
$$8 \div 2 = 4$$
Estimate: $\quad 4$

$$\frac{5}{8} \times 17\frac{1}{3}$$
$$\downarrow \quad \downarrow$$
THINK: $\quad \frac{1}{2} \times 18$
$$18 \div 2 = 9$$
Estimate: $\quad 9$

You can use compatible numbers when you estimate the quotient of 2 mixed numbers.

1. Find compatible whole numbers that are close in value to the given divisor and dividend.

2. Divide, using the compatible numbers.

Examples

$$12\frac{3}{4} \div 3\frac{1}{3}$$
$$\downarrow \quad \downarrow$$
THINK: $\quad 12 \div 3 = 4$
Estimate: $\quad 4$

$$7\frac{5}{8} \div 4\frac{3}{5}$$
$$\downarrow \quad \downarrow$$
THINK: $\quad 8 \div 4 = 2$
Estimate: $\quad 2$

Estimate the product. Look for factors close to $\frac{1}{2}$.

1. $\frac{2}{5} \times 6\frac{1}{4}$

2. $10\frac{1}{2} \times \frac{3}{8}$

3. $\frac{4}{9} \times 12\frac{1}{3}$

4. $\frac{5}{8} \times 9\frac{3}{4}$

5. $15\frac{3}{8} \times \frac{3}{5}$

6. $\frac{7}{15} \times 2\frac{1}{2}$

7. $23\frac{1}{10} \times \frac{5}{9}$

8. $\frac{7}{12} \times 13\frac{3}{4}$

9. $31\frac{2}{5} \times \frac{9}{16}$

Estimate the quotient. Use compatible numbers.

10. $9\frac{1}{4} \div 1\frac{3}{4}$

11. $10\frac{1}{3} \div 4\frac{2}{5}$

12. $37\frac{1}{2} \div 9\frac{1}{8}$

13. $17\frac{3}{8} \div 2\frac{4}{5}$

14. $14\frac{1}{4} \div 2\frac{3}{5}$

15. $28\frac{3}{4} \div 5\frac{1}{2}$

16. $23\frac{7}{8} \div 5\frac{1}{2}$

17. $26\frac{3}{4} \div 3\frac{5}{8}$

18. $38\frac{1}{2} \div 7\frac{5}{8}$

SKILLS BANK

TABLE OF CONTENTS

382 SKILLS BANK

PART D RATIO, PROPORTION, AND PERCENT

PART E MEASUREMENT

THE DECIMAL SYSTEM

Skill 1: Identify whole-number place value

The table shows the names of the places through the thousands **period.** You can use the table to identify **place values** and the values of the digits in a number.

Name the place and the value of 7 in the number 792,834.

THOUSANDS			ONES		
hundred-thousands	ten-thousands	thousands	hundreds	tens	ones
7	9	2	8	3	4

In the number 792,834, the 7 is in the hundred-thousands place. The value of 7 is 7 × 100,000, or 700,000.

Name the place of the underlined digit.

1. 7̲86
2. 4̲2,051
3. 65̲,319
4. 18̲9,231

Name the value of the underlined digit.

5. 6̲,513
6. 8̲2,045
7. 68,3̲61
8. 5̲01,632

Skill 2: Read and write whole numbers

You can read numbers by using the **period names** and **commas.**

To write a number from a word name, start with the digit in the greatest place. Then write the digit for each place to its right. Write zeros as placeholders when necessary.

Read the number 792,834.
The number 792,834 is read as 792 thousand, 834.

Write the number for fifty-six thousand, two hundred nine.

THOUSANDS		ONES		
ten-thousands	thousands	hundreds	tens	ones
5	6	2	0	9

The number is 56,209.

Write the number.

9. 6 thousand, 242
10. 16 thousand, 17
11. 23 thousand, 504
12. 418 thousand, 984
13. nine hundred eighty-one
14. sixty-three thousand, forty
15. four thousand, three hundred nineteen
16. three hundred forty thousand, two hundred ten

THE DECIMAL SYSTEM

Skill 3: Identify decimal place value

This table shows the names of the decimal places through hundred-thousandths. You can use the table to identify decimal place values and the values of the digits in a decimal.

Find the value of the 6 in the number 2.456.

ones	.	tenths	hundredths	thousandths	ten-thousandths	hundred-thousandths
2	.	4	5	6		

In the number 2.456, 6 is in the thousandths place. The value of 6 is 6 thousandths, or 0.006.

Name the place of the underlined digit.

17. 0.4<u>3</u>

18. 0.20<u>7</u>

19. 0.413<u>5</u>

20. 14.9850<u>7</u>

Name the value of the underlined digit.

21. 0.<u>9</u>

22. 0.3<u>8</u>

23. 1.76<u>2</u>5

24. 29.1876<u>2</u>

Skill 4: Read and write decimals

When you read decimals, first read the whole-number part. Then read the decimal part. Use the name of the place of the last decimal digit. Remember to use the word *and* for the decimal point.

You can use a table to write numbers from short word names and word names. Remember to use zeros as placeholders when necessary.

Read the decimal 2.456.

The number 2.456 is read as 2 and 456 thousandths.

Write the number for two hundred seventeen ten-thousandths.

THINK: Ten-thousandths means 4 decimal places.

ones	.	tenths	hundredths	thousandths	ten-thousandths
0	.	0	2	1	7

Write the number.

25. 23 hundredths

26. 417 thousandths

27. 685 ten-thousandths

28. 69 hundred-thousandths

29. nine and seven tenths

30. twenty-four and eight hundredths

31. sixty and seven hundred fifty-three thousandths

32. thirteen and four hundred eighteen ten-thousandths

COMPARE AND ORDER WHOLE NUMBERS AND DECIMALS

Skill 1: Compare whole numbers

To compare whole numbers, write the numbers in a column, aligning the places. The whole number with the greater number of digits is the greater number. If both numbers have the same number of digits, compare the digits in order from left to right.

Remember: = means *is equal to*
> means *is greater than*
< means *is less than*

Compare 4,523 and 4,517.
Use >, <, or =.

```
4,  5   2  3
↕   ↕   ↕
4,  5   1  7
```

2 tens > 1 ten, so
4,523 > 4,517

Compare. Write >, <, or =.

1. 317 ● 324   2. 4,812 ● 946   3. 6,509 ● 6,549   4. 547,213 ● 547,138

Skill 2: Order whole numbers

To order whole numbers, write the numbers in a column, aligning the places. In the example, 80,016 has the greatest number of digits. It is the greatest number. Now compare the digits from left to right in the numbers 8,916 and 8,016. Since 0 hundreds < 9 hundreds, 8,016 < 8,916.

Write in order from least to greatest:
8,916; 8,016; and 80,016.

```
8,916
8,016
80,016     ← greatest
```

```
8,  9   1  6
↕   ↕
8,  0   1  6     ← least   THINK: 0 < 9
```

The ordered numbers are 8,016; 8,916; and 80,016.

Write in order from least to greatest.

5. 85, 80, 850

6. 1,243; 1,236; 236

7. 1,436; 1,514; 1,504; 15,006

8. 6,217; 6,207; 6,200; 6,102

9. 27,026; 127,020; 29,002; 27,206

10. 158,216; 58,214; 59,006; 58,137

Write in order from greatest to least.

11. 4,016; 4,006; 4,106

12. 8,612; 86,012; 86,112

13. 87,395; 87,935; 87,305; 87,359

14. 93,406; 93,604; 93,064; 93,046

15. 314,654; 314,564; 314,645; 314,456

16. 612,253; 612,532; 612,325; 612,352

COMPARE AND ORDER WHOLE NUMBERS AND DECIMALS

Skill 3: Compare decimals

To compare decimals, write the numbers in a column. Line up the **decimal points** and **places.** Compare the digits from left to right. In the example, note that the decimal with the greater number of digits is not the greater number.

Compare 0.4317 and 0.452.

$$
\begin{array}{ccccc}
0. & 4 & 3 & 1 & 7 \\
 & \updownarrow & \updownarrow & \updownarrow & \\
0. & 4 & 5 & 2 &
\end{array}
$$

3 hundredths $<$ 5 hundredths, so
$$0.4317 < 0.452$$

Compare. Write $>$, $<$, or $=$.

17. 0.41 ● 0.81   **18.** 2.784 ● 2.84

19. 0.406 ● 0.409   **20.** 0.86956 ● 0.8692

Skill 4: Order decimals

To order decimals, write the numbers in a column, aligning the decimal points and places. Write additional zeros as needed so that each number will have an equal number of decimal places. Compare the digits from left to right.

Write in order from least to greatest:
0.54, 0.546, and 0.12.

$$
\begin{array}{cccc}
0. & 5 & 4 & 0 \\
\updownarrow & \updownarrow & \updownarrow & \updownarrow \\
0. & 5 & 4 & 6 \quad \leftarrow \text{greatest} \\
\updownarrow & \updownarrow & & \\
0. & 1 & 2 & 0 \quad \leftarrow \text{least}
\end{array}
$$

The ordered decimals are
0.12, 0.54, and 0.546.

Write in order from least to greatest.

21. 0.35, 0.31, 0.3

22. 0.07, 0.007, 0.7

23. 0.216, 0.206, 0.26, 2.1606

24. 0.761, 7.6101, 7.0101, 7.61015

Skill 5: Order money amounts

To order money amounts, write them in a column, aligning the **cents points.** Then compare the digits from left to right as you did with decimals. In the example, $2.31 has the least number of digits. It is the least. Now compare $23.14 and $23.59.

Write in order from least to greatest:
$23.14, $23.59, and $2.31.

$$
\begin{array}{cccc}
\$2 & 3. & 1 & 4 \\
\updownarrow & \updownarrow & \updownarrow & \\
\$2 & 3. & 5 & 9 \quad \leftarrow \text{greatest} \\
\$ & 2. & 3 & 1 \quad \leftarrow \text{least}
\end{array}
$$

The ordered money amounts are
$2.31, $23.14, and $23.59.

Write in order from least to greatest.

25. $0.21, $2.12, $0.12

26. $3.45, $3.54, $3.05

27. $16.41, $1.64, $16.40

28. $45.86, $45.80, $45.26

ROUND WHOLE NUMBERS AND DECIMALS

Skill 1: Round whole numbers using the number line

You can use the number line to round numbers. For example, 110 is nearer to 100 than to 200. So 110 rounds to 100. Notice that 180 is nearer to 200 than to 100. So 180 rounds to 200. When a number is located halfway between 2 numbers, it is rounded to the greater number. So 150 rounds to 200.

Round 110, 150, and 180 to the nearest hundred.

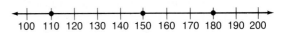

110 rounds to 100.
180 rounds to 200.
150 rounds to 200.

Round to the nearest hundred. Use the number line.

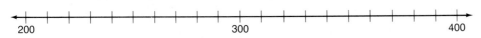

1. 220   **2.** 250   **3.** 290   **4.** 330   **5.** 370

Skill 2: Round any whole number

When you round greater numbers to a certain place, ring the digit to the right of that place. If the ringed digit is less than 5, round down. If the ringed digit is 5 or greater, round up.

Round 1,237 to the nearest hundred.

1, 2 ③ 7   ← Ring the digit to the right of the hundreds place.
↓ ↓ ↓ ↓
1, 2 0 0   ← Since 3 < 5, the hundreds place stays the same. Replace the tens and ones with zeros.

1,237 rounds to 1,200.

Round 3,546 to the nearest thousand.

3, ⑤ 4 6   ← Ring the digit to the right of the thousands place.
↓ ↓ ↓ ↓
4, 0 0 0   ← Since 5 = 5, add 1 to the thousands place. Replace the hundreds, tens, and ones with zeros.

3,546 rounds to 4,000.

Round to the nearest hundred.

6. 236   **7.** 695   **8.** 853   **9.** 907   **10.** 3,852

Round to the nearest thousand.

11. 4,281   **12.** 6,929   **13.** 7,723   **14.** 9,583   **15.** 65,100

Round to the nearest ten-thousand.

16. 10,599   **17.** 25,099   **18.** 42,999   **19.** 58,924   **20.** 151,000

ROUND WHOLE NUMBERS AND DECIMALS

Skill 3: Round any decimal

When you round decimals, follow the same rounding rules used for whole numbers. When you round to a certain place, look at the digit to its right.

Remember:

If this digit is less than 5, round down. If this digit is 5 or greater, round up.

Round 0.423 to the nearest hundredth.

0. 4 2 ③ ← 3 is to the right.
    ↓ ↓ ↓
0. 4 2   ← Drop all digits to the right.

0.423 rounds to 0.42.

Round 0.658 to the nearest tenth.

0. 6 ⑤ 8   ← 5 is to the right.
    ↓ ↓
0. 7   ← Add 1 to the tenths place.
               Drop all digits to the right.

0.658 rounds to 0.7.

Round to the nearest whole number.

21. 1.6   **22.** 2.3   **23.** 17.5

Round to the nearest hundredth.

27. 0.865   **28.** 0.679   **29.** 0.005

Round to the nearest tenth.

24. 0.42   **25.** 0.65   **26.** 0.89

Round to the nearest thousandth.

30. 0.4456   **31.** 0.6981   **32.** 0.3105

Skill 4: Round money amounts

When you round money amounts to the nearest ten dollars, dollar, or cent, follow the same rounding rules used for whole numbers and decimals.

Round $46.915 to the nearest dollar.

$4 6. ⑨ 1 5 ← 9 is to the right.
    ↓ ↓
$4 7. 0 0   ← Add 1 to the dollars place.

$46.915 rounds to $47.00.

Round $46.915 to the nearest cent.

$4 6. 9 1 ⑤ ← 5 is to the right.
    ↓ ↓ ↓ ↓
$4 6. 9 2   ← Add 1 to the cents place.

$46.915 rounds to $46.92.

Round to the nearest ten dollars.

33. $26.49   **34.** $35.79   **35.** $81.99

Round to the nearest cent.

39. $0.865   **40.** $1.426   **41.** $19.981   **42.** $0.4231   **43.** $1.8926

Round to the nearest dollar.

36. $6.42   **37.** $8.96   **38.** $10.82

USE INTEGERS

Skill 1: Graph integers

Integers to the right of 0 are called **positive integers.** The set of positive integers is written as +1, +2, +3, +4,... (positive 1, positive 2, positive 3, positive 4, and so on).

Integers to the left of 0 are called **negative integers.** The set of negative integers is written as −1, −2, −3, −4,... (negative 1, negative 2, negative 3, negative 4, and so on).

Zero is an integer that is neither positive nor negative.

Graph A at −2 and B at +4.

Point A is the graph of −2.
−2 is the **coordinate** of Point A.

Point B is the graph of +4.
+4 is the coordinate of Point B.

Draw a number line from −5 to +5. Then graph the point.

1. A at −5   **2.** B at −3   **3.** C at 0   **4.** D at +2   **5.** E at +3   **6.** F at +5

Skill 2: Find opposites

On the number line, the coordinate of point C is −2. The coordinate of point D is +2. −2 and +2 are called **opposites.** They are the same distance from 0, but on opposite sides.

Write the opposite.

7. +6   **8.** −7   **9.** 0   **10.** +15   **11.** −25   **12.** +31

13. −9   **14.** +66   **15.** +72   **16.** −115   **17.** +200   **18.** −650

Skill 3: Compare integers

You can use the number line to compare integers. Notice that, on the number line, numbers become greater as you go from left to right.

Compare −3 and −7.

The integer to the right is always the greater number. So −3 is greater than −7. Write −3 > −7.

Compare. Write >, <, or =.

19. +7 ● +5   **20.** −2 ● −3   **21.** 0 ● +4   **22.** +8 ● +5

23. −11 ● −15   **24.** −14 ● +13   **25.** +22 ● +32   **26.** −38 ● −30

USE INTEGERS

Skill 4: Order integers

To order integers, graph the integers on a number line. Remember that numbers become greater as you go from left to right.

Order +1, −5, −4, and +3.

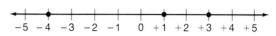

The order from least to greatest is −5, −4, +1, and +3.

The order from greatest to least is +3, +1, −4, and −5.

Order the integers from least to greatest.

27. +6, −3, 0, −4   **28.** +5, −3, −4, −1   **29.** +6, +3, +1, −4   **30.** 0, −5, −6, −7

31. +1, −1, −3, −7   **32.** 0, −6, +2, −3   **33.** +1, +3, −8, +2   **34.** +5, 0, −8, −9

35. −1, 0, −11, +6   **36.** +2, −5, −9, −6   **37.** +3, +5, 0, −8   **38.** −9, −7, +1, −5

39. 0, −6, +3, −5   **40.** +3, −6, +2, +4   **41.** −9, −7, −6, −8   **42.** +2, +8, +11, −6

43. +6, +1, 0, −12   **44.** −13, −9, +2, 0   **45.** −6, −2, −9, −4   **46.** +4, +2, −9, −7

Order the integers from greatest to least.

47. +6, 0, −3, +4   **48.** −7, −8, +1, +6   **49.** 0, +5, −6, −2   **50.** +3, +5, −4, −7

51. +4, +13, +12, 0   **52.** +1, +6, +3, +4   **53.** +8, +11, 0, −9   **54.** +2, 0, +4, −1

55. −7, −9, +2, +1   **56.** −8, +8, −2, +1   **57.** −6, +2, −3, −1   **58.** 0, +5, +2, −4

59. −6, −11, −4, −1   **60.** +9, −5, −2, +3   **61.** +8, 0, +1, −2   **62.** −4, +5, −3, −1

63. −8, 0, +2, +5   **64.** +3, −6, −8, +7   **65.** −9, +5, +4, +6   **66.** −7, −11, 0, +3

Skill 5: Find absolute value

The **absolute value** of a number is the number of units that number is from 0. The absolute value of −3 is 3 because −3 is 3 units from 0 on the number line. This is written as $|-3| = 3$.

Find the absolute values of $|-2|$ and $|+3|$. First graph the numbers.

$|-2| = 2$ because −2 is 2 units from 0.

$|+3| = 3$ because +3 is 3 units from 0.

Find the absolute value.

67. $|-9|$ **68.** $|+11|$ **69.** $|-16|$ **70.** $|-23|$ **71.** $|+31|$ **72.** $|+46|$

ADD WITH WHOLE NUMBERS AND DECIMALS

Skill 1: Add whole numbers with no regrouping

When you add numbers, write the addends in columns. Then work from right to left. Add the ones, then the tens, then the hundreds, and so on.

Add: 4,123 + 615.

th	h	t	o
4,	1	2	3
+	6	1	5
4,	7	3	8

Add.

1. 256 + 123
2. 6,534 + 163
3. 7,053 + 1,426
4. 12,435 + 7,520
5. 35,081 + 40,718
6. 642,537 + 56,412
7. 235,014 + 162,873

Skill 2: Add whole numbers with regrouping

Sometimes you must **regroup** when you add numbers. For example, 3 + 9 = 12 ones. Regroup 12 ones as 1 ten 2 ones. Write 2 in the ones column. Regroup 1 ten. Then continue to add, regrouping as necessary.

Add: 3,453 + 1,679.

th	h	t	o
^{1}3,	^{1}4	^{1}5	3
+ 1,	6	7	9
5,	1	3	2

Add.

8. 352 + 419
9. 674 + 387
10. 296 + 417
11. 585 + 805
12. 3,684 + 198
13. 7,046 + 3,497
14. 2,308 + 4,746
15. 85,721 + 69,852
16. 98,453 + 2,597
17. 21,532 + 17,009
18. 345,892 + 89,407
19. 736,495 + 573,889
20. 430,098 + 56,917

Skill 3: Add decimals with the same number of places

When you add decimals, align the decimal points in the addends. Place the decimal point in the sum. Then add as with whole numbers. If the sum ends in 1 or more zeros after the decimal point, the zeros can be dropped.

Add: 62.54 + 37.26.

$$\begin{array}{r} 6\,2.\overset{1}{5}\,4 \\ +\,3\,7.2\,6 \\ \hline 9\,9.8\,0 = 99.8 \end{array}$$

Add.

21. 4.3 + 1.6
22. 5.2 + 4.1
23. 8.9 + 7.3
24. 23.2 + 16.8
25. 7.35 + 1.83
26. 92.1 + 18.59
27. 43.36 + 29.84
28. 6.428 + 2.837
29. 26.017 + 51.984
30. 35.606 + 11.794
31. 1.3265 + 8.7316
32. 51.0604 + 27.8594
33. 44.0845 + 27.8186

ADD WITH WHOLE NUMBERS AND DECIMALS

Skill 4: Add decimals with different numbers of places

When you add decimals with different numbers of places, align the decimal points in the numbers. Place the decimal point in the sum. Write additional zeros as needed and then add as with whole numbers.

Add: 8.236 + 27.9.

$$\begin{array}{r} {\scriptstyle 1\ 1} \\ 8.236 \\ +27.900 \\ \hline 36.136 \end{array}$$

Add.

34. 8.94 + 0.2 **35.** 29.8 + 4.98 **36.** 43.76 + 16.5 **37.** 6.987 + 4.5

38. 86.907 + 4.26 **39.** 234.895 + 83.63 **40.** 7.8643 + 1.907

41. 9.31 + 27.0604 **42.** 763.5 + 1.8168 **43.** 37.245 + 416.9855

Skill 5: Add more than 2 numbers

When you add more than 2 numbers, remember to align the numbers properly.

Add: 4.3 + 23.7 + 36.

$$\begin{array}{r} {\scriptstyle 1\ 1} \\ 4.3 \\ 23.7 \\ +36.0 \\ \hline 64.0 = 64 \end{array}$$

Add.

44. 38 + 42 + 18 **45.** 5,937 + 89 + 351 **46.** 6,436 + 2,831 + 439

47. 8.6 + 0.9 + 1.5 **48.** 7.8 + 23.41 + 35.16 **49.** 9.356 + 12.607 + 2.51

50. 24.617 + 0.5 + 6.54 **51.** 16.64 + 8.9 + 0.7256 **52.** 5.642 + 13.096 + 2.7314

Skill 6: Add money amounts

When you add money amounts, align the cents points in the addends. Place the dollar sign and cents point in the sum. Then add.

Add: $657.89 + $56.13.

$$\begin{array}{r} {\scriptstyle 1\ 1\ 1\ \ 1} \\ \$657.89 \\ +\ \ 56.13 \\ \hline \$714.02 \end{array}$$

Add.

53. $5.86 + $7.83 **54.** $46.24 + $32.53 **55.** $77.10 + $3.09 **56.** $132.76 + $67.99

57. $456.67 + $39.03 + $2.55 **58.** $1,436.43 + $156 + $32.01

59. $67.45 + $0.23 + $35.86 **60.** $25.25 + $6.87 + 1,468.31

61. $57 + $23,460.26 + $6,400.19 **62.** $2.07 + $32,461 + $146,800.73

SUBTRACT WITH WHOLE NUMBERS AND DECIMALS

Skill 1: Subtract whole numbers with no regrouping

When you subtract numbers, write the numbers in columns. Then work from right to left. Subtract the ones, then the tens, then the hundreds, and so on.

Subtract: 6,345 − 4,102.

th	h	t	o
6,	3	4	5
− 4,	1	0	2
2,	2	4	3

Subtract.

1. 516 − 403
2. 8,394 − 273
3. 7,896 − 6,245
4. 28,403 − 6,100
5. 67,214 − 56,113
6. 439,453 − 28,113
7. 672,435 − 501,332

Skill 2: Subtract whole numbers with regrouping

Sometimes you must regroup when you subtract numbers. For example, you cannot subtract 8 ones from 5 ones. Regroup 3 tens 5 ones as 2 tens 15 ones. Subtract: 15 ones − 8 ones = 7 ones. Write 7 in the ones column. Then continue to subtract, regrouping as necessary.

Subtract: 8,435 − 6,548.

th	h	t	o
	13	12	
7	3	2	15
8,	4	3	5
− 6,	5	4	8
1,	8	8	7

Subtract.

8. 865 − 629
9. 4,563 − 475
10. 9,523 − 7,684
11. 36,413 − 9,534
12. 46,438 − 39,159
13. 845,126 − 39,429
14. 892,453 − 128,698

Skill 3: Subtract across zeros

When subtracting with zeros, regroup carefully. For example, when subtracting 2,987 from 4,000, you cannot subtract 7 ones from 0 ones. You must regroup thousands, hundreds, tens, and ones.

Subtract: 4,000 − 2,987.

th	h	t	o
	9	9	
3	10	10	10
4,	0	0	0
− 2,	9	8	7
1,	0	1	3

Subtract.

15. 500 − 198
16. 8,000 − 289
17. 9,006 − 8,857
18. 36,000 − 5,762
19. 50,006 − 48,195
20. 760,004 − 89,475
21. 810,000 − 768,541

SUBTRACT WITH WHOLE NUMBERS AND DECIMALS

Skill 4: Subtract decimals with no regrouping

When you subtract decimals, align the decimal points. Place the decimal point in the answer. Then subtract as with whole numbers. If the answer ends in 1 or more zeros after the decimal point, the zeros can be dropped.

Subtract: $79.43 - 58.13$.

$$\begin{array}{r} 79.43 \\ -58.13 \\ \hline 21.30 = 21.3 \end{array}$$

Subtract.

22. $5.32 - 4.01$ **23.** $61.8 - 31.6$ **24.** $79.54 - 9.13$ **25.** $8.436 - 5.106$

26. $56.636 - 42.513$ **27.** $235.48 - 120.18$ **28.** $415.123 - 303.021$

29. $362.421 - 201.310$ **30.** $752.846 - 31.021$ **31.** $504.816 - 3.602$

Skill 5: Subtract decimals with regrouping

Sometimes you must regroup when you subtract decimals. Place the decimal point in the answer. Write additional zeros as needed and then subtract as with whole numbers.

Subtract: $52 - 41.5$.

$$\begin{array}{r} 5\overset{1}{\cancel{2}}.\overset{10}{\cancel{0}} \\ -41.5 \\ \hline 10.5 \end{array}$$

Subtract.

32. $6.1 - 0.8$ **33.** $81.43 - 16.59$ **34.** $80 - 10.84$ **35.** $8.431 - 4.952$

36. $14.003 - 11.98$ **37.** $129.043 - 118.95$ **38.** $23.4982 - 10.0095$

39. $50.105 - 6.97$ **40.** $231.6425 - 75.316$ **41.** $25.73 - 7.8265$

Skill 6: Subtract money amounts

When you subtract money amounts, align the cents points. Place the dollar sign and the cents point in the answer. Then subtract.

Subtract: $\$829.43 - \$76.51$.

$$\begin{array}{r} \$8\overset{7}{\cancel{2}}\overset{12}{\cancel{9}}.\overset{8}{\cancel{4}}\overset{14}{3} \\ -\quad 76.51 \\ \hline \$752.92 \end{array}$$

Subtract.

42. $\$19.85 - \$7.13$ **43.** $\$54.76 - \$23.14$ **44.** $\$60 - \$42.98$ **45.** $\$138.41 - \$56.83$

46. $\$146.83 - \$37.98$ **47.** $\$359.86 - \$186.49$ **48.** $\$1,800 - \$186.43$

49. $\$2,000 - \$1,643.25$ **50.** $\$700.01 - \$283.99$ **51.** $\$7,002 - \$3,420.01$

52. $\$23,468 - \$5,401.76$ **53.** $\$984.77 - \$16.89$ **54.** $\$22,000.06 - \$721.97$

MULTIPLY WITH WHOLE NUMBERS

Skill 1: Multiply with multiples of 10, 100, or 1,000

When multiplying powers of 10, count the number of end zeros in each factor. For example, when multiplying $2 \times 4,000$, write 3 zeros in the answer, then multiply 2×4. Write 8,000 as the answer.

Multiply: $2 \times 4,000$.

$$
\begin{array}{r}
4,000 \leftarrow \textbf{3 zeros} \\
\times \quad\quad 2 \\
\hline
8,000 \leftarrow \textbf{3 zeros}
\end{array}
$$

When both factors are a power of 10, remember to count the number of zeros in each factor. For example, the first factor, 6,000, has 3 zeros and the second factor, 100, has 2 zeros. Write 5 zeros in the answer, then multiply 1×6. Write 600,000 as the answer.

Multiply: $100 \times 6,000$.

$$
\begin{array}{r}
6,000 \leftarrow \textbf{3 zeros} \\
\times \quad\quad 100 \leftarrow \textbf{2 zeros} \\
\hline
600,000 \leftarrow \textbf{5 zeros}
\end{array}
$$

Multiply.

1. 2×40
2. 3×200
3. 3×800
4. $8 \times 6,000$

5. 10×20
6. 10×300
7. 200×800
8. $50 \times 4,000$

9. $30 \times 2,000$
10. $60 \times 7,000$
11. $700 \times 2,000$
12. $400 \times 8,000$

13. $5,000 \times 3,000$
14. $8,000 \times 4,000$
15. $9,000 \times 3,000$
16. $6,000 \times 5,000$

17. $1,000 \times 8,000$
18. $300 \times 8,000$
19. $20 \times 5,000$
20. $400 \times 4,000$

21. $7,000 \times 6,000$
22. $70 \times 7,000$
23. $40 \times 9,000$
24. $10 \times 6,000$

Skill 2: Multiply by 1-digit numbers with no regrouping

When multiplying by a 1-digit number, multiply the ones, then the tens, then the hundreds, and so on.

Multiply: $2 \times 4,321$.

th	h	t	o
4,	3	2	1
$\times$			2
8,	6	4	2

Multiply.

25. 2×314
26. 2×401
27. 3×201
28. 3×122

29. $3 \times 2,110$
30. $4 \times 2,002$
31. $2 \times 3,102$
32. $2 \times 4,233$

33. $3 \times 31,210$
34. $4 \times 12,020$
35. $2 \times 44,421$
36. $5 \times 10,001$

37. $2 \times 433,202$
38. $3 \times 132,231$
39. $4 \times 122,021$
40. $2 \times 341,002$

MULTIPLY WITH WHOLE NUMBERS

Skill 3: Multiply by 1-digit numbers with regrouping

When multiplying with regrouping, remember you must first multiply and then add the regrouped number.

In the example:
- Multiply the ones: 7×4 ones = 28 ones. Regroup 28 ones as 2 tens 8 ones. Write 8 in the ones column. Regroup the 2 tens.
- Multiply the tens and add the regrouped number: $(7 \times 5) + 2 = 37$. Write 7 in the tens column. Regroup the 3.
- Then continue to multiply, regrouping as necessary.

Multiply: $7 \times 1{,}354$.

th	h	t	O
$\overset{2}{1},$	$\overset{3}{3}$	$\overset{2}{5}$	4
$\times$			7
9,	4	7	8

Multiply.

41. 2×353	**42.** 4×613	**43.** 8×916	**44.** 4×108
45. 6×872	**46.** 9×427	**47.** 9×162	**48.** 6×843
49. $3 \times 1{,}423$	**50.** $4 \times 2{,}621$	**51.** $2 \times 4{,}704$	**52.** $5 \times 1{,}017$
53. $6 \times 5{,}872$	**54.** $9 \times 8{,}427$	**55.** $9 \times 7{,}162$	**56.** $6 \times 7{,}843$
57. $3 \times 23{,}574$	**58.** $6 \times 14{,}817$	**59.** $8 \times 32{,}061$	**60.** $7 \times 42{,}136$
61. $4 \times 123{,}065$	**62.** $2 \times 236{,}456$	**63.** $7 \times 141{,}219$	**64.** $5 \times 215{,}076$

Skill 4: Multiply by 2-digit numbers

When multiplying greater numbers, work in columns. Multiply the ones and then the tens in the multiplier. Be sure to line up all numbers correctly. You may want to write zeros to help. Then add the partial products.

Multiply: 43×986.

```
    3 2
    2 1
    9 8 6
  ×   4 3
    2 9 5 8   ← 3 × 986
  3 9 4 4 0   ← 40 × 986
  4 2 , 3 9 8
```

Multiply.

65. 22×42	**66.** 31×32	**67.** 12×13	**68.** 33×33
69. 36×84	**70.** 36×29	**71.** 28×43	**72.** 65×56
73. 23×133	**74.** 42×203	**75.** 13×233	**76.** 24×113
77. 47×486	**78.** 53×309	**79.** 63×425	**80.** 75×468
81. $31 \times 2{,}702$	**82.** $42 \times 4{,}116$	**83.** $22 \times 2{,}543$	**84.** $32 \times 1{,}833$

MULTIPLY WITH WHOLE NUMBERS

Skill 5: Multiply by 3-digit numbers

When you multiply by a 3-digit number, multiply by the ones, then the tens, and then the hundreds in the multiplier. When you write the partial products, remember to align the numbers properly. Then add.

Multiply: 461×839.

$$
\begin{array}{r}
\scriptstyle 1\ \ 3 \\[-2pt]
\scriptstyle 2\ \ 5 \\[-2pt]
839 \\
\times 461 \\
\hline
839 \leftarrow 1 \times 839 \\
50\ 340 \leftarrow 60 \times 839 \\
335\ 600 \leftarrow 400 \times 839 \\
\hline
386,779
\end{array}
$$

Multiply.

85. 112×213	**86.** 221×224	**87.** 136×458	**88.** 342×563
89. 132×121	**90.** 212×123	**91.** 416×218	**92.** 428×295
93. $426 \times 1{,}325$	**94.** $734 \times 2{,}068$	**95.** $574 \times 6{,}616$	**96.** $212 \times 3{,}844$
97. $555 \times 6{,}734$	**98.** $735 \times 8{,}206$	**99.** $452 \times 3{,}119$	**100.** $817 \times 6{,}044$
101. $189 \times 7{,}016$	**102.** $313 \times 2{,}910$	**103.** $745 \times 8{,}013$	**104.** $952 \times 9{,}604$

Skill 6: Omit zeros in partial products

You can save time when you multiply with zeros by omitting them in the partial products. For example, when 0 is in the multiplier, omit the partial product of zeros. However, watch the alignment of the next partial product.

Multiply: 206×751.

$$
\begin{array}{r}
\scriptstyle 1 \\[-2pt]
\scriptstyle 3 \\[-2pt]
751 \\
\times 206 \\
\hline
4\ 506 \\
0\ \ 00 \\
150\ 2 \\
\hline
154,706
\end{array}
\qquad
\begin{array}{r}
\scriptstyle 1 \\[-2pt]
\scriptstyle 3 \\[-2pt]
751 \\
\times 206 \\
\hline
4\ 506 \\
150\ 2 \\
\hline
154,706
\end{array}
$$

Multiply.

105. 105×238	**106.** 208×359	**107.** 409×123	**108.** 606×987
109. 707×346	**110.** 202×435	**111.** 609×231	**112.** 807×983
113. $501 \times 3{,}604$	**114.** $708 \times 5{,}039$	**115.** $201 \times 8{,}670$	**116.** $709 \times 3{,}005$
117. $302 \times 6{,}502$	**118.** $803 \times 5{,}070$	**119.** $604 \times 1{,}623$	**120.** $801 \times 7{,}110$
121. $107 \times 4{,}301$	**122.** $407 \times 7{,}040$	**123.** $601 \times 8{,}302$	**124.** $909 \times 6{,}030$

MULTIPLY WITH DECIMALS

Skill 1: Multiply decimals by 10, 100, or 1,000

When you multiply a decimal by 10, move the decimal point 1 place to the right.

Multiply: 10×4.2.

$10 \times 4.2 \rightarrow 4.2 \rightarrow 42.$

When you multiply a decimal by 100, move the decimal point 2 places to the right.

Multiply: 100×8.931.

$100 \times 8.931 \rightarrow 8.931 \rightarrow 893.1$

When you multiply a decimal by 1,000, move the decimal point 3 places to the right. Remember to write additional zeros when necessary. For example, when multiplying 0.16 by 1,000, write 1 additional zero before you move the decimal point.

Multiply: $1,000 \times 0.16$.

$1,000 \times 0.16 \rightarrow 0.160 \rightarrow 160.$

Multiply.

1. 10×0.8
2. 10×1.56
3. 10×23.43
4. 10×136.425

5. 100×0.43
6. 100×1.896
7. 100×14.8631
8. 100×185.2

9. $1,000 \times 0.871$
10. $1,000 \times 1.0433$
11. $1,000 \times 21.1$
12. $1,000 \times 361.5$

Skill 2: Multiply decimals by whole numbers

To multiply a decimal by a whole number, multiply as with whole numbers. The product should have the same number of decimal places as the decimal factor.

Multiply: 43×3.172.

$$
\begin{array}{r}
3.172 \leftarrow \text{3 decimal places} \\
\times \qquad 43 \\
\hline
9\ 516 \\
126\ 88 \\
\hline
136.396 \leftarrow \text{3 decimal places}
\end{array}
$$

If the product ends in 1 or more zeros after the decimal point, the zeros can be dropped.

Multiply: 86×4.25.

$$
\begin{array}{r}
4.25 \leftarrow \text{2 decimal places} \\
\times \qquad 86 \\
\hline
25\ 50 \\
340\ 0 \\
\hline
365.50 \leftarrow \text{2 decimal places}
\end{array}
$$

$365.50 = 365.5$

Multiply.

13. 9×8.9
14. 18×24.6
15. 5×23.52
16. 67×76.32

17. 8×59.041
18. 65×95.434
19. 7×0.8236
20. 6×7.5954

21. 6×2.9308
22. 24×0.876
23. 51×72.394
24. 26×3.505

MULTIPLY WITH DECIMALS

Skill 3: Multiply decimals by 0.1, 0.01, or 0.001

When you multiply a decimal by 0.1, move the decimal point 1 place to the left. Remember to write a zero in the ones place.

Multiply: 0.1×8.6.

$0.1 \times 8.6 \rightarrow 8.6 \rightarrow 0.86$

When you multiply a decimal by 0.01, move the decimal point 2 places to the left.

Multiply: 0.01×14.92.

$0.01 \times 14.92 \rightarrow 14.92 \rightarrow 0.1492$

When you multiply a decimal by 0.001, move the decimal point 3 places to the left. Remember to write additional zeros when necessary.

Multiply: 0.001×3.57.

$0.001 \times 3.57 \rightarrow 003.57 \rightarrow 0.00357$

Multiply.

25. 0.1×0.5
26. 0.1×41.83
27. 0.1×251.436
28. 0.01×4.954

29. 0.01×36.4235
30. 0.001×0.421
31. 0.001×61.7
32. 0.001×254.6

Skill 4: Multiply 2 decimals

To multiply decimals, multiply as with whole numbers. Add the numbers of decimal places in the factors to find the number of decimal places in the product. Write zeros in the product when necessary.

Multiply: 0.2×0.306.

$$
\begin{array}{r}
0.306 \leftarrow \textbf{3 decimal places} \\
\times \quad 0.2 \leftarrow \textbf{1 decimal place} \\
\hline
0.0612 \leftarrow \textbf{4 decimal places}
\end{array}
$$

Multiply.

33. 0.8×0.9
34. 0.8×0.43
35. 0.12×0.85
36. 0.49×0.78

37. 0.86×1.47
38. 0.03×1.004
39. 1.59×3.809
40. 0.2×0.4305

Skill 5: Multiply money amounts

When you multiply money amounts, follow the rules for multiplying with decimals. When necessary, round the product to the nearest cent.

Multiply: $4.6 \times \$23.84$.

$$
\begin{array}{r}
\$23.84 \leftarrow \textbf{2 decimal places} \\
\times \quad 4.6 \leftarrow \textbf{1 decimal place} \\
\hline
14 \quad 304 \\
95 \quad 36 \\
\hline
\$109.664 \leftarrow \textbf{3 decimal places}
\end{array}
$$

$\$109.664 \approx \$109.66$

Multiply. Round the product to the nearest cent when necessary.

41. $16 \times \$17.86$
42. $0.8 \times \$23.45$
43. $1.23 \times \$0.49$
44. $13.82 \times \$41.89$

DIVIDE WITH WHOLE NUMBERS

Skill 1: Divide with multiples of 10, 100, or 1,000

When dividing powers of 10 by a number less than 10, think of the related multiplication sentence.

Divide: $1,200 \div 6$.

THINK: $200 \times 6 = 1,200$, so $1,200 \div 6 = 200$

When you divide with 2 powers of 10, cross out an equal number of zeros in the divisor and the dividend. Then divide.

Divide: $860 \div 10$.

$86\cancel{0} \div 1\cancel{0} = 86$

Divide: $900 \div 30$.

$90\cancel{0} \div 3\cancel{0} = 30$

Divide.

1. $400 \div 4$
2. $8,000 \div 4$
3. $5,100 \div 10$
4. $83,000 \div 10$

5. $900 \div 100$
6. $6,400 \div 100$
7. $71,000 \div 100$
8. $80,000 \div 400$

9. $7,000 \div 1,000$
10. $23,000 \div 1,000$
11. $817,000 \div 1,000$
12. $600,000 \div 2,000$

Skill 2: Divide by 1-digit numbers

Divide in order from left to right. THINK: Divide, multiply, subtract, bring down. If the difference is greater than the divisor, the partial quotient is an **underestimate.** Align the digits in the quotient over the digits in the dividend. Remember to include the remainder as part of the answer.

Divide: $6,123 \div 5$.

```
     1,224 R3
5)6,123
  5 ↓||
  1 1 |
  1 0↓|
    1 2|
    1 0↓
      2 3
      2 0
        3
```

Divide.

13. $354 \div 3$
14. $721 \div 3$
15. $8,616 \div 4$
16. $9,523 \div 6$

17. $25,926 \div 2$
18. $93,827 \div 4$
19. $976,624 \div 4$
20. $564,267 \div 5$

Skill 3: Locate the first digit in a quotient

Sometimes the divisor will not divide into the first digit in the dividend. For example, 9 does not go into 4. It goes into 46. Place the first digit of the quotient above the 6 in the hundreds place.

Divide: $4,613 \div 9$.

```
     5 1 2 R5
9)4,613
  4 5↓|
    1 1|
      9↓
    2 3
    1 8
      5
```

DIVIDE WITH WHOLE NUMBERS

Divide.

21. $288 \div 8$ **22.** $256 \div 5$ **23.** $7,512 \div 8$ **24.** $4,139 \div 7$

25. $19,614 \div 6$ **26.** $66,419 \div 8$ **27.** $325,116 \div 4$ **28.** $133,916 \div 9$

Skill 4: Divide with zeros in a quotient

Sometimes there is a zero in the quotient. Be careful to align the digits in the quotient over the digits in the dividend.

Divide: $634 \div 7$.

$$
\begin{array}{r}
9\,0 \text{ R4} \\
7\overline{)6\,3\,4} \\
\underline{6\,3}\downarrow \\
4 \\
\underline{0} \\
4
\end{array}
$$

Divide.

29. $315 \div 3$ **30.** $143 \div 7$ **31.** $8,020 \div 4$ **32.** $4,041 \div 5$

33. $42,091 \div 7$ **34.** $48,302 \div 6$ **35.** $234,009 \div 9$ **36.** $728,034 \div 8$

Skill 5: Divide using a shortcut

You can use a shortcut when you divide by 1-digit numbers. For example, when dividing 456 by 3, divide 4 by 3. Write 1 over the 4. Multiply and subtract mentally. THINK: $1 \times 3 = 3$ and $4 - 3 = 1$. Write 1 next to the 5 in 56. Continue this process until you complete the division.

Divide: $456 \div 3$.

$$
\begin{array}{r}
1\,5\,2 \\
3\overline{)4^{1}5\,6}
\end{array}
$$

Divide: $7,654 \div 4$.

$$
\begin{array}{r}
1\,,9\,1\,3 \text{ R2} \\
4\overline{)7\,,{}^{3}6\,5^{1}4}
\end{array}
$$

Divide, using the shortcut method.

37. $576 \div 3$ **38.** $670 \div 5$ **39.** $1,218 \div 2$ **40.** $3,314 \div 4$

41. $76,206 \div 6$ **42.** $81,512 \div 7$ **43.** $911,628 \div 9$ **44.** $456,127 \div 8$

Skill 6: Divide by 2-digit numbers

Divide in order from left to right. Estimate first. In the example, use the 4 in the tens place in the divisor to estimate. Then divide, multiply, subtract, and bring down. Align the digits in the quotient over the digits in the dividend. Remember to include the remainder as part of the answer.

Divide: $8,899 \div 41$.

$$
\begin{array}{r}
2\,1\,7 \text{ R2} \\
4\,1\overline{)8\,8\,9\,9} \\
\underline{8\,2}\downarrow\downarrow \\
6\,9 \\
\underline{4\,1}\downarrow \\
2\,8\,9 \\
\underline{2\,8\,7} \\
2
\end{array}
$$

← Estimate: $4\overline{)8}$. Try 2×41.

← Estimate: $4\overline{)6}$. Try 1×41.

← Estimate: $4\overline{)28}$. Try 7×41.

DIVIDE WITH WHOLE NUMBERS

Divide.

45. $860 \div 40$

46. $8,750 \div 50$

47. $891 \div 42$

48. $8,965 \div 55$

49. $4,189 \div 63$

50. $49,975 \div 31$

51. $58,474 \div 61$

52. $183,663 \div 54$

Skill 7: Divide when estimates are too great

Sometimes your first estimate may be too great. In this case, adjust your estimate and try again.

Divide: $3,476 \div 44$.

$$
\begin{array}{r}
8 \\
44)\overline{3,476} \\
3\ 52 \\
\end{array}
$$
← Estimate: 4)$\overline{34}$. Try 8 × 44.
← Cannot subtract.

$$
\begin{array}{r}
79 \\
44)\overline{3,476} \\
3\ 08 \downarrow \\
396 \\
396 \\
\hline
0
\end{array}
$$
← Try 7 × 44.
← Estimate: 4)$\overline{39}$. Try 9 × 44.

Divide.

53. $367 \div 17$

54. $290 \div 42$

55. $2,642 \div 57$

56. $2,870 \div 78$

57. $21,143 \div 29$

58. $62,115 \div 35$

59. $721,054 \div 48$

60. $642,219 \div 73$

Skill 8: Divide by 3-digit numbers

When you divide by a 3-digit number, follow the same rules as dividing by a 2-digit number. In the example, use the 2 in the hundreds place in the divisor to estimate. Remember to adjust your estimate when necessary.

Divide: $82,198 \div 214$.

$$
\begin{array}{r}
4 \\
214)\overline{82,198} \\
85\ 6 \\
\end{array}
$$
← Estimate: 2)$\overline{8}$. Try 4 × 214.
← Cannot subtract.

$$
\begin{array}{r}
384 \text{ R}22 \\
214)\overline{82,198} \\
64\ 2 \downarrow \\
17\ 99 \\
17\ 12 \downarrow \\
878 \\
856 \\
\hline
22
\end{array}
$$
← Try 3 × 214.
← Estimate: 2)$\overline{17}$. Try 8 × 214.
← Estimate: 2)$\overline{8}$. Try 4 × 214.

Divide.

61. $73,521 \div 389$

62. $42,729 \div 436$

63. $35,264 \div 341$

64. $32,509 \div 563$

65. $576,081 \div 194$

66. $243,167 \div 231$

67. $412,018 \div 176$

68. $108,432 \div 251$

DIVIDE WITH DECIMALS

Skill 1: Divide decimals by multiples of 10, 100, or 1,000

When you divide a decimal by 10, move the decimal point 1 place to the left.

Divide: $6.3 \div 10$.

$6.3 \div 10 \rightarrow 6.3 \rightarrow 0.63$

When you divide a decimal by 100, move the decimal point 2 places to the left.

Divide: $34.96 \div 100$.

$34.96 \div 100 \rightarrow 34.96 \rightarrow 0.3496$

When you divide a decimal by 1,000, move the decimal point 3 places to the left. Remember to write additional zeros when necessary.

Divide: $1.23 \div 1,000$.

$1.23 \div 1,000 \rightarrow 001.23 \rightarrow 0.00123$

Divide.

1. $0.9 \div 10$	**2.** $2.13 \div 10$	**3.** $14.58 \div 10$	**4.** $234.13 \div 10$
5. $0.89 \div 100$	**6.** $1.214 \div 100$	**7.** $36.34 \div 100$	**8.** $138.4 \div 100$
9. $0.23 \div 1,000$	**10.** $2.43 \div 1,000$	**11.** $43.8 \div 1,000$	**12.** $489.6 \div 1,000$

Skill 2: Divide decimals by whole numbers

When dividing by a whole number, place the decimal point in the quotient directly above the decimal point in the dividend. Then divide as with whole numbers. Sometimes you must write additional zeros in the quotient as placeholders. Remember, if the quotient is less than 1, write 0 in the ones place.

Divide: $36.42 \div 6$.

```
    6.07
6)36.42
  36
    4
    0
   42
   42
    0
```

Divide: $0.208 \div 4$.

```
   0.052
4)0.208
   20
    8
    8
    0
```

Divide.

13. $25.5 \div 3$	**14.** $102.2 \div 7$	**15.** $187.72 \div 19$	**16.** $858.636 \div 36$
17. $20.36 \div 4$	**18.** $0.544 \div 8$	**19.** $310.52 \div 28$	**20.** $0.8366 \div 47$

Skill 3: Divide by tenths

When you divide by tenths, multiply both the divisor and the dividend by 10 to get a whole-number divisor. Move each decimal point 1 place to the right. Then divide as with whole numbers.

Divide: $3.224 \div 5.2$.

```
      0.62
5.2)3.2.24
    3 12
      104
      104
        0
```

or

```
      0.62
52)32.24
   31 2
     1 04
     1 04
        0
```

DIVIDE WITH DECIMALS

Write an equivalent example that has a whole-number divisor.

21. $3.24 \div 0.4$ **22.** $0.4132 \div 0.8$ **23.** $84.58 \div 1.2$ **24.** $0.1865 \div 2.5$

Divide.

25. $1.888 \div 0.8$ **26.** $0.0486 \div 0.6$ **27.** $28.914 \div 6.1$ **28.** $0.2852 \div 9.2$

Skill 4: Divide by hundredths

When you divide by hundredths, move the decimal point in the divisor and the dividend 2 places to the right. Then divide as with whole numbers.

Divide: $0.0144 \div 0.03$.

$$
\begin{array}{r}
0.48 \\
0.03\overline{)0.0144} \\
12 \downarrow \\
24 \\
24 \\
\hline
0
\end{array}
\quad \text{or} \quad
\begin{array}{r}
0.48 \\
3\overline{)1.44} \\
12 \downarrow \\
24 \\
24 \\
\hline
0
\end{array}
$$

Write an equivalent example that has a whole-number divisor.

29. $0.1235 \div 0.03$ **30.** $0.2356 \div 0.04$ **31.** $4.2314 \div 0.36$ **32.** $39.128 \div 3.59$

Divide.

33. $0.0085 \div 0.05$ **34.** $0.0927 \div 0.09$ **35.** $1.8936 \div 0.24$ **36.** $12.985 \div 2.45$

Skill 5: Divide by thousandths

When you divide by thousandths, move the decimal point in the divisor and the dividend 3 places to the right. Then divide as with whole numbers.

Divide: $0.0432 \div 0.072$.

$$
\begin{array}{r}
0.6 \\
0.072\overline{)0.0432} \\
432 \\
\hline
0
\end{array}
\quad \text{or} \quad
\begin{array}{r}
0.6 \\
72\overline{)43.2} \\
432 \\
\hline
0
\end{array}
$$

Divide.

37. $0.0054 \div 0.009$ **38.** $0.0279 \div 0.031$ **39.** $0.0212 \div 0.106$ **40.** $1.02193 \div 1.123$

Skill 6: Write additional zeros in dividends

Sometimes you need to write additional zeros in the dividend. For example, when dividing 2.7 by 0.15, the decimal points must be moved 2 places to the right.

Sometimes additional zeros may also be needed in a dividend in order to continue dividing. For example, when dividing 7.3 by 0.2, 1 additional zero is needed to get a zero remainder.

Divide: $2.7 \div 0.15$.

$$
\begin{array}{r}
18. \\
0.15\overline{)2.70} \\
15 \downarrow \\
120 \\
120 \\
\hline
0
\end{array}
$$

Divide: $7.3 \div 0.2$.

$$
\begin{array}{r}
36.5 \\
0.2\overline{)7.3.0} \\
6 \downarrow \\
13 \\
12 \\
10 \\
10 \\
\hline
0
\end{array}
$$

DIVIDE WITH DECIMALS

Divide.

41. $301 \div 4.3$ **42.** $0.8 \div 0.16$ **43.** $46 \div 1.15$ **44.** $52.54 \div 0.071$

45. $8.26 \div 4$ **46.** $4.21 \div 25$ **47.** $0.0144 \div 0.45$ **48.** $108.84 \div 0.24$

Skill 7: Round quotients

To find a quotient to the nearest tenth, divide through the hundredths place. Then round the quotient to tenths.

To find a quotient to the nearest hundredth, divide through the thousandths place. Then round the quotient to hundredths.

Divide to the nearest tenth: $1.04 \div 5.6$.

$$
\begin{array}{r}
0.18 \approx 0.2 \\
5.6\overline{)1.0\,40} \\
\underline{5\,6} \\
4\,80 \\
\underline{4\,48} \\
3\,2
\end{array}
$$

Divide to the nearest tenth.

49. $14.03 \div 16$ **50.** $1.09 \div 0.8$ **51.** $3.4626 \div 0.76$ **52.** $14.9805 \div 1.83$

53. $25.374 \div 11$ **54.** $9.321 \div 1.77$ **55.** $62.596 \div 0.88$ **56.** $5.1362 \div 4.54$

Divide to the nearest hundredth.

57. $18.43 \div 23$ **58.** $5.0376 \div 0.6$ **59.** $25.3 \div 0.75$ **60.** $59.8312 \div 1.69$

61. $22.6 \div 0.77$ **62.** $3.521 \div 6.9$ **63.** $7.3425 \div 2.24$ **64.** $0.873 \div 41.9$

Skill 8: Divide money amounts

When you divide money amounts, follow the rules for dividing decimals. When necessary, round the quotient to the nearest cent by dividing through 1 place to the right of the cents place. Then round to the nearest cent.

Divide: $\$10.89 \div 0.4$.

$$
\begin{array}{r}
\$27.225 \approx \$27.23 \\
0.4\overline{)\$10.8\,900} \\
\underline{8} \\
2\,8 \\
\underline{2\,8} \\
0\,9 \\
\underline{8} \\
1\,0 \\
\underline{8} \\
2\,0 \\
\underline{2\,0} \\
0
\end{array}
$$

Divide. Round to the nearest cent when necessary.

65. $\$103.80 \div 5$ **66.** $\$124.65 \div 6$ **67.** $\$521.16 \div 8$ **68.** $\$999.99 \div 2$

69. $\$2.48 \div 0.8$ **70.** $\$386.45 \div 1.13$ **71.** $\$654.21 \div 5.3$ **72.** $\$936.07 \div 0.234$

EXPONENTS

Skill 1: Write powers of 10 in exponent form

Powers of 10 can be written in **exponent form** to show repeated multiplication. The **exponent** tells the numbers of zeros in the product.

$$1 = 10^0 \qquad 10 = 10^1 \qquad 100 = 10^2$$

Write 1,000 in exponent form.

THINK: 3 zeros $\qquad 1{,}000 \rightarrow 10^3 \;\leftarrow$ **exponent**

$\qquad\qquad\qquad\qquad\qquad\quad\; \llcorner$ **base**

Write the product of 10^5.

THINK: $10 \times 10 \times 10 \times 10 \times 10$, or 5 zeros

$10^5 \rightarrow 100{,}000$

Write in exponent form.

1. 10,000,000
2. 100,000,000
3. 1,000,000,000
4. $10 \times 10 \times 10 \times 10$
5. $10 \times 10 \times 10$
6. $10 \times 10 \times 10 \times 10 \times 10 \times 10$

Write the product.

7. 10^3
8. 10^4
9. 10^2
10. 10^6
11. 10^7
12. 10^9

Skill 2: 2 as an exponent

When a number is used as a factor 2 times, the exponent is 2. For example, 4^2 is read as 4 **to the second power** or 4 **squared.**

Write 4×4 in exponent form.

THINK: 2 fours $\qquad$ 4 is the base.

$\qquad\qquad\qquad\qquad\;$ 2 is the exponent.

$$4 \times 4 \rightarrow 4^2$$

Write in exponent form.

13. 3×3
14. 7×7
15. 17×17
16. 20×20

Write the product.

17. 4^2
18. 6^2
19. 9^2
20. 12^2
21. 14^2
22. 21^2

Skill 3: 3 as an exponent

When a number is used as a factor 3 times, the exponent is 3. For example, 2^3 is read as 2 **to the third power** or 2 **cubed.**

Write $2 \times 2 \times 2$ in exponent form.

THINK: 3 twos $\qquad$ 2 is the base.

$\qquad\qquad\qquad\qquad\;$ 3 is the exponent.

$$2 \times 2 \times 2 \rightarrow 2^3$$

Write in exponent form.

23. $1 \times 1 \times 1$
24. $4 \times 4 \times 4$
25. $13 \times 13 \times 13$
26. $25 \times 25 \times 25$

Write the product.

27. 2^3
28. 3^3
29. 5^3
30. 6^3
31. 7^3
32. 11^3

ADD WITH INTEGERS

Skill 1: Add integers using the number line

You can add integers using the number line. Always start at 0. Moving to the right means adding a positive integer. Moving to the left means adding a negative integer.

Add: $-2 + (-1)$.

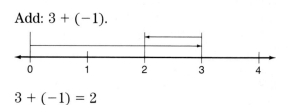

$-2 + (-1) = -3$

Since positive 3 can be written +3 or 3, write 3 (without the plus sign) from now on. Also, when a negative number follows an operation sign, use parentheses. For example, $-2 + (-1)$.

Add: $3 + (-1)$.

$3 + (-1) = 2$

Add. Use the number line.

1. $5 + 1$
2. $-3 + (-2)$
3. $5 + (-2)$
4. $-1 + (-3)$
5. $6 + (-3)$
6. $5 + 5$
7. $8 + (-4)$
8. $-6 + (-2)$

Skill 2: Add integers with like signs

The sum of 2 positive integers is a positive integer. The sum of 2 negative integers is a negative integer.

Add: $2 + 1$.
$2 + 1 = 3$

Add: $-4 + (-3)$.
$-4 + (-3) = -7$

Add.

9. $3 + 4$
10. $4 + 2$
11. $21 + 5$
12. $18 + 17$
13. $-1 + (-1)$
14. $-3 + (-5)$
15. $-11 + (-3)$
16. $-23 + (-25)$
17. $-18 + (-18)$
18. $-12 + (-32)$
19. $-28 + (-13)$
20. $-35 + (-23)$

Skill 3: Add integers with unlike signs

When you add integers with unlike signs, first subtract the absolute values of the integers (ignoring the signs). The answer has the same sign as the addend with the greater absolute value.

Add: $-5 + 2$.

THINK: $|-5| = 5$ $|2| = 2$ $5 - 2 = 3$
Since $|-5| > |2|$, the answer is negative.

$-5 + 2 = -3$

Add.

21. $-3 + 1$
22. $-8 + 4$
23. $-16 + 14$
24. $-28 + 34$
25. $5 + (-4)$
26. $6 + (-7)$
27. $23 + (-21)$
28. $34 + (-16)$
29. $16 + (-20)$
30. $30 + (-22)$
31. $33 + (-17)$
32. $27 + (-38)$

SUBTRACT WITH INTEGERS

Skill 1: Subtract integers with like signs

When you subtract an integer, add its opposite. For example, when you subtract $-4 - (-3)$, note that 3 is the opposite of -3. So add 3 to -4.

When you add $-4 + 3$, remember the rules for adding integers with unlike signs. First subtract the absolute values of the integers. The answer has the same sign as the addend with the greater absolute value.

Remember that positive 3 can be written as 3 and to use parentheses when a negative number follows an operation sign.

Subtract: $-4 - (-3)$.

$$-4 - (-3) = -4 + 3$$

$\qquad$ opposites

THINK: $|-4| = 4 \qquad |3| = 3 \qquad 4 - 3 = 1$

Since $|-4| > |3|$, the answer is negative.

$$-4 - (-3) = -4 + 3 = -1$$

Subtract.

1. $5 - 3$	**2.** $5 - 9$	**3.** $9 - 6$	**4.** $3 - 7$
5. $11 - 12$	**6.** $21 - 36$	**7.** $14 - 32$	**8.** $16 - 11$
9. $-8 - (-4)$	**10.** $-3 - (-6)$	**11.** $-17 - (-18)$	**12.** $-35 - (-43)$
13. $-9 - (-1)$	**14.** $-2 - (-8)$	**15.** $-4 - (-2)$	**16.** $-6 - (-7)$

Skill 2: Subtract integers with unlike signs

When you subtract an integer, add its opposite. For example, when you subtract $-5 - 6$, note that -6 is the opposite of 6. So add $-5 + (-6)$.

When you add $-5 + (-6)$, remember the rules for adding integers with like signs. The sum of 2 positive integers is positive. The sum of 2 negative integers is negative.

Subtract: $-5 - 6$.

$$-5 - 6 = -5 + (-6)$$

$\qquad$ opposites

THINK: $5 + 6 = 11$

$$-5 - 6 = -5 + (-6) = -11$$

Subtract: $3 - (-7)$.

$$3 - (-7) = 3 + 7$$
$$3 - (-7) = 3 + 7 = 10$$

Subtract.

17. $-5 - 7$	**18.** $-1 - 7$	**19.** $-5 - 9$	**20.** $-9 - 4$
21. $-14 - 15$	**22.** $-54 - 39$	**23.** $8 - (-3)$	**24.** $4 - (-9)$
25. $6 - (-3)$	**26.** $2 - (-9)$	**27.** $13 - (-24)$	**28.** $41 - (-34)$
29. $-16 - 9$	**30.** $-21 - 26$	**31.** $9 - (-4)$	**32.** $13 - (-15)$

MULTIPLY WITH INTEGERS

Skill 1: Multiply integers with like signs

When you multiply integers with like signs, the product is a positive number.

Remember that positive 4 can be written as 4 and to use parentheses when a negative number follows an operation sign.

Multiply: 4×4.

$4 \times 4 = 16$

Multiply: $-3 \times (-5)$.

$-3 \times (-5) = 15$

Multiply.

1. 5×3 2. 9×2 3. 6×7 4. 8×8

5. 11×2 6. 4×12 7. 25×3 8. 16×7

9. 14×8 10. 19×5 11. 7×26 12. 8×28

13. 39×8 14. 45×7 15. 38×8 16. 6×24

17. $-9 \times (-9)$ 18. $-3 \times (-26)$ 19. $-24 \times (-3)$ 20. $-1 \times (-72)$

21. $-3 \times (-11)$ 22. $-6 \times (-12)$ 23. $-18 \times (-4)$ 24. $-8 \times (-50)$

25. $-5 \times (-21)$ 26. $-4 \times (-16)$ 27. $-21 \times (-9)$ 28. $-11 \times (-12)$

29. $-6 \times (-4)$ 30. $-4 \times (-1)$ 31. $-5 \times (-5)$ 32. $-7 \times (-8)$

33. $-17 \times (-5)$ 34. $-6 \times (-11)$ 35. $-21 \times (-4)$ 36. $-24 \times (-9)$

Skill 2: Multiply integers with unlike signs

When you multiply integers with unlike signs, the product is negative.

Multiply: -6×3.

$-6 \times 3 = -18$

Multiply: $7 \times (-4)$.

$7 \times (-4) = -28$

Multiply.

37. -4×1 38. -3×9 39. -7×6 40. -9×9

41. -13×3 42. -4×17 43. -6×12 44. -24×7

45. -5×9 46. -11×5 47. -2×45 48. -5×61

49. -17×4 50. -24×8 51. -26×9 52. -3×22

53. $3 \times (-12)$ 54. $16 \times (-1)$ 55. $34 \times (-4)$ 56. $15 \times (-5)$

57. $7 \times (-21)$ 58. $23 \times (-5)$ 59. $47 \times (-8)$ 60. $5 \times (-61)$

61. $6 \times (-30)$ 62. $28 \times (-7)$ 63. $36 \times (-4)$ 64. $15 \times (-11)$

65. $5 \times (-1)$ 66. $7 \times (-3)$ 67. $6 \times (-4)$ 68. $2 \times (-9)$

69. $16 \times (-2)$ 70. $7 \times (-14)$ 71. $13 \times (-5)$ 72. $32 \times (-4)$

DIVIDE WITH INTEGERS

Skill 1: Divide integers with like signs

When you divide integers with like signs, the quotient is a positive number.

Remember that positive 8 can be written as 8 and to use parentheses when a negative number follows an operation sign.

Divide: $8 \div 4$.

$8 \div 4 = 2$

Divide $-9 \div (-3)$.

$-9 \div (-3) = 3$

Divide.

1. $4 \div 2$	2. $5 \div 1$	3. $12 \div 6$	4. $18 \div 3$
5. $45 \div 15$	6. $60 \div 10$	7. $75 \div 5$	8. $84 \div 12$
9. $9 \div 3$	10. $60 \div 12$	11. $90 \div 30$	12. $45 \div 9$
13. $44 \div 11$	14. $100 \div 10$	15. $65 \div 13$	16. $100 \div 25$
17. $-12 \div (-2)$	18. $-72 \div (-9)$	19. $-70 \div (-10)$	20. $-64 \div (-8)$
21. $-64 \div (-16)$	22. $-84 \div (-21)$	23. $-40 \div (-5)$	24. $-600 \div (-6)$
25. $-65 \div (-13)$	26. $-36 \div (-6)$	27. $-81 \div (-9)$	28. $-378 \div (-7)$
29. $-6 \div (-3)$	30. $-8 \div (-2)$	31. $-15 \div (-5)$	32. $-14 \div (-7)$
33. $-54 \div (-2)$	34. $-75 \div (-15)$	35. $-80 \div (-4)$	36. $-90 \div (-5)$

Skill 2: Divide integers with unlike signs

When you divide integers with unlike signs, the quotient is negative.

Divide: $-6 \div 2$.

$-6 \div 2 = 3$

Divide: $4 \div (-1)$.

$4 \div (-1) = -4$

Divide.

37. $-6 \div 1$	38. $-6 \div 3$	39. $-8 \div 4$	40. $-15 \div 5$
41. $-60 \div 5$	42. $-68 \div 4$	43. $-78 \div 2$	44. $-96 \div 32$
45. $-9 \div 9$	46. $-8 \div 2$	47. $-20 \div 4$	48. $-86 \div 2$
49. $-88 \div 4$	50. $-35 \div 1$	51. $-72 \div 18$	52. $-45 \div 15$
53. $16 \div (-8)$	54. $28 \div (-7)$	55. $80 \div (-16)$	56. $88 \div (-44)$
57. $48 \div (-6)$	58. $81 \div (-9)$	59. $77 \div (-11)$	60. $40 \div (-4)$
61. $64 \div (-8)$	62. $121 \div (-11)$	63. $60 \div (-12)$	64. $84 \div (-14)$
65. $9 \div (-3)$	66. $10 \div (-1)$	67. $14 \div (-7)$	68. $20 \div (-2)$
69. $50 \div (-25)$	70. $55 \div (-11)$	71. $90 \div (-15)$	72. $93 \div (-3)$

ORDER OF OPERATIONS

Skill 1: Simplify expressions with no parentheses

To simplify expressions with no parentheses:

- First multiply and divide in order from left to right.

- Then add and subtract in order from left to right.

Compute: $6 + 4 \times 6$.

THINK: **Multiply first.**
$$4 \times 6 = 24$$
$$6 + 4 \times 6 = 6 + 24 = 30$$

Compute: $4 \times 2 - 15 \div 5$.

THINK: **Multiply and divide in order first.**
$$4 \times 2 = 8 \qquad 15 \div 5 = 3$$
$$4 \times 2 - 15 \div 5 = 8 - 3 = 5$$

Compute.

1. $4 + 2 + 3$	**2.** $5 \times 2 + 3$	**3.** $3 + 6 \times 4$
4. $5 - 4 + 2$	**5.** $25 - 12 \times 2$	**6.** $20 \div 5 \times 2$
7. $4 \times 3 - 6 \times 1$	**8.** $25 \div 5 + 4 \times 1$	**9.** $6 + 3 - 2 + 4$
10. $8 \div 4 - 4 \div 2$	**11.** $8 + 6 \div 2 + 1$	**12.** $16 \div 8 \times 4 + 1$
13. $6 \times 4 \div 12 - 8$	**14.** $8 + 3 \div 3 - 2$	**15.** $20 - 9 \times 2 + 4$

Skill 2: Simplify expressions with parentheses

The following are the rules for the **Order of Operations:**

1. Do operations inside parentheses.

2. Multiply and divide in order from left to right.

3. Add and subtract in order from left to right.

Compute: $(5 + 4) \times 2$.

THINK: **Compute inside parentheses first.**
$$5 + 4 = 9$$
$$(5 + 4) \times 2 = 9 \times 2 = 18$$

Compute: $(7 + 1) \div (7 - 5)$.

THINK: **Compute inside parentheses first.**
$$7 + 1 = 8 \qquad 7 - 5 = 2$$
$$(7 + 1) \div (7 - 5) = 8 \div 2 = 4$$

Compute.

16. $(3 + 2) \times 4$	**17.** $(6 - 4) \times 7$	**18.** $11 - (9 \div 3)$
19. $12 \div (4 + 2)$	**20.** $8 \times (9 - 5)$	**21.** $25 \div (4 + 1)$
22. $(6 + 2) \div (4 - 2)$	**23.** $(7 - 1) \times (9 \div 3)$	**24.** $(16 \div 4) \times (8 \times 1)$
25. $(5 \times 3) - (10 \div 5)$	**26.** $(7 + 6) + (20 \times 2)$	**27.** $(13 + 5) \div (21 \div 7)$
28. $(14 - 8) \div (12 \div 4)$	**29.** $(27 \div 9) \times (15 - 6)$	**30.** $(7 \times 7) + (24 \div 4)$

FRACTIONS AND MIXED NUMBERS

Skill 1: Write fractions and mixed numbers for shaded regions

A **fraction** can be used to describe part of a whole. The **numerator** (top) of a fraction shows how many parts are shaded. The **denominator** (bottom) shows the total number of parts.

Write a fraction for the shaded region.

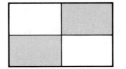

$$\frac{\text{parts shaded}}{\text{total parts}} \to \frac{2}{4}$$

A **mixed number** consists of a whole number part and a fraction part.

For example, $1\frac{1}{3}$ is a mixed number.

Write a mixed number for the shaded regions.

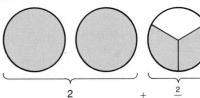

$$2 \quad + \quad \frac{2}{3} \quad = 2\frac{2}{3}$$

Write a fraction for the shaded region.

1.   **2.**

3.  **4.**

Write a mixed number for the shaded regions.

5. 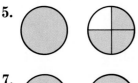 **6.**

7.  **8.**

9. 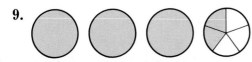 **10.**

Skill 2: Round fractions and mixed numbers using the number line

To round fractions and mixed numbers, you can use the number line. First graph the number on the number line. Then determine to which whole number it is closer.

Round $\frac{3}{4}$ and $1\frac{1}{2}$ using a number line.

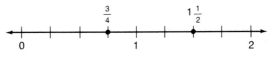

$\frac{3}{4}$ is closer to 1 than 0. Round $\frac{3}{4}$ to 1.

$1\frac{1}{2}$ is halfway between 1 and 2. Round $1\frac{1}{2}$ to 2.

FRACTIONS AND MIXED NUMBERS

Round using the number line.

11. $\frac{1}{2}$ 12. $\frac{1}{3}$ 13. $\frac{2}{3}$ 14. $\frac{1}{4}$ 15. $\frac{1}{8}$

16. $1\frac{1}{3}$ 17. $1\frac{3}{4}$ 18. $2\frac{1}{2}$ 19. $2\frac{7}{8}$ 20. $3\frac{1}{4}$

Skill 3: Rename an improper fraction as a mixed number

An **improper fraction** is a fraction in which the numerator is equal to or greater than the denominator. For example, $\frac{6}{4}$ is an improper fraction.

To rename an improper fraction as a mixed number, divide the numerator by the denominator.

Rename $\frac{6}{4}$ as a mixed number.

$$\frac{6}{4} \rightarrow 4\overline{)6} \rightarrow 1\frac{2}{4} \begin{array}{l}\leftarrow \text{remainder} \\ \leftarrow \text{divisor}\end{array}$$

$\frac{6}{4}$ is renamed as $1\frac{2}{4}$.

Rename as a mixed number or a whole number.

21. $\frac{5}{4}$ 22. $\frac{7}{3}$ 23. $\frac{7}{5}$ 24. $\frac{6}{2}$ 25. $\frac{9}{3}$ 26. $\frac{60}{5}$

27. $\frac{10}{4}$ 28. $\frac{34}{8}$ 29. $\frac{75}{9}$ 30. $\frac{25}{10}$ 31. $\frac{40}{12}$ 32. $\frac{60}{14}$

33. $\frac{5}{2}$ 34. $\frac{12}{5}$ 35. $\frac{24}{7}$ 36. $\frac{7}{6}$ 37. $\frac{10}{8}$ 38. $\frac{9}{2}$

39. $\frac{9}{6}$ 40. $\frac{10}{3}$ 41. $\frac{32}{10}$ 42. $\frac{22}{5}$ 43. $\frac{26}{6}$ 44. $\frac{42}{12}$

Skill 4: Rename a mixed number as an improper fraction

To rename a mixed number as an improper fraction, multiply the whole number by the denominator and add the numerator. This is the numerator of the improper fraction. The denominator of the improper fraction is the same as the original denominator.

Rename $1\frac{3}{4}$ as an improper fraction.

$$1\frac{3}{4} \rightarrow 1\frac{3}{4} \enspace 4+3 \rightarrow \frac{7}{4}$$
$$1 \times 4$$

$1\frac{3}{4}$ is renamed as $\frac{7}{4}$.

Rename as an improper fraction.

45. $1\frac{1}{3}$ 46. $2\frac{2}{5}$ 47. $3\frac{4}{5}$ 48. $4\frac{3}{5}$ 49. $9\frac{1}{3}$ 50. $11\frac{3}{5}$

51. $3\frac{2}{10}$ 52. $4\frac{4}{12}$ 53. $6\frac{5}{15}$ 54. $7\frac{1}{4}$ 55. $9\frac{1}{2}$ 56. $14\frac{1}{2}$

57. $7\frac{2}{3}$ 58. $3\frac{6}{11}$ 59. $5\frac{4}{5}$ 60. $9\frac{7}{10}$ 61. $13\frac{1}{6}$ 62. $8\frac{7}{12}$

63. $16\frac{2}{5}$ 64. $11\frac{5}{6}$ 65. $10\frac{3}{4}$ 66. $8\frac{5}{6}$ 67. $12\frac{3}{10}$ 68. $10\frac{1}{5}$

EQUIVALENT FRACTIONS

Skill 1: Rename fractions to higher terms

To rename fractions to higher terms, multiply the numerator and denominator of the fraction by the same nonzero number.

Rename: $\frac{2}{3} = \frac{\blacksquare}{15}$.

THINK: $3 \times \blacksquare = 15$ $3 \times 5 = 15$

$\frac{2}{3} = \frac{2 \times 5}{3 \times 5} = \frac{10}{15}$ So $\frac{2}{3} = \frac{10}{15}$.

Rename.

1. $\frac{1}{2} = \frac{\blacksquare}{4}$

2. $\frac{3}{5} = \frac{\blacksquare}{10}$

3. $\frac{5}{6} = \frac{\blacksquare}{18}$

4. $\frac{2}{9} = \frac{\blacksquare}{36}$

5. $1\frac{1}{2} = 1\frac{\blacksquare}{10}$

6. $2\frac{1}{3} = 2\frac{\blacksquare}{9}$

7. $3\frac{4}{5} = 3\frac{\blacksquare}{15}$

8. $5\frac{1}{6} = 5\frac{\blacksquare}{12}$

Skill 2: Find the LCD when there are common factors

To rename fractions using the **least common denominator (LCD),** first see if the denominators have a common factor. If they do, list the multiples of both denominators until you find a common multiple.

Rename $\frac{1}{4}$ and $\frac{5}{6}$ using the LCD.

THINK: Do 4 and 6 have a common factor? Yes, 2.

List the multiples.
4, 8, 12, 16, 20, $\cdots$ 6, 12, $\cdots$
12 is the least common multiple of 4 and 6. 12 is the LCD.

$\frac{1}{4} = \frac{1 \times 3}{4 \times 3} = \frac{3}{12}$ $\frac{5}{6} = \frac{5 \times 2}{6 \times 2} = \frac{10}{12}$

Rename both fractions using the LCD.

9. $\frac{1}{2}, \frac{3}{4}$

10. $\frac{2}{3}, \frac{4}{9}$

11. $\frac{1}{4}, \frac{7}{8}$

12. $\frac{2}{6}, \frac{5}{12}$

13. $\frac{1}{6}, \frac{3}{4}$

14. $\frac{1}{6}, \frac{7}{8}$

15. $\frac{1}{9}, \frac{5}{12}$

16. $\frac{1}{10}, \frac{2}{15}$

Skill 3: Find the LCD when there are no common factors

To rename fractions using the LCD, first find if the denominators have a common factor. If they do not, multiply the 2 denominators to find the LCD.

Rename $\frac{1}{5}$ and $\frac{5}{6}$ using the LCD.

THINK: Do 5 and 6 have a common factor? No.

$5 \times 6 = 30$ Use 30 as the LCD.

$\frac{1}{5} = \frac{1 \times 6}{5 \times 6} = \frac{6}{30}$ $\frac{5}{6} = \frac{5 \times 5}{6 \times 5} = \frac{25}{30}$

Rename the fractions using the LCD.

17. $\frac{1}{2}, \frac{2}{3}$

18. $\frac{1}{4}, \frac{2}{5}$

19. $\frac{1}{2}, \frac{3}{7}$

20. $\frac{5}{7}, \frac{3}{4}$

21. $\frac{1}{2}, \frac{2}{9}$

22. $\frac{2}{5}, \frac{7}{9}$

23. $\frac{2}{7}, \frac{3}{8}$

24. $\frac{5}{9}, \frac{7}{10}$

LOWEST TERMS

Skill 1: Find the GCF

The **greatest common factor (GCF)** of 2 or more numbers is the greatest number that is a factor of each number. To find the GCF, first list the factors of each number. Then list all the common factors.

Find the GCF of 12 and 18.

Factors of 12: 1, 2, 3, 4, 6, 12
Factors of 18: 1, 2, 3, 6, 9, 18
Common factors: 1, 2, 3, 6

The GCF of 12 and 18 is 6.

Find the GCF.

1. 2 and 6

2. 4 and 8

3. 10 and 12

4. 16 and 24

5. 2, 4, and 8

6. 3, 12, and 24

7. 4, 8, and 12

8. 12, 20, and 40

Skill 2: Rename a fraction in lowest terms

A fraction is in **lowest terms** when the only common factor of the numerator and denominator is 1. To write a fraction in lowest terms, divide the numerator and denominator by the GCF.

Write $\frac{4}{12}$ in lowest terms.

Factors of 4: 1, 2, 4
Factors of 12: 1, 2, 3, 4, 6, 12
The GCF of 4 and 12 is 4.

$$\frac{4}{12} = \frac{4 \div 4}{12 \div 4} = \frac{1}{3}$$

$\frac{4}{12}$, in lowest terms, is $\frac{1}{3}$.

Write the fraction in lowest terms.

9. $\frac{2}{4}$

10. $\frac{3}{9}$

11. $\frac{4}{24}$

12. $\frac{7}{21}$

13. $\frac{9}{36}$

14. $\frac{8}{12}$

15. $\frac{9}{21}$

16. $\frac{12}{20}$

17. $\frac{25}{35}$

18. $\frac{28}{36}$

Skill 3: Simplify mixed numbers

To **simplify** mixed numbers, write the fraction part in lowest terms.

Simplify: $1\frac{15}{20}$.

The GCF of 15 and 20 is 5.

$$1\frac{15}{20} = 1\frac{15 \div 5}{20 \div 5} = 1\frac{3}{4}$$

Simplify: $3\frac{3}{2}$.

$$3\frac{3}{2} = 3 + \frac{3}{2}$$
$$= 3 + 1\frac{1}{2} = 4\frac{1}{2}$$

Simplify.

19. $1\frac{4}{16}$

20. $2\frac{7}{21}$

21. $2\frac{8}{20}$

22. $3\frac{10}{25}$

23. $14\frac{6}{27}$

24. $1\frac{4}{3}$

25. $2\frac{5}{4}$

26. $3\frac{9}{7}$

27. $12\frac{12}{9}$

28. $16\frac{20}{15}$

COMPARE AND ORDER FRACTIONS AND MIXED NUMBERS

Skill 1: Compare fractions and mixed numbers

When you compare fractions and mixed numbers, the fractions must have the same denominator. If they do not, rename the fractions using the LCD. Then compare the numerators.

Compare $1\frac{1}{2}$ and $1\frac{1}{3}$ using $>$, $<$, or $=$.

$1\frac{1}{2} \bullet 1\frac{1}{3}$ ← unlike denominators

Use 6 as the LCD.

$\frac{1}{2} = \frac{3}{6}$ $\qquad$ $\frac{1}{3} = \frac{2}{6}$

$\frac{3}{6} > \frac{2}{6}$ ← **The numerator 3 is greater than 2.**

So $1\frac{1}{2} > 1\frac{1}{3}$.

Compare. Write $>$, $<$, or $=$.

1. $\frac{1}{4} \bullet \frac{1}{8}$

2. $\frac{3}{4} \bullet \frac{9}{16}$

3. $\frac{1}{8} \bullet \frac{1}{3}$

4. $\frac{5}{12} \bullet \frac{7}{8}$

5. $1\frac{1}{2} \bullet 1\frac{1}{4}$

6. $2\frac{1}{5} \bullet 2\frac{3}{10}$

7. $8\frac{1}{4} \bullet 8\frac{3}{12}$

8. $11\frac{2}{3} \bullet 11\frac{3}{4}$

Skill 2: Order fractions and mixed numbers

To order fractions and mixed numbers, the fractions must have the same denominator. If they do not, rename the fractions using the LCD. Then compare the numerators.

Order $1\frac{1}{4}$, $1\frac{1}{2}$, and $1\frac{3}{8}$ from least to greatest.

$1\frac{1}{4}$, $1\frac{1}{2}$, $1\frac{3}{8}$ ← unlike denominators

Use 8 as the LCD.

$1\frac{1}{4} = 1\frac{2}{8}$ $\qquad$ $1\frac{1}{2} = 1\frac{4}{8}$ $\qquad$ $1\frac{3}{8}$

$1\frac{2}{8}$, $1\frac{3}{8}$, $1\frac{4}{8}$ ← **Since the whole-number parts are the same, order the numerators.**

$1\frac{1}{4}$, $1\frac{3}{8}$, and $1\frac{1}{2}$ are the ordered numbers.

Order from least to greatest.

9. $\frac{1}{2}, \frac{3}{4}, \frac{7}{8}$

10. $\frac{2}{3}, \frac{5}{6}, \frac{4}{9}$

11. $\frac{1}{4}, \frac{1}{3}, \frac{1}{5}$

12. $\frac{5}{6}, \frac{5}{12}, \frac{5}{18}$

13. $1\frac{1}{3}, 1\frac{1}{6}, 1\frac{5}{12}$

14. $2\frac{3}{4}, 2\frac{1}{2}, 2\frac{3}{8}$

15. $9\frac{1}{6}, 9\frac{3}{8}, 9\frac{5}{12}$

16. $11\frac{4}{7}, 11\frac{5}{21}, 11\frac{7}{14}$

Order from greatest to least.

17. $\frac{1}{2}, \frac{3}{8}, \frac{1}{4}$

18. $\frac{1}{5}, \frac{2}{3}, \frac{7}{15}$

19. $\frac{1}{2}, \frac{1}{3}, \frac{1}{4}$

20. $\frac{3}{5}, \frac{5}{6}, \frac{7}{20}$

21. $1\frac{1}{4}, 1\frac{1}{3}, 1\frac{5}{12}$

22. $2\frac{1}{3}, 2\frac{5}{6}, 2\frac{7}{18}$

23. $8\frac{2}{5}, 8\frac{4}{7}, 8\frac{1}{2}$

24. $13\frac{2}{3}, 13\frac{1}{4}, 13\frac{5}{6}$

MULTIPLY WITH FRACTIONS AND MIXED NUMBERS

Skill 1: Multiply 2 fractions

When you multiply fractions, multiply the numerators and then multiply the denominators. Write the answer in lowest terms.

Multiply: $\frac{1}{3} \times \frac{3}{5}$.

$$\frac{1}{3} \times \frac{3}{5} = \frac{1 \times 3}{3 \times 5} = \frac{3}{15}$$

$$\frac{3}{15} = \frac{3 \div 3}{15 \div 3} = \frac{1}{5} \leftarrow \text{lowest terms}$$

So $\frac{1}{3} \times \frac{3}{5} = \frac{1}{5}$.

Multiply. Write the answer in lowest terms.

1. $\frac{1}{2} \times \frac{1}{4}$ 2. $\frac{2}{5} \times \frac{2}{3}$ 3. $\frac{4}{9} \times \frac{4}{5}$ 4. $\frac{5}{12} \times \frac{1}{3}$

5. $\frac{3}{4} \times \frac{1}{3}$ 6. $\frac{1}{5} \times \frac{5}{6}$ 7. $\frac{5}{6} \times \frac{2}{7}$ 8. $\frac{7}{8} \times \frac{8}{9}$

9. $\frac{2}{3} \times \frac{1}{2}$ 10. $\frac{3}{5} \times \frac{2}{3}$ 11. $\frac{4}{7} \times \frac{1}{2}$ 12. $\frac{1}{3} \times \frac{6}{7}$

13. $\frac{7}{10} \times \frac{4}{5}$ 14. $\frac{2}{3} \times \frac{7}{8}$ 15. $\frac{5}{6} \times \frac{1}{2}$ 16. $\frac{3}{4} \times \frac{2}{3}$

17. $\frac{1}{9} \times \frac{3}{4}$ 18. $\frac{4}{5} \times \frac{3}{4}$ 19. $\frac{8}{9} \times \frac{1}{2}$ 20. $\frac{7}{8} \times \frac{4}{5}$

Skill 2: Multiply 2 fractions using a shortcut

You can use a multiplication shortcut when there is a common factor in any numerator and denominator. First find the common factor(s). Simplify by dividing by the common factor(s). Then multiply.

For example, the common factor of 3 and 27 is 3 and the common factor of 7 and 14 is 7.

Multiply: $\frac{3}{7} \times \frac{14}{27}$.

$$\overset{1}{\underset{1}{\cancel{\frac{3}{7}}}} \times \overset{2}{\underset{9}{\cancel{\frac{14}{27}}}} = \frac{1 \times 2}{1 \times 9} = \frac{2}{9}$$

So $\frac{3}{7} \times \frac{14}{27} = \frac{2}{9}$.

Multiply using the shortcut.

21. $\frac{1}{2} \times \frac{6}{11}$ 22. $\frac{2}{3} \times \frac{1}{4}$ 23. $\frac{2}{9} \times \frac{6}{7}$ 24. $\frac{3}{4} \times \frac{14}{17}$

25. $\frac{1}{3} \times \frac{6}{8}$ 26. $\frac{1}{2} \times \frac{10}{15}$ 27. $\frac{7}{9} \times \frac{3}{5}$ 28. $\frac{4}{5} \times \frac{5}{7}$

29. $\frac{3}{4} \times \frac{8}{9}$ 30. $\frac{5}{6} \times \frac{3}{5}$ 31. $\frac{7}{8} \times \frac{12}{21}$ 32. $\frac{4}{9} \times \frac{15}{28}$

33. $\frac{2}{8} \times \frac{4}{6}$ 34. $\frac{4}{5} \times \frac{5}{6}$ 35. $\frac{3}{4} \times \frac{12}{15}$ 36. $\frac{4}{9} \times \frac{3}{8}$

37. $\frac{6}{9} \times \frac{3}{4}$ 38. $\frac{2}{7} \times \frac{14}{20}$ 39. $\frac{7}{8} \times \frac{2}{14}$ 40. $\frac{3}{4} \times \frac{8}{15}$

MULTIPLY WITH FRACTIONS AND MIXED NUMBERS

Skill 3: Multiply a fraction and a whole number

To multiply a fraction and a whole number, rename the whole number as a fraction. For example, rename 5 as $\frac{5}{1}$.

Then multiply and simplify the answer when possible.

Multiply: $\frac{1}{2} \times 5$.

$$\frac{1}{2} \times 5 = \frac{1}{2} \times \frac{5}{1} = \frac{5}{2} = 2\frac{1}{2}$$

Multiply: $\frac{5}{6} \times 8$.

$$\frac{5}{6} \times 8 = \frac{5}{6} \times \frac{8}{1} = \frac{5}{\overset{}{\underset{3}{6}}} \times \frac{\overset{4}{8}}{1} = \frac{20}{3} = 6\frac{2}{3}$$

Multiply. Write the answer in simplest form.

41. $\frac{1}{3} \times 7$

42. $\frac{1}{4} \times 13$

43. $\frac{1}{2} \times 4$

44. $\frac{1}{5} \times 20$

45. $\frac{2}{5} \times 25$

46. $\frac{3}{7} \times 21$

47. $\frac{3}{8} \times 18$

48. $\frac{9}{10} \times 35$

Skill 4: Multiply a fraction and a mixed number

When you multiply a fraction and a mixed number, rename the mixed number as a fraction. For example, rename $1\frac{1}{3}$ as $\frac{4}{3}$.

Then multiply and simplify the answer when possible.

Multiply: $\frac{7}{8} \times 1\frac{1}{3}$.

$$\frac{7}{8} \times 1\frac{1}{3} = \frac{7}{8} \times \frac{4}{3} = \frac{7}{\overset{}{\underset{2}{8}}} \times \frac{\overset{1}{4}}{3} = \frac{7}{6} = 1\frac{1}{6}$$

Multiply. Write the answer in simplest form.

49. $\frac{1}{3} \times 1\frac{1}{4}$

50. $2\frac{1}{3} \times \frac{1}{4}$

51. $\frac{1}{3} \times 1\frac{1}{2}$

52. $1\frac{1}{5} \times \frac{1}{2}$

53. $\frac{4}{13} \times 1\frac{3}{10}$

54. $\frac{2}{7} \times 1\frac{3}{4}$

55. $6\frac{3}{4} \times \frac{8}{15}$

56. $\frac{2}{3} \times 3\frac{3}{8}$

57. $\frac{3}{4} \times 1\frac{1}{3}$

58. $2\frac{1}{10} \times \frac{5}{7}$

59. $2\frac{1}{4} \times \frac{2}{3}$

60. $\frac{5}{6} \times 1\frac{4}{5}$

Skill 5: Multiply 2 mixed numbers

When you multiply 2 mixed numbers, rename the mixed numbers as fractions. Then multiply and simplify the answer when possible.

Multiply: $1\frac{1}{3} \times 2\frac{5}{6}$.

$$1\frac{1}{3} \times 2\frac{5}{6} = \frac{4}{3} \times \frac{17}{6} = \frac{4}{3} \times \frac{17}{\overset{}{\underset{3}{6}}} = \frac{34}{9} = 3\frac{7}{9}$$

Multiply. Write the answer in simplest form.

61. $2\frac{1}{4} \times 1\frac{1}{4}$

62. $3\frac{1}{4} \times 2\frac{1}{2}$

63. $3\frac{3}{5} \times 4\frac{2}{3}$

64. $4\frac{2}{5} \times 5\frac{1}{2}$

65. $1\frac{1}{2} \times 1\frac{1}{3}$

66. $6\frac{2}{3} \times 4\frac{1}{2}$

67. $4\frac{2}{7} \times 9\frac{1}{3}$

68. $5\frac{2}{5} \times 6\frac{2}{3}$

DIVIDE WITH FRACTIONS AND MIXED NUMBERS

Skill 1: Find the reciprocal of a fraction

Two numbers whose product is 1 are called **reciprocals**. For example, 2 and $\frac{1}{2}$ are reciprocals. To find the reciprocal of a whole or mixed number, first rename it as a fraction.

Find the reciprocal of $1\frac{1}{3}$.

THINK: $1\frac{1}{3} = \frac{4}{3}$

The reciprocal of $\frac{4}{3}$ is $\frac{3}{4}$ because $\frac{4}{3} \times \frac{3}{4} = 1$.

Find the reciprocal.

1. $\frac{3}{4}$ 2. $\frac{7}{8}$ 3. $\frac{1}{3}$ 4. 4   5. $1\frac{1}{2}$ 6. $2\frac{1}{4}$

Skill 2: Divide 2 fractions

When you divide by a fraction, write the reciprocal of the divisor. For example, $\frac{3}{2}$ is the reciprocal of the divisor, $\frac{2}{3}$. Then multiply and write the answer in lowest terms.

Divide: $\frac{4}{7} \div \frac{2}{3}$.

$$\frac{4}{7} \div \frac{2}{3} = \frac{4}{7} \times \frac{3}{2} = \frac{\overset{2}{\cancel{4}}}{7} \times \frac{3}{\underset{1}{\cancel{2}}} = \frac{6}{7}$$

Divide. Write the answer in lowest terms.

7. $\frac{1}{2} \div \frac{4}{7}$ 8. $\frac{1}{4} \div \frac{2}{3}$ 9. $\frac{3}{4} \div \frac{1}{3}$ 10. $\frac{7}{8} \div \frac{4}{5}$

11. $\frac{1}{12} \div \frac{3}{4}$ 12. $\frac{3}{10} \div \frac{1}{5}$ 13. $\frac{4}{9} \div \frac{2}{3}$ 14. $\frac{9}{14} \div \frac{3}{7}$

Skill 3: Divide a fraction and a whole number

When you divide a fraction and a whole number, rename the whole number as a fraction. For example, rename 2 as $\frac{2}{1}$.

Then write the reciprocal of the divisor and multiply. Simplify the answer when possible.

Divide: $\frac{1}{4} \div 2$.

$$\frac{1}{4} \div 2 = \frac{1}{4} \div \frac{2}{1} = \frac{1}{4} \times \frac{1}{2} = \frac{1}{8}$$

Divide: $3 \div \frac{6}{7}$.

$$3 \div \frac{6}{7} = \frac{3}{1} \div \frac{6}{7} = \frac{\overset{1}{\cancel{3}}}{1} \times \frac{7}{\underset{2}{\cancel{6}}} = \frac{7}{2} = 3\frac{1}{2}$$

Divide. Write the answer in simplest form.

15. $\frac{1}{3} \div 4$ 16. $\frac{5}{6} \div 10$ 17. $\frac{8}{9} \div 12$ 18. $\frac{10}{11} \div 20$

19. $8 \div \frac{1}{2}$ 20. $9 \div \frac{3}{5}$ 21. $10 \div \frac{2}{5}$ 22. $14 \div \frac{3}{4}$

23. $6 \div \frac{6}{7}$ 24. $5 \div \frac{10}{11}$ 25. $\frac{3}{4} \div 9$ 26. $\frac{5}{6} \div 15$

DIVIDE WITH FRACTIONS AND MIXED NUMBERS

Skill 4: Divide a fraction and a mixed number

When you divide a fraction and a mixed number, rename the mixed number as a fraction. Then write the reciprocal of the divisor and multiply. Simplify the answer when possible.

Divide: $3\frac{1}{2} \div \frac{4}{5}$.

$$3\frac{1}{2} \div \frac{4}{5} = \frac{7}{2} \div \frac{4}{5} = \frac{7}{2} \times \frac{5}{4} = \frac{35}{8} = 4\frac{3}{8}$$

Divide: $\frac{7}{8} \div 1\frac{1}{4}$.

$$\frac{7}{8} \div 1\frac{1}{4} = \frac{7}{8} \div \frac{5}{4} = \frac{7}{\overset{}{\underset{2}{8}}} \times \frac{\overset{1}{4}}{5} = \frac{7}{10}$$

Divide. Write the answer in simplest form.

27. $\frac{5}{8} \div 1\frac{1}{3}$

28. $\frac{4}{9} \div 2\frac{1}{5}$

29. $\frac{3}{4} \div 1\frac{1}{2}$

30. $\frac{7}{8} \div 2\frac{1}{4}$

31. $1\frac{1}{3} \div \frac{1}{2}$

32. $2\frac{5}{6} \div \frac{1}{5}$

33. $3\frac{1}{6} \div \frac{7}{8}$

34. $4\frac{7}{8} \div \frac{3}{4}$

35. $1\frac{3}{7} \div \frac{5}{7}$

36. $\frac{6}{9} \div 1\frac{1}{3}$

37. $\frac{3}{4} \div 3\frac{1}{2}$

38. $4\frac{1}{3} \div \frac{5}{9}$

39. $3\frac{1}{3} \div \frac{2}{5}$

40. $\frac{7}{10} \div 1\frac{1}{5}$

41. $2\frac{1}{3} \div \frac{7}{9}$

42. $\frac{2}{3} \div 1\frac{1}{5}$

43. $\frac{2}{5} \div 3\frac{1}{3}$

44. $1\frac{1}{5} \div \frac{7}{10}$

45. $\frac{5}{9} \div 4\frac{1}{3}$

46. $1\frac{1}{5} \div \frac{2}{3}$

Skill 5: Divide 2 mixed numbers

To divide with mixed numbers, rename the mixed numbers as fractions. Then write the reciprocal of the divisor and multiply. Simplify the answer when possible.

Divide: $2\frac{1}{2} \div 1\frac{1}{4}$.

$$2\frac{1}{2} \div 1\frac{1}{4} = \frac{5}{2} \div \frac{5}{4} = \frac{\overset{1}{5}}{\underset{1}{2}} \times \frac{\overset{2}{4}}{\underset{1}{5}} = \frac{2}{1} = 2$$

Divide. Write the answer in simplest form.

47. $2\frac{1}{3} \div 1\frac{1}{4}$

48. $6\frac{1}{2} \div 2\frac{1}{3}$

49. $9\frac{1}{2} \div 1\frac{1}{4}$

50. $8\frac{7}{9} \div 2\frac{2}{3}$

51. $3\frac{2}{3} \div 2\frac{4}{9}$

52. $5\frac{3}{5} \div 2\frac{1}{10}$

53. $3\frac{1}{5} \div 1\frac{11}{25}$

54. $6\frac{5}{6} \div 3\frac{5}{12}$

55. $1\frac{1}{3} \div 1\frac{1}{9}$

56. $1\frac{1}{7} \div 1\frac{1}{3}$

57. $2\frac{3}{4} \div 3\frac{1}{2}$

58. $3\frac{1}{2} \div 1\frac{1}{6}$

59. $1\frac{5}{7} \div 1\frac{1}{3}$

60. $4\frac{2}{3} \div 1\frac{1}{6}$

61. $3\frac{1}{2} \div 1\frac{3}{4}$

62. $2\frac{1}{4} \div 1\frac{1}{8}$

63. $1\frac{1}{3} \div 1\frac{5}{7}$

64. $1\frac{1}{6} \div 4\frac{2}{3}$

65. $1\frac{3}{4} \div 3\frac{1}{2}$

66. $1\frac{1}{8} \div 2\frac{1}{4}$

ADD WITH FRACTIONS AND MIXED NUMBERS

Skill 1: Add like fractions with sums less than 1

Fractions with the same denominator are called **like fractions.** To add like fractions, add the numerators.

For example, $2 + 1 = 3$. Use the same denominator, 5. Write the answer in lowest terms.

Add: $\frac{2}{5} + \frac{1}{5}$.

$$\begin{array}{r} \frac{2}{5} \\ + \frac{1}{5} \\ \hline \frac{3}{5} \end{array}$$
Add: 2 + 1

Add: $\frac{1}{8} + \frac{3}{8}$.

$$\begin{array}{r} \frac{1}{8} \\ + \frac{3}{8} \\ \hline \frac{4}{8} = \frac{1}{2} \end{array}$$
Add: 1 + 3

Add. Write the answer in lowest terms.

1. $\frac{1}{3} + \frac{1}{3}$

2. $\frac{1}{7} + \frac{2}{7}$

3. $\frac{1}{9} + \frac{4}{9}$

4. $\frac{4}{11} + \frac{3}{11}$

5. $\frac{1}{8} + \frac{3}{8}$

6. $\frac{3}{10} + \frac{1}{10}$

7. $\frac{9}{12} + \frac{1}{12}$

8. $\frac{1}{16} + \frac{1}{16}$

9. $\frac{2}{6} + \frac{2}{6}$

10. $\frac{2}{8} + \frac{4}{8}$

11. $\frac{1}{4} + \frac{1}{4}$

12. $\frac{3}{9} + \frac{3}{9}$

13. $\frac{6}{10} + \frac{2}{10}$

14. $\frac{3}{5} + \frac{1}{5}$

15. $\frac{2}{12} + \frac{4}{12}$

16. $\frac{3}{16} + \frac{5}{16}$

17. $\frac{6}{14} + \frac{4}{14}$

18. $\frac{2}{7} + \frac{3}{7}$

19. $\frac{1}{8} + \frac{1}{8}$

20. $\frac{5}{12} + \frac{3}{12}$

Skill 2: Add like fractions with sums equal to or greater than 1

Sometimes when you add like fractions, the sum will be equal to or greater than 1. Follow the rules for adding like fractions. Remember to simplify the answer.

Since $\frac{10}{8}$ is an improper fraction, rename it as a mixed number in simplest form.

Add: $\frac{5}{8} + \frac{5}{8}$.

$$\begin{array}{r} \frac{5}{8} \\ + \frac{5}{8} \\ \hline \frac{10}{8} = 1\frac{2}{8} = 1\frac{1}{4} \end{array}$$
Add: 5 + 5

Add. Write the answer in simplest form.

21. $\frac{1}{4} + \frac{3}{4}$

22. $\frac{3}{8} + \frac{5}{8}$

23. $\frac{8}{11} + \frac{7}{11}$

24. $\frac{4}{15} + \frac{13}{15}$

25. $\frac{5}{6} + \frac{5}{6}$

26. $\frac{7}{8} + \frac{3}{8}$

27. $\frac{5}{12} + \frac{11}{12}$

28. $\frac{11}{16} + \frac{9}{16}$

29. $\frac{2}{3} + \frac{1}{3}$

30. $\frac{3}{5} + \frac{4}{5}$

31. $\frac{6}{8} + \frac{6}{8}$

32. $\frac{1}{7} + \frac{6}{7}$

33. $\frac{7}{9} + \frac{5}{9}$

34. $\frac{2}{4} + \frac{3}{4}$

35. $\frac{4}{6} + \frac{4}{6}$

36. $\frac{3}{12} + \frac{11}{12}$

37. $\frac{11}{15} + \frac{4}{15}$

38. $\frac{9}{11} + \frac{4}{11}$

39. $\frac{6}{10} + \frac{8}{10}$

40. $\frac{8}{9} + \frac{7}{9}$

ADD WITH FRACTIONS AND MIXED NUMBERS

Skill 3: Add mixed numbers with like fractions

When you add mixed numbers with like fractions, add the fractions first. Then add the whole numbers. Simplify the answer when possible.

Add: $1\frac{1}{8} + 1\frac{3}{8}$.

$$1\frac{1}{8}$$
$$+1\frac{3}{8}$$
$$\overline{2\frac{4}{8} = 2\frac{1}{2}}$$

Add: $2\frac{3}{4} + 1\frac{3}{4}$.

$$2\frac{3}{4}$$
$$+1\frac{3}{4}$$
$$\overline{3\frac{6}{4} = 3 + 1\frac{2}{4} = 4\frac{2}{4} = 4\frac{1}{2}}$$

Add. Write the answer in simplest form.

41. $2\frac{2}{5} + 1\frac{1}{5}$

42. $1\frac{2}{7} + 1\frac{3}{7}$

43. $3\frac{1}{8} + 1\frac{1}{8}$

44. $4\frac{1}{6} + 2\frac{1}{6}$

45. $2\frac{1}{3} + 1\frac{2}{3}$

46. $4\frac{7}{8} + 2\frac{3}{8}$

47. $3\frac{7}{10} + 2\frac{9}{10}$

48. $5\frac{7}{12} + 3\frac{11}{12}$

Skill 4: Add unlike fractions

Fractions with different denominators are called **unlike fractions.** To add unlike fractions, first rename the fractions using the LCD. Then add the numerators and use the same denominator. Simplify the answer when possible.

Add: $\frac{1}{2} + \frac{1}{3}$.

$$\frac{1}{2} = \frac{3}{6}$$
$$+\frac{1}{3} = \frac{2}{6}$$
$$\overline{\frac{5}{6}}$$

Add: $\frac{2}{3} + \frac{5}{6}$.

$$\frac{2}{3} = \frac{4}{6}$$
$$+\frac{5}{6} = \frac{5}{6}$$
$$\overline{\frac{9}{6} = 1\frac{3}{6} = 1\frac{1}{2}}$$

Add. Write the answer in simplest form.

49. $\frac{1}{2} + \frac{1}{6}$

50. $\frac{3}{5} + \frac{1}{15}$

51. $\frac{1}{2} + \frac{3}{4}$

52. $\frac{7}{8} + \frac{3}{16}$

53. $\frac{1}{4} + \frac{2}{5}$

54. $\frac{3}{8} + \frac{1}{5}$

55. $\frac{1}{2} + \frac{3}{5}$

56. $\frac{5}{12} + \frac{7}{20}$

Skill 5: Add mixed numbers with unlike fractions

When you add mixed numbers with unlike fractions, first rename the fractions using the LCD. Then add the numerators and use the same denominator. Simplify the answer when possible.

Add: $2\frac{5}{6} + 1\frac{1}{3}$.

$$2\frac{5}{6} = 2\frac{5}{6}$$
$$+1\frac{1}{3} = 1\frac{2}{6}$$
$$\overline{3\frac{7}{6} + 3 + 1\frac{1}{6} = 4\frac{1}{6}}$$

Add. Write the answer in simplest form.

57. $1\frac{3}{8} + 1\frac{1}{4}$

58. $3\frac{3}{10} + 1\frac{1}{5}$

59. $1\frac{1}{2} + 1\frac{1}{3}$

60. $13\frac{3}{8} + 1\frac{1}{10}$

61. $3\frac{3}{4} + 1\frac{1}{8}$

62. $5\frac{5}{6} + 4\frac{7}{12}$

63. $8\frac{7}{12} + 5\frac{3}{4}$

64. $14\frac{9}{10} + 3\frac{1}{2}$

SUBTRACT WITH FRACTIONS AND MIXED NUMBERS

Skill 1: Subtract like fractions

To subtract **like fractions**, subtract the numerators. For example, $7 - 3 = 4$. Use the same denominator, 8. Write the answer in lowest terms.

Subtract: $\frac{7}{8} - \frac{3}{8}$.

$$\frac{7}{8}$$

Subtract: $7 - 3$

$$-\frac{3}{8}$$

$$\frac{4}{8} = \frac{1}{2}$$

Subtract. Write the answer in lowest terms.

1. $\frac{2}{3} - \frac{1}{3}$

2. $\frac{4}{5} - \frac{2}{5}$

3. $\frac{8}{9} - \frac{3}{9}$

4. $\frac{7}{11} - \frac{4}{11}$

5. $\frac{5}{6} - \frac{1}{6}$

6. $\frac{9}{10} - \frac{3}{10}$

7. $\frac{11}{12} - \frac{7}{12}$

8. $\frac{7}{20} - \frac{3}{20}$

9. $\frac{3}{4} - \frac{1}{4}$

10. $\frac{5}{7} - \frac{3}{7}$

11. $\frac{5}{10} - \frac{3}{10}$

12. $\frac{6}{8} - \frac{4}{8}$

Skill 2: Subtract unlike fractions

To subtract **unlike fractions**, first rename the fractions using the LCD. Then subtract the numerators and use the same denominator. Write the answer in lowest terms.

Subtract: $\frac{11}{12} - \frac{1}{4}$.

$$\frac{11}{12} = \frac{11}{12}$$

$$-\frac{1}{4} = \frac{3}{12}$$

$$\frac{8}{12} = \frac{2}{3}$$

Subtract. Write the answer in lowest terms.

13. $\frac{4}{9} - \frac{1}{3}$

14. $\frac{7}{8} - \frac{1}{4}$

15. $\frac{1}{3} - \frac{1}{4}$

16. $\frac{5}{6} - \frac{1}{5}$

17. $\frac{11}{14} - \frac{2}{7}$

18. $\frac{11}{15} - \frac{2}{5}$

19. $\frac{3}{4} - \frac{1}{6}$

20. $\frac{5}{6} - \frac{3}{10}$

21. $\frac{3}{5} - \frac{2}{10}$

22. $\frac{3}{4} - \frac{1}{2}$

23. $\frac{2}{3} - \frac{2}{5}$

24. $\frac{4}{5} - \frac{1}{2}$

Skill 3: Subtract mixed numbers with no renaming

To subtract mixed numbers, first subtract the fractions. For example, when subtracting $\frac{3}{5}$ and $\frac{1}{3}$, find the LCD first.

Then subtract the whole numbers. Simplify the answer when possible.

Subtract: $3\frac{3}{5} - 1\frac{1}{3}$.

$$3\frac{3}{5} = 3\frac{9}{15}$$

$$-1\frac{1}{3} = 1\frac{5}{15}$$

$$2\frac{4}{15}$$

SUBTRACT WITH FRACTIONS AND MIXED NUMBERS

Subtract. Write the answer in simplest form.

25. $5\frac{2}{3} - 2\frac{1}{3}$

26. $6\frac{4}{5} - 1\frac{1}{5}$

27. $6\frac{5}{12} - 4\frac{1}{12}$

28. $9\frac{11}{16} - 3\frac{9}{16}$

29. $2\frac{8}{9} - 1\frac{1}{3}$

30. $7\frac{7}{16} - 1\frac{1}{4}$

31. $9\frac{4}{5} - 2\frac{1}{2}$

32. $8\frac{5}{6} - 2\frac{1}{8}$

33. $4\frac{5}{6} - 2\frac{1}{3}$

34. $5\frac{11}{12} - 1\frac{2}{3}$

35. $5\frac{3}{4} - 1\frac{1}{2}$

36. $3\frac{9}{10} - 2\frac{3}{5}$

37. $11\frac{2}{3} - 3\frac{1}{2}$

38. $9\frac{3}{4} - 3\frac{1}{3}$

39. $7\frac{7}{12} - 6\frac{1}{4}$

40. $11\frac{3}{5} - 2\frac{1}{15}$

Skill 4: Rename whole numbers and mixed numbers

Sometimes you need to rename a whole number or a mixed number before you can subtract. For example, when subtracting 5 and $3\frac{2}{3}$, you must rename 5 as $4\frac{3}{3}$.

Rename: $5 = 4\frac{\blacksquare}{3}$.

$$5 = 4 + 1 = 4 + \frac{3}{3} = 4\frac{3}{3}$$

Rename: $2\frac{1}{3} = 1\frac{\blacksquare}{3}$.

$$2\frac{1}{3} = 1 + 1 + \frac{1}{3} = 1 + \frac{3}{3} + \frac{1}{3} = 1\frac{4}{3}$$

Rename.

41. $3 = 2\frac{\blacksquare}{3}$

42. $4 = 3\frac{\blacksquare}{5}$

43. $6 = 5\frac{\blacksquare}{7}$

44. $8 = 7\frac{\blacksquare}{11}$

45. $12 = 11\frac{\blacksquare}{15}$

46. $8\frac{1}{2} = 7\frac{\blacksquare}{2}$

47. $9\frac{3}{4} = 8\frac{\blacksquare}{4}$

48. $10\frac{7}{8} = 9\frac{\blacksquare}{8}$

49. $11\frac{1}{12} = 10\frac{\blacksquare}{12}$

50. $15\frac{2}{5} = 14\frac{\blacksquare}{5}$

Skill 5: Subtract mixed numbers with renaming

When you subtract mixed numbers, first find the LCD, if necessary. Then subtract the fractions. Rename when necessary. Finally, subtract the whole numbers. Simplify the answer when possible.

Subtract: $4\frac{1}{3} - 2\frac{1}{2}$.

$$4\frac{1}{3} = 4\frac{2}{6} = 3\frac{8}{6}$$
$$-2\frac{1}{2} = 2\frac{3}{6} = 2\frac{3}{6}$$
$$\overline{1\frac{5}{6}}$$

Subtract. Write the answer in simplest form.

51. $4 - 2\frac{1}{2}$

52. $5 - 3\frac{4}{5}$

53. $7 - 5\frac{2}{9}$

54. $18 - 13\frac{5}{11}$

55. $3\frac{1}{3} - 1\frac{2}{3}$

56. $5\frac{1}{6} - 3\frac{5}{6}$

57. $8\frac{3}{8} - 6\frac{7}{8}$

58. $11\frac{1}{16} - 8\frac{3}{16}$

59. $2\frac{1}{2} - 1\frac{2}{3}$

60. $6\frac{1}{3} - 3\frac{4}{5}$

61. $8\frac{1}{4} - 5\frac{1}{3}$

62. $11\frac{1}{2} - 3\frac{9}{10}$

63. $11\frac{1}{2} - 6\frac{4}{5}$

64. $10\frac{1}{4} - 6\frac{2}{3}$

65. $12\frac{1}{5} - 7\frac{5}{6}$

66. $14\frac{1}{6} - 9\frac{2}{3}$

RENAME FRACTIONS AS DECIMALS

Skill 1: Rename fractions as decimals

Some fractions can be renamed as decimals by first writing an equivalent fraction or mixed number with a denominator of 10, 100, 1,000, or so on.

Rename $\frac{3}{4}$ and $\frac{3}{2}$ as decimals.

$$\frac{3}{4} = \frac{75}{100} = 0.75 \qquad \frac{3}{2} = 1\frac{1}{2} = 1\frac{5}{10} = 1.5$$

Rename as a decimal.

1. $\frac{1}{10}$　　2. $\frac{7}{10}$　　3. $\frac{31}{100}$　　4. $\frac{47}{100}$　　5. $\frac{89}{100}$　　6. $\frac{123}{1,000}$　　7. $\frac{463}{1,000}$　　8. $\frac{620}{1,000}$

9. $\frac{1}{2}$　　10. $\frac{1}{4}$　　11. $\frac{2}{5}$　　12. $\frac{4}{5}$　　13. $\frac{7}{20}$　　14. $\frac{8}{25}$　　15. $\frac{16}{250}$　　16. $\frac{37}{500}$

17. $\frac{5}{2}$　　18. $\frac{5}{4}$　　19. $\frac{7}{5}$　　20. $\frac{11}{10}$　　21. $\frac{24}{20}$　　22. $\frac{55}{50}$　　23. $\frac{105}{100}$　　24. $\frac{125}{100}$

Skill 2: Rename fractions as terminating decimals

To rename any fraction as a decimal, divide the numerator by the denominator. If you can divide until the remainder is 0, the decimal is called a **terminating decimal.** For example, 0.375 is a terminating decimal.

Rename $\frac{3}{8}$ as a decimal.

$$\frac{3}{8} \rightarrow 8)\overline{3.000} \quad \leftarrow \textbf{Write additional}$$

```
        0.375
    8)3.000   ← Write additional
      2 4         zeros if necessary.
       60
       56
       40
       40
        0
```

Rename as a decimal.

25. $\frac{1}{8}$　　26. $\frac{5}{8}$　　27. $\frac{1}{16}$　　28. $\frac{14}{16}$　　29. $\frac{3}{40}$　　30. $\frac{9}{40}$　　31. $\frac{1}{80}$　　32. $\frac{7}{80}$

33. $\frac{11}{8}$　　34. $\frac{33}{8}$　　35. $\frac{22}{16}$　　36. $\frac{24}{16}$　　37. $\frac{45}{40}$　　38. $\frac{87}{40}$　　39. $\frac{90}{80}$　　40. $\frac{105}{80}$

Skill 3: Rename fractions as decimals rounded to given places

Sometimes it is more convenient to use a decimal rounded to a given place. In this case, divide the numerator by the denominator to 1 more place than the given place. Then round. For example, $0.833 \approx 0.83$ when rounded to the nearest hundredth.

Rename $\frac{5}{6}$ as a decimal to the nearest hundredth.

```
         0.833 ≈ 0.83
    6)5.000   ← Write 3 additional
      4 8         zeros.
       20
       18
        20
        18
         2
```

$$\frac{5}{6} \rightarrow 6)\overline{5.000}$$

RENAME FRACTIONS AS DECIMALS

Rename as a decimal to the nearest tenth.

41. $\frac{1}{9}$ **42.** $\frac{2}{11}$ **43.** $\frac{5}{11}$ **44.** $\frac{7}{15}$ **45.** $\frac{4}{21}$ **46.** $\frac{2}{30}$ **47.** $\frac{9}{40}$ **48.** $\frac{25}{60}$

49. $\frac{11}{9}$ **50.** $\frac{14}{13}$ **51.** $\frac{19}{15}$ **52.** $\frac{21}{20}$ **53.** $\frac{31}{25}$ **54.** $\frac{35}{30}$ **55.** $\frac{45}{40}$ **56.** $\frac{70}{60}$

Rename as a decimal to the nearest hundredth.

57. $\frac{4}{9}$ **58.** $\frac{6}{11}$ **59.** $\frac{8}{15}$ **60.** $\frac{1}{19}$ **61.** $\frac{2}{21}$ **62.** $\frac{6}{27}$ **63.** $\frac{7}{40}$ **64.** $\frac{8}{75}$

65. $\frac{8}{7}$ **66.** $\frac{13}{11}$ **67.** $\frac{15}{14}$ **68.** $\frac{37}{30}$ **69.** $\frac{60}{35}$ **70.** $\frac{67}{40}$ **71.** $\frac{65}{60}$ **72.** $\frac{80}{75}$

Skill 4: Rename fractions as repeating decimals

When you rename a fraction as a decimal by dividing, a digit or group of digits may repeat. For example, $\frac{1}{3}$ is a **repeating decimal** and can be written as $0.3333\ldots$ or $0.\overline{3}$. Both notations mean that the 3 repeats without end.

Rename $\frac{1}{3}$ and $\frac{13}{11}$ as a decimal.

$$\frac{1}{3} \rightarrow 3\overline{)1.0000} \quad \begin{array}{l}\leftarrow \textbf{Write 4 additional} \\ \textbf{zeros.}\end{array}$$

$$\frac{0.3333}{} \qquad \frac{1}{3} \approx 0.\overline{3}$$

$$\frac{13}{11} \rightarrow 11\overline{)13.0000} \quad \begin{array}{l}\leftarrow \textbf{Write 4 additional} \\ \textbf{zeros.}\end{array}$$

$$\frac{1.1818}{} \qquad \frac{13}{11} \approx 0.\overline{18}$$

Rename as a repeating decimal.

73. $\frac{2}{3}$ **74.** $\frac{1}{6}$ **75.** $\frac{5}{6}$ **76.** $\frac{5}{9}$ **77.** $\frac{1}{11}$ **78.** $\frac{5}{11}$ **79.** $\frac{1}{12}$ **80.** $\frac{5}{12}$

81. $\frac{4}{3}$ **82.** $\frac{7}{6}$ **83.** $\frac{10}{9}$ **84.** $\frac{13}{9}$ **85.** $\frac{13}{11}$ **86.** $\frac{17}{12}$ **87.** $\frac{20}{12}$ **88.** $\frac{40}{30}$

RATIOS, RATES, AND EQUAL RATIOS

Skill 1: Write ratios

A **ratio** is used to compare 2 quantities. A ratio is usually written using a fraction or a colon. The ratio $\frac{3}{4}$ or 3:4 can be read as 3 to 4, 3 for 4, or 3 out of 4.

There are 15 girls and 14 boys. Write each ratio in 2 ways.

Girls to boys: $\frac{15}{14}$ or 15:14

Girls to students: $\frac{15}{29}$ or 15 to 29

Write the ratio in 2 ways.

1. 7 girls and 11 boys; ratio of girls to boys

2. 25 records and 16 tapes; ratio of tapes to records

3. 8 African elephants and 4 Asian elephants; ratio of African elephants to all elephants

4. 16 club members and 23 nonmembers; ratio of club members to total people

Skill 2: Simplify ratios

To **simplify a ratio,** write it as a fraction with similar units. Then simplify the ratio by writing the fraction in lowest terms.

Simplify the ratio: 400 cm to 8 m.

THINK: **You need the same unit, cm.**
        8 m = 800 cm

$$\frac{400}{800} = \frac{1}{2}$$

Simplify the ratio.

5. 16 m to 2 m

6. 18 oz to 6 oz

7. 18 in. to 12 in.

8. 23 min to 46 min

9. 15 mL to 25 mL

10. 10 qt to 8 qt

11. 24 min to 1 h

12. 12 oz to 1 lb

13. 54 pennies to 5 dimes

14. 18 in. to 1 ft

15. 15 in. to 1 yd

16. 1 dime to 1 dollar

Skill 3: Compare ratios

To compare ratios, write both as fractions. Then use the **cross-product rule** to test if they are equal, that is, if they have the same value.

Write = or ≠.

3:4 ● 4:5 or $\frac{3}{4}$ ● $\frac{4}{5}$

$3 \times 5 \stackrel{?}{=} 4 \times 4$

15 ≠ 16   So $\frac{3}{4} \neq \frac{4}{5}$.

Write = or ≠.

17. 1:2 ● 3:4

18. 2:3 ● 4:6

19. 6:8 ● 3:4

20. 5:10 ● 1:3

21. 7:10 ● 8:11

22. 1:3 ● 2:6

RATIOS, RATES, AND EQUAL RATIOS

Skill 4: Find equal ratios

Ratios that have the same value are called **equal ratios.** To find equal ratios, write the ratios as fractions. Then find the equal ratios by writing the fractions with a common denominator.

Which are equal ratios?
2:3, 1:5, 4 to 5, 10 to 15

$\frac{2}{3} = \frac{10}{15}$ $\frac{1}{5} = \frac{3}{15}$ $\frac{4}{5} = \frac{12}{15}$ $\frac{10}{15} = \frac{10}{15}$

So 2:3 = 10:15.

Which are equal ratios?

23. 1:5, 1:3, 3:15

24. 1:2, 2:4, 3:5

25. 2:3, 5 to 6, 4 to 6

26. 3 to 4, 7 to 8, 12 to 16

27. 1 to 2, 3 to 5, 6 to 10, 1 to 5

28. 3 to 12, 1 to 4, 2 to 6, 1 to 2

Skill 5: Write rates

A **rate** compares 2 quantities with unlike units. Rates, like ratios, can be written using a fraction or a colon.

Write the rate in 2 ways.

30 mi per h: $\frac{30}{1}$ or 30:1

Write the rate in 2 ways.

29. $25 for 2 tapes

30. 35 mi per h

31. 25 mi per gal

32. 3 pens for 79¢

33. 2 jars for $1.53

34. 30 revolutions per min

Skill 6: Find unit rates

The rate for 1 unit is called the **unit rate.** To find a unit rate, write the rate as a fraction. Then divide the numerator by the denominator.

Find the unit rate.
Five pieces of gum cost 55¢.
How much does 1 piece cost?

cost → $\frac{55¢}{5}$ ← number 55¢ ÷ 5 = 11¢

The unit rate is 11¢ per piece.

Find the unit rate.

35. You traveled 165 mi in 3 h. How many miles did you average per hour?

36. If 5 cucumbers cost $1.20, how much does 1 cost?

37. Roy serviced 150 cars in 3 h. About how many did he service each hour?

38. Gail used 28 gal of gas this week. About how many gallons of gas did she use each day?

PROPORTIONS AND SOLVING PROPORTIONS

Skill 1: Write proportions

A **proportion** is a statement that 2 ratios are equal. For example, $\frac{1}{2}$ and $\frac{2}{4}$ are equal ratios, so $\frac{1}{2} = \frac{2}{4}$ is a proportion. Proportions can be written in 2 ways, using fractions or colons.

Write the proportion in 2 ways:
1 is to 3 as 2 is to 6.

Using fractions: $\frac{1}{3} = \frac{2}{6}$

Using colons: $1:3 = 2:6$

Write the proportion in 2 ways.

1. 4 is to 8 as 8 is to 16

2. 1 is to 4 as 3 is to 12

3. 4 is to 10 as 40 is to 100

4. 0.2 is to 0.4 as 0.3 is to 0.6

5. 1 is to 16 as 2 is to 32

6. 1 is to 7 as 2 is to 14

7. 3 is to 5 as 9 is to 15

8. 1 is to 2 as 25 is to 50

9. 2 is to 3 as 6 is to 9

10. 2 is to 5 as 4 is to 10

11. 3 is to 10 as 30 is to 100

12. 3 is to 4 as 12 is to 16

13. 0.6 is to 1.2 as 1.8 is to 3.6

14. 0.5 is to 1.5 as 2 is to 6

Skill 2: Determine if 2 ratios form a proportion

Two ratios form a proportion if the **cross products** are equal. To determine whether you have a proportion, write the proportion using fractions. Then check if the cross products are equal.

Is this a proportion?
$3:6 \overset{?}{=} 4:8$

$\frac{3}{6} \bowtie \frac{4}{8}$

$3 \times 8 \overset{?}{=} 4 \times 6$
$24 = 24$

Yes, it is a proportion.

Is it a proportion? Write *yes* or *no*.

15. $3:15 \overset{?}{=} 4:20$

16. $6:8 \overset{?}{=} 7:10$

17. $\frac{2}{5} \overset{?}{=} \frac{3}{10}$

18. $\frac{3}{7} \overset{?}{=} \frac{6}{14}$

19. $\frac{1}{0.2} \overset{?}{=} \frac{5}{1.0}$

20. $\frac{3}{0.2} \overset{?}{=} \frac{6}{0.4}$

21. $3:4 \overset{?}{=} 6:8$

22. $9:27 \overset{?}{=} 14:52$

23. $2:7 \overset{?}{=} 6:21$

24. $3:5 \overset{?}{=} 8:10$

25. $\frac{7}{10} \overset{?}{=} \frac{40}{45}$

26. $\frac{3}{4} \overset{?}{=} \frac{15}{20}$

PROPORTIONS AND SOLVING PROPORTIONS

Skill 3: Solve proportions with whole numbers

To solve a proportion, use the fact that in a proportion the cross products are equal. Remember to write a proportion using fractions first. Use cross products to write an equation. Then solve and check.

Solve: $\frac{n}{7} = \frac{3}{21}$.

$$\frac{n}{7} \bowtie \frac{3}{21}$$

$$n \times 21 = 3 \times 7$$

$$n \times 21 = 21$$

$$n = 21 \div 21$$

$$n = 1$$

Solve the proportion.

27. $\frac{n}{3} = \frac{2}{6}$ **28.** $\frac{1}{n} = \frac{3}{12}$ **29.** $\frac{1}{2} = \frac{n}{20}$ **30.** $\frac{1}{5} = \frac{4}{n}$ **31.** $\frac{1}{20} = \frac{5}{n}$

32. $\frac{n}{5} = \frac{10}{25}$ **33.** $\frac{n}{7} = \frac{12}{42}$ **34.** $\frac{n}{9} = \frac{49}{63}$ **35.** $\frac{8}{9} = \frac{64}{n}$ **36.** $\frac{2}{11} = \frac{8}{n}$

37. $\frac{3}{n} = \frac{30}{100}$ **38.** $\frac{7}{n} = \frac{63}{72}$ **39.** $\frac{9}{n} = \frac{99}{121}$ **40.** $\frac{3}{7} = \frac{n}{91}$ **41.** $\frac{12}{17} = \frac{n}{34}$

42. $\frac{6}{10} = \frac{n}{100}$ **43.** $\frac{7}{12} = \frac{21}{n}$ **44.** $\frac{9}{15} = \frac{n}{30}$ **45.** $\frac{19}{20} = \frac{57}{n}$ **46.** $\frac{5}{6} = \frac{n}{48}$

Skill 4: Solve proportions with fractions or decimals

To solve a proportion with fractions or decimals, use the same cross-product method you used with whole numbers.

Solve: $\frac{4}{0.7} = \frac{n}{7}$.

$$\frac{4}{0.7} \bowtie \frac{n}{7}$$

$$4 \times 7 = n \times 0.7$$

$$28 = n \times 0.7$$

$$28 \div 0.7 = n$$

$$40 = n$$

Solve the proportion.

47. $\frac{2}{4} = \frac{n}{3}$ **48.** $\frac{3}{4} = \frac{n}{22}$ **49.** $\frac{1}{4} = \frac{n}{31}$ **50.** $\frac{n}{2} = \frac{48}{10}$ **51.** $\frac{n}{15} = \frac{30}{60}$

52. $\frac{1}{4} = \frac{0.2}{n}$ **53.** $\frac{0.4}{1} = \frac{n}{2}$ **54.** $\frac{n}{4.2} = \frac{1}{6}$ **55.** $\frac{1}{0.5} = \frac{5}{n}$ **56.** $\frac{n}{2} = \frac{1.6}{4}$

57. $\frac{1}{3.2} = \frac{5}{n}$ **58.** $\frac{1}{0.7} = \frac{n}{2.8}$ **59.** $\frac{n}{4.9} = \frac{1}{7}$ **60.** $\frac{2.4}{n} = \frac{3}{5}$ **61.** $\frac{n}{6.5} = \frac{2}{26}$

62. $\frac{\frac{1}{2}}{2} = \frac{n}{4}$ **63.** $\frac{\frac{2}{3}}{3} = \frac{2}{n}$ **64.** $\frac{n}{49} = \frac{\frac{4}{7}}{7}$ **65.** $\frac{n}{25} = \frac{\frac{2}{5}}{10}$ **66.** $\frac{3}{n} = \frac{\frac{3}{4}}{3}$

EQUIVALENT FRACTIONS, DECIMALS, AND PERCENTS

Skill 1: Rename fractions with denominators of 100 as percents

Percent means **per hundred** or **hundredths.** The symbol % is used for percent. Remember that 1 (whole) = $\frac{100}{100}$ = 100%.

Rename $\frac{46}{100}$ and $\frac{138}{100}$ as percents.

$\frac{46}{100}$ = 46 hundredths = 46%

$\frac{138}{100}$ = 138 hundredths = 138%

Rename as a percent.

1. $\frac{7}{100}$　　2. $\frac{11}{100}$　　3. $\frac{21}{100}$　　4. $\frac{30}{100}$　　5. $\frac{47}{100}$　　6. $\frac{99}{100}$

7. $\frac{109}{100}$　　8. $\frac{113}{100}$　　9. $\frac{137}{100}$　　10. $\frac{151}{100}$　　11. $\frac{169}{100}$　　12. $\frac{183}{100}$

Skill 2: Rename percents as fractions in lowest terms

When you rename a percent as a fraction, first write it as a fraction with a denominator of 100. Then write the fraction in lowest terms.

Rename 16% and $33\frac{1}{3}$% as fractions or mixed numbers in lowest terms.

16% = 16 hundredths = $\frac{16}{100}$ = $\frac{4}{25}$

$33\frac{1}{3}$% = $33\frac{1}{3}$ hundredths = $\frac{33\frac{1}{3}}{100}$

$= 33\frac{1}{3} \div 100 = \frac{\overset{1}{\cancel{100}}}{3} \times \frac{1}{\underset{1}{\cancel{100}}} = \frac{1}{3}$

Rename as a fraction or a mixed number in lowest terms.

13. 13%　　14. 21%　　15. 53%　　16. 67%　　17. 71%　　18. 99%

19. 15%　　20. 26%　　21. 40%　　22. 75%　　23. 82%　　24. 94%

25. 101%　　26. 117%　　27. 123%　　28. 145%　　29. 150%　　30. 175%

31. $\frac{1}{4}$%　　32. $\frac{1}{2}$%　　33. $\frac{9}{10}$%　　34. $12\frac{1}{2}$%　　35. $66\frac{2}{3}$%　　36. $83\frac{1}{3}$%

Skill 3: Rename decimals as percents

When you rename a decimal as a percent, move the decimal point 2 places to the right and add a percent sign.

Rename 0.21 as a percent.

0.21 → 0.21 → 21%

Sometimes it is necessary to write additional zeros before you move the decimal.

Rename 0.8 as a percent.

0.8 → 0.80 → 80%

EQUIVALENT FRACTIONS, DECIMALS, AND PERCENTS

Rename as a percent.

37. 0.17	38. 0.26	39. 0.31	40. 0.67	41. 0.72	42. 0.91
43. 0.432	44. 0.587	45. 0.621	46. 0.789	47. 0.801	48. 0.907
49. 0.1	50. 0.3	51. 0.4	52. 0.5	53. 0.6	54. 0.9
55. 1	56. 1.5	57. 2	58. 2.25	59. 2.5	60. 3

Skill 4: Rename percents as decimals

To rename a percent as a decimal, move the decimal point 2 places to the left and drop the percent sign.

Sometimes it is necessary to write additional zeros before you move the decimal point.

Rename 32% as a decimal.

$32\% \rightarrow \underset{\smile}{32} \rightarrow 0.32$

Rename 7% as a decimal.

$7\% \rightarrow \underset{\smile}{07} \rightarrow 0.07$

Rename as a decimal.

61. 11%	62. 18%	63. 37%	64. 42%	65. 79%	66. 83%
67. 24.3%	68. 36.8%	69. 42.7%	70. 59.3%	71. 67.2%	72. 81.4%
73. 1%	74. 2%	75. 5%	76. 6%	77. 8%	78. 9%
79. 100%	80. 125%	81. 150%	82. 175%	83. 200%	84. 300%

Skill 5: Rename fractions as percents using division

You can rename a fraction as a percent. First rename the fraction as a decimal using division. Then rename the decimal as a percent.

Rename $\frac{1}{4}$ and $\frac{4}{3}$ as percents.

$$\frac{1}{4} \rightarrow 4\overline{)1.00}^{\,0.25} \rightarrow 0.\underset{\smile}{25} \rightarrow 25\%$$

$$\frac{4}{3} \rightarrow 3\overline{)4.00}^{\,1.33\frac{1}{3}} \rightarrow 1.\underset{\smile}{33}\tfrac{1}{3} \rightarrow 133\tfrac{1}{3}\%$$

Rename as a percent using division.

85. $\frac{1}{10}$	86. $\frac{1}{5}$	87. $\frac{1}{4}$	88. $\frac{3}{10}$	89. $\frac{1}{2}$	90. $\frac{3}{4}$
91. $\frac{11}{10}$	92. $\frac{6}{5}$	93. $\frac{5}{4}$	94. $\frac{14}{10}$	95. $\frac{3}{2}$	96. $\frac{7}{4}$
97. $\frac{1}{3}$	98. $\frac{1}{6}$	99. $\frac{1}{8}$	100. $\frac{2}{9}$	101. $\frac{4}{7}$	102. $\frac{7}{8}$
103. $\frac{5}{3}$	104. $\frac{7}{6}$	105. $\frac{9}{8}$	106. $\frac{11}{9}$	107. $\frac{11}{7}$	108. $\frac{13}{8}$

FIND THE PERCENT OF A NUMBER

Skill 1: Find the percent of a number using a fraction

To find the percent of a number, you solve an equation of the form $a\%$ of $b = c$. First substitute the values you know. Then solve for the unknown value. Rename the percent as a fraction and then multiply.

Find $5\frac{1}{2}\%$ of 50.

$$\begin{array}{cccc} a\% & \text{of} & b & = & c \\ \downarrow & & \downarrow & & \downarrow \\ 5\frac{1}{2}\% & \times & 50 & = & c \end{array}$$

THINK: $5\frac{1}{2}\% = \dfrac{5\frac{1}{2}}{100}$

$$= 5\frac{1}{2} \div 100 = \frac{11}{2} \times \frac{1}{100} = \frac{11}{200}$$

$$\frac{11}{200} \times 50 = \frac{11}{\underset{4}{200}} \times \frac{\overset{1}{50}}{1} = \frac{11}{4} = 2\frac{3}{4}$$

Find the answer using a fraction.

1. 11% of 25
2. 17% of 32
3. 21% of 58
4. 47% of 89

5. 10% of 60
6. 44% of 100
7. 40% of 125
8. 95% of 200

9. 15% of 50
10. 25% of 110
11. 90% of 175
12. 75% of 150

13. 8% of 20
14. 13% of 60
15. 21% of 44
16. 35% of 75

17. 51% of 90
18. 69% of 200
19. 75% of 700
20. 80% of 800

21. $\frac{1}{4}\%$ of 10
22. $\frac{1}{2}\%$ of 25
23. $6\frac{1}{2}\%$ of 100
24. $33\frac{1}{3}\%$ of 150

25. $\frac{1}{2}\%$ of 50
26. $\frac{1}{5}\%$ of 20
27. $4\frac{1}{4}\%$ of 200
28. $6\frac{1}{3}\%$ of 300

29. $\frac{1}{8}\%$ of 40
30. $\frac{1}{10}\%$ of 300
31. $17\frac{1}{2}\%$ of 600
32. $66\frac{2}{3}\%$ of 900

33. $\frac{1}{2}\%$ of 60
34. $\frac{1}{4}\%$ of 25
35. $7\frac{1}{3}\%$ of 90
36. $19\frac{3}{5}\%$ of 950

37. $\frac{1}{5}\%$ of 125
38. $\frac{1}{3}\%$ of 150
39. $24\frac{2}{5}\%$ of 50
40. $17\frac{2}{3}\%$ of 150

Skill 2: Find the percent of a number using a decimal

To find the percent of a number, you can first rename the percent as a decimal and then multiply.

Find 6.5% of 100.

$$\begin{array}{cccc} a\% & \text{of} & b & = & c \\ \downarrow & & \downarrow & & \downarrow \\ 6.5\% & \times & 100 & = & c \end{array}$$

THINK: $6.5\% \rightarrow 06.5 \rightarrow 0.065$

$0.065 \times 100 = 6.5$

FIND THE PERCENT OF A NUMBER

Find the answer using a decimal.

41. 10% of 30	**42.** 25% of 50	**43.** 36% of 25	**44.** 75% of 63
45. 10% of 110	**46.** 25% of 160	**47.** 45% of 300	**48.** 75% of 500
49. 15% of 90	**50.** 21% of 85	**51.** 52% of 98	**52.** 84% of 156
53. 10% of 70	**54.** 75% of 100	**55.** 30% of 40	**56.** 27% of 80
57. 11% of 56	**58.** 19% of 28	**59.** 45% of 150	**60.** 88% of 230
61. 7.5% of 30	**62.** 15.5% of 45	**63.** 25.5% of 86	**64.** 80.5% of 91
65. 13.4% of 94	**66.** 26.8% of 72	**67.** 16.45% of 40	**68.** 24.33% of 69
69. 12.5% of 96	**70.** 15.5% of 50	**71.** 2.5% of 120	**72.** 5.5% of 24
73. 9.2% of 30	**74.** 6.4% of 25	**75.** 15.8% of 75	**76.** 12.6% of 50
77. 15.75% of 100	**78.** 2.25% of 80	**79.** 11.33% of 20	**80.** 14.125% of 40

Skill 3: Find the percent of a number when the percent is greater than 100%

When you find the percent of a number when the percent is greater than 100%, the answer will be greater than the original number. For example, 150% of 300 = 450. Notice that the answer, 450, is greater than the original number, 300.

Find 150% of 300.

$$a\% \quad \text{of} \quad b = c$$
$$\downarrow \quad \downarrow \quad \downarrow \quad \quad \downarrow$$
$$150\% \times 300 = c$$

THINK: $150\% \rightarrow 1\underline{50} \rightarrow 1.5$

$1.5 \times 300 = 450$

Find the percent of the number.

81. 111% of 200	**82.** 150% of 400	**83.** 150% of 44	**84.** 160% of 85
85. 170% of 150	**86.** 175% of 400	**87.** 180% of 500	**88.** 200% of 225
89. 103% of 50	**90.** 117% of 120	**91.** 125% of 50	**92.** 165% of 222
93. 200% of 6.4	**94.** 300% of 105.5	**95.** 150% of 4.4	**96.** 175% of 55.7
97. 225% of 3.5	**98.** 450% of 2.4	**99.** 375% of 50.6	**100.** 290% of 99.9
101. 500% of 200	**102.** 250% of 400	**103.** 875% of 212	**104.** 999% of 100
105. 120% of 100	**106.** 140% of 125	**107.** 160% of 350	**108.** 180% of 36
109. 125% of 225	**110.** 132% of 70	**111.** 220% of 400	**112.** 275% of 500
113. 111% of 7.2	**114.** 120% of 8.9	**115.** 200% of 2.8	**116.** 360% of 9.8
117. 240% of 20.5	**118.** 350% of 50.5	**119.** 425% of 75.2	**120.** 600% of 80.5

FIND THE PERCENT ONE NUMBER IS OF ANOTHER

Skill 1: Find the percent using a fraction

When you solve equations of the form $a\%$ of $b = c$, substitute the values that you know. Then solve for the unknown value.

What percent of 100 is 25?

$$
\begin{array}{cccc}
a\% & \text{of} & b & = c \\
\downarrow & \downarrow & \downarrow & \downarrow \\
a & \times & 100 & = 25
\end{array}
$$

$$a = 25 \div 100 = \frac{25}{100} = 25\%$$

Find the answer using a fraction.

1. What percent of 100 is 30?

2. What percent of 100 is 45?

3. What percent of 5 is 4?

4. What percent of 25 is 5?

5. What percent of 12 is 4?

6. What percent of 24 is 21?

7. What percent of 200 is 100?

8. What percent of 90 is 15 ?

9. What percent of 100 is 10?

10. What percent of 4 is 2?

11. What percent of 36 is 9?

12. 8 is what percent of 32?

13. 50 is what percent of 500?

14. 7 is what percent of 28?

15. 60 is what percent of 100?

16. 90 is what percent of 100?

17. 16 is what percent of 64?

18. 10 is what percent of 50?

19. 6 is what percent of 36?

20. 8 is what percent of 64?

Skill 2: Find the percent using a decimal

When you find the percent one number is of another, you can use a decimal.

What percent of 80 is 20?

$$
\begin{array}{cccc}
a\% & \text{of} & b & = c \\
\downarrow & \downarrow & \downarrow & \downarrow \\
a & \times & 80 & = 20
\end{array}
$$

$$a = 20 \div 80 = 0.25$$

$$a = 0.25 \rightarrow 0.\underset{\smile}{25} \rightarrow 25\%$$

FIND THE PERCENT ONE NUMBER IS OF ANOTHER

Find the answer using a decimal.

21. What percent of 100 is 80?

22. What percent of 10 is 6?

23. What percent of 5 is 3?

24. What percent of 75 is 15?

25. What percent of 200 is 75?

26. What percent of 11 is 5.5?

27. What percent of 500 is 25?

28. What percent of 125 is 10.5?

29. What percent of 100 is 15?

30. What percent of 9 is 3?

31. What percent of 300 is 45?

32. 70 is what percent of 100?

33. 25 is what percent of 50?

34. 8 is what percent of 10?

35. 4 is what percent of 32?

36. 4.2 is what percent of 42?

37. 9 is what percent of 45?

38. 6.7 is what percent of 20.1?

39. 6 is what percent of 15?

40. 25 is what percent of 75?

Skill 3: Find a percent greater than 100%

Sometimes the percent can be greater than 100%. You can estimate that your answer will be greater than 100%. For example, notice that in $a \times 40 = 60$, $c > b$, or $60 > 40$. Therefore, the answer (%) is greater than 100%.

What percent of 40 is 60?

$$a\% \text{ of } b = c$$
$$\downarrow \quad \downarrow \; \downarrow \qquad \downarrow$$
$$a \; \times \; 40 = 60$$
$$a = 60 \div 40 = 1.5$$
$$a = 1.5 = 1.50 \rightarrow 150\%$$

Find the answer.

41. What percent of 100 is 150?

42. What percent of 100 is 200?

43. What percent of 25 is 60?

44. What percent of 40 is 160?

45. What percent of 10 is 55?

46. What percent of 10.25 is 20.5?

47. What percent of 5 is 60?

48. What percent of 2.5 is 6.25?

49. 130 is what percent of 100?

50. 165 is what percent of 100?

51. 150 is what percent of 50?

52. 90 is what percent of 30?

53. 90 is what percent of 40?

54. 76.5 is what percent of 25.5?

FIND A NUMBER WHEN A PERCENT OF IT IS KNOWN

Skill 1: Find the number using a fraction

To find a number when a percent of it is known, you solve an equation of the form $a\%$ of $b = c$. First substitute the values that you know. Then solve for the unknown value.

16 is 20% of what number?

$$a\% \text{ of } b = c$$
$$\downarrow \quad \downarrow \quad \downarrow \quad \quad \downarrow$$
$$20\% \times b = 16$$

THINK: $20\% = \frac{20}{100}$

$$\frac{20}{100} \times b = 16$$

$$b = \frac{16}{1} \div \frac{20}{100} = \frac{\overset{4}{\cancel{16}}}{1} \times \frac{100}{\underset{5}{\cancel{20}}} = \frac{400}{5} = 80$$

Find the answer using a fraction.

1. 10 is 10% of what number?

2. 30 is 30% of what number?

3. 22 is 11% of what number?

4. 52 is 13% of what number?

5. 65 is 25% of what number?

6. 75 is 50% of what number?

7. 150 is 75% of what number?

8. 200 is 80% of what number?

9. 20 is 5% of what number?

10. 60 is 40% of what number?

11. 36 is 15% of what number?

12. 85 is 25% of what number?

13. 294 is $4\frac{1}{5}\%$ of what number?

14. 150 is $7\frac{1}{2}\%$ of what number?

15. 44 is $5\frac{1}{2}\%$ of what number?

16. 105 is $10\frac{1}{2}\%$ of what number?

17. 45 is $2\frac{1}{4}\%$ of what number?

18. 110 is $4\frac{2}{5}\%$ of what number?

Skill 2: Find the number using a decimal

To find a number when a percent of it is known, you can use a decimal.

21 is 7% of what number?

$$a\% \text{ of } b = c$$
$$\downarrow \quad \downarrow \quad \downarrow \quad \quad \downarrow$$
$$7\% \times b = 21$$

THINK: $7\% \rightarrow \underset{\smile}{.07.} \rightarrow 0.07$

$$0.07 \times b = 21$$

$$b = 21 \div 0.07 = 300$$

FIND A NUMBER WHEN A PERCENT OF IT IS KNOWN

Find the answer using a decimal.

19. 9 is 9% of what number?

20. 23 is 23% of what number?

21. 15 is 20% of what number?

22. 18 is 30% of what number?

23. 105 is 75% of what number?

24. 120 is 50% of what number?

25. 11 is 20% of what number?

26. 20 is 80% of what number?

27. 16 is 80% of what number?

28. 36 is 12% of what number?

29. 30.5 is 50% of what number?

30. 7.2 is 10% of what number?

31. 20.25 is 50% of what number?

32. 200.4 is 80% of what number?

33. 7.5 is 20% of what number?

34. 9.75 is 75% of what number?

35. 130.5 is 25% of what number?

36. 89.3 is 38% of what number?

Skill 3: Find the number when the percent is greater than 100%

Remember, sometimes the percent is greater than 100%. Notice that when this happens $c > b$, for example, $84 > 70$.

84 is 120% of what number?

$$a\% \quad \text{of} \quad b = c$$
$$\downarrow \quad \downarrow \quad \downarrow \quad \quad \downarrow$$
$$120\% \times \quad b = 84$$

THINK: $120\% \rightarrow 1\underline{20}. \rightarrow 1.2$

$1.2 \times b = 84$

$b = 84 \div 1.2 = 70$

Find the answer.

37. 30 is 100% of what number?

38. 170 is 100% of what number?

39. 222 is 111% of what number?

40. 286 is 143% of what number?

41. 25 is 125% of what number?

42. 105 is 150% of what number?

43. 22 is 125% of what number?

44. 480 is 150% of what number?

45. 85.6 is 200% of what number?

46. 16.5 is 300% of what number?

47. 6.4 is 128% of what number?

48. 26.4 is 132% of what number?

49. 45.5 is 455% of what number?

50. 36.5 is 200% of what number?

PERCENT AND PROPORTION

Skill 1: Find the percent of a number

Percent problems can be solved using the percent formula, $a\%$ of $b = c$, or using the proportion, $\frac{a}{100} = \frac{c}{b}$. First substitute the values you know. Then solve for the unknown value. Remember, use cross products to solve the proportion.

Find 6% of 50.

THINK: $a = 6$, $b = 50$, $c = ?$

$$\frac{a}{100} = \frac{c}{b}$$

$$\frac{6}{100} = \frac{c}{50}$$

$$\frac{6}{100} \bowtie \frac{c}{50}$$

$$6 \times 50 = c \times 100$$

$$300 = c \times 100$$

$$300 \div 100 = c$$

$$3 = c$$

So 6% of 50 is 3.

Find the answer using a proportion.

1. 10% of 50

2. 20% of 80

3. 25% of 60

4. 30% of 90

5. 10% of 160

6. 25% of 180

7. 50% of 150

8. 75% of 120

9. 11% of 50

10. 42% of 85

11. 41.5% of 60

12. 25.5% of 36

13. $\frac{1}{4}\%$ of 20

14. $\frac{1}{2}\%$ of 50

15. $3\frac{1}{2}\%$ of 50

16. $33\frac{1}{3}\%$ of 250

17. 100% of 16

18. 150% of 54

19. 200% of 52

20. 300% of 75

Skill 2: Find the percent one number is of another

To find the percent, you can use the percent formula, $a\%$ of $b = c$, or the proportion, $\frac{a}{100} = \frac{c}{b}$. When finding the percent, remember to include the % sign in your final answer.

What percent of 16 is 4?

THINK: $a = ?$, $b = 16$, $c = 4$

$$\frac{a}{100} = \frac{c}{b}$$

$$\frac{a}{100} = \frac{4}{16}$$

$$\frac{a}{100} \bowtie \frac{4}{16}$$

$$a \times 16 = 4 \times 100$$

$$a \times 16 = 400$$

$$a = 400 \div 16 = 25$$

So 4 is 25% of 16.

PERCENT AND PROPORTION

Find the answer using a proportion.

21. What percent of 100 is 40?

22. What percent of 100 is 75?

23. What percent of 10 is 8?

24. What percent of 20 is 4?

25. What percent of 150 is 75?

26. What percent of 400 is 200?

27. 4 is what percent of 12?

28. 150 is what percent of 400?

29. 5.4 is what percent of 54?

30. 7.8 is what percent of 39?

31. 140 is what percent of 100?

32. 160 is what percent of 80?

Skill 3: Find a number when a percent of it is known

To find a number when a percent of it is known, you can use the percent formula, $a\%$ of $b = c$, or the proportion, $\frac{a}{100} = \frac{c}{b}$.
Remember, sometimes the percent is greater than 100%. When this happens $c > b$, for example, $30 > 20$.

30 is 150% of what number?

THINK: $a = 150$, $b = ?$, c 30

$$\frac{a}{100} = \frac{c}{b}$$

$$\frac{150}{100} = \frac{30}{b}$$

$$\frac{150}{100} \bowtie \frac{30}{b}$$

$$150 \times b = 30 \times 100$$

$$150 \times b = 3,000$$

$$b = 3,000 \div 150 = 20$$

So 30 is 150% of 20.

Find the answer using a proportion.

33. 20 is 100% of what number?

34. 40 is 400% of what number?

35. 15 is 125% of what number?

36. 36 is 120% of what number?

37. 210 is 175% of what number?

38. 240 is 150% of what number?

39. 87.9 is 300% of what number?

40. 210 is 150% of what number?

41. 16.3 is 500% of what number?

42. 8.3 is 100% of what number?

43. 30 is 125% of what number?

44. 140 is 200% of what number?

45. 8.7 is 150% of what number?

46. 500 is 125% of what number?

47. 13.2 is 200% of what number?

48. 4.23 is 150% of what number?

PERCENT OF INCREASE AND DECREASE

Skill 1: Find percent of increase using the equation method

To find **percent of increase** using the equation method, first find the amount of change (increase). Then use this formula:

AMOUNT OF CHANGE = RATE × ORIGINAL AMOUNT

Finally, rename the answer as a percent.

Find the percent of increase.
Last week: $20
This week: $30

THINK: The amount of change is 30 − 20 = 10.

AMOUNT OF CHANGE = RATE × ORIGINAL AMOUNT

$$10 = r \times 20$$
$$10 \div 20 = r$$
$$0.5 = r$$

$$0.5 \rightarrow 0.5\underset{\smile}{0} \rightarrow 50\%$$

So the percent of increase is 50%.

Find the percent of increase.

1. Last week: $50
   This week: $60

2. Test 1: 80
   Test 2: 100

3. Game 1: 15
   Game 2: 18

4. Last year: 250
   This year: 320

5. Morning: $500
   Afternoon: $850

6. Bought: $520
   Sold: $650

7. Semester 1: 80
   Semester 2: 90

8. Last week: 600
   This week: 800

9. Game 1: 30
   Game 2: 50

Skill 2: Find percent of increase using the ratio method

To find percent of increase using the ratio method, first find the amount of change. Then find this ratio:

$$\frac{\text{AMOUNT OF CHANGE}}{\text{ORIGINAL AMOUNT}}$$

Finally, rename the answer as a percent.

Find the percent of increase.
Game 1: 10
Game 2: 30

THINK: The amount of change is 30 − 10 = 20.

$$\frac{\text{AMOUNT OF CHANGE}}{\text{ORIGINAL AMOUNT}} = \frac{20}{10} = 2$$

$$2 \rightarrow 200 \rightarrow 2\underset{\smile}{00}\%$$

So the percent of increase is 200%.

Find the percent of increase.

10. Last year: 50
    This year: 75

11. Week 1: 25
    Week 2: 30

12. Bought: 60
    Sold: 90

13. Bought: $40
    Sold: $80

14. Year 1: 140
    Year 2: 175

15. Last year: $750
    This year: $3,000

16. Game 1: 64
    Game 2: 72

17. Last week: 160
    This week: 180

18. Month 1: $120
    Month 2: $160

PERCENT OF INCREASE AND DECREASE

Skill 3: Find percent of decrease using the equation method

To find **percent of decrease** using the equation method, first find the amount of change (decrease). Then use this formula:

AMOUNT OF CHANGE = RATE × ORIGINAL AMOUNT

Finally, rename the answer as a percent.

Find the percent of decrease.
Last week: 60
This week: 48

THINK: The amount of change is 60 − 48 = 12.

AMOUNT OF CHANGE = RATE × ORIGINAL AMOUNT
$$12 = r \times 60$$
$$12 \div 60 = r$$
$$0.2 = r$$

$$0.2 \rightarrow 0.2\underset{\smile}{0} \rightarrow 20\%$$

So the percent of decrease is 20%.

Find the percent of decrease.

19. Last year: 100
This year: 60

20. Morning: 80
Afternoon: 40

21. Bought: 25
Sold: 5

22. Last week: $150
This week: $90

23. Year 1: 300
Year 2: 180

24. Period 1: 500
Period 2: 450

25. Week 1: $90
Week 2: $60

26. Last year: 800
This year: 700

27. 10 years ago: 600
5 years ago: 420

Skill 4: Find percent of decrease using the ratio method

To find the percent of decrease using the ratio method, first find the amount of change. Then find this ratio:

$$\frac{\text{AMOUNT OF CHANGE}}{\text{ORIGINAL AMOUNT}}$$

Finally, rename the answer as a percent.

Find the percent of decrease.
Week 1: 400
Week 2: 218

**THINK: The amount of change is
400 − 218 = 182.**

$$\frac{\text{AMOUNT OF CHANGE}}{\text{ORIGINAL AMOUNT}} = \frac{182}{400} = 0.455$$

$$0.455 \rightarrow 0.4\underset{\smile}{55} \rightarrow 45.5\%$$

So the percent of decrease is 45.5%.

Find the percent of decrease.

28. Morning: 80
Afternoon: 60

29. Year 1: 50
Year 2: 10

30. Last week: 25
This week: 20

31. Bought: 500
Sold: 250

32. Last year: $500
This year: $420

33. Month 1: $750
Month 2: $525

34. Session 1: 800
Session 2: 700

35. Last week: $600
This week: $200

36. Week 1: 1,000
Week 2: 450

METRIC UNITS OF LENGTH

Skill 1: Identify the correct unit of length

kilometer (km)	centimeter (cm)
meter (m)	millimeter (mm)

Which unit of length would you use?

Distance from N.Y. to L.A.: km

Length of a car: m   Height of a glass: cm

Length of a mosquito: mm

Which unit would you use to measure? Write km, m, cm, or mm.

1. Length of your foot

2. Height of a bus

3. Thickness of a knife

4. Distance from Houston to San Diego

Skill 2: Measure to the nearest centimeter and millimeter

A centimeter is used to measure very small lengths. On a metric ruler, each centimeter is subdivided into 10 millimeters.

Measure the line segment.

It measures 3 cm to the nearest cm.

It measures 32 mm to the nearest mm.

Measure to the nearest centimeter and to the nearest millimeter.

5. string: about ■ cm

6. string: about ■ mm

7. chalk: about ■ cm

8. chalk: about ■ mm

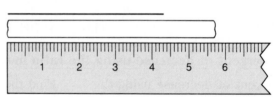

Skill 3: Convert between kilometers, meters, centimeters, and millimeters

1 centimeter = 10 millimeters
1 meter = 100 centimeters
1 kilometer = 1,000 meters

- To rename larger units to smaller units, multiply.
- To rename smaller units to larger units, divide.

Complete: 3 cm = ■ mm.

THINK: Larger to smaller, so multiply.

1 cm = 10 mm

3 cm = ■ mm   3 × 10 = 30

3 cm = 30 mm

Complete: 4,300 m = ■ km.

THINK: Smaller to larger, so divide.

1,000 m = 1 km

4,300 m = ■ km   4,300 ÷ 1,000 = 4.3

4,300 m = 4.3 km

Complete.

9. 6 m = ■ cm

10. 7 km = ■ m

11. 1.2 cm = ■ mm

12. 13 mm = ■ cm

13. 20 mm = ■ cm

14. 300 cm = ■ m

METRIC UNITS OF CAPACITY AND MASS

Skill 1: Identify the correct unit of capacity or mass

UNITS OF CAPACITY
kiloliter (kL)
liter (L)
milliliter (mL)

UNITS OF MASS
kilogram (kg)
gram (g)
milligram (mg)

Which unit of capacity or mass would you use?

Capacity of a pail: L
Capacity of a dropper: mL
Mass of a person: kg
Mass of a grape: g

Which unit would you use to measure? Write kL, L, mL, kg, g, or mg.

1. Capacity of a dropper

2. Capacity of a water tower

3. Mass of a person

4. Capacity of a gas tank

5. Mass of an insect

6. Mass of a banana

Skill 2: Convert between kiloliters, liters, and milliliters

1 liter = 1,000 milliliters
1 kiloliter = 1,000 liters

Remember: Larger to smaller → multiply
Smaller to larger → divide

Complete.

Complete: 3,000 mL = ■ L.

THINK: Smaller to larger, so divide.

$1 L = 1,000 mL$
$3,000 mL = ■ L$ $3,000 ÷ 1,000 = 3$
$3,000 mL = 3 L$

7. $3 L = ■ mL$

8. $5,000 mL = ■ L$

9. $3 kL = ■ L$

10. $6,000 L = ■ kL$

11. $2,500 mL = ■ L$

12. $3,500 L = ■ kL$

Skill 3: Convert between kilograms, grams, and milligrams

1 gram = 1,000 milligrams
1 kilogram = 1,000 grams

Remember: Larger to smaller → multiply
Smaller to larger → divide

Complete.

Complete: 6 kg = ■ g.

THINK: Larger to smaller, so multiply.

$1 kg = 1,000 g$
$6 kg = ■ g$ $6 × 1,000 = 6,000$
$6 kg = 6,000 g$

13. $2 g = ■ mg$

14. $4,000 g = ■ kg$

15. $3,000 mg = ■ g$

16. $5 kg = ■ g$

17. $1,500 g = ■ kg$

18. $5,500 mg = ■ g$

CUSTOMARY UNITS OF LENGTH

Skill 1: Identify the correct unit of length

mile (mi)	foot (ft)
yard (yd)	inch (in.)

Which unit of length would you use?
Distance from Tampa to Dallas: mi
Length of a room: ft   Height of a cup: in.

Which unit would you use to measure? Write mi, yd, ft, or in.

1. Height of a person

2. Length of a pencil

3. Height of a bookcase

4. Distance to a planet

5. Length of fabric on a bolt

6. Thickness of a book

Skill 2: Measure to the nearest inch, $\frac{1}{2}$-inch, and $\frac{1}{4}$-inch

An inch is used to measure the lengths of small objects to the nearest inch, nearest $\frac{1}{2}$-inch, and nearest $\frac{1}{4}$-inch.

Measure the line segment.

It measures 1 in. to the nearest inch.
It measures $1\frac{1}{2}$ in. to the nearest $\frac{1}{2}$-inch.
It measures $1\frac{1}{2}$ in. to the nearest $\frac{1}{4}$-inch.

Use a ruler to draw the line segment.

7. 3 in.   **8.** 5 in.   **9.** $2\frac{1}{2}$ in.   **10.** $4\frac{1}{2}$ in.   **11.** $1\frac{1}{4}$ in.   **12.** $3\frac{3}{4}$ in.

Skill 3: Convert between miles, yards, feet, and inches

1 foot (ft) = 12 inches (in.)
1 yard (yd) = 3 feet = 36 inches
1 mile (mi) = 1,760 yards = 5,280 feet

- To rename larger units to smaller units, multiply.
- To rename smaller units to larger units, divide.

Complete: 3 ft = ■ in.

THINK: Larger to smaller, so multiply.

1 ft = 36 in.
3 ft = ■ in. $3 \times 36 = 108$
3 ft = 108 in.

Complete: 17 ft = ■ yd.

THINK: Smaller to larger, so divide.

3 ft = 1 yd
17 ft = ■ yd $17 \div 3 = 5\frac{2}{3}$
17 ft = $5\frac{2}{3}$ yd

Complete.

13. 2 ft = ■ in.

14. 72 in. = ■ yd

15. 7 ft = ■ yd

16. 2 mi = ■ ft

17. $1\frac{1}{2}$ yd = ■ in.

18. 3,520 yd = ■ mi

CUSTOMARY UNITS OF CAPACITY AND WEIGHT

Skill 1: Identify the correct unit of capacity or weight

UNITS OF CAPACITY	
gallon (gal)	cup (c)
quart (qt)	fluid ounce (fl oz)
pint (pt)	

UNITS OF WEIGHT		
ton (T)	pound (lb)	ounce (oz)

Which unit of capacity or weight would you use?

Capacity of a gas tank: gal
Capacity of a glass: fl oz
Weight of a person: lb
Weight of a bird: oz

Which unit would you use to measure? Write gal, qt, pt, c, fl oz, T, lb, or oz.

1. Weight of an elephant
2. Capacity of a small juice glass
3. Capacity of a pool
4. Weight of a bunch of bananas
5. Capacity of a thermos
6. Weight of a pencil

Skill 2: Convert between gallons, quarts, pints, cups, and fluid ounces

1 cup = 8 fluid ounces	
1 pint = 2 cups	
1 quart = 2 pints	
1 gallon = 4 quarts	

Remember: Larger to smaller → multiply
Smaller to larger → divide

Complete: 2 qt = ■ pt.

THINK: Larger to smaller, so multiply.

1 qt = 2 pt
2 qt = ■ pt $2 \times 2 = 4$
2 qt = 4 pt

Complete.

7. 2 c = ■ fl oz
8. 8 c = ■ pt
9. 6 pt = ■ qt
10. 3 gal = ■ qt
11. 24 fl oz = ■ c
12. $1\frac{1}{2}$ qt = ■ pt

Skill 3: Convert between tons, pounds, and ounces

1 pound = 16 ounces	
1 ton = 2,000 pounds	

Remember: Larger to smaller → multiply
Smaller to larger → divide

Complete: 32 oz = ■ lb.

THINK: Smaller to larger, so divide.

1 lb = 16 oz
32 oz = ■ lb $32 \div 16 = 2$
32 oz = 2 lb

Complete.

13. 2 T = ■ lb
14. 48 oz = ■ lb
15. 6,000 lb = ■ T
16. 4 lb = ■ oz
17. $1\frac{1}{2}$ T = ■ lb
18. 3,000 lb = ■ T

PERIMETER

Skill 1: Find the perimeter of any polygon

The **perimeter** of any polygon is the distance around it. To find the perimeter of any polygon, add the lengths of all the sides.

Find the perimeter.

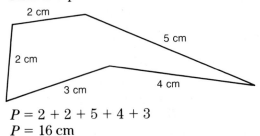

$$P = 2 + 2 + 5 + 4 + 3$$
$$P = 16 \text{ cm}$$

Find the perimeter.

1.
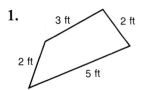

2.
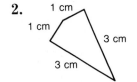

3.
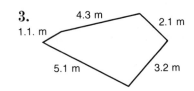

Skill 2: Find the perimeters of rectangles

Remember that a **rectangle** has opposite sides that are equal in length. In rectangle *ABCD*, sides *BC* and *AD* both measure 4 cm. So the length of the rectangle is 4 cm. Sides *AB* and *CD* both measure 2 cm. So the width of the rectangle is 2 cm. The perimeter of any rectangle can be found by using this formula: $P = (2 \times l) + (2 \times w)$.

Find the perimeter of rectangle *ABCD*.

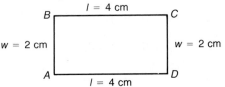

$$P = (2 \times l) + (2 \times w)$$
$$= (2 \times 4) + (2 \times 2)$$
$$= 8 + 4$$
$$P = 12 \text{ cm}$$

Find the perimeter of the rectangle.

4. $l = 4$ ft, $w = 3$ ft

5. $l = 5.2$ m, $w = 4.1$ m

6. $l = 6.1$ ft, $w = 2.3$ ft

Skill 3: Find the perimeters of squares

Remember that a **square** has all sides equal in length. In square *EFGH*, all sides measure 2 in. The perimeter of any square can be found by using this formula: $P = 4 \times s$.

Find the perimeter of square *EFGH*.

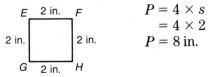

$$P = 4 \times s$$
$$= 4 \times 2$$
$$P = 8 \text{ in.}$$

Find the perimeter of the square.

7. $s = 3$ cm

8. $s = 4$ ft

9. $s = 5$ m

10. $s = 15.1$ yd

CIRCUMFERENCE

Skill 1: Identify the parts of a circle

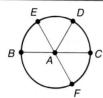

In the circle, A is the **center,** $\overline{BC}$ is a **diameter,** and $\overline{AD}$ is a **radius.** The radius of a circle is $\frac{1}{2}$ the diameter. This relationship can be written as $d = 2 \times r$ or $r = \frac{1}{2} \times d$.

Complete. Use circle A.
If $\overline{BA} = 3$ cm, then $\overline{BC} = \blacksquare$?

THINK: $\overline{BA}$ is a radius.
$\overline{BC}$ is a diameter.

$$d = 2 \times r$$
$$= 2 \times 3$$
$$d = 6 \text{ cm}$$

Find the diameter.

1. $r = 1$ in. 2. $r = 2$ cm 3. $r = 4$ ft 4. $r = 5$ m 5. $r = 10.4$ ft 6. $r = 11.6$ yd

Find the radius.

7. $d = 4$ in. 8. $d = 6$ cm 9. $d = 8$ ft 10. $d = 12$ m 11. $d = 20$ yd 12. $d = 30.6$ km

Skill 2: Find the circumference

The **circumference** of a circle is the distance around it. To find the circumference use one of the following formulas:
$C = \pi \times d$ or $C = 2 \times \pi \times r$
Remember to use 3.14 for π (**pi**).

Find the circumference when $r = 3$ in.
$$C = 2 \times \pi \times r$$
$$\approx 2 \times 3.14 \times 3$$
$$\approx 6.28 \times 3$$
$$C \approx 18.84 \text{ in.}$$

Find the circumference.

13. $d = 3$ in. 14. $d = 5$ cm 15. $d = 11$ ft 16. $r = 4$ m 17. $r = 7$ yd 18. $r = 12$ km

Skill 3: Find the radius and diameter given the circumference

To find the radius or diameter of a circle given the circumference, use the following formulas:
$C = \pi \times d$ or $C = 2 \times \pi \times r$
Remember to use 3.14 for π.

Find the diameter of a circle when the circumference is 6.28 cm.
$$C = \pi \times d$$
$$6.28 \approx 3.14 \times d$$
$$6.28 \div 3.14 \approx d$$
$$2 \text{ cm} \approx d$$

Find the diameter and the radius.

19. $C = 3.14$ in. 20. $C = 9.42$ cm 21. $C = 12.56$ m 22. $C = 21.98$ m 23. $C = 28.26$ ft

AREA

Skill 1: Find the areas of rectangles

The **area** of a figure is the number of square units that it contains. In **rectangle** $ABCD$, the length is 4 cm and the width is 2 cm. By counting, you can see that the area of the rectangle is 8 square cm.

You can find the area of a rectangle by multiplying. Use this formula: $A = l \times w$.

Find the area of the rectangle.

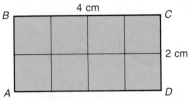

$$A = l \times w$$
$$= 4 \times 2$$
$$A = 8 \text{ square cm}$$

Find the area of the rectangle.

1. $l = 3$ cm, $w = 1$ cm

2. $l = 4$ in., $w = 3$ in.

3. $l = 5$ ft, $w = 4$ ft

4. $l = 1.4$ in., $w = 1.1$ in.

5. $l = 2.1$ m, $w = 1.2$ m

6. $l = 3.3$ cm, $w = 2.1$ cm

Skill 2: Find the areas of squares

Since a **square** is a rectangle with all sides equal in length, the length and the width are the same. You can find the area of a square by using this formula: $A = s \times s$ or $A = s^2$.

Find the area of a square with $s = 1.2$ cm.

$$A = s \times s$$
$$= 1.2 \times 1.2$$
$$A = 1.44 \text{ square cm}$$

Find the area of the square.

7. $s = 3$ in.

8. $s = 11$ cm

9. $s = 1.4$ m

10. $s = 10.1$ ft

Skill 3: Find the areas of triangles

In a **triangle,** the **height** is the perpendicular distance from any **vertex** to the opposite side. In triangle DEF, GE is a height. The height (h) = 10 in. and the **base** (b) = 32 in.

You can find the area of a triangle by using this formula: $A = \frac{1}{2} \times b \times h$.

Find the area of triangle DEF.

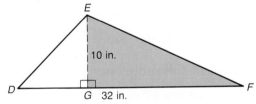

$$A = \frac{1}{2} \times b \times h$$
$$= \frac{1}{2} \times 32 \times 10$$
$$= 16 \times 10$$
$$A = 160 \text{ square in.}$$

Find the area of the triangle.

11. $b = 16$ mm, $h = 8$ mm

12. $b = 7$ ft, $h = 5$ ft

13. $b = 4.3$ cm, $h = 2.5$ cm

AREA

Skill 4: Find the areas of parallelograms

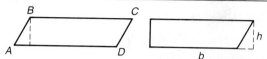

Figure *ABCD* is a **parallelogram.** A parallelogram can be changed into an equivalent rectangle. So, the area of a parallelogram is found by using this formula: $A = b \times h$.

Find the area of a parallelogram with $b = 12$ m and $h = 5$ m.

$$A = b \times h$$
$$= 12 \times 5$$
$$A = 60 \text{ square m}$$

Find the area of the parallelogram.

14. $b = 6$ ft, $h = 4$ ft

15. $b = 7.1$ cm, $h = 4.2$ cm

16. $b = 9.3$ in., $h = 4.2$ in.

Skill 5: Find the areas of circles

The area of a **circle** is found by using one of these formulas: $A = \pi \times r \times r$ or $A = \pi \times r^2$. When you must find the area of a circle given the diameter, find the radius first by using the formula: $r = \frac{1}{2} \times d$. Remember to use 3.14 for π.

Find the area of a circle when $d = 4$ ft.

THINK: $r = \frac{1}{2} \times d = \frac{1}{2} \times 4 = 2$

$$A = \pi \times r \times r$$
$$\approx 3.14 \times 2 \times 2$$
$$A \approx 12.56 \text{ square ft}$$

Find the area of the circle to the nearest hundredth.

17. $r = 3$ in.

18. $r = 5$ m

19. $r = 10.2$ ft

20. $r = 15.1$ km

21. $d = 6$ cm

22. $d = 10$ in.

23. $d = 12.2$ yd

24. $d = 16.8$ m

Skill 6: Find the areas of combined regions

To find the area of combined regions, divide them into known polygons. Find the area of each polygon. Then add all the areas.

Find the area of the figure.

THINK: Triangle with $b = 2$ cm, $h = 2$ cm
Square with $s = 2$ cm

$$A = \frac{1}{2} \times b \times h \qquad\qquad A = s \times s$$
$$= \frac{1}{2} \times 2 \times 2 \qquad\qquad = 2 \times 2$$
$$A = 2 \text{ square cm} \qquad\qquad A = 4 \text{ square cm}$$

So the area of the combined regions is 2 square cm + 4 square cm = 6 square cm.

Find the area.

25.

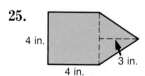

26.

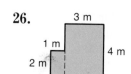

27.

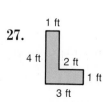

SURFACE AREA AND VOLUME

Skill 1: Identify solid figures

Here are some solid figures.

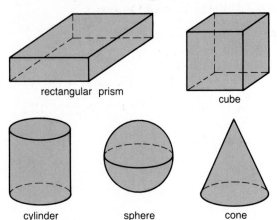

rectangular prism

cube

cylinder   sphere   cone

Name the solid figure.

Coffee mug: cylinder
Basketball: sphere
Party hat: cone
Shirt box: rectangular prism

Name the solid figure.

1. Cereal box

2. Juice glass

3. Funnel

4. Baseball

5. Globe

6. Brick

Skill 2: Find the surface areas of rectangular prisms and cubes

In a rectangular prism, each **face** (side) is a rectangle. There are 6 faces and the opposite faces have equal areas. The surface area of a rectangular prism is the sum of the area of the 6 faces.

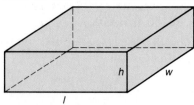

Find the surface area of the rectangular prism below.

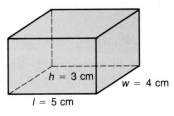

$h = 3$ cm $w = 4$ cm

$l = 5$ cm

To find the surface area of a rectangular prism, use the following formula:

SURFACE AREA	=	AREA OF FRONT AND BACK	+	AREA OF TOP AND BOTTOM	+	AREA OF SIDES
SA	=	$(2 \times l \times h)$	+	$(2 \times l \times w)$	+	$(2 \times w \times h)$

$$SA = (2 \times l \times h) + (2 \times l \times w) + (2 \times w \times h)$$
$$= (2 \times 5 \times 3) + (2 \times 5 \times 4) + (2 \times 4 \times 3)$$
$$= 30 + 40 + 24$$
$$SA = 94 \text{ square cm}$$

Since a cube is a special rectangular prism, you can use the above formula or $SA = 6 \times s \times s$.

SURFACE AREA AND VOLUME

Find the surface area.

7. rectangular prism:
$l = 4$ cm, $w = 3$ cm, $h = 1$ cm

8. rectangular prism:
$l = 16$ in., $w = 14$ in., $h = 2$ in.

9. rectangular prism:
$l = 5$ ft, $w = 4$ ft, $h = 6$ ft

10. rectangular prism:
$l = 8$ m, $w = 2$ m, $h = 3$ m

11. cube: $s = 8$ cm   **12.** cube: $s = 1$ in.   **13.** cube: $s = 20$ m   **14.** cube: $s = 3$ yd

15. cube: $s = 4$ ft   **16.** cube: $s = 7$ m   **17.** cube: $s = 11$ yd   **18.** cube: $s = 15$ cm

Skill 3: Find the volumes of rectangular prisms and cubes

The **volume** of a figure is the number of cubic units it contains. In the rectangular prism, the length is 4 in., the width is 3 in., and the height is 2 in. By counting, you can see the volume is 24 cubic in.

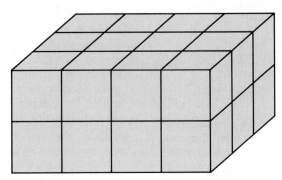

You can also find the volume of a rectangular prism by multiplying. Use the formula: $V = l \times w \times h$.

Since a cube is a special rectangular prism, you can use the above formula or $V = s \times s \times s$ or $V = s^3$.

Find the volume of a rectangular prism with $l = 4$ in., $w = 3$ in., and $h = 2$ in.

$$V = l \times w \times h$$
$$= 4 \times 3 \times 2$$
$$V = 24 \text{ cubic in.}$$

Find the volume.

19. rectangular prism:
$l = 3$ m, $w = 2$ m, $h = 4$ m

20. rectangular prism:
$l = 14$ in., $w = 13$ in., $h = 5$ in.

21. rectangular prism:
$l = 6$ m, $w = 5$ m, $h = 4$ m

22. rectangular prism:
$l = 20$ cm, $w = 10$ cm, $h = 8$ cm

23. cube: $s = 3$ ft   **24.** cube: $s = 7$ m   **25.** cube: $s = 11$ in.   **26.** cube: $s = 15$ yd

27. cube: $s = 14$ m   **28.** cube: $s = 2$ in.   **29.** cube: $s = 21$ cm   **30.** cube: $s = 16$ m

GLOSSARY

addends   Numbers to be added. [2]

additive inverses   Two numbers are additive inverses of each other if their sum is 0.

Example: 6 and −6 are additive inverses, since 6 + (−6) = 0.
[371]

adjustable rate mortgage (ARM)   A mortgage on which the interest rate may go up or down as interest rates in general fluctuate. [241]

all-day pass   A general admission ticket that allows unlimited use of activities without paying separate admissions. [86]

algebraic expression   An expression that contains one or more **variables,** with or without operational signs. [366]

annual expense   [304] (See budget)

Annual Percentage Rate (APR)   The true rate of interest charged on the actual amount of the outstanding loan. [145; 151]

appreciation   An increase in value as general market values go up. In housing, this may be because of inflation, greater demand, rising building costs, population increase, or scarcity of vacant land. [236; 237]

area   The number of square units needed to cover the surface bounded by a 2-dimensional figure such as a rectangle or a circle. [249; 262; 268]

assessed valuation   The value of a property, as officially determined by a local government for taxation purposes.

$$\frac{\text{ASSESSED}}{\text{VALUATION}} = \frac{\text{ASSESSMENT}}{\text{RATE}} \times \frac{\text{MARKET}}{\text{VALUE}}$$
[242]

asset   [310] (See net worth)

automobile loan   Money lent to help the borrower buy a car and have the use of it while paying for it in periodic installments.

The car is the security for the loan, since the lender holds the title (a registered paper that shows legal ownership) until the loan is repaid. [170]

automobile purchase price   The amount paid for a car. Beginning with the sticker (offering) price, a trade-in allowance may be subtracted if the buyer owns a car to turn over to the dealer.

Other possible price adjustments are: special discounts, down payment, the cost of extra items (options), finance charges, vehicle registration fee, and taxes. [168]

average daily balance   [150] (See Money Market checking account)

beneficiary   The person named in an insurance policy to receive money from the insurance company should the person die who is protected under the policy. [72]

board foot   The amount of wood in a board 1 in. thick by 1 ft wide by 1 ft long. [262]

bond   A corporate or municipal bond is a certificate received by a person who lends money to a corporation or to a local (state or city) government. The holder of a bond is paid interest for a set period of time and is repaid the full amount (face, or par, value) on the maturity date. [327]

budget   An organized plan for spending money. **Fixed expenses,** such as rent, are the same each month and are not easily changed or controlled. **Variable expenses,** such as clothing, food, and entertainment, can be changed to some extent according to necessity or choice. **Annual expenses,** such as vacation and insurance premiums, may actually be paid only once a year, but should be shown in the budget in monthly shares. [304; 306]

buying in bulk   Buying in a quantity larger than is usual for normal individual use. It may also mean buying loose goods—not in packages, boxes, or bags. [275]

canceled checks   [127] (See checking account statement)

cash value   For insurance, the amount you would receive if you canceled a straight life policy or borrowed money with the policy as security. The cash value depends upon how much has been paid in premiums. [74]

catalog   A publication that pictures and describes merchandise that can be ordered at home and received by mail. [110]

certificate of deposit (CD)   A paper that is evidence of money deposited for investment. It tells the set period of time the money must be left on deposit to avoid a penalty charge for withdrawal. [322]

checking account   An agreement with a bank that allows the customer to deposit money and write checks against it. [124, 135]

checking account statement   A monthly statement from the bank that lists all changes in a checking account such as deposits, amounts paid by check, service charges, and interest. Checks written by the customer and stamped by the bank, to verify payment, are called **canceled** checks and are usually returned to the customer along with the monthly statement. [127]

closing costs   Fees related to buying a house or condominium, and paid by the buyer before moving in. Closing costs vary, but may include lawyer's services, title search, and inspection of the property. Bank service charges, referred to as **points,** may be included. Each point is 1% of the mortgage amount. [240]

collectible   Something such as a piece of fine art, stamps, or coins, bought as an investment with the expectation that its value will increase. [316]

collision insurance   Insurance that pays for damage to the insured car. [175]

column-inch   A measure of newspaper space, computed by multiplying the number of columns wide the space is by the number of inches long. [282]

combination   A selection of objects without regard to their order. [357]

commission   Money paid to an agent or salesperson, often a percentage of the gross amount of business that person generates. A **straight commission** plan pays only commission. A **graduated commission** plan pays a different percent (**rate of commission**) for different levels of sales. [66]

compatible numbers   Numbers used to estimate answers in division. They are close in value to the given divisor and dividend, and divide evenly. [257; 381]

compound interest   Interest calculated by periodically (quarterly, or even daily) adding earned interest to an account. The principal then increases more rapidly than with simple interest. [132]

comprehensive insurance   Insurance that gives financial protection in case of fire, theft, vandalism, and weather damage that involves an insured car. [175]

computer simulation   For a product, imitation by a computer of how the product will react under certain conditions. [363]

condominium   An apartment that is owned, rather than rented. Each owner pays a monthly **maintenance fee** for the care of the building and grounds. [238]

Consumer Price Index (CPI)   A number that represents the value of a "market basket" of goods and services bought by a typical city family. Social Security benefits and the wages of many union workers change according to how much a dollar will buy (**purchasing power** of a dollar), as indicated by the CPI. [302]

contractor   A person or company who agrees to provide materials and perform work, usually for a certain price and in a given length of time. [249]

corporate stock   An investment that represents shares in the ownership of a company that is organized as a corporation so that its stock can be traded by stockbrokers on a stock exchange. Owners of stock are paid **dividends** when the corporation makes a profit. [319; 324; 330; 336]

credit card   A card that allows the person to whom it is issued to receive purchases and services, but pay for them at a later time. If the entire balance shown on a **monthly statement** is paid by the date due, there is no extra charge. A **minimum payment** is usually required. A **finance charge** is calculated on any **unpaid balance.** [144; 147]

credit union   A cooperative group that makes loans to its members (sometimes a company's employees) at a low rate. [151]

daily interest rate   [149] (See overdraft)

decimal A base-ten numeral that uses a decimal point and place value. [2]

deductible clause The section of an insurance policy (health, auto) that specifies how much of any incurred expense the insured person must pay. The insurance company then agrees to pay all or part of the remaining expense. [70; 175]

deflation The opposite of inflation. During a period of deflation, money is relatively scarce and of greater value. Prices fall, business activity is slowed, and unemployment is high. [303]

dependent events [352] (See event)

depreciation For automobiles, the regular decrease in the value of a car. This decrease occurs even if the car is not used heavily. Such depreciation affects the trade-in value of a car. [174]

diameter of a circle Any chord of a circle that contains the center of the circle. [264]

difference The number found by subtracting. [4]

discount The amount that is subtracted from the regular price of an item. Also called a **markdown**. [104]

dividend An amount of money paid to the shareholders of a corporation out of its earnings. [324; 330; 336]

dividend in division [8] (See divisor)

divisor The number by which another number, the **dividend,** is divided.

Example: In $6\overline{)24}$, or $24 \div 6$, 6 is the divisor and 24 is the dividend. [8]

down payment [154; 170; 240] (See automobile purchase price; installment buying; mortgage)

EPA Fuel Economy Rating (mpg) The result of tests done by the Federal Environmental Protection Agency (EPA) to find how many miles a car can go on a gallon of gasoline (miles per gallon, or mpg).

$$\text{mpg} = \frac{\text{MILES}}{\text{DRIVEN}} \div \frac{\text{GALLONS OF}}{\text{GASOLINE USED}}$$

[168; 172]

equation A mathematical sentence that contains an is-equal-to sign, indicating that 2 expressions are equal. [366]

estimate To calculate roughly, when an approximation is sufficient. Used also to check the accuracy of computation. [26]

evaluate an algebraic expression To replace each variable by a given value; then, simplify the resulting expression. [368]

event A subset of all possible outcomes of an experiment. Events are independent of one another if the probability of one is not affected by the probability of another.

The probability of a series of **independent events** occurring together is found by multiplying the probabilities of the individual events.

Events are **dependent** upon one another if the probability of one affects the probability of another. [346; 350; 352]

exchange rate The fluctuating ratio of the values of the money of 2 countries (as the ratio of the U.S. dollar to the English pound). [286; 287]

face value For an insurance policy, the amount printed on the policy. That is, the amount the insurance company agrees to pay. [72; 320; 327]

factors Numbers to be multiplied. [6]

Federal withholding tax A percentage of an employee's taxable pay, deducted and paid directly by the employer to the Internal Revenue Service of the Federal government. State and city income taxes are collected in a similar way. [68; 214]

finance charge [144; 154] (See credit card; installment buying)

fixed expense [304] (See budget)

fixed rate mortgage A mortgage on which the interest rate remains the same throughout the term of the mortgage. [252]

formula An equation that expresses the rule for a frequently used relationship, often among quantities such as measurements. [368]

fraction The division of 2 numbers written in the form $\frac{a}{b}$. The denominator (divisor), cannot be 0.

Examples: $\frac{1}{3}$; $\frac{7}{8}$; $\frac{12}{5}$

[10]

fringe benefit A benefit, such as free insurance, a discount on purchases, or child care, that is received by an employee in addition to regular pay. [70]

front-end estimation A procedure for estimating answers.
1. Find the greatest number.
2. Identify the place of its leading nonzero digit.
3. Compute only with the digits in that place.
[79; 121; 163; 361]

graduated commission [66] (See commission)

gross pay [68; 212] (See payroll deductions)

group rate A special reduced price for admission when tickets for a group of people are ordered at the same time. [87]

health insurance A contract by which a person regularly pays a **premium** to an insurance company. In return, the company promises to help pay medical expenses, as specified in a written policy, in case the person becomes ill or is injured. [70]

home equity loan Money borrowed to buy a house. The house is the security for the loan. That is, the lender has the right to take over the house if the loan is not repaid. [152]

homeowner's insurance A contract by which a person pays a **premium** to an insurance company. In return, the company agrees to pay money, as specified in a written policy, to cover loss or damage to the property (by fire, for example). Such insurance usually excludes causes of loss such as flood, earthquake, and nuclear accident.
   Most owners insure a property for its full **replacement value,** which would cover reconstruction if it were destroyed. [244]

idle time In taxicab fares, time during which a customer is in the cab, but the cab is not moving. [201]

income tax [68] (See Federal withholding tax)

independent events [350] (See event)

Individual Retirement Account (IRA) [333] (See pension)

inflation A continuous and relatively large rise in prices caused by expansion in paper money, or bank credit, which decreases the value of money. The **inflation** rate is the percent prices increase, by comparison with a previous month or year. [302]

installment buying plan A plan by which the buyer begins using the item purchased at once, but pays for it in periodic **installments.** A **finance charge,** or interest, is added to the cash price. If there is a **down payment,** that amount is deducted before the finance charge is figured. The installment price is the total of the installment payments. [154]

insurance [70; 72; 175; 244] (See automobile insurance; health insurance; homeowner's insurance; life insurance)

interest rate [132] (See compound interest; simple interest)

inverse operations Operations that "undo" each other.

Examples: Adding and subtracting the same number
Multiplying and dividing by the same number

[370; 372]

kilowatt-hour A unit of energy, equivalent to 1,000 watts of electricity used for 1 hour. [246]

liability [310] (See net worth)

liability coverage For automobiles, insurance that gives financial protection for injury to others and damage to their property.
   For homes, liability coverage provides financial protection in case someone is injured on the insured property. [175; 244]

life insurance A contract by which a person regularly pays a **premium** to an insurance company. In return, the company agrees to pay money, as specified in a written **policy,** to a **beneficiary** in case the insured person dies. A **straight life** insurance policy provides protection for as long as premiums are paid. [72]

loan Money lent at interest. The interest depends upon the amount borrowed, the interest rate (Annual Percentage Rate), and the time it takes to repay the loan. [151]

maintenance fee [238; 239] (See condominium)

map scale A rate (ratio) between two sets of measurements. It tells how many miles are represented by a unit (usually an inch) on a map. [190]

markdown [104] (See discount)

market research Gathering and analyzing data about consumer preferences and buying power. Such information is important in planning the development and marketing of new products. [282]

market value An approximation of the amount a property could be sold for. [242]

markup The difference between the retail and the wholesale prices of an item. The amount of the markup is found by multiplying the wholesale price by an established percent, which is the **markup rate.** [104]

mean (average) A single number used to represent a set of numbers; found by dividing the sum of the numbers by the number of numbers.

Example:

$2 + 3 + 4 + 5 + 6 = 20$ and $20 \div 5 = 4$.

4 is the mean, since $4 + 4 + 4 + 4 + 4 = 20$. [16]

median The middle value when a set of numbers are listed in order.

Example: 6 is the median of 2, 4, 6, 8, 9. 6 is also the median of 2, 3, 4, 8, 9, 10, since $\frac{4+8}{2} = 6$. [16]

membership fee Money paid to allow access to the facilities of an organization such as a health or swim club. [92]

mental computation Ways devised to think about operations on numbers so that external help (paper and pencil, calculator) is not needed to arrive at exact answers. [24]

minimum wage The least amount of money a person can be paid per hour; set by federal law so that it applies in all states. [42]

mixed number A number that indicates the sum of a whole number and a fraction.

Example: $3\frac{3}{4} = 3 + \frac{3}{4}$

[10]

mode The number that occurs most often in a set of numbers.
Example:

7 is the mode of 1, 1, 4, 7, 7, 7, 8, 9.
[16]

Money Market checking account A special checking account that earns interest. To earn interest and to avoid a service charge, most such accounts require that a minimum balance be kept in the account. Interest is usually compounded daily and paid monthly on the basis of the **average daily balance.** Most Money Market accounts limit the number of checks that can be written each month. [134; 135]

mortgage Money borrowed to buy a house or a condominium. The amount is approximately the purchase price less the **down payment**. The mortgage is repaid in periodic payments that include interest, and sometimes taxes. [240]

move-in costs Costs, in addition to rent, that must be paid when a renter moves into a residence. These may include a **fee** to the rental agent and a **security deposit** to the landlord. Occasionally, utility deposits are also required. [234]

mutual fund Money from a group of investors, used to buy and sell a mixture of stocks or other investments. **Dividends** are paid to members of the fund when there are profits. The price of a **share** in the fund goes up or down depending upon the changing value of the stocks held.

A "no load" fund does not charge a seller's fee; that is, the **buy** and **sell** prices of a share are the same. [330]

negotiated price [168] (See automobile purchase price)

net pay [68] (See payroll deductions)

net worth The difference between what is owned (**assets**) and what is owed (**liabilities**). [310]

NOW checking account A special checking account that earns interest. To earn interest and to avoid a service charge, most such accounts require that a minimum balance be kept in the account. Interest is usually compounded daily and paid monthly on the basis of the **average daily balance.** [134; 135]

odometer A gauge that automatically measures distance passed over by a wheeled vehicle. [172]

options [168] (See sticker price)

order of operations The order in which an expression is simplified when there is more than 1 operation. [23; 364]

outcome [346] (See event; probability; sample space, tree diagram)

overdraft A check written for more than the balance in the account. The bank may lend money to cover overdrafts up to an agreed amount. A **daily interest rate** times the **sum of the daily balances** is the usual way to compute the interest charge on overdrafts. The daily interest rate is based on an Annual Percentage Rate (APR). [149]

overestimate The result when estimating is intentionally done to make the approximation higher than the exact answer can be, as in estimating whether an amount of money is adequate for a given purpose. [32]

overtime [58; 295] (See wages)

package deal In travel, an overall charge. It includes many individual expenses (such as transportation, hotel, and meals). [203]

payroll deductions Money subtracted from a worker's full (**gross**) pay. The deductions cover taxes, insurance, and sometimes special amounts such as contributions or investments. The amount the worker receives, after deductions, is called the **net** (or take-home) pay. [68; 214]

pension Money received from a worker's pension plan after the worker retires. The amount received (annual pension benefit) depends upon the number of years the worker has belonged to the pension plan and upon her/his average annual earnings.

   People can save for their retirement on their own by investing in **Individual Retirement Accounts (IRAs)**. [332]

percent A ratio that compares a number to 100. 10% means 10 hundredths, or 10 per 100.

Example: $75\% = 0.75 = \frac{75}{100}$, or $\frac{3}{4}$ [10]

perimeter The distance around the outer boundary of a 2-dimensional figure such as a rectangle or a square. [249]

permutation Any arrangement of a number of objects in a definite order. [356]

piecework A method of paying a worker on the basis of the number of items produced or jobs completed. [64]

premium In insurance, money paid by the policyholder for coverage under a contract (policy). [70; 72; 175; 244]

preventive maintenance For automobiles, periodic servicing to prevent the need for more serious and expensive repairs. [173]

probability A measure of chance. The probability, or chance, of an event occurring is a ratio: [346; 354]

$$P(\text{Event}) = \frac{\text{no. of favorable outcomes}}{\text{no. of possible outcomes}}$$

product The number found by multiplying. [6]

promotion On a job, advancement in rank or position. [295]

proportion A statement that 2 rates, or ratios, are equal. [250; 270; 286; 288]

purchasing power [302] (See Consumer Price Index)

quality control A system of inspection for making sure that an agreed-upon standard of quality is maintained in a production process. [288]

quotient The number obtained by dividing.

Example: In $6\overline{)27}$, 4 is the quotient. The **remainder** is 3.

$$\begin{array}{r} 4\text{ R}3 \\ 6\overline{)27} \end{array}$$

[8]

rate of commission [66] (See commission)

real estate taxes Money collected by local governments and used to pay for municipal services and schools. The real estate tax is based on the **assessed valuation** of a property, which is a percent of the property's **market value.** [242]

reconciled balance A checking account balance that reflects any changes that are needed to make the bank's monthly statement and the customer's check register agree. [127]

remainder [8] (See quotient)

remodeling Rebuilding all or part of a structure. [249]

renewable policy [74] (See term insurance)

retail Related to the sale of goods directly to the consumer, as in retail store, retail price, or "to sell at retail." [104]

rounding Replacing a number with an approximation to a nearest given unit, such as to the nearest hundred or tenth. Also, a mixed number can be rounded to the nearest whole number.

Examples: $1{,}721 \approx 1{,}700$
$1.645 \approx 1.65$
$$4\tfrac{3}{4} \approx 5$$

[26]

salary A fixed amount of money paid periodically for work or services. Most often salaries are paid monthly, semimonthly (twice a month), biweekly (every other week), or weekly. Salaries are often quoted on a "per year" basis, as in "$20,000 per year." [62]

sales tax A percent of the total price of goods and services. The money collected from sales taxes is a major source of revenue in many states and municipalities. Sales tax rates vary from state to state and from city to city. [108]

sample space A list of all possible outcomes of an experiment. [348]

sampling In manufacturing, a system of selecting a sample for testing or analysis, for the purpose of checking quality. [288]

savings account An agreement with a bank whereby a customer deposits money and in return, the bank pays **interest** out of what it earns by investing the money.

Careful records are kept of all changes in a savings account. The customer completes **deposit** and **withdrawal** slips. The bank records all changes, including the addition of interest, in a **passbook** kept by the customer. This makes a current balance available at all times. [130]

savings bond [320] (See U.S. savings bond)

scale drawing A diagram, with dimensions that are in a fixed ratio to the object it represents.

A scale drawing may be a reduction (as the blueprints of a house) or an enlargement (as a diagram of a small insect). [250]

schedules (bus, train, flight, subway) Charts, or tables, that give information about service including routes, arrival and departure times, and frequency of service. [192; 193; 195; 198]

season ticket A ticket for a series of events such as sporting events, concerts, or plays— usually at a reduced rate. [86]

secured/unsecured loans A secured loan is money lent with the understanding that if it is not repaid, some property (house, automobile, furniture) can be taken by the person who made the loan. The property is usually whatever has been bought with the borrowed money.

An unsecured loan has the guarantee of the borrower's word that the money will be repaid, but there is no property held as security. [152]

security deposit Money (usually one or two month's rent) collected and held during the period a renter occupies a residence. All or part of the deposit can be retained by the landlord if the dwelling is damaged by the renter. [234]

service contract A written agreement by which the purchaser of an appliance or a machine agrees to pay a fee regularly (usually monthly) whether or not the equipment needs any repair. In return, the serviceperson promises to make as many service calls as are needed to keep the equipment in good repair. [278]

simple interest A payment for the use of money. The amount of interest depends on the interest **rate** (expressed as an annual percent), on the **principal** (the amount of money in the account), and on the length of **time** (in years) that the money is used.

$\text{INTEREST} = \text{PRINCIPAL} \times \text{RATE} \times \text{TIME}$,
or
$$I = p \times r \times t$$

[132]

Social Security (FICA) The Federal Insurance Contributions Act; an insurance and pension plan contributed to, in equal shares, by employees and employers. The plan covers the cost of medical, retirement, and disability benefits paid to employees who have contributed, or to their families. [46]

sticker price   The suggested price shown on a paper (**sticker**) that is taped to the window of a car that is for sale. Other information about the car is shown such as a list of items (**options**) available, but not included in the regular price, and the **EPA Fuel Economy Rating.** [168]

stock exchange   An organized market for buying and selling stocks and bonds listed by that exchange. [319; 324; 330; 336]

straight commission   [66] (See commission)

sum   The number found by adding. [2]

sum of daily balances   [149] (See overdraft)

take-home pay   [54] (See payroll deductions)

term insurance   Life insurance, provided for a specified number of years only. The face value is paid to the beneficiary in case the insured person dies. However, no equity, or investment, accumulates. [72]

tip   The amount of money a customer leaves as a gift for a person who has provided service. [44]

title   [170] (See automobile loan)

trade-in allowance   [168; 170] (See automobile purchase price)

trade industry   A line of skilled manual or mechanical work such as the construction, printing, or auto repair trades. [261]

tree diagram   A diagram used to list all possible outcomes (the **sample space**) of a compound experiment such as rolling a die *and* tossing a coin. [348]

twofer coupon   A coupon that may be exchanged at a theater box office for tickets at a discounted price. "Twofer" is short for "two for the price of one." [85]

underestimate   The result when estimating is intentionally done to make the approximation less than the exact answer, as in estimating whether a certain amount has been reached. [32]

United States savings bonds   (Series EE) Bonds issued by the U.S. Federal government. They are often bought through payroll deductions and at a purchase price that is half the value printed on the face of the bond (the **face value**). Such bonds can be cashed in (redeemed) at any time after 6 mo. The variable interest rate increases the longer the bond is held. [320]

unit price   The price of an item given in terms of an appropriate unit of measure such as per pound, ounce, quart, or yard. [112]

unpaid balance   [144] (See credit card)

utilities   Goods and services such as electricity, natural gas, water, oil, and telephone. [234; 246]

value checking   A checking account that requires no minimum balance. A very limited number of checks are allowed per month without charge. [135]

variable   A symbol, usually a letter, used to stand for a number. [366]

variable expense   [304] (See budget)

wages   (hourly) Money paid for work when the amount varies according to the number of hours worked. **Overtime** is extra time worked (often any hours over 40 per wk). The hourly rate for overtime is usually $1\frac{1}{2}$ times the regular rate. [58; 294]

whole number   A number in the set 0, 1, 2, 3, and so on in the same pattern. There is no greatest whole number. [2]

wholesale   Related to the sale of goods in large quantities to merchants (retailers) who, in turn, sell to consumers. [104]

withholding tax   [68] (See Federal withholding tax)

SELECTED ANSWERS

CHAPTER 1

Page 3
1. 757   7. 29.8   13. 1,202   19. 15.0   37. $44.45

Page 5
1. 432   7. 1,878   10. 3.6   12. 38.92   37. 385 mi

Page 7
1. 48   13. 9.6   19. 8.64   49. 2,653 mi

Page 9
1. 42   4. 47   9. 1,465   31. 2.5   36. 1.39   41. $0.49

Page 11
1. 23%   7. 63%   13. 0.25; 25%   19. 3.5; 350%   25. 0.24   31. 0.028   37. $\frac{7}{10}$ 43. 0.25   44. $\frac{1}{20}$

Page 13
1. 4   2. 6   13. 6   14. 5   25. 21   26. 10.8   37. 36 mi   38. 288 pages

Page 15
4. 150 cars and trucks   8. 4-door sedan   12. pick-up truck

Page 17
1. 90   9. 13   13. 3   15. 75.3; 78; none

CHAPTER 2

Page 23
1. 1,263,602   2. 948,405   15. 49.1   19. 70.62   23. 324.004   27. $44.84

Page 25
1. 75   11. 42   21. 1,270   29. 32   37. $40.42   38. $491

Page 27
1. 80   6. $10   13. 500   18. $0.60   32. $1.90

Page 29
1. 140   5. $14   21. 30   28. 2   41. $6   45. $64

Page 31
1. 19   9. 5   17. 35   25. 8   33. 15 h   37. 32 in.

Page 33
1. b   5. c   9. 10 wk   13. yes

Page 35
1. mental computation   3. paper and pencil or calculator   9. $1.05; mental computation

CHAPTER 3

Page 41
1. $51.75   2. $41.15   7. $19.50

Page 43
1. $4.65   2. $51.00   7. Camp Crestmont; Hamburger Barn; Ray's Dept. Store   8. $120

Page 45
1. $2.10   3. $12.30   4. $27

Page 47
1. $15.30   2. $53.55   11. $31.50   12. $135

Page 49
3. 95 h, 75 h   4. 11 quarters, 5 dimes

Page 50
1. T, W, 4–8   3. 13h   11. Big Time Burger   12. Dime Department Store

CHAPTER 4

Page 59
1. $194   2. $184.75   7. $246.24   8. $0   22. $5.75

Page 61
1. 7:00   2. 3:15

Page 63
1. $168.27   5. $12,872.60   9. Job B; $2,400   15. $9,200 per y job; $320

Page 65
1. $12.25   2. $161.20   13. $218.75   14. $151.20

Page 67
1. $133.75   2. $162.50   9. $277.50   10. $1,480.96

Page 69
1. $153.00   2. $123.09   11. $402.38   13. $75.40   18. $3,920.80

Page 71
1. $248   2. $227   11. $19.35   12. $232.20   19. $29.45

Page 73
1. $114.45   2. $789

Page 75
1. term   3. $3.40   11. $130; $170; $475   12. SBLI

CHAPTER 5

Page 85
1. $22.75; $2.25   2. $22.00; $8.00   7. $56   9. $82.50; $17.50

Page 87
1. $17.25; pay separately

Page 89
1. $21.44   4. 9 packets; $1.35

Page 91
1. $35   2. $103

Page 93
1. $2.38   2. $4.18   11. $0.46

Page 95
3. 23 cartons   7. 3 classes

Page 97
1. indoor   4. $19.13   16. tennis   20. tennis inside, racquetball, skiing

CHAPTER 6

Page 105
1. $18.19   6. 18%   11. $135.00

Page 107
1. $28.00   2. $26.98   18. $34   19. $25.98

Page 109
1. $0.17   2. $1.37   7. $0.94   8. $4.95   13. $0.63   14. $0.64   19. $0.88   20. $18.38

Page 111
4. $58.75   7. $58.45

Page 113
1. does make sense   2. does not make sense   7. 8.2¢ per oz; 6.9¢ per oz; 10 oz for 69¢
8. 9.9¢ per oz; 10.6¢ per oz; 9 oz for 89¢

Page 115
1. less than $5.00   2. more than $5.00   7. $6.42; $13.58   8. $5.87; $14.13   13. $1.72; $3.44

Page 117
1. $3.60   2. $8.00   17. home   20. $6.31

CHAPTER 7

Page 126
6. total deposit: $160.86   11. $386.16

Page 128
1. $414.09   2. $398.99

Page 131
1. total deposit: $128.29   9. $188.57   10. $41.95   15. $128.85   16. $83.85

Page 134
1. $60; $310   2. $75; $575   9. $50.63; $1,050.63   13. $5,375.60

Page 136
1. $1,000   2. None   13. Money Market   17. $8.00; $96.00

Page 137
23. $5   24. $1,500   29. Regular savings   30. Money Market savings

CHAPTER 8

Page 146
1. 123 789 456 2   2. 2/22/94   7. Feb. 28, 1994   9. $158.88

Page 148
1. $218.35; $3.28; $257.12   2. $80.45; $0.80; $181.10   10. $7.95   15. $234.00; $3.51; $582.51

Page 150
1. $1.53   6. $1.90; $3,846.90   8. $12.35; $807.35

Page 152
1. $403.86; $18.86   2. $864.72; $55.72

Page 153
7. $19.87; $86.65   8. $56.02; $89.56   17. $137.28; $2,236.80   18. $115.29; $5,634.80

Page 155
1. $90; $5   2. $126; $24   9. $99; $9.05

Page 157
3. $2.55

Page 159
1. 19.8%   4. $100.00   15. School's Tuition Plan   17. School's Tuition Plan

CHAPTER 9

Page 169
1. $9,958.00   5. $12,463   8. $14,687.76

Page 171
1. $11,189   2. $13,751.04   33. $2,292.92; $15,168.92

Page 174
1. 199   2. 2,356   13. $40   14. $40   25. Van

Page 177
1. $479.17   5. 3.40   6. 2.10   11. $223.10   12. $183.42

Page 179
1. $56.82   5. $36   6. 100 mi   29. about $300

Page 181
1. $14,509.86   3. $276.50   15. Car C   21. $67.34

CHAPTER 10

Page 189
1. 1,387 mi   5. 1,000 mi   9. 45 mi   13. 20 h   14. 18 h

Page 191
1. 4.0 mi   5. 15   9. 2.0 mi

Page 194
1. 2:35 P.M.   2. 9:45 P.M.   11. 10:25 A.M.   12. 1:23 P.M.

Page 196
1. Sierra Airlines Flight #272   2. Central Airlines Flight #244   7. 3 h and 15 min
15. $725   19. $130

Page 199
1. Red Line 5 stops   2. Red Line 3 stops to Metro Center, change to the Orange or Blue
Line, and go 8 more stops   7. $0.80   8. $1.25   13. 14 min   14. 27 min

Page 201
1. $8.10   2. $4.40   7. $1.20   12. $8.05 + $1.20 tip = $9.25

Page 203
1. $13.13   2. $10.50   7. $150   8. $300

Page 205
1. $7\frac{1}{2}$ h   2. 42 h   10. plane   13. $192

CHAPTER 11

Page 213
1. $1,647.90 5. $17,731 6. $24,080 11. $21,546.82 12. $4,524.34

Page 215
4. $19,074; $2,861 8. owe $296.65

Page 218
1. $21,050.37 2. $21,292.05 7. 11,253.82 8. 319.56

Page 221
1. $1,163 2. $75 7. $1,096; standard

Page 223
1. $137.44 2. $355.34 10. $628.41 11. $69.72(R)

Page 225
1. $2,600 6. $212.50 7. $45

Page 227
1. Married, joint return 3. $46,820 17. A:1040EZ; B:1040A; C:1040EZ 18. A:1040EZ; B:1040A; C:1040EZ

CHAPTER 12

Page 235
4. $934; $261.52 5. $1,245; $348.60 10. $371 11. $446

Page 237
1. $82,000; $100,000 2. $73,000; $114,600 7. $5,000 8. $55,000

Page 239
1. $35,600; $1,660 4. $2,000 9. $8,760; $810

Page 241
1. $445.50 6. $24,800 7. $99,200 8. $907.68 18. $2,160

Page 243
1. $76,000 6. $2,391.96 11. $721 16. $87,500 17. $52,250

Page 245
1. $7,800 2. $39,000 13. $760 14. 1,520

Page 248
4. 2,873 5. $141.64 12. $82.89 16. 3.051 18. $43.87

Page 250
1. 58 ft 5. 2 gal; $27.90

Page 251
8. $1,512 11. l = 10 in.; w = 8 in.

Page 253
1. 11% 3. Fixed 14. Intown Bank 18. The APR, and therefore the monthly payment, may decrease.

CHAPTER 13

Page 263
1. $5,400   4. $11,250   8. 12   9. $4.50   18. $36   19. $43.20

Page 265
1. $1\frac{3}{8}$ in.   2. $2\frac{1}{2}$ in.   7. 102 ft   8. 6

Page 267
1. 3   2. $89.85   11. $234.00

Page 269
1. 108 square ft   2. 51 square ft   26. $336.00   30. 500 square ft

Page 271
1. 120   2. $72   9. 1,080   10. $162

Page 273
3. 12 posts   4. 5 times

Page 275
1. $107.88   3. Very good   9. Good   10. Deluxe   15. 12.25¢   17. 400 bricks
23. Truckload   24. Loose

CHAPTER 14

Page 283
1. 3.5   2. $59.05   9. 16   10. $375.68   17. 3 d

Page 287
1. 4,557 francs   6. 46 pounds   11. $20.57   12. $58.78

Page 289
1. 37   2. 160   9. 58   10. 3

Page 291
1. 3   2. 2.5   11. 28 drops per min

Page 293
1. 22 min and 31 s   7. $178.75   11. 15 spots

Page 294
1. $5,590   2. $220   21. Job 2

Page 295
26. $11,611.60   27. $12,900   36. Yes   37. No

CHAPTER 15

Page 303
1. $2.00   2. $16.00   15. $1,900   16. $1,800

Page 305
1. $214   2. $133   8. $75   9. $38   17. $38   18. $472

Page 307
1. $64   2. $108   9. $177   10. $14

Page 309
1. $6,000   2. $19,000   17. $315,060   18. $294,130

Page 311
1. $3,892   2. $38,433   7. $111,500   8. $15,650

Page 313
1. $911   2. $1,096   15. Plan A   19. $75

CHAPTER 16

Page 321
1. $50   2. $37.50   7. $302.90   8. $344.40   13. $946.20   14. $196.20

Page 323
1. 7.92%   6. $198   7. $79.20   12. $1,131

Page 326
1. $18   2. 30\frac{3}{4}$ 8. $1,012.50   9. $660   14. (P) $217.50   18. $0.56   19. $5.60

Page 329
1. Chapman International   2. Finch Township   7. $4,200   11. 95%   12. 87.5%   17. $525
21. 9.0%

Page 331
1. $38.12   2. $1,906   13. $4,124   14. $14,340   19. 509 shares

Page 333
1. 2.0%   2. $9,600

Page 335
3. $27,000   4. $9,000

Page 336
1. $37.50   2. 0.5%

Page 337
28. Technics   29. Jetstorm

CHAPTER 17

Page 347

1. $\frac{1}{2}$ 2. $\frac{1}{3}$ 7. $\frac{1}{20}$ 8. $\frac{3}{20}$ 17. $\frac{1}{52}$ 18. $\frac{1}{26}$

Page 349

1. (H, H) (H, T) (T, H) (T, T) 2. (T, H, T) (H, T, T) (T, T, T) (H, H, H) (H, H, T) (H, T, H) (T, H, H) (T, T, H) 9. 15 outfits

Page 351

1. $\frac{1}{36}$ 2. 0 7. $\frac{1}{4}$ 8. $\frac{3}{20}$ 13. $\frac{1}{4}$ 14. $\frac{1}{4}$ 19. $\frac{3}{10}$ 20. $\frac{1}{5}$

Page 353

1. independent 6. $\frac{2}{9}$ 7. $\frac{1}{6}$ 12. $\frac{3}{14}$ 13. $\frac{1}{14}$ 18. $\frac{25}{102}$ 19. $\frac{13}{51}$

Page 355

1. 8 d 2. 6 d 7. 48 doubles 8. 22 home runs 13. 42 games

Page 357

1. Martin, Jane, Eli; Martin, Eli, Jane; Jane, Martin, Eli; Jane, Eli, Martin; Eli, Martin, Jane; Eli, Jane, Martin 2. 48, 49, 84, 89, 94, 98

CHAPTER 18

Page 365
1. 5   2. 21   10. 11   16. 42

Page 367
1. $x + 9$ 2. $15 \div x$ or $\frac{15}{x}$ 11. $10 + 6 = y$ 12. $6(3) = x$ 22. $p = \$40 \div 5$ or $p = \frac{\$40}{5}$

Page 369
1. 11   2. 2   9. 6   10. 2   17. 9   18. 2   27. 86° F

Page 371
1. 60   2. 4.4   25. $p - \$6 = \$38$; $44   26. $t + 8 = 89$; 81 points

Page 373
1. 32   2. 48   25. $\frac{n}{5} = 9$; 45   26. $7n = 56$; 8

Page 375
4. 7   5. 12   22. $3n + 5 = 32$; 9   23. $\frac{2}{5}n - 6 = 49$; 137.5

Page 377
3. $24.75

TABLES

UNITED STATES CUSTOMARY SYSTEM OF MEASUREMENT

Length	12 inches (in.) = 1 foot (ft)
	3 feet 36 inches $\Big\}$ = 1 yard (yd)
	1,760 yards 5,280 feet $\Big\}$ = 1 mile (mi)
	6,076 feet = 1 nautical mile
Area	144 square inches (square in.) = 1 square foot (square ft)
	9 square feet = 1 square yard (square yd)
	4,840 square yards = 1 acre (A)
Volume	1,728 cubic inches (cubic in.) = 1 cubic foot (cubic ft)
	27 cubic feet = 1 cubic yard (cubic yd)
Weight	16 ounces (oz) = 1 pound (lb)
	2,000 pounds = 1 ton (T)
Capacity	8 fluid ounces (fl. oz) = 1 cup (c)
	2 cups = 1 pint (pt)
	2 pints = 1 quart (qt)
	4 quarts = 1 gallon (gal)

SYMBOLS

=	is equal to	>	is greater than
≠	is not equal to	<	is less than
$a \overset{?}{=} b$	is a equal to b?	%	percent
≈	is approximately equal to	π	pi
		⊥	right angles

METRIC SYSTEM OF MEASUREMENT

Length	10 millimeters (mm) = 1 centimeter (cm)
	$\left.\begin{array}{l}\text{10 centimeters}\\\text{100 millimeters}\end{array}\right\}$ = 1 decimeter (dm)
	$\left.\begin{array}{l}\text{10 decimeters}\\\text{100 centimeters}\end{array}\right\}$ = 1 meter (m)
	1,000 meters = 1 kilometer (km)
Area	100 square millimeters (square mm) = 1 square centimeter (square cm)
	10,000 square centimeters = 1 square meter (square m)
	100 square meters = 1 are (a)
	10,000 square meters = 1 hectare (ha)
Volume	1,000 cubic millimeters (cubic mm) = 1 cubic centimeter (cubic cm)
	1,000 cubic centimeters = 1 cubic decimeter (cubic dm)
	1,000,000 cubic centimeters = 1 cubic meter (cubic m)
Mass	1,000 milligrams (mg) = 1 gram (g)
	1,000 grams = 1 kilogram (kg)
	1,000 kilograms = 1 metric ton (t)
Capacity	100 milliliters (mL) = 1 liter (L)
	1,000 liters = 1 kiloliter (kL)

GEOMETRIC FORMULAS

Perimeter		**Surface Area**	
rectangle	$P = 2l + 2w$	rectangular prism	$SA = 2lw + 2lh + 2wh$
square	$P = 4s$	cube	$SA = 6s^2$
Circumference		cylinder	$SA = 2\pi rh + 2\pi r^2$
circle	$C = \pi d$ or $C = 2\pi r$	sphere	$SA = 4\pi r^2$
Area		**Volume**	
rectangle	$A = lw$	rectangular prism	$V = lwh$
square	$A = s^2$	cube	$V = s^3$
parallelogram	$A = bh$	cylinder	$V = \pi r^2 h$
triangle	$A = \frac{1}{2}bh$	rectangular pyramid	$V = \frac{1}{3}lwh$
trapezoid	$A = \frac{1}{2}h(b_1 + b_2)$	cone	$V = \frac{1}{3}\pi r^2 h$
circle	$A = \pi r^2$	sphere	$V = \frac{4}{3}\pi r^3$

FRACTION, DECIMAL, AND PERCENT EQUIVALENCIES

Fraction	Decimal	Percent	Fraction	Decimal	Percent
$\frac{1}{10}$	0.1	10%	$\frac{1}{6}$	$0.16\overline{6}$	$16\frac{2}{3}\%$
$\frac{1}{5}$	0.2	20%	$\frac{1}{3}$	$0.33\overline{3}$	$33\frac{1}{3}\%$
$\frac{1}{4}$	0.25	25%	$\frac{2}{3}$	$0.66\overline{6}$	$66\frac{2}{3}\%$
$\frac{2}{5}$	0.4	40%	$\frac{5}{6}$	$0.83\overline{3}$	$83\frac{1}{3}\%$
$\frac{1}{2}$	0.5	50%	$\frac{1}{8}$	0.125	$12\frac{1}{2}\%$
$\frac{3}{5}$	0.6	60%	$\frac{3}{8}$	0.375	$37\frac{1}{2}\%$
$\frac{3}{4}$	0.75	75%	$\frac{5}{8}$	0.625	$62\frac{1}{2}\%$
$\frac{4}{5}$	0.8	80%	$\frac{7}{8}$	0.875	$87\frac{1}{2}\%$

COMPOUND INTEREST

No. of Periods	1.5%	2%	2.5%	3%	3.5%	4%	5%	6%	7%	8%
1	1.0150	1.0200	1.0250	1.0300	1.0350	1.0400	1.0500	1.0600	1.0700	1.0800
2	1.0302	1.0404	1.0506	1.0609	1.0712	1.0816	1.1025	1.1236	1.1449	1.1664
3	1.0457	1.0612	1.0769	1.0927	1.1087	1.1248	1.1576	1.1910	1.2250	1.2597
4	1.0614	1.0824	1.1038	1.1255	1.1475	1.1699	1.2155	1.2625	1.3108	1.3605
5	1.0773	1.1041	1.1314	1.1593	1.1877	1.2167	1.2763	1.3382	1.4026	1.4693
6	1.0934	1.1262	1.1597	1.1941	1.2293	1.2653	1.3401	1.4186	1.5007	1.5869
7	1.1098	1.1487	1.1887	1.2299	1.2723	1.3159	1.4071	1.5036	1.6058	1.7138
8	1.1265	1.1717	1.2184	1.2668	1.3168	1.3686	1.4775	1.5938	1.7182	1.8059
9	1.1434	1.1951	1.2489	1.3048	1.3629	1.4233	1.5513	1.6895	1.8385	1.9990
10	1.1605	1.2190	1.2801	1.3439	1.4106	1.4802	1.6289	1.7908	1.9672	2.1589
11	1.1779	1.2434	1.3121	1.3842	1.4600	1.5395	1.7103	1.8983	2.1049	2.3316
12	1.1956	1.2682	1.3449	1.4258	1.5111	1.6010	1.7959	2.0122	2.2522	2.5182
13	1.2136	1.2936	1.3785	1.4685	1.5640	1.6651	1.8856	2.1329	2.4098	2.7196
14	1.2318	1.3195	1.4130	1.5126	1.6187	1.7317	1.9799	2.2609	2.5785	2.9372
15	1.2502	1.3459	1.4483	1.5580	1.6753	1.8009	2.0789	2.3966	2.7590	3.1722
16	1.2690	1.3728	1.4845	1.6047	1.7340	1.8730	2.1829	2.5404	2.9522	3.4259
17	1.2880	1.4002	1.5216	1.6528	1.7947	1.9479	2.2920	2.6928	3.1588	3.7000
18	1.3073	1.4282	1.5597	1.7024	1.8575	2.0258	2.4066	2.8543	3.3799	3.9960
19	1.3270	1.4568	1.5987	1.7535	1.9225	2.1068	2.5270	3.0256	3.6165	4.3157
20	1.3469	1.4859	1.6386	1.8061	1.9898	2.1911	2.6533	3.2071	3.8697	4.6610
21	1.3671	1.5157	1.6796	1.8603	2.0594	2.2788	2.7860	3.3996	4.1406	5.0338
22	1.3876	1.5460	1.7216	1.9161	2.1315	2.3699	2.9253	3.6035	4.4304	5.4365
23	1.4084	1.5769	1.7646	1.9736	2.2061	2.4647	3.0715	3.8198	4.7405	5.8715
24	1.4295	1.6084	1.8087	2.0328	2.2833	2.5633	3.2251	4.0489	5.0724	6.3412
25	1.4509	1.6407	1.8539	2.0938	2.3673	2.6658	3.3864	4.2919	5.4274	6.8485

1991 Tax Table

Use if your taxable income is less than $50,000. If $50,000 or more, use the Tax Rate Schedules.

Example: *Mr. and Mrs. Brown are filing a joint return. Their taxable income on line 37 of form 1040 is $25,300. First, they find the $25,300–25,350 income line. Next, they find the column for married filing jointly and read down the column. The amount shown where the income line and filing status column meet is $3,799. This is the tax amount they must write on line 38 of their return.*

Sample Table

At least	But less than	Single	Married filing jointly	Married filing separately	Head of a household
			Your tax is—		
25,200	25,250	4,418	3,784	4,853	3,784
25,250	25,300	4,432	3,791	4,867	3,791
25,300	25,350	4,446	(3,799)	4,881	3,799
25,350	25,400	4,460	3,806	4,895	3,806

If line 37 (taxable income) is— At least	But less than	Single	Married filing jointly *	Married filing separately *	Head of a household
			Your tax is—		
$0	$5	$0	$0	$0	$0
5	15	2	2	2	2
15	25	3	3	3	3
25	50	6	6	6	6
50	75	9	9	9	9
75	100	13	13	13	13
100	125	17	17	17	17
125	150	21	21	21	21
150	175	24	24	24	24
175	200	28	28	28	28
200	225	32	32	32	32
225	250	36	36	36	36
250	275	39	39	39	39
275	300	43	43	43	43
300	325	47	47	47	47
325	350	51	51	51	51
350	375	54	54	54	54
375	400	58	58	58	58
400	425	62	62	62	62
425	450	66	66	66	66
450	475	69	69	69	69
475	500	73	73	73	73
500	525	77	77	77	77
525	550	81	81	81	81
550	575	84	84	84	84
575	600	88	88	88	88
600	625	92	92	92	92
625	650	96	96	96	96
650	675	99	99	99	99
675	700	103	103	103	103
700	725	107	107	107	107
725	750	111	111	111	111
750	775	114	114	114	114
775	800	118	118	118	118
800	825	122	122	122	122
825	850	126	126	126	126
850	875	129	129	129	129
875	900	133	133	133	133
900	925	137	137	137	137
925	950	141	141	141	141
950	975	144	144	144	144
975	1,000	148	148	148	148

1,000

At least	But less than	Single	Married filing jointly	Married filing separately	Head of a household
1,000	1,025	152	152	152	152
1,025	1,050	156	156	156	156
1,050	1,075	159	159	159	159
1,075	1,100	163	163	163	163
1,100	1,125	167	167	167	167
1,125	1,150	171	171	171	171
1,150	1,175	174	174	174	174
1,175	1,200	178	178	178	178
1,200	1,225	182	182	182	182
1,225	1,250	186	186	186	186
1,250	1,275	189	189	189	189
1,275	1,300	193	193	193	193

If line 37 (taxable income) is— At least	But less than	Single	Married filing jointly	Married filing separately	Head of a household
			Your tax is—		
1,300	1,325	197	197	197	197
1,325	1,350	201	201	201	201
1,350	1,375	204	204	204	204
1,375	1,400	208	208	208	208
1,400	1,425	212	212	212	212
1,425	1,450	216	216	216	216
1,450	1,475	219	219	219	219
1,475	1,500	223	223	223	223
1,500	1,525	227	227	227	227
1,525	1,550	231	231	231	231
1,550	1,575	234	234	234	234
1,575	1,600	238	238	238	238
1,600	1,625	242	242	242	242
1,625	1,650	246	246	246	246
1,650	1,675	249	249	249	249
1,675	1,700	253	253	253	253
1,700	1,725	257	257	257	257
1,725	1,750	261	261	261	261
1,750	1,775	264	264	264	264
1,775	1,800	268	268	268	268
1,800	1,825	272	272	272	272
1,825	1,850	276	276	276	176
1,850	1,875	279	279	279	279
1,875	1,900	283	283	283	283
1,900	1,925	287	287	287	287
1,925	1,950	291	291	291	291
1,950	1,975	294	294	294	294
1,975	2,000	298	298	298	298

2,000

At least	But less than	Single	Married filing jointly	Married filing separately	Head of a household
2,000	2,025	302	302	302	302
2,025	2,050	306	306	306	306
2,050	2,075	309	309	309	309
2,075	2,100	313	313	313	313
2,100	2,125	317	317	317	317
2,125	2,150	321	321	321	321
2,150	2,175	324	324	324	324
2,175	2,200	328	328	328	328
2,200	2,225	332	332	332	332
2,225	2,250	336	336	336	336
2,250	2,275	339	339	339	339
2,275	2,300	343	343	343	343
2,300	2,325	347	347	347	347
2,325	2,350	351	351	351	351
2,350	2,375	354	354	354	354
2,375	2,400	358	358	358	358
2,400	2,425	362	362	362	362
2,425	2,450	366	366	366	366
2,450	2,475	369	369	369	369
2,475	2,500	373	373	373	373
2,500	2,525	377	377	377	377
2,525	2,550	381	381	381	381
2,550	2,575	384	384	384	384
2,575	2,600	388	388	388	388
2,600	2,625	392	392	392	392
2,625	2,650	396	396	396	396
2,650	2,675	399	399	399	399
2,675	2,700	403	403	403	403

If line 37 (taxable income) is— At least	But less than	Single	Married filing jointly	Married filing separately	Head of a household
			Your tax is—		
2,700	2,725	407	407	407	407
2,725	2,750	411	411	411	411
2,750	2,775	414	414	414	414
2,775	2,800	418	418	418	418
2,800	2,825	422	422	422	422
2,825	2,850	426	426	426	426
2,850	2,875	429	429	429	429
2,875	2,900	433	433	433	433
2,900	2,925	437	437	437	437
2,925	2,950	441	441	441	441
2,950	2,975	444	444	444	444
2,975	3,000	448	448	448	448

3,000

At least	But less than	Single	Married filing jointly	Married filing separately	Head of a household
3,000	3,050	454	454	454	454
3,050	3,100	461	461	461	461
3,100	3,150	469	469	469	469
3,150	3,200	476	476	476	476
3,200	3,250	484	484	484	484
3,250	3,300	491	491	491	491
3,300	3,350	499	499	499	499
3,350	3,400	506	506	506	506
3,400	3,450	514	514	514	514
3,450	3,500	521	521	521	521
3,500	3,550	529	529	529	529
3,550	3,600	536	536	536	536
3,600	3,650	544	544	544	544
3,650	3,700	551	551	551	551
3,700	3,750	559	559	559	559
3,750	3,800	566	566	566	566
3,800	3,850	574	574	574	574
3,850	3,900	581	581	581	581
3,900	3,950	589	589	589	589
3,950	4,000	596	596	596	596

4,000

At least	But less than	Single	Married filing jointly	Married filing separately	Head of a household
4,000	4,050	604	604	604	604
4,050	4,100	611	611	611	611
4,100	4,150	619	619	619	619
4,150	4,200	626	626	626	626
4,200	4,250	634	634	634	634
4,250	4,300	641	641	641	641
4,300	4,350	649	649	649	649
4,350	4,400	656	656	656	656
4,400	4,450	664	664	664	664
4,450	4,500	671	671	671	671
4,500	4,550	679	679	679	679
4,550	4,600	686	686	686	686
4,600	4,650	694	694	694	694
4,650	4,700	701	701	701	701
4,700	4,750	709	709	709	709
4,750	4,800	716	716	716	716
4,800	4,850	724	724	724	724
4,850	4,900	731	731	731	731
4,900	4,950	739	739	739	739
4,950	5,000	746	746	746	746

Continued on next page

1991 Tax Table—*Continued*

5,000

At least	But less than	Single	Married filing jointly*	Married filing separately	Head of a household
5,000	5,050	754	754	754	754
5,050	5,100	761	761	761	761
5,100	5,150	769	769	769	769
5,150	5,200	776	776	776	776
5,200	5,250	784	784	784	784
5,250	5,300	791	791	791	791
5,300	5,350	799	799	799	799
5,350	5,400	806	806	806	806
5,400	5,450	814	814	814	814
5,450	5,500	821	821	821	821
5,500	5,550	829	829	829	829
5,550	5,600	836	836	836	836
5,600	5,650	844	844	844	844
5,650	5,700	851	851	851	851
5,700	5,750	859	859	859	859
5,750	5,800	866	866	866	866
5,800	5,850	874	874	874	874
5,850	5,900	881	881	881	881
5,900	5,950	889	889	889	889
5,950	6,000	896	896	896	896

6,000

At least	But less than	Single	Married filing jointly*	Married filing separately	Head of a household
6,000	6,050	904	904	904	904
6,050	6,100	911	911	911	911
6,100	6,150	919	919	919	919
6,150	6,200	926	926	926	926
6,200	6,250	934	934	934	934
6,250	6,300	941	941	941	941
6,300	6,350	949	949	949	949
6,350	6,400	956	956	956	956
6,400	6,450	964	964	964	964
6,450	6,500	971	971	971	971
6,500	6,550	979	979	979	979
6,550	6,600	986	986	986	986
6,600	6,650	994	994	994	994
6,650	6,700	1,001	1,001	1,001	1,001
6,700	6,750	1,009	1,009	1,009	1,009
6,750	6,800	1,016	1,016	1,016	1,016
6,800	6,850	1,024	1,024	1,024	1,024
6,850	6,900	1,031	1,031	1,031	1,031
6,900	6,950	1,039	1,039	1,039	1,039
6,950	7,000	1,046	1,046	1,046	1,046

7,000

At least	But less than	Single	Married filing jointly*	Married filing separately	Head of a household
7,000	7,050	1,054	1,054	1,054	1,054
7,050	7,100	1,061	1,061	1,061	1,061
7,100	7,150	1,069	1,069	1,069	1,069
7,150	7,200	1,076	1,076	1,076	1,076
7,200	7,250	1,084	1,084	1,084	1,084
7,250	7,300	1,091	1,091	1,091	1,091
7,300	7,350	1,099	1,099	1,099	1,099
7,350	7,400	1,106	1,106	1,106	1,106
7,400	7,450	1,114	1,114	1,114	1,114
7,450	7,500	1,121	1,121	1,121	1,121
7,500	7,550	1,129	1,129	1,129	1,129
7,550	7,600	1,136	1,136	1,136	1,136
7,600	7,650	1,144	1,144	1,144	1,144
7,650	7,700	1,151	1,151	1,151	1,151
7,700	7,750	1,159	1,159	1,159	1,159
7,750	7,800	1,166	1,166	1,166	1,166
7,800	7,850	1,174	1,174	1,174	1,174
7,850	7,900	1,181	1,181	1,181	1,181
7,900	7,950	1,189	1,189	1,189	1,189
7,950	8,000	1,196	1,196	1,196	1,196

8,000

At least	But less than	Single	Married filing jointly*	Married filing separately	Head of a household
8,000	8,050	1,204	1,204	1,204	1,204
8,050	8,100	1,211	1,211	1,211	1,211
8,100	8,150	1,219	1,219	1,219	1,219
8,150	8,200	1,226	1,226	1,226	1,226
8,200	8,250	1,234	1,234	1,234	1,234
8,250	8,300	1,241	1,241	1,241	1,241
8,300	8,350	1,249	1,249	1,249	1,249
8,350	8,400	1,256	1,256	1,256	1,256
8,400	8,450	1,264	1,264	1,264	1,264
8,450	8,500	1,271	1,271	1,271	1,271
8,500	8,550	1,279	1,279	1,279	1,279
8,550	8,600	1,286	1,286	1,286	1,286
8,600	8,650	1,294	1,294	1,294	1,294
8,650	8,700	1,301	1,301	1,301	1,301
8,700	8,750	1,309	1,309	1,309	1,309
8,750	8,800	1,316	1,316	1,316	1,316
8,800	8,850	1,324	1,324	1,324	1,324
8,850	8,900	1,331	1,331	1,331	1,331
8,900	8,950	1,339	1,339	1,339	1,339
8,950	9,000	1,346	1,346	1,346	1,346

9,000

At least	But less than	Single	Married filing jointly*	Married filing separately	Head of a household
9,000	9,050	1,354	1,354	1,354	1,354
9,050	9,100	1,361	1,361	1,361	1,361
9,100	9,150	1,369	1,369	1,369	1,369
9,150	9,200	1,376	1,376	1,376	1,376
9,200	9,250	1,384	1,384	1,384	1,384
9,250	9,300	1,391	1,391	1,391	1,391
9,300	9,350	1,399	1,399	1,399	1,399
9,350	9,400	1,406	1,406	1,406	1,406
9,400	9,450	1,414	1,414	1,414	1,414
9,450	9,500	1,421	1,421	1,421	1,421
9,500	9,550	1,429	1,429	1,429	1,429
9,550	9,600	1,436	1,436	1,436	1,436
9,600	9,650	1,444	1,444	1,444	1,444
9,650	9,700	1,451	1,451	1,451	1,451
9,700	9,750	1,459	1,459	1,459	1,459
9,750	9,800	1,466	1,466	1,466	1,466
9,800	9,850	1,474	1,474	1,474	1,474
9,850	9,900	1,481	1,481	1,481	1,481
9,900	9,950	1,489	1,489	1,489	1,489
9,950	10,000	1,496	1,496	1,496	1,496

10,000

At least	But less than	Single	Married filing jointly*	Married filing separately	Head of a household
10,000	10,050	1,540	1,504	1,504	1,504
10,050	10,100	1,511	1,511	1,511	1,511
10,100	10,150	1,519	1,519	1,519	1,519
10,150	10,200	1,526	1,526	1,526	1,526
10,200	10,250	1,534	1,534	1,534	1,534
10,250	10,300	1,541	1,541	1,541	1,541
10,300	10,350	1,549	1,549	1,549	1,549
10,350	10,400	1,556	1,556	1,556	1,556
10,400	10,450	1,564	1,564	1,564	1,564
10,450	10,500	1,571	1,571	1,571	1,571
10,500	10,550	1,579	1,579	1,579	1,579
10,550	10,600	1,586	1,586	1,586	1,586
10,600	10,650	1,594	1,594	1,594	1,594
10,650	10,700	1,601	1,601	1,601	1,601
10,700	10,750	1,609	1,609	1,609	1,609
10,750	10,800	1,616	1,616	1,616	1,616
10,800	10,850	1,624	1,624	1,624	1,624
10,850	10,900	1,631	1,631	1,631	1,631
10,900	10,950	1,639	1,639	1,639	1,639
10,950	11,000	1,646	1,646	1,646	1,646

11,000

At least	But less than	Single	Married filing jointly*	Married filing separately	Head of a household
11,000	11,050	1,654	1,654	1,654	1,654
11,050	11,100	1,661	1,661	1,661	1,661
11,100	11,150	1,669	1,669	1,669	1,669
11,150	11,200	1,676	1,676	1,676	1,676
11,200	11,250	1,684	1,684	1,684	1,684
11,250	11,300	1,691	1,691	1,691	1,691
11,300	11,350	1,699	1,699	1,699	1,699
11,350	11,400	1,706	1,706	1,706	1,706
11,400	11,450	1,714	1,714	1,714	1,714
11,450	11,500	1,721	1,721	1,721	1,721
11,500	11,550	1,729	1,729	1,729	1,729
11,550	11,600	1,736	1,736	1,736	1,736
11,600	11,650	1,744	1,744	1,744	1,744
11,650	11,700	1,751	1,751	1,751	1,751
11,700	11,750	1,759	1,759	1,759	1,759
11,750	11,800	1,766	1,766	1,766	1,766
11,800	11,850	1,774	1,774	1,774	1,774
11,850	11,900	1,781	1,781	1,781	1,781
11,900	11,950	1,789	1,789	1,789	1,789
11,950	12,000	1,796	1,796	1,796	1,796

12,000

At least	But less than	Single	Married filing jointly*	Married filing separately	Head of a household
12,000	12,050	1,804	1,804	1,804	1,804
12,050	12,100	1,811	1,811	1,811	1,811
12,100	12,150	1,819	1,819	1,819	1,819
12,150	12,200	1,826	1,826	1,826	1,826
12,200	12,250	1,834	1,834	1,834	1,834
12,250	12,300	1,841	1,841	1,841	1,841
12,300	12,350	1,849	1,849	1,849	1,849
12,350	12,400	1,856	1,856	1,856	1,856
12,400	12,450	1,864	1,864	1,864	1,864
12,450	12,500	1,871	1,871	1,871	1,871
12,500	12,550	1,879	1,879	1,879	1,879
12,550	12,600	1,886	1,886	1,886	1,886
12,600	12,650	1,894	1,894	1,894	1,894
12,650	12,700	1,901	1,901	1,901	1,901
12,700	12,750	1,909	1,909	1,909	1,909
12,750	12,800	1,916	1,916	1,916	1,916
12,800	12,850	1,924	1,924	1,924	1,924
12,850	12,900	1,931	1,931	1,931	1,931
12,900	12,950	1,939	1,939	1,939	1,939
12,950	13,000	1,946	1,946	1,946	1,946

13,000

At least	But less than	Single	Married filing jointly*	Married filing separately	Head of a household
13,000	13,050	1,954	1,954	1,954	1,954
13,050	13,100	1,961	1,961	1,961	1,961
13,100	13,150	1,969	1,969	1,969	1,969
13,150	13,200	1,976	1,976	1,976	1,976
13,200	13,250	1,984	1,984	1,984	1,984
13,250	13,300	1,991	1,991	1,991	1,991
13,300	13,350	1,999	1,999	1,999	1,999
13,350	13,400	2,006	2,006	2,006	2,006
13,400	13,450	2,014	2,014	2,014	2,014
13,450	13,500	2,021	2,021	2,021	2,021
13,500	13,550	2,029	2,029	2,029	2,029
13,550	13,600	2,036	2,036	2,036	2,036
13,600	13,650	2,044	2,044	2,044	2,044
13,650	13,700	2,051	2,051	2,051	2,051
13,700	13,750	2,059	2,059	2,059	2,059
13,750	13,800	2,066	2,066	2,066	2,066
13,800	13,850	2,074	2,074	2,074	2,074
13,850	13,900	2,081	2,081	2,081	2,081
13,900	13,950	2,089	2,089	2,089	2,089
13,950	14,000	2,096	2,096	2,096	2,096

* This column must also be used by a qualifying widow(er).

Continued on next page

Page 32

If line 37 (taxable income) is—		And you are—				If line 37 (taxable income) is—		And you are—				If line 37 (taxable income) is—		And you are—			
At least	But less than	Single	Married filing jointly *	Married filing separately	Head of a household	At least	But less than	Single	Married filing jointly *	Married filing separately	Head of a household	At least	But less than	Single	Married filing jointly *	Married filing separately	Head of a household
		Your tax is—						Your tax is—						Your tax is—			

14,000 / 17,000 / 20,000

At least	But less than	Single	MFJ	MFS	HoH	At least	But less than	Single	MFJ	MFS	HoH	At least	But less than	Single	MFJ	MFS	HoH
14,000	14,050	2,104	2,104	2,104	2,104	17,000	17,050	2,554	2,554	2,557	2,554	20,000	20,050	3,004	3,004	3,397	3,004
14,050	14,100	2,111	2,111	2,111	2,111	17,050	17,100	2,561	2,561	2,571	2,561	20,050	20,100	3,011	3,011	3,411	3,011
14,100	14,150	2,119	2,119	2,119	2,119	17,100	17,150	2,569	2,569	2,585	2,569	20,100	20,150	3,019	3,019	3,425	3,019
14,150	14,200	2,126	2,126	2,126	2,126	17,150	17,200	2,576	2,576	2,599	2,576	20,150	20,200	3,026	3,026	3,439	3,026
14,200	14,250	2,134	2,134	2,134	2,134	17,200	17,250	2,584	2,584	2,613	2,584	20,200	20,250	3,034	3,034	3,453	3,034
14,250	14,300	2,141	2,141	2,141	2,141	17,250	17,300	2,591	2,591	2,627	2,591	20,250	20,300	3,041	3,041	3,467	3,041
14,300	14,350	2,149	2,149	2,149	2,149	17,300	17,350	2,599	2,599	2,641	2,599	20,300	20,350	3,049	3,049	3,481	3,049
14,350	14,400	2,156	2,156	2,156	2,156	17,350	17,400	2,606	2,606	2,655	2,606	20,350	20,400	3,060	3,056	3,495	3,056
14,400	14,450	2,164	2,164	2,164	2,164	17,400	17,450	2,614	2,614	2,669	2,614	20,400	20,450	3,074	3,064	3,509	3,064
14,450	14,500	2,171	2,171	2,171	2,171	17,450	17,500	2,621	2,621	2,683	2,621	20,450	20,500	3,088	3,071	3,523	3,071
14,500	14,550	2,179	2,179	2,179	2,179	17,500	17,550	2,629	2,629	2,697	2,629	20,500	20,550	3,102	3,079	3,537	3,079
14,550	14,600	2,186	2,186	2,186	2,186	17,550	17,600	2,636	2,636	2,711	2,636	20,550	20,600	3,116	3,086	3,551	3,086
14,600	14,650	2,194	2,194	2,194	2,194	17,600	17,650	2,644	2,644	2,725	2,644	20,600	20,650	3,130	3,094	3,565	3,094
14,650	14,700	2,201	2,201	2,201	2,201	17,650	17,700	2,651	2,651	2,739	2,651	20,650	20,700	3,144	3,101	3,579	3,101
14,700	14,750	2,209	2,209	2,209	2,209	17,700	17,750	2,659	2,659	2,753	2,659	20,700	20,750	3,158	3,109	3,593	3,109
14,750	14,800	2,216	2,216	2,216	2,216	17,750	17,800	2,666	2,666	2,767	2,666	20,750	20,800	3,172	3,116	3,607	3,116
14,800	14,850	2,224	2,224	2,224	2,224	17,800	17,850	2,674	2,674	2,781	2,674	20,800	20,850	3,186	3,124	3,621	3,124
14,850	14,900	2,231	2,231	2,231	2,231	17,850	17,900	2,681	2,681	2,795	2,681	20,850	20,900	3,200	3,131	3,635	3,131
14,900	14,950	2,239	2,239	2,239	2,239	17,900	17,950	2,689	2,689	2,809	2,689	20,900	20,950	3,214	3,139	3,649	3,139
14,950	15,000	2,246	2,246	2,246	2,246	17,950	18,000	2,696	2,696	2,823	2,696	20,950	21,000	3,228	3,146	3,663	3,146

15,000 / 18,000 / 21,000

At least	But less than	Single	MFJ	MFS	HoH	At least	But less than	Single	MFJ	MFS	HoH	At least	But less than	Single	MFJ	MFS	HoH
15,000	15,050	2,254	2,254	2,254	2,254	18,000	18,050	2,704	2,704	2,837	2,704	21,000	21,050	3,242	3,154	3,677	3,154
15,050	15,100	2,261	2,261	2,261	2,261	18,050	18,100	2,711	2,711	2,851	2,711	21,050	21,100	3,256	3,161	3,691	3,161
15,100	15,150	2,269	2,269	2,269	2,269	18,100	18,150	2,719	2,719	2,865	2,719	21,100	21,150	3,270	3,169	3,705	3,169
15,150	15,200	2,276	2,276	2,276	2,276	18,150	18,200	2,726	2,726	2,879	2,726	21,150	21,200	3,284	3,176	3,719	3,176
15,200	15,250	2,284	2,284	2,284	2,284	18,200	18,250	2,734	2,734	2,893	2,734	21,200	21,250	3,298	3,184	3,733	3,184
15,250	15,300	2,291	2,291	2,291	2,291	18,250	18,300	2,741	2,741	2,907	2,741	21,250	21,300	3,312	3,191	3,747	3,191
15,300	15,350	2,299	2,299	2,299	2,299	18,300	18,350	2,749	2,749	2,921	2,749	21,300	21,350	3,326	3,199	3,761	3,199
15,350	15,400	2,306	2,306	2,306	2,306	18,350	18,400	2,756	2,756	2,935	2,756	21,350	21,400	3,340	3,206	3,775	3,206
15,400	15,450	2,314	2,314	2,314	2,314	18,400	18,450	2,764	2,764	2,949	2,764	21,400	21,450	3,354	3,214	3,789	3,214
15,450	15,500	2,321	2,321	2,321	2,321	18,450	18,500	2,771	2,771	2,963	2,771	21,450	21,500	3,368	3,221	3,803	3,221
15,500	15,550	2,329	2,329	2,329	2,329	18,500	18,550	2,779	2,779	2,977	2,779	21,500	21,550	3,382	3,229	3,817	3,229
15,550	15,600	2,336	2,336	2,336	2,336	18,550	18,600	2,786	2,786	2,991	2,786	21,550	21,600	3,396	3,236	3,831	3,236
15,600	15,650	2,344	2,344	2,344	2,344	18,600	18,650	2,794	2,794	3,005	2,794	21,600	21,650	3,410	3,244	3,845	3,244
15,650	15,700	2,351	2,351	2,351	2,351	18,650	18,700	2,801	2,801	3,019	2,801	21,650	21,700	3,424	3,251	3,859	3,251
15,700	15,750	2,359	2,359	2,359	2,359	18,700	18,750	2,809	2,809	3,033	2,809	21,700	21,750	3,438	3,259	3,873	3,259
15,750	15,800	2,366	2,366	2,366	2,366	18,750	18,800	2,816	2,816	3,047	2,816	21,750	21,800	3,452	3,266	3,887	3,266
15,800	15,850	2,374	2,374	2,374	2,374	18,800	18,850	2,824	2,824	3,061	2,824	21,800	21,850	3,466	3,274	3,901	3,274
15,850	15,900	2,381	2,381	2,381	2,381	18,850	18,900	2,831	2,831	3,075	2,831	21,850	21,900	3,480	3,281	3,915	3,281
15,900	15,950	2,389	2,389	2,389	2,389	18,900	18,950	2,839	2,839	3,089	2,839	21,900	21,950	3,494	3,289	3,929	3,289
15,950	16,000	2,396	2,396	2,396	2,396	18,950	19,000	2,846	2,846	3,103	2,846	21,950	22,000	3,508	3,296	3,943	3,296

16,000 / 19,000 / 22,000

At least	But less than	Single	MFJ	MFS	HoH	At least	But less than	Single	MFJ	MFS	HoH	At least	But less than	Single	MFJ	MFS	HoH
16,000	16,050	2,404	2,404	2,404	2,404	19,000	19,050	2,854	2,854	3,117	2,854	22,000	22,050	3,522	3,304	3,957	3,304
16,050	16,100	2,411	2,411	2,411	2,411	19,050	19,100	2,861	2,861	3,131	2,861	22,050	22,100	3,536	3,311	3,971	3,311
16,100	16,150	2,419	2,419	2,419	2,419	19,100	19,150	2,869	2,869	3,145	2,869	22,100	22,150	3,550	3,319	3,985	3,319
16,150	16,200	2,426	2,426	2,426	2,426	19,150	19,200	2,876	2,876	3,159	2,876	22,150	22,200	3,564	3,326	3,999	3,326
16,200	16,250	2,434	2,434	2,434	2,434	19,200	19,250	2,884	2,884	3,173	2,884	22,200	22,250	3,578	3,334	4,013	3,334
16,250	16,300	2,441	2,441	2,441	2,441	19,250	19,300	2,891	2,891	3,187	2,891	22,250	22,300	3,592	3,341	4,027	3,341
16,300	16,350	2,449	2,449	2,449	2,449	19,300	19,350	2,899	2,899	3,201	2,899	22,300	22,350	3,606	3,349	4,041	3,349
16,350	16,400	2,456	2,456	2,456	2,456	19,350	19,400	2,906	2,906	3,215	2,906	22,350	22,400	3,620	3,356	4,055	3,356
16,400	16,450	2,464	2,464	2,464	2,464	19,400	19,450	2,914	2,914	3,229	2,914	22,400	22,450	3,634	3,364	4,069	3,364
16,450	16,500	2,471	2,471	2,471	2,471	19,450	19,500	2,921	2,921	3,243	2,921	22,450	22,500	3,648	3,371	4,083	3,371
16,500	16,550	2,479	2,479	2,479	2,479	19,500	19,550	2,929	2,929	3,257	2,929	22,500	22,550	3,662	3,379	4,097	3,379
16,550	16,600	2,486	2,486	2,486	2,486	19,550	19,600	2,936	2,936	3,271	2,936	22,550	22,600	3,676	3,386	4,111	3,386
16,600	16,650	2,494	2,494	2,494	2,494	19,600	19,650	2,944	2,944	3,285	2,944	22,600	22,650	3,690	3,394	4,125	3,394
16,650	16,700	2,501	2,501	2,501	2,501	19,650	19,700	2,951	2,951	3,299	2,951	22,650	22,700	3,704	3,401	4,139	3,401
16,700	16,750	2,509	2,509	2,509	2,509	19,700	19,750	2,959	2,959	3,313	2,959	22,700	22,750	3,718	3,409	4,153	3,409
16,750	16,800	2,516	2,516	2,516	2,516	19,750	19,800	2,966	2,966	3,327	2,966	22,750	22,800	3,732	3,416	4,167	3,416
16,800	16,850	2,524	2,524	2,524	2,524	19,800	19,850	2,974	2,974	3,341	2,974	22,800	22,850	3,746	3,424	4,181	3,424
16,850	16,900	2,531	2,531	2,531	2,531	19,850	19,900	2,981	2,981	3,355	2,981	22,850	22,900	3,760	3,431	4,195	3,431
16,900	16,950	2,539	2,539	2,539	2,539	19,900	19,950	2,989	2,989	3,369	2,989	22,900	22,950	3,774	3,439	4,209	3,439
16,950	17,000	2,546	2,546	2,546	2,546	19,950	20,000	2,996	2,996	3,383	2,996	22,950	23,000	3,788	3,446	4,223	3,446

* This column must also be used by a qualifying widow(er).

Continued on next page

1991 Tax Table—*Continued*

If line 37 (taxable income) is—		And you are—			
At least	But less than	Single	Married filing jointly *	Married filing separately	Head of a household
		Your tax is—			

23,000

At least	But less than	Single	Married filing jointly	Married filing separately	Head of a household
23,000	23,050	3,802	3,454	4,237	3,454
23,050	23,100	3,816	3,461	4,251	3,461
23,100	23,150	3,830	3,469	4,265	3,469
23,150	23,200	3,844	3,476	4,279	3,476
23,200	23,250	3,858	3,484	4,293	3,484
23,250	23,300	3,872	3,491	4,307	3,491
23,300	23,350	3,886	3,499	4,321	3,499
23,350	23,400	3,900	3,506	4,335	3,506
23,400	23,450	3,914	3,514	4,349	3,514
23,450	23,500	3,928	3,521	4,363	3,521
23,500	23,550	3,942	3,529	4,377	3,529
23,550	23,600	3,956	3,536	4,391	3,536
23,600	23,650	3,970	3,544	4,405	3,544
23,650	23,700	3,984	3,551	4,419	3,551
23,700	23,750	3,998	3,559	4,433	3,559
23,750	23,800	4,012	3,566	4,447	3,566
23,800	23,850	4,026	3,574	4,461	3,574
23,850	23,900	4,040	3,581	4,475	3,581
23,900	23,950	4,054	3,589	4,489	3,589
23,950	24,000	4,068	3,596	4,503	3,596

24,000

At least	But less than	Single	Married filing jointly	Married filing separately	Head of a household
24,000	24,050	4,082	3,604	4,517	3,604
24,050	24,100	4,096	3,611	4,531	3,611
24,100	24,150	4,110	3,619	4,545	3,619
24,150	24,200	4,124	3,626	4,559	3,626
24,200	24,250	4,138	3,634	4,573	3,634
24,250	24,300	4,152	3,641	4,587	3,641
24,300	24,350	4,166	3,649	4,601	3,649
24,350	24,400	4,180	3,656	4,615	3,656
24,400	24,450	4,194	3,664	4,629	3,664
24,450	24,500	4,208	3,671	4,643	3,671
24,500	24,550	4,222	3,679	4,657	3,679
24,550	24,600	4,236	3,686	4,671	3,686
24,600	24,650	4,250	3,694	4,685	3,694
24,650	24,700	4,264	3,701	4,699	3,701
24,700	24,750	4,278	3,709	4,713	3,709
24,750	24,800	4,292	3,716	4,727	3,716
24,800	24,850	4,306	3,724	4,741	3,724
24,850	24,900	4,320	3,731	4,755	3,731
24,900	24,950	4,334	3,739	4,769	3,739
24,950	25,000	4,348	3,746	4,783	3,746

25,000

At least	But less than	Single	Married filing jointly	Married filing separately	Head of a household
25,000	25,050	4,362	3,754	4,797	3,754
25,050	25,100	4,376	3,761	4,811	3,761
25,100	25,150	4,390	3,769	4,825	3,769
25,150	25,200	4,404	3,776	4,839	3,776
25,200	25,250	4,418	3,784	4,853	3,784
25,250	25,300	4,432	3,791	4,867	3,791
25,300	25,350	4,446	3,799	4,881	3,799
25,350	25,400	4,460	3,806	4,895	3,806
25,400	25,450	4,474	3,814	4,909	3,814
25,450	25,500	4,488	3,821	4,923	3,821
25,500	25,550	4,502	3,829	4,937	3,829
25,550	25,600	4,516	3,836	4,951	3,836
25,600	25,650	4,530	3,844	4,965	3,844
25,650	25,700	4,544	3,851	4,979	3,851
25,700	25,750	4,558	3,859	4,993	3,859
25,750	25,800	4,572	3,866	5,007	3,866
25,800	25,850	4,586	3,874	5,021	3,874
25,850	25,900	4,600	3,881	5,035	3,881
25,900	25,950	4,614	3,889	5,049	3,889
25,950	26,000	4,628	3,896	5,063	3,896

26,000

At least	But less than	Single	Married filing jointly	Married filing separately	Head of a household
26,000	26,050	4,642	3,904	5,077	3,904
26,050	26,100	4,656	3,911	5,091	3,911
26,100	26,150	4,670	3,919	5,105	3,919
26,150	26,200	4,684	3,926	5,119	3,926
26,200	26,250	4,698	3,934	5,133	3,934
26,250	26,300	4,712	3,941	5,147	3,941
26,300	26,350	4,726	3,949	5,161	3,949
26,350	26,400	4,740	3,956	5,175	3,956
26,400	26,450	4,754	3,964	5,189	3,964
26,450	26,500	4,768	3,971	5,203	3,971
26,500	26,550	4,782	3,979	5,217	3,979
26,550	26,600	4,796	3,986	5,231	3,986
26,600	26,650	4,810	3,994	5,245	3,994
26,650	26,700	4,824	4,001	5,259	4,001
26,700	26,750	4,838	4,009	5,273	4,009
26,750	26,800	4,852	4,016	5,287	4,016
26,800	26,850	4,866	4,024	5,301	4,024
26,850	26,900	4,880	4,031	5,315	4,031
26,900	26,950	4,894	4,039	5,329	4,039
26,950	27,000	4,908	4,046	5,343	4,046

27,000

At least	But less than	Single	Married filing jointly	Married filing separately	Head of a household
27,000	27,050	4,922	4,054	5,357	4,054
27,050	27,100	4,936	4,061	5,371	4,061
27,100	27,150	4,950	4,069	5,385	4,069
27,150	27,200	4,964	4,076	5,399	4,076
27,200	27,250	4,978	4,084	5,413	4,084
27,250	27,300	4,992	4,091	5,427	4,091
27,300	27,350	5,006	4,099	5,441	4,102
27,350	27,400	5,020	4,106	5,455	4,116
27,400	27,450	5,034	4,114	5,469	4,130
27,450	27,500	5,048	4,121	5,483	4,144
27,500	27,550	5,062	4,129	5,497	4,158
27,550	27,600	5,076	4,136	5,511	4,172
27,600	27,650	5,090	4,144	5,525	4,186
27,650	27,700	5,104	4,151	5,539	4,200
27,700	27,750	5,118	4,159	5,553	4,214
27,750	27,800	5,132	4,166	5,567	4,228
27,800	27,850	5,146	4,174	5,581	4,242
27,850	27,900	5,160	4,181	5,595	4,256
27,900	27,950	5,174	4,189	5,609	4,270
27,950	28,000	5,188	4,196	5,623	4,284

28,000

At least	But less than	Single	Married filing jointly	Married filing separately	Head of a household
28,000	28,050	5,202	4,204	5,637	4,298
28,050	28,100	5,216	4,211	5,651	4,312
28,100	28,150	5,230	4,219	5,665	4,326
28,150	28,200	5,244	4,226	5,679	4,340
28,200	28,250	5,258	4,234	5,693	4,354
28,250	28,300	5,272	4,241	5,707	4,368
28,300	28,350	5,286	4,249	5,721	4,382
28,350	28,400	5,300	4,256	5,735	4,396
28,400	28,450	5,314	4,264	5,749	4,410
28,450	28,500	5,328	4,271	5,763	4,424
28,500	28,550	5,342	4,279	5,777	4,438
28,550	28,600	5,356	4,286	5,791	4,452
28,600	28,650	5,370	4,294	5,805	4,466
28,650	28,700	5,384	4,301	5,819	4,480
28,700	28,750	5,398	4,309	5,833	4,494
28,750	28,800	5,412	4,316	5,847	4,508
28,800	28,850	5,426	4,324	5,861	4,522
28,850	28,900	5,440	4,331	5,875	4,536
28,900	28,950	5,454	4,339	5,889	4,550
28,950	29,000	5,468	4,346	5,903	4,564

29,000

At least	But less than	Single	Married filing jointly	Married filing separately	Head of a household
29,000	29,050	5,482	4,354	5,917	4,578
29,050	29,100	5,496	4,361	5,931	4,592
29,100	29,150	5,510	4,369	5,945	4,606
29,150	29,200	5,524	4,376	5,959	4,620
29,200	29,250	5,538	4,384	5,973	4,634
29,250	29,300	5,552	4,391	5,987	4,648
29,300	29,350	5,566	4,399	6,001	4,662
29,350	29,400	5,580	4,406	6,015	4,676
29,400	29,450	5,594	4,414	6,029	4,690
29,450	29,500	5,608	4,421	6,043	4,704
29,500	29,550	5,622	4,429	6,057	4,718
29,550	29,600	5,636	4,436	6,071	4,732
29,600	29,650	5,650	4,444	6,085	4,746
29,650	29,700	5,664	4,451	6,099	4,760
29,700	29,750	5,678	4,459	6,113	4,774
29,750	29,800	5,692	4,466	6,127	4,788
29,800	29,850	5,706	4,474	6,141	4,802
29,850	29,900	5,720	4,481	6,155	4,816
29,900	29,950	5,734	4,489	6,169	4,830
29,950	30,000	5,748	4,496	6,183	4,844

30,000

At least	But less than	Single	Married filing jointly	Married filing separately	Head of a household
30,000	30,050	5,762	4,504	6,197	4,858
30,050	30,100	5,776	4,511	6,211	4,872
30,100	30,150	5,790	4,519	6,225	4,886
30,150	30,200	5,804	4,526	6,239	4,900
30,200	30,250	5,818	4,534	6,253	4,914
30,250	30,300	5,832	4,541	6,267	4,928
30,300	30,350	5,846	4,549	6,281	4,942
30,350	30,400	5,860	4,556	6,295	4,956
30,400	30,450	5,874	4,564	6,309	4,970
30,450	30,500	5,888	4,571	6,323	4,984
30,500	30,550	5,902	4,579	6,337	4,998
30,550	30,600	5,916	4,586	6,351	5,012
30,600	30,650	5,930	4,594	6,365	5,026
30,650	30,700	5,944	4,601	6,379	5,040
30,700	30,750	5,958	4,609	6,393	5,054
30,750	30,800	5,972	4,616	6,407	5,068
30,800	30,850	5,986	4,624	6,421	5,082
30,850	30,900	6,000	4,631	6,435	5,096
30,900	30,950	6,014	4,639	6,449	5,110
30,950	31,000	6,028	4,646	6,463	5,124

31,000

At least	But less than	Single	Married filing jointly	Married filing separately	Head of a household
31,000	31,050	6,042	4,654	6,477	5,138
31,050	31,100	6,056	4,661	6,491	5,152
31,100	31,150	6,070	4,669	6,505	5,166
31,150	31,200	6,084	4,676	6,519	5,180
31,200	31,250	6,098	4,684	6,533	5,194
31,250	31,300	6,112	4,691	6,547	5,208
31,300	31,350	6,126	4,699	6,561	5,222
31,350	31,400	6,140	4,706	6,575	5,236
31,400	31,450	6,154	4,714	6,589	5,250
31,450	31,500	6,168	4,721	6,603	5,264
31,500	31,550	6,182	4,729	6,617	5,278
31,550	31,600	6,196	4,736	6,631	5,292
31,600	31,650	6,210	4,744	6,645	5,306
31,650	31,700	6,224	4,751	6,659	5,320
31,700	31,750	6,238	4,759	6,673	5,334
31,750	31,800	6,252	4,766	6,687	5,348
31,800	31,850	6,266	4,774	6,701	5,362
31,850	31,900	6,280	4,781	6,715	5,376
31,900	31,950	6,294	4,789	6,729	5,390
31,950	32,000	6,308	4,796	6,743	5,404

* This column must also be used by a qualifying widow(er).

Continued on next page

Page 34

1991 Tax Table—*Continued*

If line 37 (taxable income) is—		And you are—			
At least	But less than	Single	Married filing jointly *	Married filing separately	Head of a household
		Your tax is—			

32,000

At least	But less than	Single	Married filing jointly	Married filing separately	Head of a household
32,000	32,050	6,322	4,804	6,757	5,418
32,050	32,100	6,336	4,811	6,771	5,432
32,100	32,150	6,350	4,819	6,785	5,446
32,150	32,200	6,364	4,826	6,799	5,460
32,200	32,250	6,378	4,834	6,813	5,474
32,250	32,300	6,392	4,841	6,827	5,488
32,300	32,350	6,406	4,849	6,841	5,502
32,350	32,400	6,420	4,856	6,855	5,516
32,400	32,450	6,434	4,864	6,869	5,530
32,450	32,500	6,448	4,871	6,883	5,544
32,500	32,550	6,462	4,879	6,897	5,558
32,550	32,600	6,476	4,886	6,911	5,572
32,600	32,650	6,490	4,894	6,925	5,586
32,650	32,700	6,504	4,901	6,939	5,600
32,700	32,750	6,518	4,909	6,953	5,614
32,750	32,800	6,532	4,916	6,967	5,628
32,800	32,850	6,546	4,924	6,981	5,642
32,850	32,900	6,560	4,931	6,995	5,656
32,900	32,950	6,574	4,939	7,009	5,670
32,950	33,000	6,588	4,946	7,023	5,684

33,000

At least	But less than	Single	Married filing jointly	Married filing separately	Head of a household
33,000	33,050	6,602	4,954	7,037	5,698
33,050	33,100	6,616	4,961	7,051	5,712
33,100	33,150	6,630	4,969	7,065	5,726
33,150	33,200	6,644	4,976	7,079	5,740
33,200	33,250	6,658	4,984	7,093	5,754
33,250	33,300	6,672	4,991	7,107	5,768
33,300	33,350	6,686	4,999	7,121	5,782
33,350	33,400	6,700	5,006	7,135	5,796
33,400	33,450	6,714	5,014	7,149	5,810
33,450	33,500	6,728	5,021	7,163	5,824
33,500	33,550	6,742	5,029	7,177	5,838
33,550	33,600	6,756	5,036	7,191	5,852
33,600	33,650	6,770	5,044	7,205	5,866
33,650	33,700	6,784	5,051	7,219	5,880
33,700	33,750	6,798	5,059	7,233	5,894
33,750	33,800	6,812	5,066	7,247	5,908
33,800	33,850	6,826	5,074	7,261	5,922
33,850	33,900	6,840	5,081	7,275	5,936
33,900	33,950	6,854	5,089	7,289	5,950
33,950	34,000	6,868	5,096	7,303	5,964

34,000

At least	But less than	Single	Married filing jointly	Married filing separately	Head of a household
34,000	34,050	6,882	5,107	7,317	5,978
34,050	34,100	6,896	5,121	7,331	5,992
34,100	34,150	6,910	5,135	7,345	6,006
34,150	34,200	6,924	5,149	7,359	6,020
34,200	34,250	6,938	5,163	7,373	6,034
34,250	34,300	6,952	5,177	7,387	6,048
34,300	34,350	6,966	5,191	7,401	6,062
34,350	34,400	6,980	5,205	7,415	6,076
34,400	34,450	6,994	5,219	7,429	6,090
34,450	34,500	7,008	5,233	7,443	6,104
34,500	34,550	7,022	5,247	7,457	6,118
34,550	34,600	7,036	5,261	7,471	6,132
34,600	34,650	7,050	5,275	7,485	6,146
34,650	34,700	7,064	5,289	7,499	6,160
34,700	34,750	7,078	5,303	7,513	6,174
34,750	34,800	7,092	5,317	7,527	6,188
34,800	34,850	7,106	5,331	7,541	6,202
34,850	34,900	7,120	5,345	7,555	6,216
34,900	34,950	7,134	5,359	7,569	6,230
34,950	35,000	7,148	5,373	7,583	6,244

35,000

At least	But less than	Single	Married filing jointly	Married filing separately	Head of a household
35,000	35,050	7,162	5,387	7,597	6,258
35,050	35,100	7,176	5,401	7,611	6,272
35,100	35,150	7,190	5,415	7,625	6,286
35,150	35,200	7,204	5,429	7,639	6,300
35,200	35,250	7,218	5,443	7,653	6,314
35,250	35,300	7,232	5,457	7,667	6,328
35,300	35,350	7,246	5,471	7,681	6,342
35,350	35,400	7,260	5,485	7,695	6,356
35,400	35,450	7,274	5,499	7,709	6,370
35,450	35,500	7,288	5,513	7,723	6,384
35,500	35,550	7,302	5,527	7,737	6,398
35,550	35,600	7,316	5,541	7,751	6,412
35,600	35,650	7,330	5,555	7,765	6,426
35,650	35,700	7,344	5,569	7,779	6,440
35,700	35,750	7,358	5,583	7,793	6,454
35,750	35,800	7,372	5,597	7,807	6,468
35,800	35,850	7,386	5,611	7,821	6,482
35,850	35,900	7,400	5,625	7,835	6,496
35,900	35,950	7,414	5,639	7,849	6,510
35,950	36,000	7,428	5,653	7,863	6,524

36,000

At least	But less than	Single	Married filing jointly	Married filing separately	Head of a household
36,000	36,050	7,442	5,667	7,877	6,538
36,050	36,100	7,456	5,681	7,891	6,552
36,100	36,150	7,470	5,695	7,905	6,566
36,150	36,200	7,484	5,709	7,919	6,580
36,200	36,250	7,498	5,723	7,933	6,594
36,250	36,300	7,512	5,737	7,947	6,608
36,300	36,350	7,526	5,751	7,961	6,622
36,350	36,400	7,540	5,765	7,975	6,636
36,400	36,450	7,554	5,779	7,989	6,650
36,450	36,500	7,568	5,793	8,003	6,664
36,500	36,550	7,582	5,807	8,017	6,678
36,550	36,600	7,596	5,821	8,031	6,692
36,600	36,650	7,610	5,835	8,045	6,706
36,650	36,700	7,624	5,849	8,059	6,720
36,700	36,750	7,638	5,863	8,073	6,734
36,750	36,800	7,652	5,877	8,087	6,748
36,800	36,850	7,666	5,891	8,101	6,762
36,850	36,900	7,680	5,905	8,115	6,776
36,900	36,950	7,694	5,919	8,129	6,790
36,950	37,000	7,708	5,933	8,143	6,804

37,000

At least	But less than	Single	Married filing jointly	Married filing separately	Head of a household
37,000	37,050	7,722	5,947	8,157	6,818
37,050	37,100	7,736	5,961	8,171	6,832
37,100	37,150	7,750	5,975	8,185	6,846
37,150	37,200	7,764	5,989	8,199	6,860
37,200	37,250	7,778	6,003	8,213	6,874
37,250	37,300	7,792	6,017	8,227	6,888
37,300	37,350	7,806	6,031	8,241	6,902
37,350	37,400	7,820	6,045	8,255	6,916
37,400	37,450	7,834	6,059	8,269	6,930
37,450	37,500	7,848	6,073	8,283	6,944
37,500	37,550	7,862	6,087	8,297	6,958
37,550	37,600	7,876	6,101	8,311	6,972
37,600	37,650	7,890	6,115	8,325	6,986
37,650	37,700	7,904	6,129	8,339	7,000
37,700	37,750	7,918	6,143	8,353	7,014
37,750	37,800	7,932	6,157	8,367	7,028
37,800	37,850	7,946	6,171	8,381	7,042
37,850	37,900	7,960	6,185	8,395	7,056
37,900	37,950	7,974	6,199	8,409	7,070
37,950	38,000	7,988	6,213	8,423	7,084

38,000

At least	But less than	Single	Married filing jointly	Married filing separately	Head of a household
38,000	38,050	8,002	6,227	8,437	7,098
38,050	38,100	8,016	6,241	8,451	7,112
38,100	38,150	8,030	6,255	8,465	7,126
38,150	38,200	8,044	6,269	8,479	7,140
38,200	38,250	8,058	6,283	8,493	7,154
38,250	38,300	8,072	6,297	8,507	7,168
38,300	38,350	8,086	6,311	8,521	7,182
38,350	38,400	8,100	6,325	8,535	7,196
38,400	38,450	8,114	6,339	8,549	7,210
38,450	38,500	8,128	6,353	8,563	7,224
38,500	38,550	8,142	6,367	8,577	7,238
38,550	38,600	8,156	6,381	8,591	7,252
38,600	38,650	8,170	6,395	8,605	7,266
38,650	38,700	8,184	6,409	8,619	7,280
38,700	38,750	8,198	6,423	8,633	7,294
38,750	38,800	8,212	6,437	8,647	7,308
38,800	38,850	8,226	6,451	8,661	7,322
38,850	38,900	8,240	6,465	8,675	7,336
38,900	38,950	8,254	6,479	8,689	7,350
38,950	39,000	8,268	6,493	8,703	7,364

39,000

At least	But less than	Single	Married filing jointly	Married filing separately	Head of a household
39,000	39,050	8,282	6,507	8,717	7,378
39,050	39,100	8,296	6,521	8,731	7,392
39,100	39,150	8,310	6,535	8,745	7,406
39,150	39,200	8,324	6,549	8,759	7,420
39,200	39,250	8,338	6,563	8,773	7,434
39,250	39,300	8,352	6,577	8,787	7,448
39,300	39,350	8,366	6,591	8,801	7,462
39,350	39,400	8,380	6,605	8,815	7,476
39,400	39,450	8,394	6,619	8,829	7,490
39,450	39,500	8,408	6,633	8,843	7,504
39,500	39,550	8,422	6,647	8,857	7,518
39,550	39,600	8,436	6,661	8,871	7,532
39,600	39,650	8,450	6,675	8,885	7,546
39,650	39,700	8,464	6,689	8,899	7,560
39,700	39,750	8,478	6,703	8,913	7,574
39,750	39,800	8,492	6,717	8,927	7,588
39,800	39,850	8,506	6,731	8,941	7,602
39,850	39,900	8,520	6,745	8,955	7,616
39,900	39,950	8,534	6,759	8,969	7,630
39,950	40,000	8,548	6,773	8,983	7,644

40,000

At least	But less than	Single	Married filing jointly	Married filing separately	Head of a household
40,000	40,050	8,562	6,787	8,997	7,658
40,050	40,100	8,576	6,801	9,011	7,672
40,100	40,150	8,590	6,815	9,025	7,686
40,150	40,200	8,604	6,829	9,039	7,700
40,200	40,250	8,618	6,843	9,053	7,714
40,250	40,300	8,632	6,857	9,067	7,728
40,300	40,350	8,646	6,871	9,081	7,742
40,350	40,400	8,660	6,885	9,095	7,756
40,400	40,450	8,674	6,899	9,109	7,770
40,450	40,500	8,688	6,913	9,123	7,784
40,500	40,550	8,702	6,927	9,137	7,798
40,550	40,600	8,716	6,941	9,151	7,812
40,600	40,650	8,730	6,955	9,165	7,826
40,650	40,700	8,744	6,969	9,179	7,840
40,700	40,750	8,758	6,983	9,193	7,854
40,750	40,800	8,772	6,997	9,207	7,868
40,800	40,850	8,786	7,011	9,221	7,882
40,850	40,900	8,800	7,025	9,235	7,896
40,900	40,950	8,814	7,039	9,249	7,910
40,950	41,000	8,828	7,053	9,263	7,924

* This column must also be used by a qualifying widow(er).

Continued on next page

INDEX

Credits

Book Design and Production: Textart Inc.
Cover Design: Textart Inc.
Cover Photo: Robert Fishman
Technical Art: Network Graphics

Illustrations: *Eva Vagreti Cockrille* 30, 31, 37, 62, 84, 86, 87, 88, 253; *Mark Giglio* 29, 33, 81, 114, 289, 291; *Steve Marchesi* 28, 92, 119; *Samantha Smith* 106, 107, 148, 154, 197, 302; 197 Subway Map "Used by permission of the Washington Metropolitan Area Transit Authority. Designed by Michael Hertz Associates, New York, for the WMATA Office of Marketing. © 1984 WMATA."

Picture Credits:

Contents Pages: iii, iv–v, vi–vii, viii–ix
HRW photo Ken Karp

Chapter 1 Opener: Page 1 Janet Pinneau/Allsport Photographic/Woodfin Camp Assoc.; **15** Stan Tess/Stock Market

Chapter 2 Opener: Page 21 HRW Photo Michal Heron; **27** Simon Nathan/The Stock Market; **29** Craig Hammell/The Stock Market; **32** Lew Merrim/Monkmeyer Press; **34–35** HRW Photo Ken Karp

Chapter 3 Opener: Page 39 HRW Photo Michal Heron; **44** Alvis Upitis/Image Bank; **48** HRW Photo Ken Karp

Chapter 4 Opener: Page 57 Palmer Kane/The Stock Market; 58 Cliff Feulner/Image Bank, **64** HRW Photo Ken Lax; **75** HRW Photo Ken Lax

Chapter 5 Opener: Page 83 Co Rentmeester; **88** National Philatelic Collection, Smithsonian Institution; **90** Kirk Schlea/Focus West; **94–95** HRW Photo Ken Karp; **97** HRW Photo Ken Lax

Chapter 6 Opener: Page 103 HRW Photo Richard Haynes; **115** HRW Photo Richard Haynes

Chapter 7 Opener: Page 123 Chris Jones/The Stock Market; **130** Jon Ferngersh/The Stock Market

Chapter 8 Opener: Page 143 HRW Photo Richard Haynes; **150** HRW Photo Ken Lax; **157** Dan McCoy/Rainbow

Chapter 9 Opener: Page 167 HRW Photo Michal Heron; **171** Gabe Palmer/The Stock Market; **173** Jay Freis/Image Bank; **179** HRW Photo Richard Haynes

Chapter 10 Opener: Page 187 Tom Bean/The Stock Market; **200** Lew Merrim/Monkmeyer Press; **202** James Cook/Folio Inc.; **204–205** HRW Photo Ken Karp

Chapter 11 Opener: Page 211 John Ficara/Woodfin Camp Assoc.; **217** HRW Photo Ken Karp; **223** Michael Quackenbush/Image Bank; **224** HRW Photo Ken Karp

Chapter 12 Opener: Page 233 HRW Photo Richard Haynes; **236** Craig Hammell/The Stock Market; **242** Richard Hutchings/Photo Researchers; **247** HRW Photo Ken Karp; **250** John Coletti/Stock, Boston

Chapter 13 Opener: Page 261 Gabe Palmer/The Stock Market; **268** HRW Photo Ken Lax; **273** Michael Pasdzior/Image Bank; **275** HRW Photo Ken Lax

Chapter 14 Opener: Page 281 Enrico Ferorelli/Dot; **284** Hank Morgan/Rainbow; **286** HRW Photo Ken Lax; **290** Alvis Upitis/Image Bank; **292** Gabe Palmer/The Stock Market; **295** HRW Photo Ken Karp

Chapter 15 Opener: Page 301 Bettmann Archive; **304** HRW Photo Ken Lax; **307** Randy Duchaine/The Stock Market; **308** Roger Miller/Image Bank

Chapter 16 Opener: Page 319 Ted Russell/Image Bank; **323** Dan McCoy/Rainbow; **327** Charles Feil/Stock Boston; **331** Jay Freis/Image Bank; **334** Harvey Lloyd/The Stock Market; **337** HRW Photo Ken Karp

Chapter 17 Opener: Page 345 Hank Morgan/Photo Researchers; **349** HRW Photo Ken Karp; **351** HRW Photo Ken Karp; **355** J. Rettaliata/Focus West; **356** Alan Choisnet/Image Bank; **357** Ben Rose/Image Bank

Chapter 18 Opener: Page 363 Hank Morgan/Rainbow; **369** HRW Photo Richard Haynes; **371** Sepp Seitz/Woodfin Camp Assoc.; **373** HRW Photo Ken Lax; **376** HRW Photo Ken Karp

Angel
Pastor
♡'s
Christine
Aldier
4
Eve